Encyclopedia of North American
BIRDS

Encyclopedia of North American
BIRDS

DEREK HALL

THUNDER BAY
P·R·E·S·S
San Diego, California

THUNDER BAY
P·R·E·S·S

Thunder Bay Press
An imprint of the Advantage Publishers Group
5880 Oberlin Drive, San Diego, CA 92121-4794
www.thunderbaybooks.com

The Brown Reference Group plc
(incorporating Andromeda Oxford Limited)
8 Chapel Place
Rivington Street
London EC2A 3DQ

© 2004 The Brown Reference Group plc

ISBN 1-59223-190-X

Library of Congress Cataloging-in-Publication Data
available upon request.

Project Director: Graham Bateman
Editors: Marion Dent, John Woodward
Art Editor and Designer: Tony Truscott
Cartographic Editor: Tim Williams
Editorial Assistants: Marian Dreier, Rita Demetriou
Picture Manager: Claire Turner
Picture Researcher: Vickie Walters
Production: Clive Sparling
Authors: David Chandler, Dominic Couzens,
Euan Dunn, Jonathan Elphick, Rob Hume,
Derek Niemann, Tony Whitehead,
John Woodward

Printed in China
1 2 3 4 5 08 07 06 05 04

Barn swallow

Title page: **Bald eagle**
Half title: **Atlantic puffins**

Contents

Blue jay

Barn owl

Common Loon	8–13
Northern Fulmar	14–15
Sooty Shearwater	16–17
Leach's Storm Petrel	18–19
Brown Pelican	20–23
Great Cormorant	24–25
Northern Gannet	26–29
American Bittern	30–31
Glossy Ibis	32–33
Wood Stork	34–35
Mute Swan	36–39
Canada Goose	40–43
Wood Duck	44–45
Mallard	46–49
American Wigeon	50–53
King Eider	54–55
Long-Tailed Duck	56–57
California Condor	58–63
Turkey Vulture	64–67
Everglade Kite	68–69
Northern Goshawk	70–71
Golden Eagle	72–77
Bald Eagle	78–83
Osprey	84–87
Peregrine Falcon	88–91
Northern Bobwhite	92–93
Common Pheasant	94–97
Prairie Chicken	98–99
Sage Grouse	100–103
Common Turkey	104–109

Common Moorhen	**110–113**
Whooping Crane	**114–117**
American Golden Plover	**118–123**
American Black Oystercatcher	**124–125**
Greater Yellowlegs	**126–127**
Ruddy Turnstone	**128–131**
Short-Billed Dowitcher	**132–135**
Snipe	**136–137**
Red-Necked Phalarope	**138–139**
Great Skua	**140–143**
Herring Gull	**144–145**
Kittiwake	**146–151**
Arctic Tern	**152–155**
Black Skimmer	**156–157**
Dovekie	**158–159**
Black Guillemot	**160–161**
Atlantic Puffin	**162–165**
Mourning Dove	**166–167**
Rock Dove	**168–171**
Greater Roadrunner	**172–177**
Great Horned Owl	**178–179**
Snowy Owl	**180–183**
Barn Owl	**184–189**
Whippoorwill	**190–191**
Ruby-Throated Hummingbird	**192–195**
Belted Kingfisher	**196–199**
Pileated Woodpecker	**200–205**
Yellow-Throated Vireo	**206–207**
Blue Jay	**208–213**
Common Raven	**214–217**
Horned Lark	**218–219**
Barn Swallow	**220–223**

Black-Capped Chickadee	**224–229**
Red-Breasted Nuthatch	**230–231**
Winter Wren	**232–233**
American Dipper	**234–235**
Eastern Bluebird	**236–239**
American Robin	**240–241**
Northern Mockingbird	**242–245**
European Starling	**246–249**
American Redstart	**250–253**
Cardinal	**254–259**
Snow Bunting	**260–261**
Common Grackle	**262–265**
Baltimore Oriole	**266–267**
Pine Grosbeak	**268–273**
American Goldfinch	**274–275**
House Sparrow	**276–279**
Glossary	**280–282**
Further Reading/Web Sites	**283–284**
Index	**285–288**

Ruddy turnstone

Rock dove

Wood stork

Introduction

ABOUT 60 MILLION PEOPLE in North America—one-fifth of the population—watch birds for pleasure. And each year we spend millions of dollars trying to entice them into our backyards to add that extra touch of nature to our immediate surroundings

What is it that we find so fascinating about birds? For a start, there is diversity; the continent is home to around 850 species, ranging in size from the California condor with a 9-foot wingspan, to tiny hummingbirds with wingspans that measure less than the length of your hand. Birds also come in an astonishing variety of shapes, colors, and habitat choices, from the leggy, long-necked, white whooping crane

wading through a Texan swamp, to the diminutive northern cardinal, glowing bright red against the snow of a Minnesotan winter.

Part of the attraction stems from the fact that, unlike most mammals—which are shy and nocturnal—birds tend to be active during the day and so are easy to see. It is hard not to feel affection toward a creature that is confiding enough to take food from you and occupy the birdhouse you have built for it in your backyard. We hear their presence, too, as the air is filled with strident calls and melodious song, proclaiming their desirability to a potential mate, threatening a rival, or warning of danger. There is such variety in their calls that we can identify individual bird species by sound alone. We associate the changing seasons with birds: in various parts of the continent, spring is heralded by the return of the robin or the swallow, the warble of the meadowlark, or the loons nesting on the lake.

Masters of the Sky

ONE PARTICULAR CHARACTERISTIC of birds fills us with admiration and envy: they can fly. For early humans, mastery of the air was powerfully symbolic. The eagle's size, power, and above all, its ability to soar high in the sky, led most of the 500 or so Native American tribes to see it as a direct link between them and the heavens. The founding fathers of the United States adopted the bird as the emblem of their new country, a position the bald eagle still holds today.

Birds are specially adapted to achieve the technical marvel of flight. They have wings instead of arms, powered by extraordinarily strong muscles—up to one-quarter of a bird's musculature is dedicated to flight. Feathers on the wings provide aerodynamic flight surfaces, and body feathers help streamline the body as it moves through the air. Weight is a critical factor for flying animals, which is why birds have light, hollow bones and a light beak rather than bony jaws full of teeth. And of course all birds lay eggs instead of bearing heavy live young.

Evolution of Birds

OUR KNOWLEDGE of how birds evolved is sketchy, because hollow bird skeletons rarely survive to provide fossil evidence. Most scientists believe birds are descended from

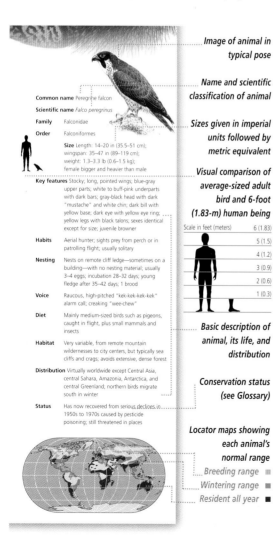

Image of animal in typical pose

Name and scientific classification of animal

Common name Peregrine falcon
Scientific name *Falco peregrinus*
Family Falconidae
Order Falconiformes
Size Length: 14–20 in (35.5–51 cm); wingspan: 35–47 in (89–119 cm); weight: 1.3–3.3 lb (0.6–1.5 kg); female bigger and heavier than male
Key features Stocky; long, pointed wings; blue-gray upper parts; white to buff-pink underparts with dark bars; gray-black head with dark "mustache" and white chin; dark bill with yellow base; dark eye with yellow eye ring; yellow legs with black talons; sexes identical except for size; juvenile browner
Habits Aerial hunter; sights prey from perch or in patrolling flight; usually solitary
Nesting Nests on remote cliff ledge—sometimes on a building—with no nesting material; usually 3–4 eggs; incubation 28–32 days; young fledge after 35–42 days; 1 brood
Voice Raucous, high-pitched "kek-kek-kek-kek" alarm call; creaking "wee-chew"
Diet Mainly medium-sized birds such as pigeons, caught in flight, plus small mammals and insects
Habitat Very variable, from remote mountain wildernesses to city centers, but typically sea cliffs and crags; avoids extensive, dense forest
Distribution Virtually worldwide except Central Asia, central Sahara, Amazonia, Antarctica, and central Greenland; northern birds migrate south in winter
Status Has now recovered from serious declines in 1950s to 1970s caused by pesticide poisoning; still threatened in places

Sizes given in imperial units followed by metric equivalent

Visual comparison of average-sized adult bird and 6-foot (1.83-m) human being

Scale in feet (meters)
6 (1.83)
5 (1.5)
4 (1.2)
3 (0.9)
2 (0.6)
1 (0.3)

Basic description of animal, its life, and distribution

Conservation status (see Glossary)

Locator maps showing each animal's normal range

Breeding range ■
Wintering range ■
Resident all year ■

⊝ *Summary panel presents basic facts and figures for each bird.*

two-footed flightless dinosaurs called theropods that roamed North America during the Jurassic Period around 150 million years ago. During the great Ice Ages, which began 2 million years ago, groups of birds became isolated as glaciers advanced and retreated. These groups of birds often developed into distinct species. As the climate began to stabilize, with the tropical south markedly different from the temperate north with its cold winters, many birds found the benefits of flying north for the summer months outweighed the enormous physical cost of journeys measuring thousands of miles. Two-thirds of our nesting bird species migrate here to feed and breed in places where there is less competition for food and fewer predators than in the tropics.

Birds and Humans

THE IMPACT of human civilizations on birds has been felt most strongly within the past 150 years with the development of efficient firearms and intensive farming. Unrestricted hunting during the 19th century saw many populations crash. Most notably, the passenger pigeon was shot to extinction, even though, with flocks of up to 2 billion birds, it may once have been the world's most numerous bird. Modern legislation that controls hunting means that this threat is far less significant. Far more important is the loss of or damage to the habitats where birds live. In our quest to provide food for expanding human populations, we have destroyed half of North America's wetlands and replaced 99 percent of the grass prairies with corn fields. The challenge now is for

conservationists to work with governments, industry, and local people to find ways of integrating our needs with those of birds and other wildlife.

There is clearly hope, for we are well equipped to understand the nature and scale of threats to birds. Efforts to tackle the problems of species that have been in steep decline have met with some success; both the bald eagle and peregrine falcon are no longer endangered, for example. But massive support for birds must be sustained if we are to safeguard their future.

The Encyclopedia of North American Birds

IN THIS ENCYCLOPEDIA you will find detailed descriptions of 78 common or familiar birds that are native to North America. Examples have been selected to give the broadest range of types from all key habitats. For each animal there is a detailed summary panel (see left) that gives all the basic facts and figures, including a distribution map (which also shows other parts of the world in which the bird occurs) and a scale drawing compared with a 6 foot high person. There then follows the main article which describes the most interesting features of each bird. Throughout there are detailed artwork portrayals and dynamic photographs of the birds in the wild.

If you find something in the following pages to inspire you, we hope you will pass it on and thus contribute in your own way to a greater awareness and appreciation of North America's magnificent bird life.

⊕ *Representative species of ground-dwelling birds.*

Prairie chicken

Northern bobwhite

Sage grouse

Common turkey

Common name Common loon (great northern diver)

Scientific name *Gavia immer*

Family Gaviidae

Order Gaviiformes

Size Length: 27–36 in (68.5–91 cm); wingspan: 50–57 in (127–147 cm); weight: 6.5–10 lb (3–4.5 kg); male slightly larger than female

Key features Heavily built, thick-necked bird; large head with big, pointed, blue-gray bill; sexes similar

Habits Almost totally aquatic; dives for food; pairs form lifelong bonds and nest well away from humans and other loons

Nesting Nest a heap of plant material close to water's edge; 1–3 eggs; incubation 24–25 days; young fledge after 63 days; 1 brood

Voice Yodeling and "tremelo" calls, and soft hoots

Diet Mainly fish, but also crustaceans, insects, mollusks, amphibians; also some vegetable matter

Habitat Large, deep freshwater lakes surrounded by conifer forests or tundra; flies south to winter on coasts and occasionally inland lakes—either alone, in pairs, or usually small flocks

Distribution Northern areas of the Northern Hemisphere and along coasts of North Atlantic and Pacific

Status Not globally threatened, but population has declined over the last 100 years, particularly as a result of human disturbance

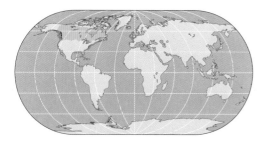

Common Loon

Gavia immer

Few sounds are more evocative of the wild, lonely northern lakes and forests of the planet than the strange call of the common loon. Fiercely territorial, this bird is remarkably well suited to living in an often harsh environment.

THE SHAPE OF A COMMON loon in the water is quite distinctive. It has a long body—often sitting low in the water—a chunky neck, and a big head flattened on top, which drops from a peak to a thick bill, always held level. In the breeding season the head is black and bears stripes down both sides of the neck with white checkered upper parts and light underparts. In winter the upper parts become grayish, and the bill becomes much lighter in color. You might see the bird's big feet when it is in flight, but you would be lucky, for the common loon spends nearly all of its time in the water.

Fish-finders

Moving slowly on the surface of a lake, a loon is constantly searching for fish. Instead of simply looking from above, however, it regularly dips its head below the surface to get a clearer view. Loons hunt their live prey almost completely by sight, so they nest in clear waters and only hunt during the day. If the water is murky, they resort to feeling their way along the bottom of the lake, hoping to detect slow-moving crustaceans such as crawfish.

Unlike grebes and cormorants, which seem to leap from the surface and then dive under with a splash, loons prefer to lower their heads and slip under silently. Although they do not actually "dive" from the surface, they can easily reach depths of 33 feet (10 m). Loons have even been recorded at depths of 230 feet (70 m). Propelled at considerable speed by their feet and steering with their wings, loons usually find their food within a minute of diving.

⊕ *A common loon in winter plumage. The common loon is considerably bigger than either the red-throated loon (Gavia stellata) or the black-throated loon (G. arctica).*

A loon's food depends both on where it lives and the season. Fish make up the bulk of most loon diets, and some individuals eat nothing else. Trout and salmon are among the most common foods, although a variety of other fish are taken. Most are eaten whole underwater, but those that prove awkward or are too large to swallow in this way are taken to the surface and pulled apart. Crustaceans such as prawns and shrimp are also caught, as well as water snails, insects, occasionally frogs and other amphibians, seeds, and plant leaves.

Mating for Life

In spring, when the ice has melted from the lakes of the north, common loons return there to breed. For the next few months they lead a deliberately isolated existence; no pair will nest within sight of another loon, and if humans disturb them, they will abandon the lake.

The two birds that arrive on a large, deep, freshwater lake will probably have been there the year before and perhaps the year before that. Loons mate for life, and these strongly bonded birds return to the same site to nest year after year. The drab grays of the birds' winter plumage have been replaced by vivid black-and-white markings. And most remarkably, their irises turn red, giving the eyes a flaming intensity.

Loons always wait to form pairs on their breeding territory, even though these normally solitary birds gather in winter flocks. Usually a young male occupies a territory and waits for a female, making loud calls to attract one. Conversely, if the male of a pair has died during the fall or winter, the female can find a new mate within a matter of days. Birds that have remained silent all winter now begin to make an extraordinary range of calls that, on a still evening, can be heard for miles around.

◉ *The breeding colors of the common loon include bold black-and-white plumage markings, distinctive "necklaces," and vivid red eyes.*

Their loudness is quite deliberate, for in most cases the wailing and yodeling calls are advertising ownership of a territory or warning away other loons. Each male has a yodeling call that studies have shown is unique to that particular bird. They also produce a rapid succession of notes described as a "tremelo" call. It can sound like manic laughter—hence the expressions "crazy as a loon" or "loony." Sometimes neighboring loons will begin a concert of calls, with both male and female responding to the calls of their neighbors—a contest between dusk and dawn that is often sustained over long periods of time.

The loons' courtship display before mating appears comical; the two birds face each other in the water, with their heads tipped forward, then begin dipping their bills in the water. The dipping grows faster, until eventually they dive past each other, turn, and begin the process all over again. Eventually the female draws her neck and head down and leads the male toward the shore. She leaps onto the land and often makes real or imaginary nest-building movements. It is enough to persuade the male loon to mate with her.

Fighting for Territory

When a pair of nesting birds occupies a fixed territory with only a relatively small amount of food available, it is essential that they defend the territory against intruders to ensure there will be enough food for the young. Given the harsh environment in which they live, it is not surprising that a male loon will fight for its territory.

Aggressive behavior begins with warning calls and a clear, threatening posture. The loon leans low and forward in the water, with its head and neck extended and its bill tipped upward. As an intruder approaches, one or both of the pair begins a ritual threat display. They will circle the intruder, dip bills in the water, jump or dive in front of it, then rush toward it and begin "fencing." The "homebird" and the intruder stand up in the water facing each other, wings stretched out, bobbing toward each other. The next stage is rarely reached; but if the loons begin to attack each other with their long, sharp bills, they can cause serious, even fatal, injuries.

Even when they nest, common loons try to minimize their contact with land. They build the rough mat of vegetation that passes for a nest as close to the water as possible—rarely more than a few feet away. They nest so close to water that heavy rains or storms can result in their nest being washed away or flooded. It appears that easy access to water makes the risk worthwhile. Besides, the female can lay a replacement clutch of eggs within a couple of weeks when necessary.

The female usually lays two eggs, two days apart. When hatched, the older, bigger chick stands a much better chance of survival because if food is short, it will be able to take most of it. It is not uncommon for the younger chick to starve within the first few days. The adults are kept busy finding food for their hungry young—a family of four will eat about a ton of fish during the breeding season.

Raising the Young

Young loons are on the water permanently within three days of hatching. To begin with, they ride on their parents' back. An eighteenth-century writer commented on a Faroe Island belief that the bird "is thought to hatch its young in a hole formed by nature under the wing for that purpose." On days when the water is calmer, the cheeping young learn to swim and dive. The adults guard the young against predators by rushing at intruders with their heads and necks outstretched. The family stays together, each hooting softly to the others to maintain contact.

It is no easy task for a young bird to learn how to fish. The parents encourage them to hunt for themselves by catching and disabling fish, bringing them to the surface, and then getting the baby birds to chase after them. Because of their rather inept first attempts, the

⊖ *The nest is usually built on an islet close to the water's edge soon after the spring thaw. Human disturbance from recreation and vacation homes has increased on lakes in the southern parts of the bird's range, causing a decline in breeding.*

young loons remain largely dependent on their parents for about seven weeks. But long after they have started to fish for themselves, they continue to take food from their parents—even when they have left the lake of their birth and flown south for the winter.

Mythical Birds

The behavior of loons has fascinated humans for thousands of years, encouraging many myths and legends. Many center around their unearthly calls. The Thompson River native Americans of British Columbia believed the sound would cause rain, and if humans imitated it, they could do likewise. In the early nineteenth century the famous U.S. ornithologist John James Audubon traveled with sailors who, when they heard the call of a loon, believed disaster would befall them. In medieval times the Scots considered the call a bad omen, and the Norwegians thought a loon call signified that a death was imminent. Much earlier human societies spanning the Northern Hemisphere, from the Inuit and native American peoples to the Scandinavians and Siberians, all had legends about the loon. Some linked its dive to the bottom of deep lakes with creation—they believed the bird brought up mud that formed the land.

Heading South

At the onset of fall the loons must leave the lake before it becomes frozen over. Most head south—usually toward the coast, although some winter on inland lakes. Their bulky, heavy bodies and narrow wings make takeoff difficult, and loons must first run across the water to get enough lift. Their slow-flapping, gooselike flight takes them to the sea, where they winter alone, in their breeding pairs, or in small, loose groups. Common loons can migrate considerable distances, for those that have nested on Canadian lakes may head to the coasts of California or Florida for the winter. The freshwater diet of the summer gives way to sea fish such as cod, herring, and haddock. However far they travel, one thing is certain— where there are loons, there is water.

Conservation Pressures

It is not surprising, given the loon's need for solitude during the breeding season, that human disturbance is the greatest threat to the bird today. Increasingly, lakes in the southern parts of its range are being opened up for recreation. Fishing and water sports cause

⬅ *For the first two or three weeks after hatching, the tiny chicks of the common loon often ride on their parents' backs for safety.*

➡ *An adult common loon offers a fish to its four-day-old chick on Bow Lake, New Hampshire. Food like this is presented whole and not regurgitated. The young are usually weaned by 11 weeks. Sexual maturity is reached after two years.*

enough disturbance for a pair to abandon a lake, and even irregularly occupied lakefront cabins are sufficient to lead to desertion. As people use lakes more, so also do the gulls, crows, and mammals such as raccoons that live alongside humans. All of these predators may take the eggs and chicks of loons.

Loons are also affected by pollution, both on their breeding lakes and at sea. Heavy industries release sulfates into the atmosphere that gather moisture from the air and fall as acid rain. Not only does this damage lakeshore vegetation, it also has a major effect on food chains within the lakes themselves. As the quantity of algae, plankton, insects, and fish are reduced, the amount of food available to loons declines, too. Heavy metals from industry also cause problems for loons because they are high predators in the food chain. Elements such as mercury dissolve in water and accumulate in the gills of fish. Over time, as loons eat more fish, they build up lethal levels of mercury in their own bodies. By examining the feathers of loons, scientists can calculate the levels of mercury in lakes. And because the mercury remains in the feathers even after death, they are able to figure out how much mercury was in a lake decades ago.

At sea loons are more at risk from oil pollution than most birds. Their tendency to stay on the water close to the coast, diving continuously, makes them especially vulnerable. Once they are coated in oil, they are unable to use their feathers to regulate their body temperature, or they die from ingesting the oil when they try to preen their feathers. Loons are also prone to getting trapped and drowned in fishing nets—that is probably the biggest cause of death outside the breeding season.

A Popular Emblem

The common loon has featured in the everyday life of Canadians for a number of years. In the late 1980s the Canadian government decided to issue a dollar coin for the first time in more than 50 years. On one side it chose to depict a loon, one of the country's most distinctive birds. The coin soon became known affectionately as "the loonie." The loon is also the state bird of Minnesota, a lake-rich state with a big breeding population of loons.

Common name Northern fulmar

Scientific name *Fulmarus glacialis*

Family	Procellariidae
Order	Procellariiformes
Size	Length: 18–20 in (46–51 cm); wingspan: 40–44 in (101–112 cm); weight: 1.5–2 lb (0.7–0.9 kg)
Key features	Stout-bodied, with thick neck and short, diamond-shaped tail; flies on stiff wings; most have gray-and-white gull-like plumage, but many high arctic breeders are darker overall; stubby, yellow bill with prominent tubular nostrils on top
Habits	Gregarious at breeding sites; feeds at sea in scattered or dense flocks
Nesting	Lays 1 white egg on bare rock ledge, a hollow, or a burrow; incubation 47–53 days by both sexes; young fledge after 46–53 days; 1 brood
Voice	Range of loud cackling, chuckling, and crooning sounds at nest; soft cooing and sneezing calls in flight; feeding flocks grunt and cackle
Diet	Fish, small squid, crustaceans, jellyfish, and other marine creatures; carrion from ships
Habitat	Breeds mainly on cliffs, sometimes on ledges of buildings; otherwise lives on open oceans
Distribution	Rocky coasts, islands, and open ocean throughout much of Arctic, northern Atlantic, and northern Pacific regions
Status	Widespread, common, and increasing

Northern Fulmar

Fulmarus glacialis

The gull-like fulmar is a skillful flyer that spends much of its life wandering the oceans. It has increased its range dramatically over the past 100 years, taking advantage of waste food from fishing boats.

AT FIRST GLANCE THE NORTHERN fulmar looks like just another "seagull," but it is completely unrelated to the gull family. A closer look reveals a thick bill of distinct plates with tubular nostrils on top, identifying it as a tubenose.

Secret Weapon
The name "fulmar" comes from the Icelandic for "foul gull." It refers to the smell of its stomach oil, which is truly disgusting. It is the basis of the bird's defense against predators such as foxes, large gulls, or birds of prey. The fulmar suddenly ejects a powerful stream of oil from its mouth, fouling the intruder's fur or plumage. This can destroy the waterproofing of a bird's feathers; and as some humans have also found, the nauseating smell of the oil can linger on clothing for years despite repeated washing.

Northern fulmars are very distinctive in flight, usually alternating bursts of powerful wingbeats with long, stiff-winged glides. They

⊕ *Fulmars often gather in flocks at rich sources of food, such as this whale carcass in the sea off Iceland.*

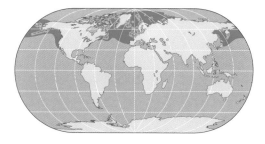

Fulmars spend a great deal of time patrolling back and forth near their nesting ledges. They often use their webbed feet to help them maneuver, riding the updrafts with grace and precision.

cope superbly with gales, using the updrafts that blow off rough seas to make long, sweeping glides, rolling and tilting through the wave troughs and over the breaking crests. Fulmars are also buoyant swimmers and often spend a good deal of time on the water.

Fatty Foods

As they plane above the waves, fulmars are always on the alert for something edible. They take a wide range of animal food, especially items rich in fat or oil, from tiny planktonic crustaceans and jellyfish to small fish, fish offal, and carrion. Once they have spotted a meal, fulmars usually descend to seize it in their bills while swimming or floating on the sea. They occasionally pursue active prey, such as fish, by plunging beneath the surface to depths of about 15 feet (4.6 m), propelling themselves with their webbed feet and half-opened wings.

Cliff Colonies

In the milder parts of their range fulmars may return to their breeding colonies as early as late October. They are faithful to both their nest sites as well as their mates, usually for life. An ideal nest site is a narrow ledge near the top of a cliff, where soil or grass and other vegetation provide a cushion for the egg. The pairs greet each other and dispute nest sites with rivals using raucous cackling and crooning calls, throwing back their heads, and opening their bills.

Most fulmars begin to lay in early May, but arctic birds may not lay until mid-June. The pair take turns incubating, and the downy white chick soon grows very plump on its diet of partly digested food.

Fulmars are long-lived, slow-breeding birds. Most do not breed until they are about nine, and some not until they are 12 or more. Their average life expectancy is about 34 years, but some are known to be over 40 years old, and a few may even live to be 100.

Population Explosion

Over the past 100 years or so there has been an extraordinary expansion of the north Atlantic fulmar population. In Britain, for instance, the species was restricted to Scotland in 1900. Only a few hundred pairs bred there, apart from a large, centuries-old population of about 20,000 pairs on the remote Scottish island of St. Kilda. Today there are over 600,000 pairs, with 63,000 on St. Kilda alone. There are also colonies all around the coasts of England, Wales, and Ireland, as well as Scotland.

A major factor in the success story of the fulmar seems to be the huge increase in availability of waste food at sea, mainly due to the great expansion of the fishing industry. The birds eagerly await the rich pickings—offal discarded as the catch is processed on board the trawlers, as well as undersized, injured, or dying fish thrown back into the sea.

Another factor is probably the fulmar's ability to use a wide range of nesting sites. In addition to traditional cliff ledges, the bird may exploit holes in low banks, walls surrounding fields, the walls or windowsills of ruined buildings, and even suitable places in old quarries some distance inland.

Sooty Shearwater

Puffinus griseus

The elegant sooty shearwater is a global wanderer that makes immensely long migrations, all the way from its breeding islands in the Southern Hemisphere to the northern Atlantic and Pacific, and back again.

Common name Sooty shearwater

Scientific name *Puffinus griseus*

Family	Procellariidae
Order	Procellariiformes
Size	Length: 16–20 in (41–51 cm); wingspan: 37–43 in (94–109 cm); weight: 1.4–2.1 lb (0.6–0.9 kg)
Key features	Small head and long, slender bill; long, pointed wings; all-dark, chocolate-brown plumage, apart from variable amount of silvery white on central part of underwings
Habits	Very gregarious, often feeding in huge flocks at sea; may breed in vast coastal colonies; migrates in long lines
Nesting	Nests in grass-lined chamber at end of long burrow; 1 white egg; incubation by both sexes for 53–56 days; young fledge after 86–106 days; 1 brood every 2 years
Voice	Repeated hoarse, rhythmic crooning calls at breeding grounds; much less vocal at sea
Diet	Small fish, squid, crustaceans, and fish offal
Habitat	Breeds mainly on coastal slopes covered with grass or other vegetation; otherwise lives far out at sea unless driven close to shore while on migration
Distribution	Throughout much of the Atlantic, Pacific, and Southern Oceans
Status	Abundant and widespread over much of its broad range

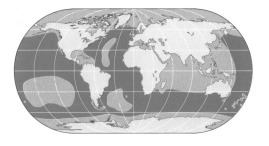

ALTHOUGH IT IS ABOUT THE size of a farmyard duck, the sooty shearwater is shaped like an albatross, with a heavy, streamlined body and long, narrow, sharply pointed wings. It has a long, slender blackish bill with a small tubenose on top and blackish legs and webbed feet tinged with a beautiful shade of lilac-purple.

Looping Migrations

Sooty shearwaters are superb flyers, capable of traveling far and fast. Although some adults stay in the southern oceans during the southern winter after breeding, most migrate immense distances to enjoy the northern summer in the north Pacific and Atlantic Oceans off Alaska, northeast Canada, Greenland, and Japan.

The annual migrations take them on huge loops as they travel north up one side of the Atlantic or Pacific Oceans, then east and back down the other side to return to their breeding colonies. This strategy enables them to make the best use of tailwinds and crosswinds and fly with minimum expenditure of energy.

Fishing for Food

Sooty shearwaters eat small shoaling fish such as anchovies as well as crustaceans and small squid. They catch most of their prey by diving from the surface while swimming or plunging more deeply beneath the waves from the air. Sometimes they simply reach out and snatch prey from the surface while swimming.

Huge flocks of many thousands of birds gather at rich feeding sites, forming a seething mass as they leapfrog one another in their eagerness to get to the prey. They often feed in

⤋ *The greatest concentrations of sooty shearwaters are found in the north Pacific and may contain as many as half a million birds. Flocks feeding at sea have been reported to make screaming or cackling sounds—the combined effect sounding like distant human voices.*

the company of other seabirds, especially other shearwaters and—in the south—penguins. They often appear behind fishing vessels to scavenge for offal thrown overboard.

Eerie Calls

Most sooty shearwaters breed on remote islands to the south and east of New Zealand, with as many as 2.75 million pairs on the Snares Islands alone. Huge colonies occur off the southernmost coasts of Chile, especially on islands around Cape Horn, while much smaller numbers breed on the Falklands, Tristan da Cunha, and on islands off southeast Australia.

The birds return to these breeding grounds in the southern spring. Usually pairing for life, they dig out a nest-burrow with their strong webbed feet and often use it year after year.

The shearwaters spend their day feeding offshore. At dusk they assemble on the sea in huge "rafts" of birds, which then rise and circle the colony before flying to the nest-burrows under cover of darkness. At this time the air is filled with an eerie cacophony of rhythmically repeated, hoarse moaning "oo-oo-ah" calls, increasing in loudness and speed before dying away. The birds may be even noisier at dawn.

The parents take turns incubating the egg in shifts lasting from one to two weeks. A few days after the egg hatches, the parents leave their chick in the nest-burrow while they go to find food. Returning at night, the parents feed their chick by regurgitating a thick, oily soup of semidigested fish from their stomachs. They may be away for up to ten nights, yet their rich diet ensures that the chick weighs twice as much as its parents before it fledges. This allows the parents to leave on their long migration, since their chick can survive on its fat reserves for three weeks until it is ready to fly away with other young birds on their first great journey northward.

Plump Plunder

In New Zealand this species is sometimes known as the muttonbird because the grossly plump young are traditionally eaten by the Maori people or processed for their oil. Half a million are currently taken annually, but introduced predators such as cats, pigs, and rats, plus destruction of nesting sites and drowning in drift nets, are more important threats. Even so, the total world population is estimated at a healthy 20 million birds.

Leach's Storm Petrel

Oceanodroma leucorhoa

The diminutive Leach's storm petrel is rarely seen by humans, for it spends most of its life at sea and nests on remote islands that it visits only at night.

Common name Leach's storm petrel

Scientific name *Oceanodroma leucorhoa*

Family Hydrobatidae

Order Procellariiformes

Size Length: 7.5–8.5 in (19–21.6 cm); wingspan: 18–19 in (45.7–48 cm); weight: 1.5–1.8 oz (42.5–51 g)

Key features Very distinctive flight, with sudden changes of speed, direction, and action; all-dark plumage except for pale, diagonal bar across upper wings and divided white rump patch above forked tail

Habits Gregarious at breeding sites, visiting only at night; otherwise mainly solitary, feeding at sea, but may flock at food source

Nesting Nests in shallow earth burrow, rock crevice, old wall, or ruined building; 1 white egg; incubation by both sexes for 41–42 days; young fledge after 63–70 days; 1 brood

Voice Very noisy at breeding colonies, uttering long sequences of purring, chattering, cackling, or screaming sounds

Diet Mainly planktonic crustaceans, mollusks, tiny fish, and squid; also morsels of oil or fat

Habitat Generally far out to sea when not breeding

Distribution Temperate and tropical Atlantic and Pacific Oceans, plus offshore islands in north

Status Little known, although some colonies huge; declines in some areas due to predation

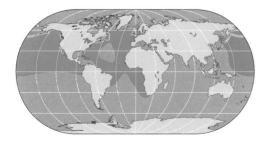

ELUSIVE AND DIFFICULT TO STUDY, Leach's storm petrel is one of the most mysterious of seabirds. Although bigger than some of its close relatives, it is only the size of a starling, and it is a matter of wonder that such a small, fragile-looking creature can survive a life largely spent flying just above the open ocean, coping with fierce gales, great waves, and driving rain.

The bird lives in the north Atlantic and north Pacific Oceans, where it can be delightful to watch as it dances over the ocean surface with constant, sudden changes of speed, direction, and technique. One moment Leach's storm petrel is hanging motionless on the wind like a miniature gull, the next shooting away with deep wingbeats like a tern, before soaring and banking on stiff wings like a shearwater. The bird's relatively long, pointed wings and forked tail help it perform its dramatic maneuvers.

⊕ In fall and early winter migrating Leach's storm petrels can be tossed around in the wind and get blown very close to shore. This sometimes produces dramatic "wrecks" of hundreds or even thousands of exhausted birds along coastlines— sometimes even far inland.

Floating Food

Leach's storm petrel feeds mainly on tiny crustaceans that drift in the plankton in the surface layers of the ocean, as well as small fish and squid. It supplements this basic diet with floating fragments of flesh, fat, and oily material from the carcasses of large animals such as whales and seals, sometimes following obviously injured or sick individuals to obtain these energy-rich morsels.

Although it dangles its legs when feeding, Leach's storm petrel does not patter its feet or "walk" on the water like most other storm petrels and only occasionally settles on the water. It usually spends a solitary life at sea and does not follow boats to scavenge for scraps.

Offshore Breeding

Leach's storm petrels breed on offshore islands in the north Pacific Ocean from Japan and Alaska south to Baja California, and in the north Atlantic Ocean from Britain and Iceland to Nova Scotia and south to Massachusetts.

They usually choose breeding sites where there is a good layer of topsoil so males can dig out their nest-burrows using their bills and feet. If it is not available, they nest in holes in cliffs or crevices among rocks. They visit the sites only at night, to avoid predators.

Breeding birds perform dramatic communal display flights in which pairs chase each other in very fast, erratic flights over their burrows, hover with legs trailing, or stand at the burrow entrances with raised wings. All this activity is accompanied by chattering, cackling, or screaming sounds and long, purring duets that emanate from deep within the burrows.

After hatching, the youngster remains in the burrow for two months, steadily putting on weight thanks to more or less nightly feeds by its parents before it is ready to depart for a life on the open ocean. It will not return until it is at least five years old. By September the Leach's storm petrels have left their breeding grounds to migrate south. Each year these tough little seabirds make journeys of 3,105 to 5,590 miles (5,000–9,000 km), reaching as far as the equatorial Galápagos Islands in the Pacific Ocean and to Brazil and South Africa in the Atlantic Ocean; a few have even reached Australia and New Zealand.

Local Dangers

Although making accurate counts of these birds is almost impossible, one estimate puts the world population at over 10 million birds. However, some local populations are suffering the effects of predators such as rats, cats, mink, and foxes introduced to their breeding islands. Other threats include disturbance by visitors, attacks by great skuas (*Catharacta skua*), and the collapse of nest-burrows due to sheep walking on them. Leach's storm petrels may be tough, but they are still vulnerable.

Brown Pelican

Pelecanus occidentalis

Ungainly and comical-looking on land, the brown pelican becomes elegant once airborne—gliding over the sea on its great, broad wings before plunging beneath the waves in search of fish.

Common name Brown pelican

Scientific name *Pelecanus occidentalis*

Family	Pelecanidae
Order	Pelecaniformes
Size	Length: 43–47 in (109–119 cm); wingspan: 75–85 in (190–216 cm); weight: 8–15 lb (3.6–6.8 kg)
Key features	Typical huge pelican bill and throat pouch; mainly brown plumage; smaller and with less bright color on head and bill than similar Peruvian pelican
Habits	Gregarious all year; plunges into sea from high in air to catch fish; young gather in crèches before fledging
Nesting	Nests mainly in trees or shrubs; variable nest of sticks and grass; 2–3 chalky white eggs; incubation 28–31 days; young fledge after 63–78 days; 1 brood
Voice	Adults make deep grunts, moans, and other sounds at breeding colonies; young utter higher-pitched noises, yelps, and screams
Diet	Mainly fish; also carrion and crustaceans
Habitat	Along coasts and islands, feeding in inshore waters, including estuaries; avoids open sea
Distribution	Pacific coasts from British Columbia to Peru, including Galápagos; Atlantic coasts from New England through Caribbean to Guiana
Status	Quite common; probably the second most numerous pelican after Peruvian pelican

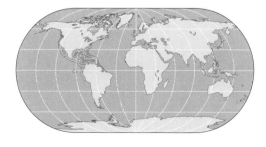

THE SMALLEST OF ALL PELICANS, the brown pelican is one of only two species in its family that are truly marine, the other being its close relative the Peruvian pelican (*Pelecanus thagus*). These two species are also distinctive because of their fishing techniques. Unlike all other pelicans, which merely dip their heads or upend their bodies beneath the water to scoop up fish in their great pouches, they catch their food by spectacular plunge-dives from midair.

Versatile Bird

Like other pelicans, the brown pelican is essentially a bird of the tropics and subtropics. But it is a versatile species, able to tolerate the cooler climate of Maryland and Virginia as well as the tropical heat of the Caribbean.

Most pelicans have white plumage with areas of gray or black; but as its name suggests, the brown pelican is mainly pale brown with darker flight feathers and a chestnut nape in

⊕ *The brown pelican draws its head back onto its shoulders in flight. This allows it to support the weight of the huge bill by resting it on its neck, which is held in an S-shape.*

the breeding season. The very closely related Peruvian pelican is similar, but much bigger, with more white streaking below, more orange on the bill, and brighter areas of bare skin on the face when breeding. It was once considered to be just a race of the brown pelican, but is now generally regarded as a separate species.

Ocean Patrol

Brown pelicans can travel nonstop for great distances by using a flap-glide technique—a few powerful beats of their wings are followed by a long glide. They usually travel in V-formations or staggered lines, a habit that may save energy as each bird rides on the upwash of air from the wingtips of the bird in front. The birds generally fly very low over the water, with their wingtips almost touching it, taking advantage of updrafts created by waves by flying along the leading edge of the wave crests. At times, however, they soar high in the air.

Brown pelicans usually search for food in small groups, flying above the water in single file and watching for the slightest sign of a fish below. On sighting a single large fish or a shoal of smaller ones, one of the party peels off and plunges down, opening its great bill to trap the fish in its huge pouch.

The sound of the splash as a brown pelican hits the water can be heard from up to almost 0.6 mile (1 km) away. Yet the bird remains unharmed thanks to the air sacs beneath the skin of its chest that cushion the impact. They also make the pelican buoyant, so it bobs to the surface quickly if it has submerged. It always surfaces facing into the wind, to ensure an easy takeoff. However, it cannot rise until it has drained off the great volume of water trapped in its pouch—which can weigh more than the bird itself—and swallowed the fish.

Feeding Flocks

Brown pelicans feed mainly on fish, especially small schooling species. Large shoals of sardines or anchovies can attract big concentrations of the birds, and they may compete with human fishing interests, particularly along Pacific coasts. However, in other places, such as off the Atlantic coast of the U.S., most of the species taken by brown pelicans are fish such as menhaden that have little commercial value.

As well as fish, brown pelicans also catch some shrimp and other crustaceans. They

⤊ When a brown pelican dives, it stretches its head and neck forward and angles its wings back to ease its passage into the water. As it strikes the water surface, it thrusts its wings and feet back to increase its speed.

⤴ Immature brown pelicans are often targeted by pirates such as large gulls, which steal the pelicans' catch before they get the chance to swallow it. This juvenile is trying to swallow a fish.

occasionally scavenge for animal remains, as well as any fish offal or dead fish they can glean from fishermen.

They feed almost entirely in the relatively shallow waters of estuaries and other sheltered inshore areas, within about 6 miles (10 km) of the coast. They are most active in the early morning or late afternoon, perhaps to avoid the glare of the Sun shining in their eyes, which makes it harder to dive accurately.

Brown pelicans often suffer from the attentions of other birds that make a habit of kleptoparasitism, or food piracy. In the Atlantic and Caribbean the most likely robbers are laughing gulls (*Larus atricilla*), which are bold enough to fly down and land on a pelican's head as it emerges from the sea with its catch, hoping to grab a free meal. In the subtropical and tropical parts of their range, from Mexico and Florida southward, the pelicans need to keep watch for another, more dedicated pirate—the very large magnificent frigatebird (*Fregata magnificens*).

When they are not feeding, brown pelicans spend a lot of time resting. Although they are powerful, buoyant swimmers, they cannot spend long periods on the water without their feathers becoming sodden, so they roost on sandbars or on trees or other perches. The birds also splash their feathers in the water before preening them, taking care to scratch their heads and necks thoroughly in an attempt to remove irritating parasitic feather lice.

Adapting to Humans

Of all pelicans, the brown pelican has adapted best to life alongside humans. Pelicans are generally shy and wary—and with good reason, since they have suffered much persecution at the hands of people. However, brown pelicans have managed to overcome this fear, particularly at fishing ports, tourist resorts, and other coastal settlements where they are regularly allowed to take discarded scraps of fish. At such places they are a common and much photographed sight as they glide in to take these offerings or digest them while resting on jetties, walls, posts, or moored boats.

⊙ *If a male succeeds in winning over a female, he presents her with a gift of some twigs or grass, and she uses it to start building the nest. The male continues to gather nesting material and is not averse to stealing it from neighboring nests.*

Remote Refuges

If they can find them, brown pelicans nest in stands of mangroves or other trees to gain protection from ground predators and flooding. Otherwise, and especially in the Pacific region, they nest on the ground on small, remote flat islands and arid stretches of coast, often on steep, rocky slopes that are free from predatory mammals and human disturbance. Some of these colonies are maintained for many years, but others may be abandoned as a result of disturbance, heavy infection of the young with parasites, or a sudden drop in the food supply.

Whatever the site, the male chooses it and advertises for a mate with head-swaying displays and repeated bowing to show off the strip of rich chestnut feathers that runs up the back of the neck; he also jerks up his wingtips rhythmically about once a second.

⊖ *Brown pelican chicks beg for food by pecking at their parents' bills, trying to make them regurgitate a meal of half-digested fish. These pelicans have nested in mangrove trees in the Galápagos.*

Brown pelican nests built on the ground are merely hollows scraped out by the birds in the soil or even the birds' droppings, sparsely lined with a few feathers; the rim builds up to as much as 10 inches (25 cm) high as the pair add their droppings to the soil and debris. Nests constructed among trees or shrubs are much more substantial structures of twigs, grass, reeds, or other vegetation piled onto a platform of large sticks interwoven into the supporting branches.

Both parents share the task of incubating the eggs, placing them gently on top of the huge, warm webs of their feet. On hatching, the chicks look like miniature pterodactyls (prehistoric flying reptiles). The grotesqueness—at least to human eyes—is often increased by the sight of many parasitic ticks scuttling over their naked bodies.

At first their parents regurgitate half-digested food onto the floor of the nest for the chicks to pick up in their bills. After about ten days the chicks start growing coats of soft, white down and begin to take food directly from their parents' pouches. Unlike their generally silent parents, the chicks are very noisy, begging for food with piercing screams.

Before they are able to fly, young brown pelicans gather together in groups known as "pods." Each chick may need as much as 176 pounds (80 kg) of fish to survive to the fledging stage. If food is in short supply, the oldest is fed first, and one or both of the others may be left to starve, so that at least one survives. Older chicks may even eat younger ones.

Many chicks also die by being trampled underfoot when a hungry pod scrambles to obtain food from a returning adult, which often beats off or tosses aside chicks that are not its own. But if they survive these and other hazards to reach adulthood, brown pelicans may live to 25 years or more.

Problems with Pesticides

During the 1960s and 1970s brown pelican populations in the U.S. suffered massive declines as the birds accumulated the pesticides DDT and dieldrin in their bodies. These widely used poisons built up in the food chain and became concentrated in the fish that the birds ate. That affected the pelicans' eggs, thinning their shells so that they broke in the nests. In parts of their northern range brown pelican numbers slumped by as much as 90 percent in just 20 years, and the bird was declared an endangered U.S. species by 1973. Fortunately, the pesticides involved were then banned, allowing the pelicans to make a dramatic recovery, and in most areas populations had reached their former levels by the late 1980s.

Great Cormorant

Phalacrocorax carbo

Largest of all the cormorants, the great cormorant is both highly adaptable and superbly equipped for diving to catch its fish prey.

Common name Great cormorant

Scientific name *Phalacrocorax carbo*

Family	Phalacrocoracidae
Order	Pelecaniformes
Size	Length: 31–39 in (79–99 cm); wingspan: 51–63 in (130–160 cm); weight: 4–6 lb (1.8–2.7 kg)
Key features	Large seabird with thick, snakelike neck and long, bulky body; powerful, hook-tipped bill; almost all-black with white face patch, variable white neck plumes, and white thigh patch in breeding plumage
Habits	Swims low in water; dives frequently; often perches with wings held out; colonial nester
Nesting	Lined, shallow cups on sea cliffs, stacks, and among boulders, also (chiefly inland) in trees, bushes, reed beds, or on ground; 2–6 (usually 3–4) eggs; incubation 27–31 days by both parents; young fledge after 50 days; 1 brood
Voice	Guttural grunting and groaning calls from adults at breeding sites; chicks beg for food with whining, warbling calls
Diet	Almost entirely fish, including flatfish and eels; also crustaceans, chicks, and small birds
Habitat	Many individuals chiefly marine; others occur mainly around inland freshwaters
Distribution	Very widespread, from northeastern North America east to Japan and south to South Africa, Australia, and New Zealand
Status	Common and widespread throughout much of range; many populations have increased over past 100 years

THE GREAT CORMORANT'S RANGE SPANS five continents, from cold, arctic coasts to warm, tropical lagoons, and it breeds both by the sea and inland, thriving in habitats ranging from remote sea cliffs and rough seas to reservoirs in major cities. Populations that are mainly marine prefer to stay within sight of the coast.

Great cormorants are specialized diving birds, and on land they are extremely clumsy, sometimes even falling over their own huge, webbed feet. Yet they are able to balance on tree branches, rocks, buoys, and other suitable perches, where they spend a great deal of time standing upright resting.

In flight they look rather like geese as they speed low over the water in loose V-formations with rapid, shallow beats of their long, angled, blunt-tipped wings. Unlike any goose, however, they alternate their flapping flight with brief glides. Over land they often fly higher and sometimes circle up until almost lost from view.

Deadly Struggle

Instead of catching fish in the upper layers of the ocean like many seabirds, great cormorants concentrate on fish that live on or just above the seabed. In coastal waters flatfish such as flounders and plaice form the bulk of their diet, and they are also fond of eels. They sometimes tackle surprisingly large prey, which may put up a dramatic struggle and take a good deal of subduing by the cormorant before it can position its catch to swallow it headfirst.

Sometimes great cormorants will eat crabs and shrimp; there are even records of them eating ducklings or snatching swallows flying low over the water.

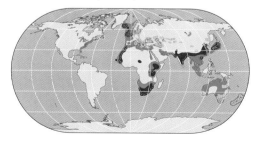

⊕ Great cormorants dive to the seabed for their prey and have plumage that absorbs water to reduce buoyancy. Each bout of diving is followed by a period spent perched with their broad wings held open, so that their waterlogged feathers dry off completely.

To find their prey, great cormorants may dive as deep as 120 feet (37 m) for up to a minute. Most dives are less ambitious, reaching to within 33 feet (10 m) of the surface and lasting about half a minute. Swimming low in the water, a cormorant often makes a small leap into the air before leading into the dive, but may also submerge by simply sinking with scarcely a ripple.

Bulky Heaps

Great cormorant pairs do not usually stay together for more than a few seasons. Their bulky nests, up to 1 foot (30 cm) high and 3 feet (90 cm) across, are made of sticks and other material—coastal breeders use mainly seaweed. The shallow cup formed at the top of the nest is lined with softer material.

In temperate regions the birds usually lay their chalky, pale bluish or greenish eggs between April and June; but in tropical regions, where the food supply is less seasonal, great cormorants may breed at any time.

Unlike all other pelican-related families apart from the darters, cormorants are able to rear more than just a single youngster. That is because they do not have to fly long distances for their food, so they can feed four or more chicks several times a day. The parent birds even continue to feed their young for up to two months after they have fledged.

Unproven Pests

Great cormorants have suffered badly from persecution in the past, but protection in parts of their range has resulted in increases at many colonies. Even so, they still come into conflict with fisherfolk and fish farmers, who accuse them of taking too many fish. As a result, they are still killed, often illegally. Research is ongoing to determine whether or not they are serious pests of fisheries.

Northern Gannet

Morus bassanus

The magnificent northern gannet is always a dramatic sight, both during its spectacular dives for fish and at its crowded breeding colonies, where the gleaming white birds festoon the rocks like fallen snow.

BIG, POWERFUL, AND SPECTACULAR, THE northern gannet is the most charismatic of north Atlantic seabirds. It is superbly adapted for both flying and plunge-diving for fish; the cigar-shaped body, daggerlike bill, and long, sharp-ended tail give the bird a streamlined profile that offers minimum resistance to air and water. Together with its long, narrow black-tipped wings, it allows the gannet to travel far and fast, at speeds of 25 to 37 miles per hour (40–60 km/h), both to reach good feeding areas and on migration.

Individuals or groups often fly low over the water, with shallow, but powerful strokes of

Plunge-diver

Wheeling and soaring high above the sea, a gannet searches for prey from heights of up to 130 feet (40 m). On spotting a shoal, it suddenly goes into a dive, beginning to fold its wings back as it accelerates. All the time it is checking the exact position of its target, taking advantage of the excellent binocular vision provided by its forward-facing eyes. Just before it hits the waves, it draws its wings right back parallel with its body, so it resembles a great white arrowhead. It reduces the resistance as it slices into the water with tremendous force, raising a great plume of spray.

Air sacs beneath its skin and a pad of spongy bone at the base of its bill act as natural shock absorbers, cushioning the gannet's head, neck, and breast against the impact. As the bird strikes the water, a protective, translucent membrane flicks across the eyes to prevent them being injured, and movable flaps seal the nostrils near the base of the bill to prevent water rushing into the mouth.

Common name Northern gannet

Scientific name *Morus bassanus*

Family Sulidae

Order Pelecaniformes

Size Length: 34–39 in (86–99 cm); wingspan: 65–71 in (165–180 cm); weight: 5–8 lb (2.3–3.6 kg)

Key features Very large white seabird; long, conical bill; long, streamlined body; long, pointed black-tipped wings; head and neck creamy-yellow; juveniles dark brown with white speckling, older immatures progressively more white

Habits Breeds mainly in large colonies; otherwise found in smaller groups that may gather at good feeding sites; plunges into sea for food

Nesting Nests on tops of steep cliffs, stacks, and islands; nests built of seaweed, grass, and flotsam; 1 pale blue egg; incubation 44 days by both sexes; young fledge after 90 days; 1 brood

Voice Chorus of loud, harsh groans, barks, and croaks at breeding colonies, with yapping sounds of young

Diet Shoaling open ocean fish, mainly mackerel, herring, sprat, and sand eels; also scavenges for offal and dead fish from fishing boats

Habitat Feeds at sea; breeds on mainland coasts and on offshore islands

Distribution Northern Atlantic, northern Caribbean, and western Mediterranean, from Arctic south to West Africa

Status Steady expansion of range and numbers; about 70 percent of total nest in British Isles

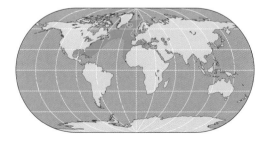

their wings alternating with short glides. Gannets relish rough weather, using the wind sweeping over the waves to soar with minimum input of energy, and making great banking glides like giant shearwaters.

Gannets are good swimmers and often alight on the sea to ride out storms or to roost at night when not at the breeding colony. Taking off from water is more difficult than from the cliffs of their nesting colonies, however, and they need a short run with vigorous wingbeats and much splashing of their big, webbed feet to get airborne.

Diving for Prey

While they are always dramatic-looking birds, gannets are at their most impressive when diving for prey from midair. When mass diving of a large flock is at its height, with the great white birds raining down from all directions and frequently crossing paths, it is astonishing that they do not impale their long, sharp bills in each other's bodies.

The northern gannet's combination of foraging far from land and deep plunge-diving enables it to concentrate on shoaling fish, such as mackerel, sprat, and herring, that gather in great numbers and at considerable depths a good distance offshore. In this way it avoids competition with other seabirds within its range.

Plumage Signals

Unlike most other seabirds, an adult northern gannet is almost entirely white. Its dazzling plumage is thought to serve as a long-range signal to others of its kind that one or more birds have found a shoal of fish, providing a marker for the watchers to home in on and share the rich feeding opportunities.

By contrast, juveniles are blackish-brown with a frosting of white speckles. It probably has the function of inhibiting the aggressive adults from attacking the youngsters. Gradually, starting with the head, neck, and underparts, the birds gain more and more white feathers, creating a distinctive wing pattern like a piano keyboard. It takes four to six years for a gannet to acquire its full adult plumage.

A gannet can dive to depths of 33 feet (10 m) or more. There are several reasons why it can dive so deeply. It is the heaviest member of its family, and this extra weight—together with its beautifully streamlined profile—allow it to penetrate well below the surface. Plunging down through the water, it seizes its target fish in its saw-edged bill and usually swallows it underwater before resurfacing.

⊕ Gannets may be expert at catching their own food, but they are not above trying to steal a meal from each other. Normally the birds avoid such squabbles by swallowing their prey under the water.

⊕ Collecting nesting material is the job of the male gannet, while his mate has the responsibility of stopping neighboring birds from stealing it from under her bill.

⊕ This elaborate bow is part of a whole range of ritual displays that help cement the bonds between mated pairs. Any gannet that fails to give the correct response is treated as a trespasser and is threatened or even attacked.

Crowded Neighborhood

In the breeding season gannets nest in dense colonies that often contain many thousands of pairs. The birds normally mate for life, renewing their pair-bonds each year as they return to the colony. Pairs use complex ritualized displays throughout the season to ensure they rein in their natural aggression and bond with each other; they include dramatic bouts of bill-fencing with outstretched wings.

The nests are so closely packed together that the birds could reach out and touch one another; but with suitable sites in short supply, each pair vigorously defends a tiny breeding territory in the immediate vicinity of the nest for up to nine months each year.

Neighbors threaten each other; and if that fails, they may fight viciously, using their formidable bills as weapons. It is not unusual for birds to be seriously injured or even killed.

The male gannet undertakes most of the nest-building, collecting seaweed and grass to be mixed with soil and the birds' droppings to form a large mound. His mate stands guard over this material to prevent other pairs from stealing it. They share the incubation of the relatively small egg by carefully placing the warm web of one foot over the egg, largely covering it, and then wrapping the other foot over on top of it to retain the heat.

Two or three days before the egg is ready to hatch, the chick inside begins to cheep. This alerts the parent on duty to transfer the egg to the upper surface of its foot-web before it hatches, so that the weakened shell does not break and suffocate the chick.

During the chick-rearing period a pair of gannets may make fishing expeditions that last as long as 13 hours and take the birds up to 373 miles (600 km) from the colony.

Eventually, the well-fed, plump youngster molts from its thick coat of fluffy white down into its first true feathers. Soon it is ready to leave its parents and plunge off the cliff edge onto the surface of the sea far below. It swims away and fasts for a while until it is light enough to take off and perfect its flying skills. It soon departs to explore warmer seas, European birds reaching as far as West Africa. Immature northern gannets do not usually return north for two or more years. They are mature at five to six years of age.

Persecution and Pollution

Despite being praised for their wild beauty in traditional folklore and ancient chronicles, northern gannets suffered badly from human persecution for centuries. The great birds were hunted for their meat, fat, and eggs, and many were pointlessly shot as a form of "sport," especially during the nineteenth century. Now, almost all the colonies enjoy legal protection; the population has made a dramatic recovery, and numbers are still increasing.

The main threats today are various forms of pollution. They include mercury, pesticides, and other poisons that can build up in the food chain and become concentrated in the gannets' bodies and eggs. Oil spills are always a risk, as is being drowned in modern synthetic fishing nets, which are indestructible and often travel great distances after being lost or discarded. Many birds are also strangled in tangled rope and other flotsam such as the plastic packaging used for packs of cans and bottles.

↑ A gannet breeding colony is a spectacular sight, with the ground almost obscured by the closely packed nesting birds and the sky filled with adults leaving to catch fish or returning to feed their young. This colony is on Grassholm off southwest Wales.

29

American Bitten

Botauris lentiginosus

Common name American bitten

Scientific name *Botauris lentiginosus*

Family	Ardeidae
Order	Ciconiiformes
Size	Length: 23.5–33.5 in (60–85 cm); wingspan: 41–49 in (105–125 cm); weight: 13–20 oz (0.4–0.6 kg)
Key features	Thickset, medium-sized, streaky brown heron; small yellow bill; juvenile lacks the black line behind the eye broadening to a patch running down neck; sexes identical
Habits	Solitary; normally secretive but occasionally seen stalking prey in open fields
Nesting	Platform of vegetation in dense marsh cover; 3–5 eggs (exceptionally 2–7); incubation 28–29 days; young fledge after 14 days; 1 brood
Voice	Male gives booming call in breeding season; alarm call is "kok-kok-kok"
Diet	Very wide: fish, amphibians, snakes, small mammals, crawfish, mollusks, and insects
Habitat	Marshes, bogs, open meadows; mangroves, and swamps outside breeding season
Distribution	North and central U.S. states and southern Canada; also southern U.S., Central America, and Caribbean
Status	Not globally threatened but declining throughout breeding range; declared as threatened or endangered in many U.S. states and Canadian provinces

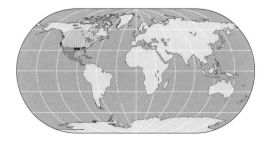

Bitterns are experts at concealment. Often hidden in the depths of a marsh, their camouflaged plumage makes them doubly difficult to see.

WHEN IT STANDS PERFECTLY STILL among the rushes or cattails of a marsh, the American bittern blends in perfectly with its surroundings. Variable shades of brown on its upper parts contrast with heavy black streaks down its neck, becoming buff-colored on the belly. The brown-black mix can be indistinguishable from the surrounding dead vegetation. When the bittern flies on its broad but pointed wings, the dark flight feathers are conspicuous.

Active Hunter

The American bittern spends much of its time in marshes, although it is unique among the larger bitterns in looking for food in open meadows and dry grasslands, too. It stands in water or on a bank with its thin, pointed bill held low, waiting to strike at prey below. Now and then it takes very slow, measured steps forward. It usually hunts fish, but it will take anything that comes close enough. Sometimes it picks insects off plant stems or catches them in the air. The American bittern is undoubtedly more active in its feeding techniques than the other large bitterns—when hunting in tall grass on land, the bird often runs quickly after prey with its wings held up.

Booming Call

At the beginning of the breeding season the male produces an extraordinary booming call that advertises his territory and attracts a mate. Crouching on a perch, the male inflates his esophagus so that it acts like a giant wind pump, expelling a loud, booming belch. It has resulted in the bittern gaining such names as "thunder pumper," "bog bull," and "mire drum." He makes the sound several times at intervals of several seconds and utters it more and more often until the birds have mated.

Bitterns conceal their nests within dense cover, usually tucked into vegetation on a marsh, but occasionally in tall grasses on land. It is likely that the male chooses the nest site, and thereafter the female assumes all the duties. She shapes reeds, rushes, and other plants into a nest platform on which she lays her brownish eggs. After incubation she feeds the yellow chicks by regurgitating food she has brought back to the nest.

Birds in southern parts of the range remain largely where they are after breeding, but those from the northern U.S. and Canada prepare to migrate south for the winter, flying at night with fast wingbeats, on huge journeys into the Caribbean and Central America. Saltwater coastal marshes, mangrove, cattail, and sawgrass swamps are all favored winter habitats. Some lose their direction or get carried by winds, and American bitterns have been known to land as far away as Norway.

Bittern Numbers

The bittern's ability to remain hidden in tall vegetation can work against it. Although bitterns are widespread, conservationists are unable to ascertain exact numbers. But evidence suggests that since the Second World War the destruction of its wetland habitats has been catastrophic. Surveys estimate that throughout North America bittern numbers have more than halved. Many wetlands have been drained to make way for agriculture or development. Others have become polluted by chemicals from farm fields or have been damaged by uncontrolled grazing by livestock. Many more have simply silted up and become unsuitable. Conservationists are working to restore and recreate the bittern's habitat.

⊕ A solitary hunter, the American bittern feeds at dawn, dusk, and at night. This one, wading through the shallows on Long Island, New York, has caught a fish. Crawfish, salamanders, gophers, ground squirrels, and garter snakes are also items on the bittern's wide diet.

Glossy Ibis

Plegadis falcinellus

From a distance the glossy ibis appears black. But on closer inspection, and with the sunlight shining on it, the bird's plumage displays the glossy chestnuts and greens from which it gets its common name.

THE GLOSSY IBIS IS AN ATTRACTIVE and widespread waterbird. The "glossy" description in the bird's name derives from its dark, shiny plumage: brown on the head and neck with green on the wings. Its underparts are black to brown in color. It is distributed across a vast range, including Australia, Asia, Africa, the U.S., and the Caribbean. These latter populations, it is thought, are relatively recent arrivals in the New World, with first records of the birds appearing in the 1880s.

Seldom Alone

The glossy ibis is a bird of extensive shallow lakes, lagoons, and estuaries with abundant vegetation. Here, at the water's edge the bird searches for its animal prey—a wide mixture of invertebrates (such as insects, water snails, leeches, worms, and crustaceans) plus occasional small fish and snakes (including, in North America, the poisonous water moccasin). The glossy ibis uses its long bill for probing mud, and its long legs enable the bird to wade comfortably in the water.

Like a number of wetland birds, the glossy ibis is a highly social species. Nesting in colonies and feeding in groups, it is rarely seen alone. Its colonies range in size from a few pairs up to thousands, where they are often found in the company of herons, egrets, and cormorants. The glossy ibis nests either in low trees and bushes of about 16–23 feet (5–7 m) in height—where it favors willow—or more commonly on the ground in reed beds or other areas where tall vegetation offers privacy and protection.

In the Northern Hemisphere nesting takes place between March and the end of May. Pairs are formed during periods of display, when

---

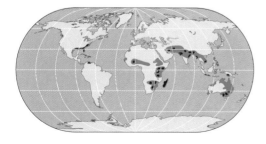

Common name Glossy ibis

Scientific name *Plegadis falcinellus*

Family Threskiornithidae

Order Ciconiiformes

Size Length: 19–22 in (48.5–56 cm); wingspan: 31.5–37.5 in (80–95 cm); weight: 1.1–1.3 lb (0.5–0.6 kg)

Key features An all-dark ibis with characteristic long legs and downcurved bill; neck and back brown with white edging between face and bill; wings and tail glossy green; male slightly larger

Habits Feeds at water's edge; highly social and rarely seen alone; nests in colonies

Nesting Nest a substantial pile of twigs in trees or bushes, or woven reeds in tall vegetation on the ground; 3–6 eggs; incubation 21 days; young fledge after 28 days; 1 brood

Voice Very occasional nasal grunts; some cooing and bleating while at nest

Diet Wide range of invertebrates; also some fish and snakes

Habitat Found in shallow water in lakes and marshes; also rivers, extensive flood plains, and estuaries

Distribution Widely distributed from Australia, India, Central Asia, eastern Europe, and Africa; also eastern U.S., Venezuela, and Caribbean

Status Across its range the glossy ibis population appears stable; in North America its numbers are increasing; there are concerns in some parts of Europe due to wetland drainage, the spread of agriculture, and hunting pressures

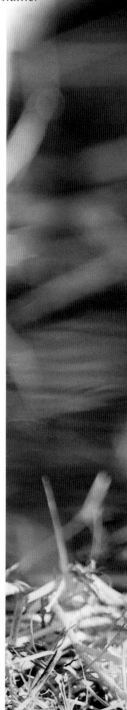

males and females indulge in ritualized actions, including the touching of bills, bowing, and mutual preening (known as allopreening).

After mating, the female lays three to six eggs. Incubation is shared, but it is usually the female that sits at night. The chicks are initially cared for by their parents when they hatch. They are fed on animal matter regurgitated from the parents' crops, which, soon after hatching, the young obtain by inserting their bills into the adults' mouths.

For the first week at least one parent is always present. From about two weeks the young birds become more mobile, wandering onto surrounding branches. As the young grow, the parents leave regurgitated food in the nest for them. Around this time each parent makes at least six trips a day to bring their offspring food in addition to feeding themselves. This is no mean feat because the parents must often make long flights to suitable feeding grounds.

By six weeks the young are starting to feed themselves. By seven weeks they will fly with their parents to feeding grounds, only returning at night to the safety of their nesting site.

Toward the end of the nesting season larger flocks of ibises form, often with young and adults in separate groups. Young birds then begin to disperse in all directions. Dispersion from the breeding grounds in parts of the Northern Hemisphere leads, from September, into migration proper. Eastern European birds, for instance, drift southward in the fall, most wintering south of the Sahara.

Local Concerns

Although the glossy ibis population appears generally stable, there are concerns for its welfare in some parts of the world. In Europe, for instance, it has declined since the 1950s as a result of large-scale drainage of wetlands and the remorseless spread of intensive agriculture.

⊜ *The almost iridescent green plumage of the glossy ibis is caught by the sunlight in this specimen preening itself in the Florida Everglades.*

Wood Stork

Mycteria americana

Known locally as "ironhead" or "flinthead" due to its gray, featherless head, the wood stork is an impressive and stoutly built bird and North America's only stork.

YEAR ROUND THE WOOD STORK relies almost entirely on fish as the main constituent of its diet. Whereas many fish-eating birds, such as herons, rely on good eyesight to locate and catch their prey, the wood stork relies on its sense of touch. Pacing slowly through shallow water, it feels for fish with its long and sensitive bill. Holding the bill slightly open, it sweeps it from side to side. On touching a fish, the bill is snapped closed, sharp edges holding the prey firmly. From touch to capture takes no longer than 25 milliseconds—one of the fastest-known responses in any vertebrate. This special method of food capture allows the birds to feed in shallow, muddy, and weed-choked waters where visibility is poor.

Raising the Young

The wood stork is colonial, nesting in large rookeries and feeding in flocks. The rookeries are located in the tops of tall trees (such as cypress in the southeastern U.S.), where each will be home to a number of nests. The colonies are often located on islands that offer greater security from predators.

On hatching, the chicks are covered in a soft, gray down and rely on their parents for food. It is regurgitated by the adults and left on the nest floor for the chicks to eat. Young storks can eat up to 60 percent of their body weight every day. It is not surprising that their development is rapid!

Around 65 days from hatching the young take to the air. Following the breeding season, birds both disperse and, in some cases, migrate in search of good places to feed. Birds nesting in the Amazon basin, for instance, may move along the Amazon River, across the Andes to Columbia or south to southern Brazil.

Common name Wood stork

Scientific name *Mycteria americana*

Family   Ciconiidae

Order   Ciconiiformes

Size Length: 33–40 in (83–102 cm); wingspan: 59 in (150 cm); weight: 4.4–6.6 lb (2–3 kg)

Key features Largely white plumage except for black on the tips and trailing edge of the wings and tail; black bill; neck and head largely bare

Habits   Nests colonially; feeds in groups

Nesting   In the tops of tall trees, often on islands; nest consists of a large pile of sticks lined with leaves; 3 eggs; incubation 28–32 days; young fledge after 65 days; 1 brood

Voice   Normally silent but will hiss when at nest site during breeding season

Diet   Mostly small fish; also invertebrates and small snakes

Habitat   Shallow water in swamps, mangroves, estuaries, and manmade habitats such as canals; prefers fresh water

Distribution Wetland areas from northern Argentina, through Mexico, to North America

Status   Not globally threatened but has suffered serious declines in the southeastern U.S.

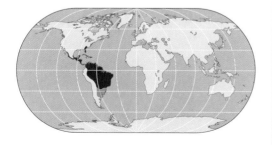

Locally Threatened

While not threatened globally, in North America the wood stork is endangered. Here its history and decline over the last 100 years are linked to the plight of natural wetlands. Traditionally, in North America the birds nested in Texas, Louisiana, Mississippi, Alabama, Florida, South Carolina, and Georgia. They were numerous in many places, and in the 1930s there were still an estimated 20,000 nesting pairs.

However, by 1960 the North American population had fallen to 10,000 pairs, and since the late 1970s only around 5,000 pairs have nested annually. At first the decline went unnoticed. But as numbers crashed, there were fears for the birds' future in the United States. The wood stork's decline is linked to its method of feeding; for it to be successful, the prey must be concentrated into small areas. Furthermore, it is vital that during the breeding season, when most food is needed, there is an even higher concentration of fish. In the wetlands that wood storks prefer, this concentration happens naturally during the dry season. At this time formerly extensive areas of water where fish have bred are reduced in size to small pools. With the reduction in water comes the concentration of fish that the bird requires. The storks use this time to nest and raise young, a time when parents can be sure of a plentiful supply of food for hungry bills.

However, from the 1930s onward there has been sustained pressure in the southeastern U.S. for both land development and for the control of water to release former natural wetlands for agriculture. In many places the wetlands on which the wood stork depended were simply built on. In other places the water levels were changed with drainage and improvement projects to allow for the growing of crops and the grazing of stock. With such alterations the wood stork no longer had the seasonal concentration of fish during the dry season. Consequently, across the bird's range in North America numbers crashed.

With luck, new conservation measures already in hand will help halt the decline of both the wood stork and other wetland species.

⊕ A wood stork (right) confronts an anhinga (Anhinga anhinga) in the Florida Everglades. Both birds raise their wings in a threat gesture designed to make them appear bigger. In four U.S. states the wood stork is listed as endangered, threatened, or of special concern. However, there are plans to restore some of the habitats that provide a home for the wood stork and other threatened wetland species.

Common name
Mute swan

Scientific name *Cygnus olor*

Family Anatidae

Order Anseriformes

Size Length: 49–63 in (125–160 cm); wingspan: 94 in (240 cm); weight: 14–33 lb (6.6–15 kg)

Key features Large, long-necked bird; adults white, juveniles brownish; females normally smaller than males with smaller knob on bill

Habits Usually on or near water; may be in pairs or family groups; often in close proximity to man—some individuals very approachable

Nesting Spring and summer; nest is a large pile of vegetation, sometimes floating; 5–7 eggs; incubation 35–36 days; young fledge at 120–150 days; 1 brood

Voice Not mute! Threatened birds hiss; other sounds include snoring, snorting, quiet trumpeting, and bubbling noises; whooshing noise heard in flight is caused by wings

Diet Mostly aquatic plants; also seeds, grasses, and herbs taken at the water's edge or when grazing on land; occasionally small animals

Habitat Lowland freshwater lakes (including manmade bodies of water), marshes, rivers, and estuaries; also sheltered sea areas

Distribution Resident populations in northern and central Europe and North America; migrant populations in eastern Europe, Scandinavia, Central Asia, and eastern China; small, feral, nonmigrating populations in South Africa, Australia, New Zealand, and Japan

Status Not threatened; range expanding due to originally ornamental swans establishing feral populations

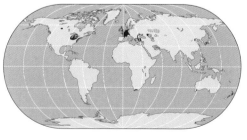

Mute Swan

Cygnus olor

Huge and awkward-looking on land, the mute swan becomes a beautiful, elegant galleon on water—often seen swimming with its neck arched back, wings slightly raised, and pointed tail cocked upward.

THIS GRACEFUL BIRD HAS BEEN known as the mute swan for just over 200 years. Before 1785 it was known as the "tame swan." The earlier name provides clues about the history and the current status of what is, to many, a very familiar bird. The "new" name is somewhat misleading in fact, since mute swans are not completely silent. When the naturalist Pennant named it the mute swan, however, the contrast between this relatively quiet bird and more vocal species, such as whooper swans (*Cygnus cygnus*), was enough to justify its new label.

The natural range of the mute swan is limited to scattered parts of eastern China and Central Asia and to a belt from the Caspian and Black Seas to northern Europe. The fairly broad distribution of the mute swan today is largely the result of domestication and its introduction to several countries outside its original range, including North America.

Underwater Feeding

The mute swan is probably more closely related to swans found in the Southern Hemisphere—the black swan (*Cygnus atratus*) of Australia and New Zealand and the black-necked swan (*Cygnus melanocorypha*) of South America—than to other Northern Hemisphere swans. No other swan has an orange bill with a black knob at the base. It takes several years for a mute swan to acquire its white, adult plumage. The downy young are grayish in color, and juvenile birds are brownish.

The mute swan's long neck makes it easy to feed on underwater plants. The neck may be thrust under water with or without the bird upending, although upending clearly increases the reach. Water plants make up most of the

⊖ *The threat display of a male mute swan includes raised wings, hissing, and a prolonged chase to drive rivals from his territory. Swans are highly protective of their surroundings and fiercely defensive of their young.*

diet, but swans have also been known to eat toads, frogs, tadpoles, mollusks, and insects. There are even a few instances of whole fish and even fruit tree blossom being eaten. The species' success is due in part to its ability to live alongside humans and to make the most of whatever food is available. Important supplementary food items include bread thrown by picnickers and others, as well as spilled grain. Adult swans sometimes make feeding easier for their offspring by paddling their feet to bring food items within reach.

Bonded for Life

Once a pair-bond is formed, the male and female usually stay together for life. The separation rate is remarkably low; in one study it was a mere 3 percent among successful breeders and 9 percent among unsuccessful breeders.

Typically, a territory will cover a large area on a lake or a mile (about 1.6 km) or more of river. It is defended passionately by the male, sometimes all year round. Both birds build the nest—a huge mound of vegetation that can be

3 feet (1 m) deep and 12–15 feet (4–5 m) across. The female incubates the eggs, covering them with plants when she leaves the nest. When the young have hatched, both parents look after them. The young birds will sometimes climb onto a parent's back, where they are carried and brooded.

There are a few places where the mute swan's strong territorial nesting instincts seem to have disappeared, and birds breed in colonies. One example is Abbotsbury, a centuries-old swannery in

⊕ Landing on water is a spectacular event when a mute swan is involved. The huge wings act as an air brake to slow the descent, while the bird pivots its body to enter feetfirst.

England. The colony was established in the eleventh century to rear cygnets for eating. Perhaps through semidomestication, or because there were many birds and few breeding sites, the nests are only about 10 feet (3 m) apart. When the eggs hatch, however, the swans spread out to feed on a large, brackish lagoon nearby.

Mute swans can live for a long time—the oldest survived for over 21 years. A recent survey looked at the life histories of over 1,600 mute swans. Surprisingly, over 50 percent died in their first two years, and only 40 lived beyond ten years. Only 177 of the birds bred, and 40 of them produced no young. So, of the original 1,600 birds, only 137 produced any young, although 22 of them produced over 27 cygnets each during their lifetime.

It takes three years for a mute swan to become sexually mature. In the meantime, nonbreeding birds are gregarious and may gather in particularly large numbers to molt. From July to September one- and two-year-olds, and older birds that have failed to breed, congregate in estuaries or on shallow seawater. As many as

Swan Upping

In twelfth-century Britain, owning swans was an important status symbol because they were regarded as a delicacy for eating. Swans' bills were marked with different patterns to identify their owners—just like branding cattle and horses today. The crown granted certain noblemen and other bodies (such as livery companies of the City of London) the right to own swans and to mark them for identification. Any unmarked swans on the Thames River automatically became the property of the crown, and in an annual "swan upping"

ceremony they were rounded up and given the royal marks. Of the companies that were allowed to own swans in the fifteenth century only two retain such rights today—the

Vintners Livery Company and the Dyers Livery Company.

Swan upping is an annual event on the Thames River. It is organized by the queen's swan marker, who looks after the queen's swans. The monarch has the right to own any unmarked swans in open water. Six traditional rowing skiffs are used for the five-day swan upping event. The queen's swan marker wears a scarlet jacket, and the skiffs fly flags and pennants. When a brood of swans is seen, "All up!" is shouted, warning everyone to get ready to catch the swans. They are then weighed, measured, banded, and released.

15,000 individuals gather off the Swedish coast.

The truly wild populations of mute swans are mainly migratory, moving from cold places to temperate zones. Populations with more domesticated origins are more or less sedentary. Populations in eastern Europe are more migratory and much more wary of people. On the whole, those in western Europe do not migrate and are more approachable.

Feathers and Molting

Adult birds molt while they are still caring for their offspring. Since they molt all of their flight feathers at the same time, they cannot fly for five or six weeks. To ensure the maximum protection for the young swans at this time, therefore, the adult female molts before the male. Thus there is always one parent that can fly. Nonbreeding mute swans of both sexes molt more or less at the same time.

The largest flight feathers, the primaries, are 16 inches (40 cm) long when fully grown. A flightless bird is very vulnerable, and it is important that the birds can fly again as soon as possible. The new primaries emerge at a rate

Polish Swans

Polish swans are mute swans with a difference. They have pale legs throughout their lives, and the downy young and juveniles are white. The name is derived from the time when swan was a food delicacy, and Polish swans were imported into markets in London, England, from areas around the Baltic Sea in Poland. The occurrence of Polish swans appears to be more common in domesticated and semidomesticated swan populations than in truly wild populations.

Adult swans are very territorial and will attack other adult swans to defend their territory, the behavior probably being triggered by the white plumage of another adult. As a result of the "white trigger," adult swans sometimes attack their Polish cygnets.

⊕ *Feather preening helps keep feathers in peak condition. This is a particularly vital task for birds such as swans that spend so much of their lives in water.*

of 0.25 inches (6–7 mm) a day. It takes almost ten weeks for the feather to grow fully, but the bird can still fly on partially grown primaries. Molting birds require a lot of energy to quickly grow new feathers. To meet these high-energy demands, a molting swan may eat half of its own body weight in vegetation each day.

Common name Canada goose

Scientific name *Branta canadensis*

Family	Anatidae
Order	Anseriformes
Size	Length: 22–43 in (55–110 cm); wingspan: 48–72 in (122–183 cm); weight: 4.5–14 lb (2–6.4 kg); male larger
Key features	Black neck and head; white cheek patches joining under chin; body mostly brown, with white on lower belly extending to undertail
Habits	Common; found in a range of habitats, usually near water; may form large flocks
Nesting	Nest built on ground from plant material, lined with feathers; 4–7 eggs; incubation 24–30 days; young fledge after 40–86 days; 1 brood
Voice	Large subspecies make a deep honk; smaller subspecies make a higher-pitched cackle or barking noise
Diet	Seeds, fruit, and grain on land; also underwater plant material such as roots and stems
Habitat	Tundra, semidesert, open cultivated areas, and wooded areas, usually near water
Distribution	Native to North America; introduced to Britain, northwest Europe, and New Zealand
Status	Common and not globally threatened, although some subspecies are declining; Aleutian islands subspecies (*B. c. leucopareia*) has benefited from conservation action

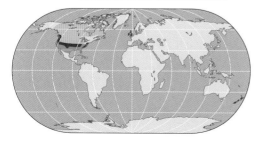

Canada Goose

Branta canadensis

The Canada goose is a bird of conflicting fortunes. On the one hand, it can be so common that some people regard it as a pest. But it also a bird with a successful conservation story. One of its subspecies was thought to be extinct until the 1960s, but thanks to longterm conservation action it is now no longer threatened.

THE CANADA GOOSE IS A HIGHLY variable bird. Although not everyone agrees, there are probably 11 different subspecies. Some ornithologists even believe that the goose is not one species, but four. The different forms vary mainly in size and breast color.

Animals living near the poles are usually bigger than their relatives elsewhere. They have a small surface area relative to their body volume and therefore lose less heat. Canada geese are different; the smallest forms breed on the high Arctic tundra. The cackling goose (*B. c. minima*) that breeds in western Alaska weighs only about 4.5 pounds (2 kg). So why is it that Canada geese do not conform to the normal pattern? The reason is because the arctic breeding season is short, and Canada geese must get their young to the flying stage so that they can migrate south for the winter. They can do that because they are small and grow fast.

The giant Canada goose (*B. c. maxima*) is at the other end of the scale. Typically, it weighs 14 pounds (6.4 kg), and exceptional individuals have tipped the scales at nearly 20 pounds (9 kg). It is the world's biggest goose. Breast color varies from pale brown on the eastern seaboard to a much darker, almost chocolate-brown in southern Alaska.

Distinctive Feature

Perhaps the most obvious plumage feature of the Canada goose is its white chinstrap, which extends from under the chin up onto both

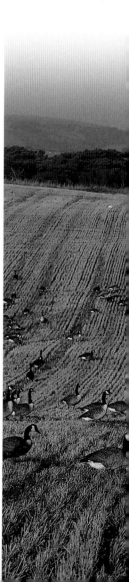

cheeks. The chinstrap is used as a social signal; the bird will lift its chin and flick its head from side to side to signal its intention to fly.

Big Feeders

Canada geese feed mostly by grazing on land, but they can also swim well and will sometimes dip their head in the water to feed or even upend like many other wildfowl. They are herbivores, and their diet includes grasses, the green parts of aquatic plants, roots, stems, leaves, fruits, and during the winter seaweed and grain.

Much of their food is low in nutrition, and that means they must eat a lot of it. The voracious feeding and resultant droppings are the cause of their unpopularity in some areas.

⊕ Canada geese are versatile feeders and can be seen grazing on land as well as feeding in and on water. Here a flock is foraging in a harvested cornfield.

Island Nest Sites

Canada geese are two or three years old when they first breed. They are monogamous and mate for life. Pairs nest individually or in colonies, and the nest is often built on an island—although the Canada goose's definition of an island also includes natural structures like muskrat and beaver lodges.

Normally, the first eggs will be buried in the nesting materials, and as more and more of the clutch is laid, the female plucks downy feathers from her belly and adds them to the nest. The female undertakes nearly all of the incubating and only leaves the nest for short periods. When she does so, she covers the eggs with her plucked feathers. This reduces heat loss, and it makes the eggs less visible to predators.

Bird Strikes

In a typical year bird and other wildlife strikes cause $500 million worth of damage to U.S. aircraft. In 2000 some 3,100 incidents were reported by the USAF and 5,800 by civilian aviation. Gulls, wildfowl, and raptors are the main culprits. A 12-pound (5.5-kg) Canada goose colliding with an airplane traveling at 150 miles per hour (241 km/h) hits it with the same force as a 1,000-pound (454-kg) weight

⊕ *Large birds such as Canada geese can do enormous damage when they are struck by aircraft.*

dropped from 10 feet (3 m). On August 23, 2000, a Boeing 747 collided with 30 Canada geese during takeoff from Philadelphia. Several geese were sucked into an engine. Although this event did not end in disaster for the passengers, the total bill for damage was $3 million!

Airports use a range of techniques to reduce bird strikes. Simple bird-scaring devices can work; but if overused, birds get accustomed to them. Research has shown that catching the offending birds and moving them to a new area can be effective, and in 2000 the U.S. Congress approved a grant to develop an oral contraceptive for Canada geese to help limit populations.

The chicks are greenish-brown above and buff colored underneath. When all the young are hatched, the family moves away from the nest to a brood-rearing area—typically somewhere with open water and good grazing. Both parents take care of the goslings, and the family bond is maintained until the next breeding season. At this point the parents become hostile to last year's offspring, and the family unit breaks down.

Migration Patterns

The native North American populations of Canada geese migrate. They head south for the winter and spend what would otherwise be cold northern months in the southern U.S. and along the North American coasts. Some Canada geese make it as far south as central Mexico. Canada geese from Minnesota are known to travel around 600 miles (966 km) nonstop on their annual fall migration. Occasionally, vagrants have been recorded in Hawaii, the Bahamas, and Jamaica. Truly wild (as opposed to introduced) Canada geese are sometimes seen in Europe, too.

Canada geese were introduced to Britain in the seventeenth century and to Norway and Sweden in the first half of the twentieth century. They were originally introduced both as ornamental birds in parks and for sport. Most of these feral populations are not migratory, although there are some exceptions. Birds in Sweden and Norway do migrate because the Scandinavian winter is so severe. These birds overwinter in Germany and the Netherlands. Interestingly, a molt migration has developed among some British Canada geese.

In North America nonbreeding native geese migrate north to molt. During their molt Canada geese are flightless, and the molt migration takes them to a relatively safe area for this vulnerable part of their life cycle. Geese from Yorkshire in northern England fly 250 miles (402 km) to the north of Scotland to molt. And just like the native birds, it is the nonbreeding birds that do this; the breeders molt while they are raising their young on their breeding territory.

On migration Canada geese usually fly in a V-formation to help conserve energy.

⊕ *Nesting beside a quarry, a Canada goose threatens an intruder. Natural predators of goose eggs include crows, ravens, gulls, coyotes, skunks, foxes, and raccoons. Some nests are lost to flooding, too.*

Partial Conservation Success

There are over 3 million Canada geese, but some subspecies are faring better than others. The large subspecies are fairly numerous, but some of the other subspecies are not doing as well. In a 20-year period the cackling goose declined from around 400,000 birds in the 1960s to just 25,000. The main cause of the decline was too much hunting and too much subsistence harvesting. One of the most amazing declines and subsequent recoveries is that of the Aleutian Canada goose (*B. c. leucopareia*), whose story is told opposite.

Canada geese are sometimes seen as pests because of the damage they do to parks, gardens, golf courses, and fields of crops. Culling has occurred in some places but has sometimes caused conflict between conservationists and animal welfare groups. The U.S. has also seen a rapid growth in the number of nonmigratory, feral Canada geese in some regions. They can cause a number of problems, including bird strikes at airports. More innovative methods are being researched for the control of these birds.

Aleutian Canada Geese

Between 1750 and 1936 red and Arctic foxes were introduced to over 190 islands in the breeding range of this unique Canada goose subspecies. By 1938 Aleutian Canada geese were thought to be extinct. Everything changed in 1963, when 200 to 300 birds were "rediscovered" on Buldir in the Western Aleutians. Captive breeding commenced, and the Aleutian Canada goose was declared an "endangered species."

From 1971 to 1982 birds reared in captivity were released onto fox-free islands. As a further measure, from 1973 to 1984 hunting was stopped on both their breeding and their wintering areas. By the spring of 1975 the population had grown to 790 birds. Foxes were then removed from the goose's original breeding habitat. In 1984 the geese bred successfully on one of the "restored" islands.

By 1990 the population totaled 6,300 geese, and for the next eight years it grew at an annual rate of about 20 percent. In 1999 there were 37,000 birds. Conservationists had succeeded in bringing this bird back from apparent extinction. It had taken nearly 40 years, and there is still work to do. For a secure future, breeding populations must be restored to other parts of the bird's historic breeding range. So far, however, this is a story of success.

Wood Duck

Aix sponsa

It is hard to believe that one of North America's most colorful and common ducks was once driven to the brink of extinction. Happily, conservationists have brought about an astonishing transformation in the fortunes of the wood duck.

THE WOOD DUCK'S SCIENTIFIC NAME *Aix sponsa* means "waterbird in bridal dress," and it is an apt description of the male's striking plumage! The sleek crest and neat white markings divide the bold patches of color on the head, neck, body, and wings of the male. The female is mostly grayish-brown, with spots on her breast and flanks, but she has a distinctive, teardrop-shaped, white eye patch. Wood ducks, and the closely related mandarin ducks, have claws on the toes of their webbed feet; both species are perching ducks, perfectly able to grip the branch of a tree.

Woodland Feeder

The wood duck is a bird of the forests, occupying beaver ponds, slow-moving river

Common name Wood duck

Scientific name *Aix sponsa*

Family   Anatidae

Order   Anseriformes

Size Length: 17–20 in (43–51 cm); wingspan: 29.5 in (75 cm); weight: 1–2 lb (0.5–0.9 kg)

Key features Medium-sized, compact duck; male very colorful with blue-green head; patches of gold, reddish-brown, orange, and white on neck and body, generally separated by white lines; female dull brownish-gray, body spotted

Habits   Forages on land and water; dabbles and upends in water

Nesting   Nests in tree holes; 9–15 eggs; incubation 30 days; young fledge after 60 days; 1, sometimes 2, broods

Voice   Soft, high-pitched squeals emitted by both sexes

Diet   Seeds, nuts, fruits, and aquatic plants; also insects and other invertebrates

Habitat   Rivers, lakes, pools, and swamps surrounded by dense forest

Distribution Found in southern Canada, U.S., Cuba, and Mexico

Status   Conservation measures begun in early 20th century led to species becoming common and widespread once more

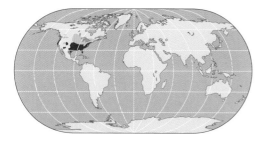

backwaters, and other inland freshwater wetlands surrounded by deciduous trees. In fall and winter it regularly forages on land for acorns and the seeds of hickory, sweet gum, buttonbush, arrow-arum, bur reed, and wild rice. Wood ducks never venture far from water, however, and by the time spring arrives, they are dabbling in shallow water most of the time for insects and other invertebrates.

Tree Nesters

The birds pair and mate in early spring. The female selects a high tree hole—often one excavated by a woodpecker. In many habitats large trees with suitable holes are in short supply, and conservationists have long provided nestboxes on wildlife preserves for the birds.

Unlike most ducks, the male stays with the female while she nests but leaves once the eggs hatch. Not that the young stay in the nest for long. Within 24 hours the downy chicks use their tiny claws to climb out of the tree hole and drop to the ground to seek water, with their mother acting as protector and teacher. For their first few weeks the young feed mainly on insects and tiny fish, but by six weeks they begin to eat pondweed, algae, and other

plants. Less than three weeks later the young ducklings are independent.

For more than 50 years human nestbox providers were baffled by the fact that the nestboxes were frequently used simultaneously by more than one duck! Other females would "dump nest"—lay their eggs in the same nest as the "official" occupant. Finding as many as 30 eggs in her nest, the rightful occupant would then usually desert. In the 1990s it was discovered that older ducks were being followed to highly visible nests by yearlings, which were simply imitating the older birds' actions. When the nestboxes were made harder to spot—as nest sites would be in the wild—dump nesting (also known as brood parasitism) fell dramatically, normal brooding behavior resumed, and chick numbers soared.

Wood ducks molt at the end of the breeding season—the male molts earlier, while the female waits until the arduous task of raising her young is over. Wood ducks breeding in Canada and northern U.S. states then usually migrate to the southern U.S. and Mexico to escape harsh winters. Birds in central states may not migrate at all in mild winters; those in states such as Georgia are resident all year long.

Hunting and forest clearance in the late nineteenth and early twentieth centuries led to the wood duck virtually disappearing from much of North America by the 1920s. However, restrictions on hunting and better management of forested wetlands saw numbers recover, and the population today is healthy at around 1.5 million birds. Below are a female (left) and a male (right).

Mallard

Anas platyrhynchos

For most people in the Northern Hemisphere the mallard is the most common and familiar species of duck. It is numerous, often lives in close association with humans, is widely hunted, and is good to eat. It is often the chief beneficiary when people go to "feed the ducks." And even with considerable hunting pressure the mallard is resilient enough to maintain large populations and remain very common.

Common name Mallard

Scientific name *Anas platyrhynchos*

Family	Anatidae
Order	Anseriformes
Size	Length: 20–26in (50–65cm); wingspan: 29–39in (75–100cm); weight: 1.6–3.4 lb (0.7–1.5 kg)

Key features Male grayish with brown chest, thin white ring around neck, bottle-green upper neck and head, and black-and-white stern; female mostly brown with darker streaks; both sexes have blue speculum

Habits Common on water, often in groups or with other waterbirds; dabbles and upends in water for food

Nesting Spring and summer; nest is built of grass lined with feathers and normally on the ground; 9–13 eggs; incubation 27–28 days; young fledge after 50–60 days; 1 brood

Voice Female makes familiar quacking noise; male's voice weaker and more rasping

Diet An opportunist; plant material includes seeds and leaves; animals include insects, mollusks, worms, and rarely fish and amphibians

Habitat Within its range found in almost all types of water—freshwater, brackish, and seawater; avoids fast-flowing streams and rivers and nutrient-poor waters

Distribution Throughout temperate latitudes in Northern Hemisphere; introduced to southeast Australia and New Zealand

Status Probably the commonest duck; in 1991 around 18 million wintered in North America despite being a common quarry for hunters

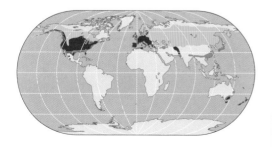

THE MALLARD'S SUCCESS IS PROBABLY due to its ability to survive in a wide variety of habitats, including those near people. Humans have intervened and introduced the species to new areas outside its natural range, and that has also benefited the species. The mallard is grouped, along with three other ducks, into a superspecies. (It is a group of very closely related species that are not normally able to breed with each other because

ⓘ *One of the mallard's favorite ways of feeding is by upending to reach food items beneath the surface. Mallards prefer to live in fairly shallow waters.*

they do not occur in the same areas.) The other three species in the superspecies are the American black duck (*Anas rubripes*) of North America, Meller's duck (*A. melleri*) of Madagascar, and the yellow-billed duck (*A. undulata*) from southern and east Africa. All the birds in a superspecies are known as allospecies.

A Very Variable Duck

Although the "typical mallard," as described opposite, is recognized by many people, it is in fact a very variable species. Its long history as a domesticated bird has produced many variations—including all-white birds and others that are mostly dark but have white patches on the chest. Some of these forms are often seen with more typical mallards and can confuse the novice birdwatcher.

Domesticated mallards may breed with wild birds, but even without this happening there is variation among the wild stock. Seven subspecies are recognized. In some subspecies male and female are similar and resemble the "classic" female mallard. Another subspecies has a white eye ring, and in yet another there is instead a white patch on the face, of varying size. This latter subspecies is known as the Laysan duck (*Anas laysanensis*) and is found only on Laysan Island to the northwest of Hawaii. In the early 1900s there were fewer

than ten Laysan ducks left. The subspecies was almost destroyed when rabbits decimated the Laysan Island vegetation. Happily, however, the population is now up to around 500.

Unfussy Feeders

To survive in the wide range of habitats that the mallard exploits, it has to be a versatile feeder. Mallards will take various sorts of plant and animal material, and those near humans will readily eat bread and other "nonnatural" foods. They avoid deep water, feeding in the shallows by dabbling, dipping their head under water, and upending to go a little deeper. Mallards will also graze vegetation on land, and birds as young as one to two months old will dive for food. Such behavior is rare in adult birds although not unknown. Dives of 3 feet (about 1 m) may occur, particularly when the birds are artificially fed or are diving for sunken acorns, one of their more surprising food items.

Extended Breeding Season

In the Northern Hemisphere the mallard's breeding range extends from the tropics to areas well inside the Arctic Circle in northern Scandinavia and Greenland. The mallard has a very long breeding season and may nest in ten months of the year. Mallards are sexually mature when they are a year old. Within a pair

47

the male and female stay together for only one season. Their average life expectancy in the wild may be less than two years, so many birds will only be alive for one breeding season. (The longest-lived banded mallard survived for over 29 years, however.)

Breeding plumage, including the male's curly black tail feathers, is often evident from October when pairs begin to form. Mallards use a range of courtship displays to attract and secure a mate. Males pull back their heads and rise up in the water and shake their heads. When one does this, others often follow. "Grunt-whistling" may come next; the bird puts its bill in the water, shakes it, then rises up, keeping its bill near the water surface. The bill is then pulled up toward the breast, producing a spray of water drops. This is followed by a sharp whistle, then a grunt. There are numerous other displays in their repertoire of complex courtship behavior.

Pairs nest alone or in loose association with

Mallards are strong flyers, taking to the air when threatened. They may also make long migrations, flying together in flocks often numbering thousands.

other pairs, with the nests a few feet apart. Mallards do not breed in colonies. Most nests are built on the ground, but some are built in the crown of pollarded trees or in tree holes. The more elevated nests have been recorded at heights of up to 33 feet (10 m). Pair-bonds break down shortly after the onset of

Domesticated Birds

Throughout history many bird species have been domesticated, primarily to produce meat, eggs, and feathers. Selective breeding of originally wild mallards has produced a wide range of domestic ducks. This domestication probably originated in China or Southeast Asia. Chickens are descendants of wild jungle fowl and may have been domesticated for 5,000 years. More surprising domesticated birds include ostriches, which have been farmed for feathers and leather; little egrets, which were farmed for their feathers; and cormorants, which were used for fishing in China and Japan.

incubation by the female, and the male normally plays no part in rearing the young.

Some of the birds' sexual behavior can be quite alarming. An incubating female that leaves the nest for a while may be pursued by a number of males. At this point in the breeding cycle the pair-bonds have broken down, and males tend to gather in small single-sex flocks. As many as 20 males will chase the female, sometimes for a considerable distance. If they are successful in bringing her down, they will try to mate with her.

Earlier in the season, when males and females are still paired, a male may harass a female paired with another male. The female will try to get away, but other males may join in and force themselves on the female. This may even include the male already paired with the female. Sexual encounters for female mallards so outnumbered by males can be very violent and may even result in the female's death.

Mallard Migration

Some mallard populations are migratory, and others are sedentary. Generally, those breeding in the far north fly south for the winter, whereas those breeding in more temperate latitudes remain in their breeding area all year round. Populations from eastern Europe east to the coast of China are almost entirely migratory, spending the winter months in Asia.

Mallard flocks may be extremely large. Where migration does occur, migrant mallards make their journeys together rather than individually. In spring, as migrating mallards return to their breeding areas, the birds within the flock are already paired. This means that no time is wasted on the breeding territory in finding and securing a mate.

Too Many Mallards

The mallard is not a conservation priority itself, although its presence can sometimes cause a problem for other species. In New Zealand and southwest Australia the mallard and the Pacific black duck (*Anas superciliosa*) are found together. Because they are in the same genus

⊕ Like most ducklings, young mallards are born well developed and quickly leave the nest to join their parents in the relative safety of the water. They may still fall victim to predators such as pike, however.

(*Anas*), they are therefore closely related. In 1960 the Pacific black duck accounted for 95 percent of all *Anas* ducks in New Zealand. Twenty-five years later the figure was only 25 percent. Introduced mallards had competed with Pacific black ducks and hybridized with them, too. Hybridization reduces the number of genetically pure Pacific black ducks and threatens the species' existence.

Hybrids

A hybrid is the offspring produced by the mating of two different species. Biological species are defined as "groups of interbreeding natural populations that are reproductively isolated from other such groups." Put simply, this means that a species does not normally breed with a different species. If it does happen, any young produced will normally be sterile. It is rare for species that are distantly related and whose ranges are far apart to hybridize. But among closely related species whose ranges meet, or between allospecies within a superspecies where their ranges overlap, hybridization is commoner.

Hybridization among birds in captivity is more common. Captivity is an artificial situation and may bring together species that would never meet in the wild. In the wild hybridization is commoner in species that form pairs quickly and in which the males play little part in nesting. Good examples are birds of paradise, hummingbirds, and ducks. Whatever the theory says, some hybrids *are* fertile. The *Anas* ducks seem particularly good at producing fertile hybrids both in captivity and in the wild. The mallard has hybridized with 23 other *Anas* species and with species from eight other wildfowl genera.

American Wigeon

Anas americana

Common name American wigeon

Scientific name *Anas americana*

Family Anatidae

Order Anseriformes

Size Length: 18–22 in (45–56 cm);
wingspan: 34 in (86 cm);
weight: 1.5–1.7 lb (0.7–0.8 kg)

Key features Male mostly brownish with white crown
and broad green eye stripe; white belly and
black stern; white shoulder patches and white
"armpits" (axillaries); female brownish with
grayish head; whitish shoulder patches and
axillaries; both sexes have a green speculum
and pale blue bill and feet

Habits Cautious; often seen with diving ducks; feeds
by grazing; also waits and snatches food
when diving ducks resurface

Nesting Starts in April/May; pairs nest alone or in
loose groups; nest hidden among plants and
lined with grass and downy feathers; 7–9
eggs; incubation 23–25 days; young fledge
at 37–48 days; 1, sometimes 2, broods

Voice Quacks; also whistles "whew-whew-whew"

Diet Water plants, crops, sedges, and grasses

Habitat Shallow fresh water, including swamps and
lakes; often winters on coastal wetlands

Distribution Found in much of Canada, the U.S.,
Central America, the Caribbean, Venezuela,
Colombia, and Japan

Status Resilient species that has remained common
despite considerable hunting pressure and
some habitat loss

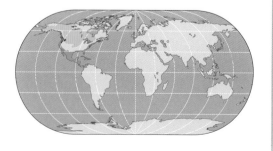

Common in many parts of North America, often in flocks of hundreds or even thousands, and easily distinguished by the white crown of the drake, the American wigeon was once known as the "baldpate."

THE AMERICAN WIGEON IS GROUPED with the Eurasian wigeon (*Anas penelope*) and the Chiloe wigeon (*A. sibilatrix*) to form a superspecies—a group of closely related species that do not normally interbreed because their ranges do not overlap. The American wigeon lives in habitats similar to the Eurasian wigeon and has a similar lifestyle. It is a monotypic species; in other words, one in which no subspecies are recognized.

Food Stealer

American wigeon feed by upending, grazing, and dabbling. They feed in shallow water, in meadows, and on drier land, including arable farmland. American wigeon eat a wide range of plant material, including aquatic plants, grasses, sedges, herbaceous plants, and the green parts of various crops. Adults eat some aquatic invertebrates, but they are mostly herbivorous. Very young American wigeon feed in a different manner, however. During their first three weeks of life the young birds eat mainly insects, only switching to a plant-based diet when they become older.

The American wigeon is one of only very few kleptoparasites among the ducks. A kleptoparasite is a bird that steals food from other birds, either of the same species or of other species. The American wigeon often associates with diving ducks, including canvasbacks (*Aythya valisineria*) and redheads (*A. americana*). While these birds dive, the American wigeon waits and then feeds on the plant material that has been disturbed by the diving birds and floats to the surface. At its more extreme American wigeon will even

The female American wigeon is brownish with a grayish head. She also has whitish shoulder patches and armpits.

snatch food from the diving species when they surface again. American wigeon feed mostly during daylight. This is a much-hunted species, however, and during the hunting season some may feed at night—clearly a useful adaptation.

Breeding Behavior

American wigeon are monogamous and first breed when they are one or two years old. Pairs are normally formed during the winter months, when the birds are away from the breeding grounds. The male uses an incitement call, a special "introductory shake," and wing preening to secure a mate. Aerial pursuits, known as pursuit flights, may also form part of the courtship ritual. When the pair-bond is secure, mating takes place. The drake swims to the rear of the female, pumps his head up and down, and then mounts her.

The white wing patches and white armpits of the male are clearly visible in flight and help identification.

The well-hidden, cuplike nests are built on dry ground and may be some distance from water. Islands are often used as nest sites, and some nests are even built in wooded areas. After the young hatch, the male normally plays little part in looking after his offspring, leaving most of the work to the female. The young may become independent of their parents before they can fly.

Occasionally, American wigeon are the victims of nest parasites. Other duck species breeding in the same area use the American wigeon as a host and deposit their own eggs in the wigeon's nest. White-winged scoters, shovelers, and lesser scaups have all been known to lay their eggs in wigeon nests.

Any birds' nests need to be protected from predators if the parents are

Pirate Birds

Piracy in birds means using force to take food from other birds. The pirates (or kleptoparasites) of the bird world steal food from their own species as well as from other bird species. Food may be snatched violently from the victim, or the victim may just give it up. Some pirates harass their victims so much that food which has already been swallowed is regurgitated. There are many examples of pirates, but 60 percent of them are birds of prey, gulls, and jaegers. The American wigeon is a very rare example of a duck pirate.

Frigatebirds are well-known pirates and obtain most of their food by harassing other birds in flight. Piracy is also common in seabird colonies, especially in those containing more than one species. Terns steal food from adult terns and from chicks. Gulls in the same colony steal from other gulls and from terns.

to successfully rear young. Birds that nest on the ground are particularly vulnerable. American wigeon nests are often well concealed, but predators such as skunks, ground squirrels, and American crows sometimes find them, with devastating results.

Long Journeys

Some American wigeon are resident, and a few populations migrate only if the weather deteriorates significantly, but most are migratory. Long migrations are undertaken, mostly within mainland North and Central America, but some birds find their way to South America, and a few winter in Japan. In most years a handful of birds turn up on the eastern side of the Atlantic, particularly in Britain and often among flocks of Eurasian wigeon.

The southbound migration takes place mainly during October and early November. Occasionally the birds migrate at night, but most migration takes place in daylight. Birds arrive back at the breeding grounds the following spring, although it can be late May before they are back in residence in the northernmost breeding areas.

Not Threatened

This common duck is not a priority for conservation action. Some of its habitat has been damaged or destroyed, and pressure from hunting has increased, but population levels remain at a healthy level. This is due, at least in part, to active protection measures being enforced at some of the sites that American wigeon depend on.

⊕ American wigeon are highly gregarious in winter and may occur on coastal lagoons and marshes in flocks several thousand strong.

⊖ A common American duck that can cope with freshwater habitats in the breeding season and coastal wetlands in winter, this male is "surfing" the waves at Jericho Beach, Canada.

Common name King eider

Scientific name *Somateria spectabilis*

Family	Anatidae
Order	Anseriformes
Size	Length: 18.5–25 in (47–63.5 cm); wingspan: 34–40 in (86–101 cm); weight: 3–4.5 lb (1.4–2 kg)
Key features	Breeding male mainly black body with small "sails" on back, salmon-pink breast, black wings with white forewing patches, bulbous multicolored head; dark in eclipse plumage; female has shorter, darker bill than common eider, with dark "smiling" gape and warmer, reddish-brown plumage with more crescent-shaped black bars; juveniles resemble female
Habits	Feeds mainly in coastal waters, taking prey from seabed; highly gregarious outside breeding season, but typically nesting in pairs
Nesting	Nest usually near water; a hollow lined mainly with down from female's breast; 3–7 pale olive eggs; incubation by female for 22–24 days; fledging period unknown; 1 brood
Voice	Male utters deep, vibrating cooing calls during courtship displays; main calls of female deep, hoarse clucking sounds
Diet	Mollusks, crustaceans, and echinoderms; also eelgrass and aquatic insects
Habitat	Breeds mainly inland on Arctic tundra, by freshwater pools, sometimes by rivers and along seacoasts; winters along seacoasts
Distribution	Throughout Arctic, ranging south to northwestern Atlantic and north Pacific
Status	Populations generally stable, but locally birds are threatened by oil pollution

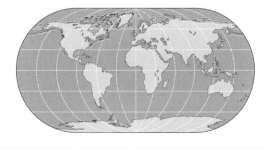

King Eider

Somateria spectabilis

This high arctic nester is usually seen only in winter, when small numbers venture further south than usual, providing an exciting find for birdwatchers.

THE MALE KING EIDER IS TRULY regal in appearance, with his stunning, crownlike "frontal shield" of bare orange skin bulging upward from his orange-red bill, separated from his pale greenish face by neat black-and-white lines. The female's exquisite camouflage plumage has a subtle beauty, which is apparent only at close range.

King eiders are among the most northerly of all ducks, breeding almost entirely north of the Arctic Circle, within a few hundred miles of the North Pole. After breeding and molting, they migrate out to sea, generally staying much further offshore than common eiders (*Somateria mollissima*). Some hardy individuals even manage to find open areas of sea among the ice in the mainly frozen Arctic basin. Most winter at the edge of the pack ice, although they may make long journeys to get there.

The largest populations winter in the Bering Sea around Kamchatka, the Aleutian Islands, and Alaska, while birds from eastern Canada and Greenland winter off Labrador and Newfoundland. West Siberian birds have been recorded in Finland, Sweden, and Iceland, and they also occur annually in Britain. In the U.S. king eiders occasionally appear as far south as California and Florida.

Seafood Diet

For much of the year king eiders feed almost entirely on small aquatic creatures. They eat mainly mussels and other bivalve mollusks, sea urchins and other echinoderms, and crabs, but they have a broad diet that includes barnacles, planktonic mollusks, and fish spawn. In places they tear off the grasslike leaves of submerged eelgrass, and during the breeding season they take more plant matter, along with a variety of aquatic insects and their larvae; they are also relished by their ducklings.

⊕ Compared with his mate, the male king eider is a dramatic sight and easy to pick out from among flocks of the less flamboyant common eider. Yet since the birds spend much of their lives in the Arctic, they are rarely seen further south, and then only in small numbers.

The cryptic plumage of the female king eider conceals her from predators such as Arctic foxes when she is sitting tight on her eggs—something she must do without feeding for the entire three-week incubation period, losing a third of her weight in the process.

King eiders feed by day, usually in flocks. They find much of their prey on the seabed, diving from the surface with their wings held partly open to depths of 50 feet (15 m) and staying under for a minute or more. They pry mussels and other firmly attached animals from rocks or dig other creatures from sand or mud with their strong, wedge-shaped bills, which they also use to crush hard-shelled prey. In shallower waters they feed by upending and reaching under the water or simply by dipping their heads beneath the surface.

Inland Breeders

Unlike the more coastal common eiders, king eiders often breed inland—in some cases as far as 130 miles (209 km) from the sea. They usually nest by pools, lakes, and rivers in a wide range of habitats from wet grassy areas, swampy hollows, and hummocky peatbogs to dry, hilly areas and sand or shingle banks.

Unlike most common eiders, they usually breed as isolated pairs, but in prime habitat—on islets in lakes and rivers—they nest in loose colonies. In places, as in eastern Siberia, they sometimes breed near nests of snowy owls (*Nyctea scandiaca*). The owls usually leave the eiders alone, but keep other predators away.

Breeding is a race against time for the females. In the northernmost parts of their range the waters used for breeding are locked in ice for most of the year, thawing for as few as 60 days. Since the breeding cycle from egg-laying to independence takes 80 days, the female must shepherd her ducklings to ice-free coastal waters while they are still very young.

The males desert their mates soon after they have laid their eggs and migrate to traditional sites on remote coasts to molt. The molting assemblies can be huge, containing 100,000 or more birds. The females must wait to molt until their young are independent.

Oil Threat

Living in such remote and inhospitable habitats, king eiders have relatively little contact with humans. So although migrating birds are shot by arctic hunters, the main threat is from oil pollution, which has the potential to devastate huge molting and wintering flocks.

Common name Long-tailed duck (oldsquaw)

Scientific name *Clangula hyemalis*

Family	Anatidae
Order	Anseriformes
Size	Length: 16–18.5 in (41–47 cm), plus up to 5 in (13 cm) of elongated central tail feathers in male; wingspan: 29–31 in (74–79 cm); weight: 1–2 lb (0.45–0.9 kg)
Key features	Domed or squarish head; triangular wings; male has long, pointed tail; summer plumage of both sexes mostly dark brown and white; male in winter almost all-white with brown patches, and female is mainly pale brown
Habits	Very gregarious outside breeding season; feeds mainly at sea by diving from surface; breeds in dispersed pairs or in loose colonies
Nesting	Nests on ground, usually in dense vegetation; 5–11 olive-buff eggs in small hollow lined with down from female's breast and plant material; incubation 24–29 days; young fledge after 35-40 days; 1 brood
Voice	Males often utter loud, melodious, yodeling calls; female calls harsher and more ducklike
Diet	Small crustaceans and mollusks; also marine worms, sea urchins, fish, and aquatic insects
Habitat	Breeds by tundra pools, lakes, marshes, and on coasts; winters mainly at sea, usually far offshore, but also on large, deep lakes and brackish lagoons in parts of winter range
Distribution	All around the Arctic, ranging south to coastal waters of north Atlantic, Baltic, Black Sea, and north Pacific
Status	One of the commonest ducks, with total population of up to 10 million, but susceptible to oil spills and entanglement in fishing nets

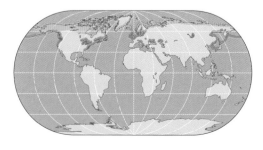

Long-Tailed Duck

Clangula hyemalis

Champion diver among the ducks, the long-tailed duck is also one of the most vocal—the male's glorious, wild musical calls carrying far across the waves.

AMONG THE MOST HANDSOME OF ALL wildfowl, these little sea ducks are dapper birds, especially the long-tailed males in their striking pied winter plumage. At home in the roughest seas, they are buoyant swimmers, bobbing around like corks in the waves. Outside the breeding season they usually gather in large flocks at night to roost far out to sea.

Long-tailed ducks are often restless and seem to dive or take to the air for no obvious reason. They are very fast, agile flyers, usually keeping low over the water, and a flock in flight is a striking sight as the birds swing from side to side, with alternate flashes of dark wings and white underparts. Instead of planing down in a shallow glide to alight on the water like most ducks, they usually drop suddenly, breastfirst, with a dramatic splash—a habit that probably makes it easier for them to land in rough seas.

Diving for Food

Long-tailed ducks feed mainly by day, often in small, scattered groups. They are skillful divers, typically holding their heads back and then bringing them forward as they make a little leap and submerge without a splash. As they slip beneath the surface, they fan their tails and partly open their wings. In the shallows they may use their webbed feet alone to propel themselves underwater, but in deeper waters their wings provide the main driving force.

Most dives are to within 33 feet (10 m), with the birds remaining submerged for up to a minute, but a long-tailed duck can descend to 180 feet (55 m). Deep diving helps them avoid competition for food with other sea ducks such as eiders (genera *Somateria* and *Polysticta*) and scaup (genus *Aythya*), which are shallow divers.

⊕ *Female long-tailed ducks, like this one, lack the distinctive tail streamers of males.*

A long-tailed duck uses its short, stout bill to seize, pry off, and crush small creatures that it finds on the seabed when it dives. Its relatively big head houses large, powerful jaw muscles for dealing with hard-shelled prey, including various kinds of mollusks such as mussels, cockles, clams, and whelks, and crustaceans such as small crabs and amphipods. Long-tailed ducks also eat marine worms and sea urchins, and chase and catch fish such as gobies, flatfish, and young cod.

During the breeding season they eat many midges and other aquatic insects taken from tundra pools, and they are the main food of the young, along with small crustaceans.

Arctic Breeding

Long-tailed ducks return to their arctic breeding grounds when the frozen ground starts to thaw in late April, May, or even June. The males are especially noisy at this time, and their combined calls have been likened to the baying of a pack of hounds or the sound of distant bagpipes.

Each pair often returns to the same nest site, usually situated some distance from their neighbors. There the female lines a slight hollow with vegetation and down that she plucks from her breast. She usually lays six to nine eggs, although she may occasionally produce more. Sometimes a female may lay her eggs in another duck's nest for her to hatch, and these so-called "dump" nests may contain as many as 17 eggs. As with other ducks, when the female leaves the nest to feed—usually twice a day and sometimes for long periods—she covers the eggs with down to keep them warm and avoid attracting predators.

The young hatch together and leave the nest within hours. Their mother leads them to the water, where they start to find their own food. She also broods the ducklings at night while they are very small. Quite often the offspring of several females form a crèche in the charge of one or two females.

Soon after fledging, the young become independent, although they do not breed until they are at least two years old. In fall both the young birds and their parents leave their breeding quarters to fly south before the arrival of the harsh arctic winter.

Common name California condor

Scientific name *Gymnogyps californianus*

Family	Cathartidae
Order	Falconiformes
Size	Length: 46–52 in (117–132 cm); wingspan: 109 in (277 cm); weight: 23 lb (10.4 kg)
Key features	Very long, broad wings with prominent "fingers" at tips; plumage largely black, white triangle on underside of wings; head and neck pink, with small black ruff; juveniles have dark head and neck
Habits	Soars on level (or slightly raised) wings, searching for prey; very stable in the air
Nesting	No nest; lays egg on ground in cave or large tree hole; 1 egg; incubation 55–60 days; young fledge after 180 days; 1 brood
Voice	Hissing and grunting at nest; otherwise silent
Diet	Carrion, mainly from large carcasses
Habitat	Hills and plains
Distribution	California and Arizona: population extinct in the wild in 1987, but now reintroduced into these two states
Status	Critically Endangered

California Condor

Gymnogyps californianus

This huge bird has dominated the skies of western North America for thousands of years. But following a long decline, it is now more famous for being on the edge of extinction than for its majestic aerial presence.

THE CALIFORNIA CONDOR IS PART of North America's history and prehistory. Thousands of years ago it soared over the hills and plains of a land populated with vast numbers of mammoths and saber-toothed cats, where almost every corpse was a giant, and the condor fed alongside other huge scavengers. The great predators and their prey died out in a great wave of extinctions around 11,000 years ago, but somehow the California condor survived, adapting to cope with smaller pickings, from elk and wild sheep to the tiniest prey, such as chipmunks and ground squirrels. This great survivor is one of our largest birds, an appropriate link with a past full of huge creatures.

Soaring Giant

It is not difficult to recognize a California condor. It dwarfs all other birds of prey with its 9-foot (2.7-m) wingspan, and it seems to fly in slow motion. Long, broad wings help the condor ride the slightest of thermal updrafts, and each of the well-spread wingtip feathers acts like a miniwing, reducing turbulence at the wingtips and enabling the great bird to fly very slowly without stalling. It is a bird of big, open skies, traveling in soaring flight from thermal to thermal with a minimal expenditure of energy, watching the ground for signs of dead and dying animals.

Its plumage is mostly black, but the adults have a large, triangular area of white under each wing that helps make them recognizable to other members of their species at a great

⊕ *Even bigger than the California condor, the colossal Andean condor* (Vultur gryphus) *of South America is the largest of all birds of prey. The naked head of the male is ornamented with a fleshy comb.*

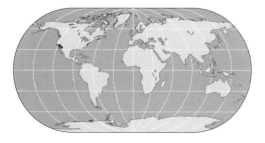

distance. In typical vulture fashion they have naked heads—orange in adults, gray in juveniles—and ruffs around their necks.

Ripping and Tearing

In common with other vultures a California condor has enormous feet that are ideal for supporting its considerable weight but useless for killing prey. Its feet are slightly webbed; and when it comes in to land, it thrusts its feet forward so the toes and webs act as airbrakes.

A condor also has a fearsome, strong hooked bill, which it can use for ripping through skin and tearing at flesh. These immense birds often tear meat from corpses by standing on them and using their weight to hold them down while heaving upward with their butcher bills.

California condors are predominantly scavengers of larger corpses, their power enabling them to tear through the skin of such animals as deer and sheep. Finding such carcasses is a relatively rare event, however, and so California condors are adapted to going for long periods without food, then gorging themselves when they do find it. The related turkey vulture (*Cathartes aura*) can go without food for two weeks without any ill effects, and the condor can probably do the same.

Once it gets lucky, a condor will eat so much that it is scarcely able to fly, its capacious crop full to the brim; a California condor has been known to eat 4.4 pounds (2 kg) of meat at a single sitting. Occasionally, if a condor is disturbed at a carcass, it will regurgitate some of what it has eaten to make itself light enough to take off and escape danger.

Dangerous Strategy

Like many large, long-lived birds, California condors have a slow reproductive rate, which is not a strategy geared to a quick recovery from any setbacks. Normally they attempt to breed only every other year in the wild, laying just one egg. The parents devote all their care to the resulting chick, which does not leave the cliff or cave nest until it is six months old, remaining

⊕ A California condor develops its white underwing patches only when it is fully mature. This bird is a subadult in its second winter, and it may be another six years before it is old enough to breed—if it survives that long.

with its parents for at least another six months. It takes five or six years to become fully adult and rarely breeds until it is about eight years old. For a bird that can live at least 45 years this breeding strategy should be perfectly adequate, but in a world where adult condors are increasingly likely to die young, it may not be sustainable.

Desperate Decline

Although they have a remarkable resistance to all kinds of natural disease and poisons, condors cannot cope with artificial ones. Being at the top of the food chain, condors accumulate toxins by eating many animals that carry small amounts of pesticides and other poisons in their bodies. When they reach a critical level, the accumulated toxins can cause breeding failure and even death.

Such poisoning has been a key factor in a long and desperate decline of the California condor, which has reduced their numbers from thousands to the very brink of extinction. Already in decline after the mass extinctions of

Air-sac Display

In common with most vultures California condors have naked skin on their heads and necks. This is an adaptation for keeping themselves clean, since feathers would quickly become matted with body fluids from the corpses into which the birds poke their scavenging bills. It is also possible that the naked skin helps a vulture regulate heat loss, since it is much easier to lose heat through skin than through insulating feathers.

A California condor also uses its baldness for another purpose: to impress a potential mate in courtship display. Every condor has a slightly different pattern and intensity of color on its neck, and when displaying, the male shows off his unique color scheme to advantage. Standing tall in front of the female, he opens his wings slightly, walks slowly toward her, and bows to display his neck. Both sexes also have air sacs, which inflate like balloons during display, emphasizing the vivid colors on their necks. Presumably the effect is so intoxicating that the pair-bond is greatly strengthened. Similar balloonlike air sacs are also found in other New World vultures, but they do not inflate to the same impressive extent as those of the California condor.

⤴ The majestic sight of a California condor soaring over the Sierra Nevada once seemed likely to become a thing of the past, but reintroductions to the wild may yet secure the future of this magnificent bird.

around 11,000 years ago, the California condor was probably already restricted to the western side of North America by the time that Europeans arrived on the eastern side of the continent in around 1500.

Over the centuries the westward expansion by settlers greatly affected condor numbers, so that by 1900 the birds were confined to California and Baja California. Many were killed through eating dead wolves and coyotes that had been lured to poisoned baits. By the late 1930s California condors were restricted to their home state, around the Sierra Nevada and the Coast Ranges near Santa Barbara, and fewer than 100 remained.

The California condor was now in dire straits, and its problems multiplied. Large and predatory to look at, some were deliberately shot in a misplaced attempt to protect livestock, while others died from lead poisoning as a result of eating animals killed by lead shot. In the 1950s and 1960s the harmful insecticide DDT found its way into the food chain, causing condor eggs to have fatally thin shells. As people and their houses encroached, the condor's habitat was increasingly disturbed. And incredibly, some unscrupulous egg collectors raided the nests of this increasingly rare bird. Little by little its numbers dwindled, until they almost reached vanishing point.

Captive Solution

In 1982 a population count of the California condor revealed the existence of only 22 birds, including just four or five breeding pairs. It was clear that the species was in imminent danger of extinction. The question was how—or indeed whether—to intervene to try and save the bird. After much discussion some conservationists advocated that the wild birds be left alone to recover by themselves or die out like their fellow prehistoric scavengers. However, a daring interventionist plan was also

⊕ In common with other vultures, the California condor does not use its clawed feet to kill prey. However, their huge size means the feet are ideal for supporting the bird's great weight on the ground.

Condors in Prehistory

Ⓣ *Confining such a magnificent bird to a cage may seem cruel, but it may be the only way of preventing its extinction. Captive breeding has allowed the California condor to multiply much faster than it does in the wild.*

California condors have been around for a very long time. Their remains have been found in the La Brea tar pits in California, dating from between 40,000 and 8,000 years ago. They once occurred throughout the North American continent, from west to east, preying on the enormous numbers of large mammals that thrived here before the last Ice Age.

Nowadays condors eat carcasses such as elk and domestic cattle, but in prehistoric times they would eat rather more spectacular corpses, such as mammoths, mastodons, saber-toothed cats, long-horned bison, camels, and great wolves. It could be said that the condor's heyday was thousands of years ago, when it shared its scavenging with several other species of giant vulture, including the enormous teratorns with their 12-foot (3.7-m) wingspans, perhaps the largest birds ever to have taken to the skies. In a sense the California condor is something of a relic from that exciting bygone era. However, its survival into modern times is a testament to its longevity and adaptability as a species. When we see a condor flying over a valley, the sight spans the millennia—reason enough for the enormous efforts that have been made to save this spectacular bird.

suggested: to take eggs from wild condors, catch some adults, and consign the fate of the condor to a captive-breeding program.

Eventually the captive-breeding option was taken up. At that time no condor had ever been bred in a zoo, so the plan was something of a gamble. Initial results were mixed; but thanks to the dedicated efforts of staff at the Zoological Societies of Los Angeles and San Diego, plus those of the Peregrine Fund, the first captive-bred condors were hatched.

Soon the decision was made to capture all the remaining wild condors to add to the breeding program, because their numbers had been progressively diminishing and were now in single figures. The very last wild condor was trapped in April 1987, and 10,000 years or more of continuous occupation of North America by these birds was at an end. The captive population totaled only 27 birds.

Breeding Breakthrough

While raising the condor chicks, staff discovered that if they took an egg from an adult pair early enough, the female would lay another, doubling the potential yield each season. Some chicks were raised by their parents and others by human foster parents wearing gloves shaped like condor heads. Many of the chicks were raised in special aviary complexes nicknamed "condorminiums." After trial and error both methods proved successful, with the numbers in captivity gradually increasing.

The year 1992 saw another breakthough. With zoos now brimming with young California condors, the first ever captive-bred birds were introduced back into the wilds of California. Each bird was radio-tagged and monitored closely, but initially several disasters occurred. Some condors died from poisoning, just as they had in the days of their decline, while others perished when they flew into electricity lines. But over the last ten years the California condor reintroduction program has been increasingly successful. Zoos have produced yet more young condors, and numbers have grown steadily in the wild thanks to more releases. Now there are three sites with released birds: two in California and a third in Arizona—with the Grand Canyon National Park providing a suitably wild and ancient setting.

By September 2002 there were 73 California condors flying free in North America: 31 in Arizona, 25 in southern California, and 17 in central California. In addition, 18 birds were awaiting release in pens, including six in a fourth release site in Baja California. At the same time, 114 were in captivity in three breeding centers, making a grand total of 205 birds. The project's immediate goal is to establish populations of around 150 birds at each site, with 10 percent of them being breeding birds.

The year 2001 was another important moment, for it marked the first breeding attempts of the reintroduced birds, with two pairs trying to nest in California and one pair in Arizona. The initial attempts failed, probably because of the inexperience of the birds involved. However, on April 11, 2002, in California the first wild-bred California condor chick for 18 years was hatched.

Has the expenditure of money, time, and resources been worthwhile? It surely will be when the California condor recovers sufficiently to shed the Critically Endangered status that has been its chief source of fame. But one thing is certain. A California condor riding the thermals over the western states is as much a celebration of America's history as the many other ancient monuments that are cherished.

Sunning Themselves

Vultures, especially those found in North and South America, are especially fond of sunning themselves, perhaps more so than any other group of birds. In the early morning and intermittently throughout the day they are often seen sitting upright with their wings outstretched as far as they will go and either facing away from or toward the sun.

Such behavior seems to have two main benefits. In the early morning some vultures use the sun's heat to warm up their bodies—their metabolic rate having dropped overnight. The other advantage concerns feather care. The vultures' soaring lifestyle puts quite a strain on their main flight feathers, since the strong updrafts often bend the primaries upward until they become slightly out of shape. When the sun shines on these feathers, it has the effect of restoring their shape by acting on the keratin from which they are made.

Turkey Vulture

Cathartes aura

The most familiar of the New World vultures, the turkey vulture is found throughout the North and South American continents. It has the largest range of any vulture and also inhabits the widest range of different habitats.

Common name Turkey vulture

Scientific name *Cathartes aura*

Family	Cathartidae
Order	Falconiformes
Size	Length: 25–32 in (64–81 cm); wingspan: 67–79 in (170–201 cm); weight: 1.9–4.4 lb (0.9–2 kg)

Key features Relatively long, broad wings; mainly black with brownish back, two-toned in flight with paler flight feathers and tail; small, naked red head; juveniles browner than adults

Habits Spends much time soaring, holding its wings in a shallow V; flies forward with slow wingbeats; unstable appearance in the air

Nesting Lays eggs on ground in cave or tree hole, sometimes under vegetation; 2 eggs; incubation 38–41 days; young fledge after 70–80 days; 1 brood

Voice Not very vocal; utters odd hiss or cluck

Diet Carrion

Habitat Broad range from deserts to rain forest

Distribution Throughout North and South America as far north as southern Canada

Status Not threatened

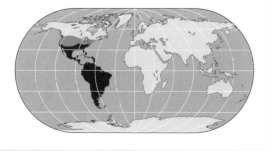

THE TURKEY VULTURE IS THE most common of the New World vultures. A familiar sight across the whole of North America as far north as southern Canada, the bird also inhabits every corner of Central and South America. Clearly it is a hugely successful species and has been for a very long time. Remains of turkey vultures have been dated from the Pleistocene era, 2 million years ago.

This medium-sized vulture has a wingspan of 6 feet (1.8 m) or more. Its plumage is largely black; but as is typical of vultures, its head is bare of feathers, revealing red skin. It gives the bird a very vague resemblance to another bald-headed bird, the common turkey (*Meleagris gallopavo*), and accounts for its name.

Across much of its range the turkey vulture coexists with the similar American black vulture (*Coragyps atratus*), but that species has a gray head and is slightly smaller. The turkey vulture also differs in having longer wings and a much longer tail, giving it a much more slimline appearance in flight.

Supreme Scavenger

All vultures are scavengers, but the turkey vulture is more dependent on carrion than most. It hardly ever kills any food for itself, relying instead on eating a very wide variety of corpses, from medium-sized mammals (including people) to the smallest of birds. It benefits greatly by scavenging along roadsides, gorging itself on the profusion of small road casualties that litter our freeways. It is likely that this opportunism has enabled the turkey vulture to expand its range recently, leaving its familiar heartland in the south to conquer the eastern

⊕ *Easily recognized by its habit of tilting from one side to another as it flies, the turkey vulture is a master of the art of riding thermal updrafts of warm air—an ability that enables it to soar for hours with barely a wingbeat.*

seaboard of North America as far north as the Atlantic provinces of Canada.

Contrary to most popular belief, turkey vultures are very discerning when it comes to choosing which carcasses to feed on. They actually avoid kills that have been lying around for some time and have become putrid, and favor much fresher food. Because carcasses do not become smelly enough to be easily detectable until some time after death, the turkey vulture has a brief window of opportunity for a few hours after an animal dies. In the tropics turkey vultures have become particularly adept at finding one-day-old carcasses, and they are usually the first scavengers to appear on the scene. But unfortunately for the turkey vultures, more aggressive species of vulture often keep careful track of their activities and arrive at the carcass in time to dominate the turkey vultures, steal their meal, and leave them with just a few leftover scraps.

Whatever the actual age of its food, any bird that eats dead matter always runs the risk of picking up bacteria that could infect it with disease. To combat this, turkey vultures and

The Migrant Vulture

The turkey vulture is the only New World vulture that migrates. Most of the birds of North America move south in the fall and north again in spring; however, they remain as permanent residents in the southeastern U.S. as far north as the Carolinas. The vultures that evacuate their breeding areas move quite a long way, wintering down in the Bahamas, Central America, and even deep into the continent of South America as far south as Argentina.

Their migration is a spectacular phenomenon. Turkey vultures cannot travel far without using thermal updrafts to carry them along. Since thermals do not develop over the sea, they must use land bridges, and enormous numbers "funnel" into the comparatively narrow part of Central America that lies between the Pacific and the Gulf of Mexico. In a recent count over one million birds passed over Veracruz in eastern Mexico during October and November. Many of the birds passed over at a height of between 19,700 and 23,000 feet (6,000–7,000 m) in large, dense flocks. At night, becalmed by lack of thermals, hundreds, if not thousands, gathered in the nearby countryside to roost. Not surprisingly, they managed to complete their migration without stopping to feed—for not even the worst outbreak of animal casualties could sustain such hordes.

Smelling It Out

Although they have highly developed senses of sight and hearing, most birds do not have much use for a sense of smell. The average bird seems almost oblivious to the vast number of scents wafting through the atmosphere, in complete contrast to mammals, which use smell all the time to find food, identify their friends and enemies, and track down breeding partners.

To date, only a few species of bird have been proven to have a strong olfactory sense. They include the kiwi (genus *Apteryx*) and various seabirds such as shearwaters (family Procellariidae) and storm-petrels (family Hydrobatidae). The three species of *Cathartes* vulture, including the turkey vulture, can be added to this list. They fly at a lower altitude than other vultures and often over thickly wooded and forested areas where their sense of smell is an excellent tool for detecting carcasses concealed on the forest floor.

Experiments show that a large area of a turkey vulture's brain is devoted to scent perception, enabling it to detect certain chemicals given off by recently dead animals. There is little doubt about the usefulness of a sense of smell for birds that eat carrion. The surprise is that among all the vultures of the world, it is just these three closely related species that use a sense of smell in this way.

⊕ *The highly adaptable turkey vulture is prepared to make a meal of almost any dead animal, provided its meat is still relatively fresh. This bird is about to eat a dead snake.*

other species of vulture have a remarkable ability to resist bacterial poisons, including such fatal diseases as botulism. Without such a mechanism vultures would be unable to clean up the remains of the dead without risking death themselves.

Courtship Displays

Vultures are often considered to be sociable birds, but in the mating season turkey vulture pairs are solitary, spacing themselves out in breeding territories. As a rule, the breeding pairs remain together for life, but in the spring each pair still indulges in courtship displays that involve flying together in so-called "follow flights," with one bird mirroring the other's aerial maneuvers. The displays reinforce the pair-bond and encourage the birds to mate. They nest in caves and hollow trees, but do not line the site with nesting material; the female lays her eggs directly onto the rock or timber. The same sites are often used year after year; over time they can begin to smell quite disgusting, but the stench does not put the birds off, despite their sensitive nostrils.

A clutch of two eggs is typical, and both chicks have a fair chance of surviving to fledging—unlike many birds of prey, which routinely raise only one because the stronger chick steals most of the food. The parents tend the chicks well and are in constant attendance, at least for the first few weeks. From the start they feed them on a diet of regurgitated food rather than fresh meat carried in the talons, which is normal among raptors. Carrion is such an unpredictable food source that the parent often provides food only once or twice a day.

The chicks are covered with down that helps them cope with the long periods between feeds when they might otherwise get cold—an adaptation to their unpredictable food supply. For the rest of their lives their feeding will follow the same pattern, as they gorge themselves at irregular feasts separated by periods of famine. It is the vulture way.

Young turkey vultures remain in the care of their parents for months. Finding carcasses is a difficult way of life, and the parents must both provide for and instruct their young during this time. Once they master the art of scavenging, the outlook for young birds is excellent. Turkey vultures have a 75–90 percent survival rate in the wild, and many live for a decade or more.

Sharing a Roost

Once breeding is over, turkey vultures become much more sociable. They gather at traditional safe sites to spend each night, sometimes with American black vultures; there may be hundreds of birds at such roosts. Once morning comes, many will take wing to forage together, scanning the ground below to see what animals have died overnight. As with all vultures, the death of another is their opportunity to live.

⬇ *Unlike the Old World vultures, which often nest in great colonies, turkey vultures breed as isolated pairs. Each pair often stays together for life, reclaiming the same breeding site each year.*

Common name Everglade kite (snail kite)

Scientific name *Rostrhamus sociabilis*
(Florida race: *R.s. plumbeus*)

Family Accipitridae

Order Falconiformes

Size Length: 16–18 in (41–46 cm);
wingspan: 45 in (114 cm);
weight: 13–14 oz (369–397 g)

Key features Slim and broad-winged; very slender, long-hooked bill and red eye; male slate-gray with black wingtips and white on tail, bare red skin on face, and red legs; female brown with paler streaked underparts, orange skin on face and legs; immature resembles female, but has brown eye

Habits Very sociable, roosting and feeding together

Nesting Nests in loose colonies; builds stick nests in reed beds, bushes, or trees; season varies with latitude; usually 2–4 eggs; incubation 26–28 days; young fledge after 40–49 days, but may leave nest earlier; 1–3 broods

Voice Bleating cry during courtship display

Diet Normally freshwater apple snails of the genus *Pomacea*; also crabs and mice when snails are scarce

Habitat Marshes

Distribution Florida Everglades, Cuba, southeast Central America, South America east of Andes

Status Rare, local, and vulnerable in Florida; common and widespread elsewhere

Everglade Kite

Rostrhamus sociabilis

Although it hovers on the edge of extinction in the swamps of Florida, the snail-eating Everglade kite is flourishing throughout most of Latin America.

THE EVERGLADE KITE FEEDS ALMOST exclusively on freshwater snails. This may seem an unusual diet for a bird of prey, but it has several advantages. Snails are very nourishing, being the freshwater equivalent of the shellfish that support vast flocks of wading birds on ocean shores. Snails often occur in huge numbers, allowing many birds to feed together. They are certainly easy to catch, and they never put up a fight. The only problem is getting into them.

The Everglade kite is equipped for the task with a slender bill ending in a very long hook like a curved blade. A captured apple snail usually retreats into its shell and seals itself in with a horny "door" called an operculum, but the kite's bill is slim enough to be slipped between the operculum and the shell. The bird feels for the muscle anchoring the snail inside its shell, slices through it, shakes the snail from its shell, and then gulps it down.

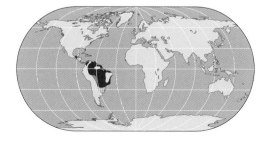

⬅ ⬇ *The kite usually hunts from a perch, swooping down to snatch each snail from the shallows with one foot before taking it back to the perch for extraction.*

Swamp Dweller

The bird is widespread over the marshy lowlands of tropical America, where it is known as the snail kite. A local race lives in the Everglades of Florida and the swamps of Cuba, and it is called the Everglade kite. The bird relies on a steady supply of *Pomacea* apple snails, and they occur only in the shallow waters of near-permanently flooded marshes and swamps. But where conditions are right, the snails can be found in their millions, supporting large populations of kites. In the Pantanal of southern Brazil, for example, groups of up to 600 kites can be seen foraging together, flying low over the marshes or perched nearby.

If there are no convenient perches from which to hunt, the birds may quarter the marsh with a slow, flapping flight. The kites target the snails visually, so where the water is overgrown with floating vegetation such as water hyacinth—a common plant in the Everglades—the snails cannot be seen, and the birds must look elsewhere. Conversely, a stretch of clear water teeming with snails can attract so many kites that each must defend its feeding patch.

The kites normally spend most of the day looking for snails, then retreat to communal roosts to spend the night. The roosts are often in dense reed beds or on wooded islands in the swamp. In the tropics a single roost may be used by 1,000 or more birds for a season or two before they are forced to move on by changing flood patterns in the marshlands. For a snail kite home is where the snails are.

Sociable Nesters

Everglade kites often breed on their roosting sites, nesting in colonies of up to 100 pairs. Each pair raises two or three chicks; but when snails are abundant, either the male or the female may desert the nest to raise a new family with another bird. Meanwhile, the abandoned bird raises the original brood on its own. Most young Everglade kites breed in their second year.

Throughout much of tropical America snail kites are very common, and in some wetland regions they outnumber all other birds of prey. In the Florida Everglades, however, the species is on the northern edge of its range and struggles to survive. The birds have also suffered badly from droughts, drainage projects, and development destroying their swampland habitat. In the mid-1960s there were only about 50 birds left. Since then careful management of water levels in selected areas has enabled the population to increase to about 500, split between three main areas. Nevertheless, in the Florida Everglades the Everglade kite remains a rare bird.

⊕ *The sharp, extralong hook on the Everglade kite's bill is the ideal tool for extracting snails from their shell.*

Northern Goshawk

Accipiter gentilis

Common name Northern goshawk

Scientific name *Accipiter gentilis*

Family Accipitridae

Order Falconiformes

Size Length: 19–27 in (48–68.5 cm); wingspan: 38–50 in (96.5–127 cm); weight: 1.1–3.3 lb (0.5–1.5 kg); female much bigger and heavier than male

Key features Big, short-winged forest hawk with medium-long tail; yellow bill base and legs; orange-yellow eye; brown-gray above, pale below with dark bars; very variable over large range; female browner above; juvenile resembles female

Habits Lone woodland hunter, using ambush and pursuit from perch

Nesting Forms longstanding pairs in spring, often reoccupying old nest; usually 3–4 eggs, rarely 5; incubation 35–41 days; young fledge after 35–40 days; 1 brood

Voice Harsh "gek-gek-gek" alarm call, plus mewing "pee-yah" from female

Diet Mainly birds ranging from medium-sized songbirds to grouse and pheasants, plus small mammals

Habitat Typically coniferous or mixed woodlands and forests with clearings

Distribution Forests of northern North America, Europe, Scandinavia, Russia, Siberia, and Japan; in winter North American birds may migrate south as far as northern Mexico

Status Recovering from sharp decline caused by persecution, forest destruction, and pesticide poisoning during 19th to late 20th centuries

The ferocious goshawk is an ambush killer: a fast, agile, yet powerful hunter that specializes in making lightning strikes from dense cover in the cold, dark forests of the north.

THE BIG, POWERFUL GOSHAWK IS THE largest of a group of more than 50 birds of prey specialized for hunting among the trees. Most of these forest hawks belong to the genus *Accipiter*, which includes species like the American sharp-shinned hawk (*A. striatus*) and the Eurasian sparrowhawk (*A. nisus*). They all have relatively short, rounded wings and long tails, giving them rapid acceleration and the ability to maneuver between branches at high speed. Coupled with their keen eyesight and sharp reflexes, the combination is deadly.

⊕ *The goshawk's nest is usually built high in a large forest tree such as a conifer. A nest from the previous year is often repaired and used again. A young bird is shown on the left.*

Forest Hunting Skills

Forests teem with life, especially small birds, and a bird of prey can find all the food it needs within quite a small area. Nevertheless, prey can easily hide among the foliage and undergrowth, and the branches and tree trunks act as a physical barrier preventing a fast, direct aerial attack. But the goshawk manages to overcome these obstacles and turn them to its advantage.

Male goshawks feed mainly on birds such as pigeons and jays, as well as on woodland mammals such as squirrels. The bigger female goshawks can take larger prey such as grouse, pheasants, and hares. They may even catch smaller hawks and owls. Goshawks are opportunists, taking whatever is available seasonally. In spring, for example, they eat a lot of nestling birds, even though they are smaller than their normal prey.

A goshawk usually perches in dense cover, waiting to launch itself into the air and dash after its quarry at high speed. The chase may involve a switchback chase over and under branches, through narrow gaps, and into dense foliage, all performed with amazing agility. If the target is a grouse or rabbit, the goshawk swoops low over the ground, often almost hovering before the final strike. It may even catch its victim by complete surprise, plucking a bird or squirrel from a branch before carrying it off to a favorite feeding perch.

Goshawks are found as far north as the fringes of the arctic tundra. In winter goshawks that breed near the tundra are sometimes forced to find food further south. Every ten years or so, North American goshawks may fly south as far as Mexico.

Nesting Time

At the end of winter the birds return to their old breeding sites. Mated pairs celebrate their reunion with dramatic aerial displays involving soaring, swooping, and vertical plunges into the nesting woods. Then they repair their old nest or build another. The female guards the young nestlings while the male keeps the family supplied with food, but both can be ferocious in defense of the nest. Most goshawks first breed in their third or fourth year.

Northern Refuge

Goshawks suffered badly from pesticide poisoning in the 1950s and 1960s, and for over a century European goshawks have been persecuted because they take game birds like grouse. Luckily, many goshawks live in remote northern forests where people are scarce, and there at least the bird is doing well.

Golden Eagle *Aquila chrysaetos*

The majestic golden eagle is an emblem of the wilderness: a spectacular, wide-ranging hunter that finds life almost impossible in regions where the landscape has been tamed by humans.

Common name Golden eagle

Scientific name *Aquila chrysaetos*

Family Accipitridae

Order Falconiformes

Size Length: 30–35 in (76–89 cm); wingspan: 75–89 in (190–226 cm); weight: 6.4–14.8 lb (2.9–6.7 kg); female bigger and heavier than male

Key features Very large with long, broad wings; mainly dark brown with golden-brown crown, nape, and wing coverts; brown eye; black-tipped bill; heavily feathered legs, yellow feet; sexes identical except for size; juvenile darker, with white patches on wings and tail

Habits Hunts on the wing, soaring and gliding, alone or in pairs

Nesting Builds big stick nest on crag or in tree in spring; usually 2 eggs, rarely 1–3; incubation 41–45 days; young fledge after 63–80 days, typically only 1 chick survives; 1 brood

Voice Generally silent, but gives whistling "twee-oo" of alarm and shrill "kya" at nest

Diet Mainly small mammals and game birds, plus carrion, but very variable

Habitat Wild, open terrain—often mountainous—from sea level to summer snow line

Distribution North America, wilder parts of Europe, Scandinavia, northern and Central Asia, North Africa; absent from most of Arctic

Status Recovering from heavy persecution, but still threatened by loss of habitat and food supply

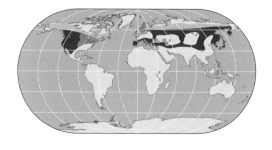

FEW BIRDS SHARE THE AURA of savage beauty that surrounds the golden eagle. Its great size and killing power make it one of the world's most formidable birds of prey; and when seen in sunlight, its golden crown gives it an impressively regal air. Yet the real source of the golden eagle's reputation may be the rugged landscapes it inhabits. As it soars over the peaks and valleys of some of the wildest terrain in the Northern Hemisphere, the golden eagle is a potent symbol of freedom.

Wide-ranging Hunter

Like most large birds of prey, the golden eagle is relatively rare because each pair requires a large hunting territory. Yet it is found over a huge range that covers most of North America and Eurasia, from the fringes of the arctic tundra to the deserts of Mexico and the Middle East. In sparsely populated regions like northern Scandinavia it often breeds in low-lying country, right down to the coast, while in the Himalayas it may hunt as high as the limit of permanent snow, at 18,000 feet (5,500 m) or more above sea level. In North America the main populations live in the mountain states of Montana, Wyoming, and Colorado, while in Europe golden eagles are most numerous in Scotland and Spain.

In Alaska, northern Canada, northern Russia, and Siberia, where winter temperatures plunge well below freezing for several months, many small animals go to ground and hibernate until spring. Live prey can become scarce, and even carrion can be hard to find in the deep snow. The golden eagles move south to find food, and at such times North American birds may fly as far south as Mexico.

⊙ *Golden eagles have large, powerful bills that enable them to rip into big, thick-skinned carcasses—a feature they share with vultures. Their scavenging habit has given them a bad reputation among farmers, who accuse them of killing healthy livestock.*

In milder regions, like western Europe, the adult eagles generally stay on their breeding grounds throughout the year, but young birds may move south to escape the worst of the winter. At one time the golden eagle probably ranged widely across Europe, but today much of the continent is too densely populated and intensively farmed for its liking.

Aerial Acrobat

Part of the golden eagle's appeal lies in its spectacular flying skills. It spends many hours on the wing every day: soaring high into the sky on updrafts, gliding fast across country, wheeling and sideslipping, and swooping and climbing—all with exquisite grace and elegance. It achieves many of these maneuvers without beating its wings at all, but when necessary it uses deep, slow wingbeats to power itself into the next glide. It can also dive at high speed with half-folded wings like a peregrine (*Falco peregrinus*), either in display or to catch its prey.

A hunting golden eagle ranges over a wide area every day. The actual area depends on the wealth of food available: In Scotland a breeding pair's hunting territory may extend over 15–30 square miles (39–78 sq km), but in the Alps a pair may cover 240 square miles (622 sq km).

Golden eagles take most of their prey on the ground, typically flying quite low and dropping onto their victims in fast, slanting dives. Their main targets are medium-sized mammals such

⊕ Golden eagles hunt over varied terrain with bare crags, moors, forested slopes, and marshes; but generally they prefer areas where the vegetation is low-growing or sparse, giving them a clear view of potential food sources.

Insurance Policy

Golden eagles nearly always lay more than one egg each season, but it is unusual for more than one chick to survive. The first to hatch gets a head start on its younger sibling and bullies it and often steals its food, so it dies in the nest. The elder chick may even kill the smaller one. In some species of eagle this happens so routinely that they never rear more than one chick. It seems a tragic waste. It also appears odd that the parents do not intervene and give the weaker chick its fair share. Yet there is a good reason why they do not.

Unless prey is extremely common, the adult birds can only manage to feed one chick properly. Trying to feed two chicks may overstretch their resources. But instead of laying just one egg, the birds lay a second egg as "insurance" in case the first egg fails to hatch or the chick is weak. Normally the first egg hatches and the chick is healthy, so the second chick is superfluous. But if the first chick is weak, the second will steal its food and survive. Either way the eagles eventually rear a single, well-fed healthy chick, which is a more satisfactory situation than rearing two underfed weaklings that may not survive the winter.

as hares, rabbits, and ground squirrels, plus various game birds. But they are opportunist hunters, ready to snatch young deer or chamoix, fox and badger cubs, rats and moles, even hedgehogs and tortoises—dropping the latter onto rocks to smash their shells. They often pounce on ducks and waders, and are sufficiently agile to catch crows, gulls, pigeons, and large songbirds. Pairs of golden eagles sometimes hunt together to increase their chances of catching elusive prey.

Golden eagles also eat a lot of carrion, especially in winter and early spring, when hard weather and starvation claim the lives of many large animals such as deer and sheep. They sometimes take live lambs, too; but like most

← *The nest, or eyrie, is usually built high in a very large tree such as an ancient pine or on an inaccessible cliff ledge. Golden eagles cannot tolerate disturbance at their nest—one of the main reasons why the birds are restricted to remote regions.*

predators, they usually target weak or diseased ones that would probably die anyway.

Long-term Care

The beginning of the breeding season is marked by breathtaking aerial displays as the birds soar high over their breeding territory, plunge to earth with their wings folded back, and climb again to repeat the performance. Sometimes the pairs grapple in the air, locking talons as one bird flies upside down.

Once the eagles have selected a nest site— they may have three or more within their territory—they set about repairing it, adding stout sticks and green spring foliage. Over the years the nest can grow into a huge pile visible from far away.

The female usually lays two eggs at an interval of three to four days, and she incubates them herself while the male brings prey to the nest. The first egg to be laid always hatches first, and the newly hatched chick usually has an advantage over its nest mate when it comes to sharing food. It often attacks the smaller chick to steal its share, and the youngest nestling often dies of the injuries inflicted on it or simply through starvation.

Fledging does not signal the start of the young birds' independence, however. Although they can fly, juvenile golden eagles are poor hunters. They rely on their parents to keep them supplied with food for several months while they learn how to catch their own prey. Once they become independent, they are still reluctant to leave their parents' territory. Sometimes they are driven south by falling temperatures in the fall. If not, the adults may tolerate them on their breeding territory until the start of the new breeding season in spring. The young eagles do not breed themselves until they are at least four to five years old.

Remote Northern Sanctuaries

Like all large birds of prey, golden eagles have suffered badly from persecution, pollution, and habitat destruction. During the nineteenth century an increase in game bird rearing in

Europe led to an extermination campaign against raptors of all kinds, and big eagles like the golden eagle were at the top of the "wanted" list. Many birds of prey already had prices on their heads, but the introduction of efficient firearms made it possible for hunters to earn a living by destroying them. Many thousands were killed, including most of the golden eagle population. Many also died through eating deliberately poisoned bait, and by the end of the 1800s the species had been virtually wiped out in lowland Europe.

Golden eagles suffered almost as badly in parts of the U.S., such as western Texas. Regarded as a threat to valuable livestock such as lambs, they were regularly killed by farmers. In the 1940s it was discovered that golden eagles could be shot from light aircraft, and the killing became a mass slaughter. For 20 years between 1,000 and 2,000 birds were shot each year in western Texas, until the practice was outlawed in 1962.

The 1960s also saw the golden eagle protected by legislation in many parts of Europe, but by this time it was suffering a new,

Size Differences in Birds of Prey

In most animal species females are either the same size as males or smaller. In birds of prey, however, the females are generally bigger than the males. A female golden eagle can weigh well over 14 pounds (6.4 kg), but a male rarely weighs more than 10 pounds (4.5 kg). The size difference is even more extreme among bird-catching hawks and falcons like the northern goshawk (*Accipiter gentilis*) and the peregrine falcon (*Falco peregrinus*).

Although the reasons for the differences are unclear, the most likely explanation is due to the way the birds care for their young. Females usually incubate the eggs and brood the chicks, while the male fetches food. If prey is scarce, it may be necessary for the female to wait some time for a meal; being bigger gives her the energy reserves to go for longer without food. The smaller male is often more agile, making him a more effective hunter. Therefore the male bird of prey is able to bring more prey to the nest for the female and her young—and also eats less of it himself.

Eagle Eyes

The golden eagle is renowned for its piercingly sharp eyesight—a quality that it shares with other birds of prey such as falcons, buzzards, and vultures. One reason for this is the sheer size of its eyes, which are bigger than human eyes. Each eye also has roughly eight times the number of visual receptor cells per square inch (6.5 sq cm) in its retina, giving far clearer definition of detail. The difference can be likened to the improvement in detail that takes place when a coarse, "pixeled" computer image over the Internet increases in definition as the pixels multiply and get smaller.

Having a high-definition retina is only part of the reason for the eagle's excellent vision, however. A raptor's eye works like a telescope, with a lens that projects a magnified image onto the retina. Because of the magnified image, seen in extrasharp detail, the eagle can detect its prey from immense distances.

A young golden eagle eagerly awaits the return of its parent. Competition for food between chicks is fierce, and normally only one of them survives to the fledging stage.

more insidious threat to its survival—pesticide poisoning. Poisoning was a particular problem in Scotland, where sheep were being routinely doused with sheep dip to kill insect parasites. The dip contained organochlorine insecticides such as dieldrin. When sheep died on the mountains, which is not uncommon in Scotland, golden eagles scavenged their remains and picked up the poison. Dieldrin is so toxic that many eagles were killed outright, and the survivors often failed to breed. The result was the eagles suffered a population crash that was only arrested when the poison was banned in the 1970s.

Today many golden eagles are still killed each year, especially in southern Europe. In the north the birds seem to command more respect, and the populations that survived in the wilder parts of northern Europe and North America are either stable or increasing. Yet they are still threatened by intensive farming, which can virtually eliminate their food supply, and by leisure activities such as hill walking and climbing, which disturb them at the nest. Many are also killed in collisions with power lines. Golden eagles are only really safe in the true wilderness areas of the far north.

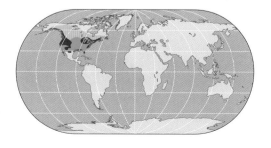

Bald Eagle

Haliaeetus leucocephalus

Common name Bald eagle

Scientific name *Haliaeetus leucocephalus*

Family Accipitridae

Order Falconiformes

Size Length: 28–38 in (71–96.5 cm); wingspan: 66–96 in (168–244 cm); weight: 6.6–13.9 lb (3–6.3 kg); female larger than male; northern race *washingtoniensis* larger than southern race *leucocephalus*

Key features Large eagle with powerful yellow bill; yellow eyes and legs; white head and tail; dark-brown body and wings; sexes identical except for size; juvenile mottled white with dark bill and eye

Habits Normally seen singly or in pairs, but gathers in larger numbers to exploit rich food sources

Nesting Large stick nest, usually in a conifer tree or on a cliff 30–60 ft (9–18 m) above the ground; reused and added to each year; nests in summer in north, winter in south; usually 2 eggs; incubation 34–36 days; young fledge after 70–92 days; 1 brood

Voice A squeaky cackle

Diet Mainly fish; also ducks, rabbits, rodents, turtles, snakes, and carrion

Habitat Usually near open water in all kinds of terrain ranging from cold conifer forest to hot deserts

Distribution Most of North America from southern Alaska and Canada to northern Mexico, plus Aleutian Islands

Status Badly hit by persecution and pesticide poisoning in the past but now flourishing, especially in far northwest of range

Despite being adopted as the national bird of the U.S. in 1782, the magnificent bald eagle has been lucky to survive extinction through the combined effects of shooting, poisoning, and habitat loss.

WITH ITS PIERCING YELLOW EYE, big hooked bill, and fearsome talons, the bald eagle is one of the most imposing of all hunting birds. The name "bald" is misleading, because it suggests a head devoid of feathers like that of a vulture. In fact, the eagle has beautiful snowy white plumage on its head, matching its tail and contrasting with the rich, dark-chocolate plumage of the rest of its body.

The bald eagle is one of eight fish eagles of the genus *Haliaeetus* that includes the white-tailed sea eagle (*H. albicilla*) of Eurasia and the colossal Steller's sea eagle (*H. pelagicus*) of eastern Siberia and Japan. Many of these eagles hunt mainly at sea, but the bald eagle lives all over North America, often far from any ocean. It certainly likes fish, however, and away from coasts it is usually found near the shores of large lakes or by big rivers.

Two Races

There are two distinct races of the bald eagle: the northern and the southern. The northern birds are bigger, and in the summer they breed among the lakes and forests of Canada and

⊕ *An adult (right) and three immature bald eagles scavenging from a garbage dump—the birds are adaptable and inventive feeders, exploiting a variety of food sources.*

⊕ When a bald eagle sees a big fish near the water surface, it swoops down, gaffs the fish with its talons, and flies off with it. Bald eagles hardly ever plunge into the water like ospreys, and they usually manage to lift their prey without getting anything other than their feet wet.

Alaska, as far north as the arctic tundra. When the northern rivers and lakes freeze over, many fly south as far as California, Arizona, or Florida. There they usually gather around rivers, lakes, and reservoirs. However, some may spend the winter far from water in dry sagebrush country or even desert, returning to their northern breeding grounds in spring.

Along the Pacific coasts and islands of Alaska and British Columbia the eagles can still feed in the sea even when lakes and rivers freeze, so they stay all year around. Most of the 100,000 or so bald eagles in North America live in this region, which is rich in fish and still largely wilderness.

The smaller, far less numerous southern race breeds in the winter in California, Texas, Louisiana, Florida, and the southern Atlantic states such as Georgia. Many young birds from the south move north toward Canada for the summer, but

other individuals, mainly older adults, stay in the steamy south all summer.

Very Varied Tastes

Bald eagles eat a wide variety of food, dead or alive, depending on the season and availability. Many breeding pairs in the southern states feed their young almost entirely on roadkills—opossums being a favorite—while Alaskan birds scavenging on the seashore may make an outsized meal of a stranded whale.

Live prey is just as important, however, and bald eagles spend a lot of time hunting fish. The eagle is equipped for the task with a pair of massive, long-clawed feet. The toes are short and strong for maximum gripping power, and the hind toe has an extralong, supersharp claw that pierces the fish's body like a dagger and often kills it almost instantly.

Often, the bald

eagle watches from a perch such as a cliff ledge or a branch before swooping down to the water. Occasionally, bald eagles search for live fish in flight, but hunting from a perch saves energy. They also steal fish from other birds of prey such as ospreys (*Pandion haliaetus*), and a bald eagle may even snatch a meal from a sea otter as it floats on its back among the seaweed, gnawing at a fish held between its front paws.

For the eagles that live on the northern shores of the Pacific Ocean, the highlight of the year arrives in the fall, when millions of Pacific salmon return to their home rivers to spawn. Once the fish have struggled upstream through the rapids to lay and fertilize their eggs in the shallows, they become exhausted and die. Now the rivers are full of dying or dead salmon, and the bald eagles simply wade into the shallows and pull them out. Hundreds of bald eagles gather for the annual feast; in mid-November as many as 4,000 birds have been counted fishing along a 10-mile (16-km) stretch of the Chilkat River in Alaska.

Bald eagles also prey on other birds, especially seabirds and wildfowl. They may dive on seabirds from a height, almost like giant peregrines (*Falco peregrinus*), or ambush them as they paddle in the water by flying at low

High Rise

When a bald eagle needs to gain height while scanning the ground for food, it does not waste energy hauling itself aloft with powerful wingbeats. Instead, it finds a thermal (an air current rising from a patch of warm ground) and then circles in the rising air with its broad wings outspread. The rising air carries it up like an elevator; and when the bird is high enough, it can leave the thermal and glide across country until it finds another. It can soar on updrafts from ridges and cliffs in the same way.

The soaring technique is used by many big birds of prey. It is very useful during migration, since the birds can travel huge distances by picking routes punctuated by thermal "hotspots" and updrafts. But they can only travel during the heat of the day and must avoid stretches of open water where there are no rising air currents. That may force them to cross at certain points, like the Straits of Gibraltar between Europe and Africa, where huge numbers of eagles and other migrants can be seen every spring and fall.

level through the troughs between waves. They use similar techniques to catch ducks, geese, and ptarmigan (genus *Lagopus*) on the treeless, hummocky subarctic tundra and may even cooperate to ensure a kill. Bald eagles also take voles, rats, rabbits, turtles, snakes, and even insects.

Paired for Life

At the beginning of the breeding season the mature males and females indulge in spectacular display flights, soaring high over their territory and tumbling out of the sky with their feet locked together. Pairs tend to stay together for life, but they still use display flights each breeding season prior to mating. The main reason pairs stay together is because both birds generally return to the same nest site every season and therefore meet up again with their partner from the previous year.

First the birds check out the nest to make sure it is still usable. Sometimes bald eagle nests become occupied by great horned owls (*Bubo virginianus*); and when this happens, the eagles must start a new nest elsewhere. Some pairs suffer from "nest squatting" quite frequently, so after three or four seasons the bald eagles may have several nests in their territory from which to choose.

Once they have chosen a nest, the birds

⊖ *Bald eagles usually add fresh sticks and other building materials to their nest each year. In time the nest can become an enormous structure weighing up to 2 tons (1.8 tonnes).*

repair it, adding more sticks and soft lining material such as grass or seaweed. When they are satisfied, the female lays her eggs, and both birds take turns incubating them. The eggs are laid at intervals of a few days and hatch at the same intervals. The last chick to hatch is smaller than the others, and competition for food in the nest often means that the youngest chick does not get enough and dies. Therefore, despite the best efforts of both parents, who share in bringing food to the nest, it is quite unusual for more than two chicks to survive to fledging time.

The young birds finally fly at about ten weeks old. At first they are dark all over; but as they grow, they become more mottled with white until they are four or five years old, when they grow their adult plumage and are ready to start families of their own. Most breed for the first time in their fifth year.

Prey Power

Before 1953 bald eagles in Alaska had a price on their heads. The state authorities believed that the eagles destroyed valuable stocks of Pacific salmon, threatening the economy, so they encouraged people to shoot them.

But they were wrong. Predators such as hunting birds very rarely destroy their own food supply. It requires a lot of fish to sustain just one family of bald eagles, so if the fish become scarce, the eagles disappear. That allows the numbers of prey to recover until there is enough to support the predators again. Therefore, the numbers of prey control the numbers of predators, and a big population of bald eagles is a sure sign that there are a lot of fish about.

Hacking Back

If nesting bald eagles lose their first clutch of eggs, the female simply lays some more. Wildlife conservators have made good use of this habit; they carefully remove eggs from bald eagle nests and put them in incubators to hatch. Meanwhile, the eagles incubate a second clutch, and the result is twice the number of chicks.

When they are about eight weeks old, the hand-reared chicks can be reintroduced to areas where bald eagles are scarce, using a technique called "hacking." Each young bald eagle is placed on a man-made nest protected by an enclosure and then fed by humans who stay out of sight. When the eagle is ready to fly, the enclosure is opened so that the bird is able to leave. Since food is still provided at the nest site, the young eagle rarely goes far. By the time it has learned to hunt for itself, it has settled into the area, and with luck the young bald eagle will breed and start a new population.

Back from the Brink

A few decades ago bald eagles were under threat for a variety of reasons. Their taste for valuable fish—particularly salmon—made them very unpopular. In Alaska in 1917 a reward of $2 was offered for every dead bald eagle. However, in 1940 Congress passed the Bald Eagle Protection Act, which made it illegal to kill or harass bald eagles throughout most of the U.S., though Alaska was excluded. The birds were not fully protected by law until 1953, and meanwhile, about 140,000 bald eagles had been shot—more than the entire population of the species alive today.

By the time shooting was outlawed, bald eagles were suffering from something even worse: pesticide poisoning. Like ospreys and many other birds of prey, bald eagles were eating prey contaminated with DDT and similar chemicals. The poisons accumulated in their bodies and had the effect of making their eggs so fragile that they broke in the nest. Eagle populations plummeted, and by the early 1960s there were only some 450 breeding pairs left in the U.S., excluding Alaska.

In 1967 the bald eagle was declared an endangered species south of the 40th parallel, and anyone found guilty of shooting one was liable to prosecution. But the real turning point came in 1972, with the virtual banning of DDT and related pesticides in the U.S. Since then eagle numbers have steadily increased. There are now some 4,500 breeding pairs south of the Canada–U.S. border.

Bald eagles are still suffering from loss of wild habitat and a shortage of natural prey, particularly in the southern part of their range. Many have also died from lead poisoning, caused by eating waterfowl that have swallowed lead shot from shotguns or from fishing lines. Lead shot has now been phased out, thanks to a five-year program instituted by the U.S. Fish and Wildlife Service. So despite these problems, bald eagle numbers are still increasing in most states, and in 1995 the eagle was taken off the endangered list and reclassified as Threatened.

Osprey

Pandion haliaetus

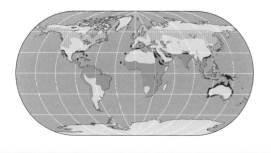

Common name Osprey

Scientific name *Pandion haliaetus*

Family   Pandionidae

Order   Falconiformes

Size Length: 22–23 in (56–58.5 cm);
wingspan: 57–67 in (145–170 cm);
weight: 2.6–4.3 lb (1.2–2 kg);
female slightly larger than male

Key features Long, narrow wings; dark-brown upper
parts and mainly white underparts with dark-
speckled breast band; white head with dark-
brown stripe through yellow eye; black
hooked bill; blue-gray legs; sexes identical;
immature paler

Habits   Hunts alone over shallow water; spends much
time perched near water

Nesting   Large, isolated nest of sticks and grasses,
usually in top of tall tree near water; season
varies with region; usually 2–3 eggs;
incubation 35–43 days; young fledge after
44–59 days; 1 brood

Voice   Loud yelping call; shrill "pyew-pyew-pyew"
during territorial display

Diet   Mainly live fish snatched from just below
surface of water, plus a few frogs, snakes,
and small birds

Habitat   Coasts, estuaries, rivers, lakes, and swamps

Distribution Breeds virtually worldwide except South
America, polar regions, deserts, and much of
Africa; breeding birds from North America
and northern Eurasia winter in warm-
temperate and tropical zones

Status   Badly affected by pesticide poisoning during
1960s and 1970s, but now flourishing
throughout most of its range

The spectacular hunting style of the fish-catching osprey makes it one of the most recognizable of all birds of prey throughout its huge, almost global range.

THE DISTINCTIVE BROWN-AND-WHITE osprey is a fish
hunter. It is so highly specialized that it is
classified in a family on its own. Other birds of
prey catch fish, but the osprey has acquired a
unique combination of adaptations that make it
the most widespread and successful of its kind.

The osprey has oily, water-resistant
plumage allowing it to plunge underwater to
catch its prey, then surface and fly off without
difficulty. It can close its nostrils as it dives to
prevent water being forced into its lungs. The
bird has extremely strong feet to absorb the
impact of the dive, reversible outer toes, and
long, curved talons. It also has a long, hooked
bill as well as a variety of unusual internal
features not seen in other birds of prey.

Adaptable Hunter

Ospreys may live in almost any habitat that
offers regular supplies of medium-sized fish,
from tropical swamps and coastal lagoons to
the cold rivers and lakes of the northern forests.
They are most numerous in rich, remote coastal
habitats such as saltmarshes and mangrove
swamps. However, they are unusually tolerant
of human activity and are often seen fishing in
suburban reservoirs and rivers flowing through

*⊕ The osprey skewers
its prey with long,
curved talons. The soles
of the feet are covered
in sharp, spiny scales
that help prevent the
slippery prize from being
dropped while being
carried back to the
feeding perch.*

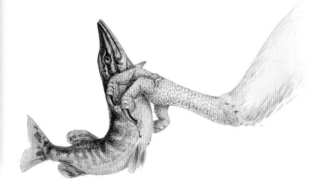

towns. They will even nest in such places, sometimes using man-made nesting platforms provided for the purpose. The willingness to exploit artificial habitats can cause conflicts with humans, however, for they may raid fish farms used for rearing trout or salmon.

Ospreys that breed in the tropics and around the coasts of Australia stay on or near their breeding grounds all year. During the northern winter the tropical residents are joined by birds that have migrated from North America, northern Europe, Scandinavia, Russia, and Siberia. The migrants breed in the north, mainly on the broad rivers and lakes of the great evergreen forests, and then fly south before their feeding waters freeze over. They fly strongly, covering distances of 2,500 to 6,000 miles (4,025–9,650 km). Unlike many birds of

prey, they fly directly toward their destinations without making detours to avoid deserts or deep seas. Therefore, they do not gather in large numbers at favored crossing points like Panama, and it is unusual to see more than one or two ospreys together on migration.

Whether it is on its breeding territory, its wintering grounds, or on migration between the two, an osprey usually hunts in the same way. Cruising some 30–100 feet (9–30 m) above the water, it pauses to hover with its head bent down and legs dangling, searching for a fish just below the surface. If the bird sees a likely prey, it may descend to get a better view before diving headfirst with half-folded wings. Just before the osprey hits the water, it throws its feet forward with talons outspread to seize the fish. Its whole body may disappear

⊕ An osprey may take almost any medium-sized fish, depending on what is locally available, up to a weight of about 3 pounds (1.4 kg).

Display Flights

Amale osprey usually returns to the breeding site before the female. As soon as he arrives, he stakes his claim with a spectacular switchback display flight, fluttering, wheeling, and diving high over the site, with shrill, whistling calls. When a female arrives, she is attracted by the display and joins him in the performance to strengthen the bond between them.

This type of display flight is common among birds of prey, particularly larger species such as eagles and harriers. In some cases the female flips onto her back in midair so the male can seize her by the talons. Locked together, the pair spiral slowly toward the ground before releasing their grip and flying up again.

underwater with a loud splash, leaving just the wings visible, but it soon struggles free, shakes the water from its feathers, and carries its struggling catch away in its talons, holding it headfirst to reduce wind resistance.

If the fish is too heavy to carry away, the osprey simply drops it, but sometimes the bird's talons are so deeply embedded that it cannot release its grip. Then the weight of the fish may drag its attacker back into the water, and ospreys have been drowned on such occasions.

Big Nests

A typical osprey nest is a big, broad pile of sticks and flotsam lined with soft grass and moss, securely wedged in the crown of a tall tree such as a fir, although the birds will also nest on cliffs, ruined buildings, artificial platforms, aerials, and even poles supporting electricity lines.

The female usually carries out most of the five-week incubation, while the male keeps her supplied with fish. He also brings food for the chicks when they hatch and keeps the whole family fed until the chicks are fledged. As soon as they can fly, the young ospreys start fishing for themselves, but it takes them weeks, even months, to become as skilled as their parents. Most young ospreys breed in their fourth year.

Brighter Future

Since ospreys build such big, conspicuous nests, they make easy targets for hunters and egg thieves, and in the past they have suffered badly from persecution. As recently as the mid-nineteenth century they bred all over Europe, but within a century shooting and nest destruction had eliminated the breeding populations from nearly all of Europe west of the Black Sea. Then the survivors were hit by a new threat: poisoning by agricultural pesticides.

The worst effects of it were seen in the northeastern U.S., where chemicals draining into waterways and lakes contaminated the fish taken by ospreys as prey. The birds accumulated the poison in their bodies and either died or failed to breed. By the 1970s they were in serious decline; but when the offending chemicals were outlawed in North America and Europe, the situation began to improve. Today osprey populations are recovering strongly in the U.S., and they are also doing well in northern Europe, thanks partly to birds being reintroduced to regions where they were once common. In Scotland, for example, ospreys became extinct in 1902, but a reintroduction plan has now created a viable breeding population of more than 80 pairs.

Each pair of ospreys returns to the same site year after year, renovating the old nest and adding more material, so it grows bigger and bigger. Eventually the nest can become so huge that it collapses, and the birds have to begin again on a new site.

Mated for Life

Like many large birds of prey, ospreys often stay faithful to their partners for life. At the end of the breeding season the birds leave the nest and go their separate ways. When the time comes to mate again, the ospreys instinctively return to the same area. Unless one of the original pair has died, they both come back to the isolated nest, get reacquainted, and start another family.

However, some birds returning to the breeding area have never mated before. If one of a pair fails to arrive, the survivor may mate with one of the unattached birds and rear a brood of chicks in the old nest. If neither of the original breeders returns, a new pair may take over the nest, repair it, and use it themselves for the next few years. The same nest may be reoccupied every year for decades or even centuries.

A juvenile osprey calling. The pale undersides act as camouflage to help the bird conceal itself from prey as it swoops over the surface of the water.

Common name Peregrine falcon

Scientific name *Falco peregrinus*

Family Falconidae

Order Falconiformes

Size Length: 14–20 in (35.5–51 cm); wingspan: 35–47 in (89–119 cm); weight: 1.3–3.3 lb (0.6–1.5 kg); female bigger and heavier than male

Key features Stocky; long, pointed wings; blue-gray upper parts; white to buff-pink underparts with dark bars; gray-black head with dark "mustache" and white chin; dark bill with yellow base; dark eye with yellow eye ring; yellow legs with black talons; sexes identical except for size; juvenile browner

Habits Aerial hunter; sights prey from perch or in patrolling flight; usually solitary

Nesting Nests on remote cliff ledge—sometimes on a building—with no nesting material; usually 3–4 eggs; incubation 28–32 days; young fledge after 35–42 days; 1 brood

Voice Raucous, high-pitched "kek-kek-kek-kek" alarm call; creaking "wee-chew"

Diet Mainly medium-sized birds such as pigeons, caught in flight, plus small mammals and insects

Habitat Very variable, from remote mountain wildernesses to city centers, but typically sea cliffs and crags; avoids extensive, dense forest

Distribution Virtually worldwide except Central Asia, central Sahara, Amazonia, Antarctica, and central Greenland; northern birds migrate south in winter

Status Has now recovered from serious declines in 1950s to 1970s caused by pesticide poisoning; still threatened in places

Peregrine Falcon

Falco peregrinus

The peregrine is probably the fastest hunter on Earth, capable of launching an airborne attack on its prey at speeds of over 100 miles per hour (160 km/h).

BIG, BURLY, AND AMAZINGLY FAST, the bird-killing peregrine falcon could claim to be the ultimate airborne hunter. It is certainly the most spectacular, likely to attack apparently out of nowhere and strike its prey dead in midair. It must be a strategy for success, because of all birds of prey it is the species that has spread most widely around the globe.

Deadly Hunter

Like nearly all falcons, the peregrine is built for speed. It has sharp-pointed wings adapted for maximum thrust, and they are powered by huge flight muscles that give the bird a heavy, broad-chested look as it perches watching for potential prey. In the air the peregrine is agile and fast, and it has the stamina to cross oceans on its long migration flights. Where there are no suitable vantage points, the bird often searches for prey by circling high in the sky, using its excellent eyesight to pick out a victim below. Once it has a target in view, it may mount an attack that, for sheer speed, has no equal in the natural world.

Already moving fast, the falcon powers into a headfirst dive, or stoop. It may fall almost vertically out of the sky, accelerating all the time

⊕ *Peregrines may pass food to each other in flight. Here a female turns on her back to receive a blackbird (*Turdus vulgaris*) from her mate.*

⊕ *A peregrine attacking an American bittern (*Botaurus lentiginosus*). Although peregrines do not usually attack such large prey, they have been known to take birds as big as geese.*

with the air roaring over the feathers of its half-closed wings. Special structures in the bird's airways prevent the rising air pressure bursting its lungs. The bird keeps its eyes open to ensure it stays on target. As the peregrine closes on its victim, it reaches out with its talons, extending a powerful hind claw to slice into its quarry like a can opener. It usually aims for the head, and the high-velocity impact is often enough to kill the victim outright, so it tumbles from the sky in a flurry of bloodstained feathers.

It is a devastating technique but not infallible. The peregrine stoops at such high speed that it cannot easily alter course; and if the intended victim manages to dodge aside at the last moment, the falcon may miss. In fact, many attacks fail at the first attempt, but a peregrine does not give up easily. Swooping around, it may try again, this time relying on active flying speed to overhaul its prey. Often it succeeds—few birds can fly faster than a peregrine, which can achieve 50 miles per hour (80 km/h) in level flight. Occasionally a hunted bird manages to escape by diving into a swirling flock of birds or simply by dropping to the ground and into cover.

Sometimes a bird is not killed by the first strike, so the peregrine has to finish it off with a lethal neck bite. Like all falcons—but not other birds of prey—it has an extra notch in its bill to help it cut through neck bones to sever the spinal cord. Then it either eats the bird where it fell or carries it to a favorite feeding perch, using its hooked bill to rip away feathers and skin to get at the flesh.

The peregrine's main victims are pigeons, crows, ducks, seabirds, or big waders; but it also takes smaller songbirds such as larks and thrushes, plus the occasional insect or small

⊕ A peregrine searches the sky and the ground below for prey. Often the bird simply perches on a suitable lookout post or branch until a likely victim is sighted.

The Falconer's Choice

As the most spectacular hunter among the falcons, the peregrine has traditionally been the bird of choice for falconry. This ancient sport has been practiced for at least 4,000 years, and it is still extremely popular, with as many as 20,000 falconers worldwide.

The birds used for falconry are usually well cared for; and since they are flown free, they have the opportunity to escape if they wish. Yet falconry has a downside. It creates a demand for young peregrines and other falcons. While many are captive-bred, there is a flourishing trade in birds taken from the wild as eggs or nestlings. That is illegal, but nest robbers are prepared to risk fines or imprisonment because they can get a huge sum for every bird they sell. This is a big problem in southern Europe, where many peregrine pairs have their young stolen each year.

⊙ A peregrine stands over its prey with arched wings before eating it. This is known as mantling. The peregrine normally ignores the wings and feet of its victim but strips everything else down to the bone.

mammal picked off the ground. The bigger female takes heavier prey than the male, and that may help a mated pair divide the spoils on their joint territory.

Rich Pickings

During the breeding season peregrines need more food, both for themselves and for their young, and many head north to prey on the huge flocks of waders and wildfowl that breed on the arctic tundra. Like all peregrines, these northern breeders prefer to nest on cliffs and crags; but where suitable nest sites are scarce, they lay their eggs in bare scrapes on the ground. Here they are vulnerable to nest robbers like Arctic foxes, so the birds must be particularly vigilant to drive away any intruders. Other breeding birds suffer in the same way, and in the Siberian Arctic rare red-breasted geese (*Branta ruficollis*) often nest near the peregrines to take advantage of their air defenses. Clearly the risk from the foxes outweighs the risk from the falcons!

Farther south, breeding peregrines favor sea cliffs near seabird nesting colonies or upland wildernesses used as breeding grounds by waders. But some peregrines regularly nest on city towers, chimneys, and bridges. In early spring the pairs perform noisy aerial displays over their nest sites, spiraling into the sky and plummeting down again, sometimes rolling over and clasping talons as they tumble earthward. The male keeps his mate supplied with food as she incubates the eggs and broods the young, but the female also starts hunting when the young are a month old. Most young birds breed in their third year.

At the end of the breeding season northern peregrines move south to warmer regions. Birds that breed in the Canadian Arctic fly all the way to Argentina and Chile, while those from northern Europe and Siberia spend the northern winter in Africa, southern Asia, and Indonesia. Peregrines breeding in milder climates may not travel so far, but in western Europe many leave their nesting sites to hunt over estuaries teeming with waders and wildfowl that have moved south from the Arctic for the winter.

Poisoned

In 1942 mass production of an insecticide called DDT began. The insecticide was effective and inexpensive, and by the 1950s DDT and other "organochlorine" insecticides were being widely used to combat crop pests. Seeds were laced with the chemicals to kill the insects that fed on them, and crop yields soared.

Yet there was a problem brewing for wildlife. Organochlorines take a long time to break down and become harmless. Pigeons and other seed-eating birds started accumulating them in their body fat. When the chemicals washed off the land into waterways, they also entered the bodies of fish. At first the effects went unnoticed. A pigeon might accumulate the DDT from 1,000 seeds and show no side effects. But the poison stays in its body. If a peregrine catches and eats 100 such pigeons, it accumulates the DDT from 100,000 seeds, with disastrous results.

In fact, the main effect of DDT on peregrines was to make their eggshells thinner, so they broke as the birds tried to incubate them. Fish-eating birds of prey like the osprey (*Pandion haliaetus*) and bald eagle (*Haliaeetus leucocephalus*) suffered in the same way. They were also killed outright by stronger organochlorines such as dieldrin and aldrin. So, by destroying both the birds of prey and their eggs, the pesticides threatened to wipe them out altogether.

By the 1970s the problem was recognized, and organochlorine pesticides were virtually banned in North America and Europe. Yet they are still used in the tropics to fight insect-borne diseases like malaria. So although many birds of prey are recovering in the north, pesticide poisoning is still a major threat to their survival.

Victim of War

Like most birds of prey, the peregrine has suffered badly from persecution. Many were shot in the past because they were considered a danger to valuable game birds, and during World War II the peregrines of southern Britain were virtually annihilated because of the threat they posed to homing pigeons carrying messages from occupied Europe.

More recently, huge numbers of peregrines shared the same fate as the osprey, wiped out by pesticide poisoning during the 1960s and 1970s. The entire peregrine population of the eastern U.S. was destroyed by pesticides, plus about 85 percent of the peregrines in the western U.S. The situation in Europe was almost as bad.

The most destructive chemicals are no longer used in North America and Europe, and now many populations of peregrines have completely recovered, thanks partly to birds being bred in captivity and released in areas where they once lived wild. And since peregrines are amazingly adaptable, being prepared to breed almost anywhere, their global future is probably secure.

⊕ *An adult peregrine offers its chick a mouthful of food. The nest has been built among rocks by a river in the Russian Arctic.*

Northern Bobwhite

Colinus virginianus

Calling loudly from low, dense cover, the northern bobwhite is a common species in North America. It will keep out of sight until almost stepped on, when it bursts into the air with a tremendous clatter of wings.

Common name Northern bobwhite (bobwhite)

Scientific name *Colinus virginianus*

Family   Phasianidae

Order   Galliformes

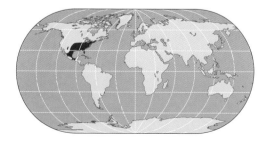

Size Length: 8–10 in (20–25 cm); wingspan: 17 in (43 cm); weight: 4 oz (113 g)

Key features Small, rounded, rusty-brown quail with tiny bill; males have very variable head pattern— according to race—from all-black to blackish, with buff or white stripe over eye and on throat; both sexes unmarked or spotted white below; females generally duller

Habits   Ground-dwelling; found in small family parties

Nesting   Shallow nest on ground; 10–15 eggs; incubation 23 days; young fledge after 14 days; 1 brood

Voice   Clear, whistled "bob-white!" and "kal-oi-kee?"

Diet   Seeds and fruits; insects in summer

Habitat   Open woodland, woodland edge and shrubbery, arable fields, pastures, and open grassland

Distribution Eastern U.S. south into Central America; also Cuba

Status   Abundant; more than 20 million shot annually in U.S.

THE NORTHERN BOBWHITE IS AN UNUSUALLY variable New World quail, with 22 races and even some variation within them. All are small, round birds with no obvious crest and a stubby, black bill. Males have fairly distinct head patterns, with a buff or white stripe over the eye and on the throat, separated by broad bands of black. Some races have all-black heads and deep rufous bodies, while those with strong head patterns tend to have paler colors with a scattering of big, pale spots.

Range and Habitat

The northern bobwhite is found as far north as the Great Lakes and west to central Texas but is mostly absent from the western U.S. In the south it extends through Mexico to Guatemala, and it is also found widely in Cuba, where it is assumed to be native but could perhaps have been introduced long ago. It has certainly been introduced, with varying success, in many parts of the world, including Hawaii and New Zealand. Introductions in Britain failed to produce any lasting presence there, however.

Within its range the bird usually occupies more or less open ground, but in some areas it lives in extensive pine woods. Fields with hedges and patches of bushes or shrubbery are also favored, especially those of arable crops that provide seed and fruit.

Calling Its Name

Northern bobwhites live in coveys (groups), consisting of several families together. They are terrestrial birds, keeping to thick cover mostly, but their loud calls betray their presence even if

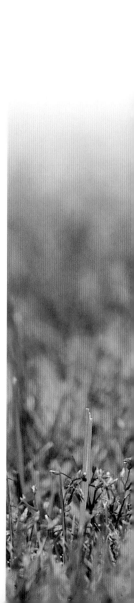

A male bobwhite (left) is distinguished by his white eye stripe and white throat markings. Females (right) have duller plumage.

they are hard to see. From these hidden coveys comes a chorus of questioning, triple-note calls with loud, two-note responses. The usual call gives the bird its name—a clearly pronounced "bob-white!" If approached too closely, northern bobwhites simply crouch quietly out of sight or scuttle away through the vegetation. Only if almost stepped on will they suddenly fly, bursting up underfoot in all directions. They spend all day feeding, dusting, or sunbathing and roost on the ground at night.

In natural habitats with plenty of coarse, herbaceous growth bobwhites eat the seeds of plants as varied as thistles, grasses, and oak trees (acorns are eaten with relish). Crops such as sunflowers, corn, soya, and tomatoes are also eaten. In summer this vegetarian diet is supplemented by insects. Insects are important to growing chicks and also to females that need a higher energy intake in order to produce a large clutch of eggs.

Large Broods

Northern bobwhites are monogamous. Each male displays to a female and pairs with her before making a simple, shallow nest on the ground with a lining of grasses and stems. The nest is well hidden in vegetation. After the eggs are laid, a second female will sometimes lay in the nest in a form of brood parasitism. By laying her eggs in other nests, she is giving her own eggs a better chance of success.

The chicks leave the nest soon after hatching, tended by the parent birds or by the female alone, and they grow quickly. As with many game-bird chicks, the wing feathers of bobwhite chicks grow especially quickly, and the birds are able to fly before they are fully grown, when just two weeks old.

Like other New World quails, northern bobwhites lay large numbers of eggs because many chicks die before they reach adulthood. Also, if a clutch is lost—for example, through predation—the birds will lay a replacement. These activities are designed to ensure the birds' populations are maintained at high levels.

Losses and Gains

Northern bobwhites have long been declining in traditional habitats in the south and west of their range because of land development and loss of habitat. However, in the east they have increased due to management of their numbers and habitats—despite the birds being shot for sport in huge numbers every year.

Common Pheasant

Phasianus colchicus

A familiar bird of the countryside, the pheasant is also commonly seen hanging in the butcher's store in the fall. The cock pheasant is an eye-catching and handsome bird, with exquisite, glossy plumage.

Common name Common pheasant (pheasant, ring-necked pheasant)

Scientific name *Phasianus colchicus*

Family Phasianidae

Order Galliformes

Size Length: male 29.5–35 in (75–89 cm), female 21–24.5 in (53–62 cm); wingspan: 27.5–36 in (70–91.5 cm); weight: 1.3–4.4 lb (0.6–2 kg)

Key features Round-bodied, triangular-tailed, small-headed game bird; male with green head, coppery or golden-brown body with dark spots, green to orange-buff rump; female dull, spotted, shorter-tailed

Habits Lives socially; terrestrial except when roosting; noisy at dusk

Nesting Males mate with several hens; small nest on ground; 9–14 eggs; incubation 22 days; young fledge after 12 days; 1 brood

Voice Loud, crowing calls and abrupt "korr-kok"

Diet Fruits, seeds, and buds; occasionally insects and small reptiles, amphibians, and mammals

Habitat Woodland edge, overgrown riversides, edges of marshes, and farmland

Distribution Natural range across Central and eastern Asia, west to eastern Europe; introduced widely in other parts of Europe, North America, and Australasia

Status Common and secure in original range

THERE ARE 31 RECOGNIZED RACES, or subspecies, of the common pheasant and much variety even within those. In most areas matters are further complicated by captive-bred and released birds mixing with others of different appearance.

Colorful Bird

All races of common pheasant have a basically similar appearance. Mature males have a broad, disklike, bright red, fleshy wattle on the face and tiny "horns" on the back of the crown, a pale bill, and a glossy green head. The head looks black from a distance, but close up it is a beautiful emerald green with a blue-and-purple sheen. Many males have a white ring around the neck or a broader white patch; in Britain those without such markings are sometimes called "Old English" pheasants. The breast is usually dark, rich coppery-red or rust colored, while the back is paler, more golden-yellow, with or without large, pale spots. Bold, dark spots on the breast and flanks appear solid black unless seen close up, when they reveal a gloss of iridescent purple, lilac, and blue.

Long, drooping feathers on the rump form a kind of shawl of orange, brown, or pale green. Some races (in Russia and Afghanistan) have white wing coverts. This feature may be combined with or without a wide, white collar. The tail is long and stiff; and although it does not have the remarkably long, arched, or beautifully patterned appearance of the tails of the more exotic-looking Lady Amherst's (*Chrysolophus amherstiae*), golden (*C. pictus*), and Reeves' (*Syrmaticus reevesii*) pheasants, it is still eye-catching.

⊕ *During territorial disputes between male common pheasants, each leaps off the ground and tries to attack the other with his claws and spurs.*

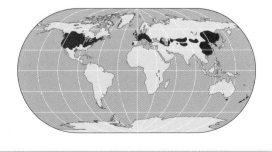

Females are pale buff-brown with spots of black. They have round, plain heads and shorter, but still elongated, spikelike tails that distinguish them from partridges.

Pheasants are rather short-legged birds, but more upstanding than the partridges, and more elegant and long-striding when walking on the ground. They are much more likely to run than to fly if disturbed. On the back of the leg is a short, stubby spur that males use for fighting.

⊕ Before a fight over territory ensues, males may display to each other by raising and lowering their tails and heads.

Versatile Bill

The common pheasant has a stout, arched, but very short bill. It looks like a typical seed-eater's beak, but in fact it is able to perform a wider variety of functions. Like a farmyard chicken, a pheasant picks food from the ground with a series of rhythmic, fast, and accurate pecks, using its sinuous neck to dart the head forward and back. This same action can also stab and hammer small ground-dwelling animals such as voles, mice, or even young birds. Pheasants can be quite predatory; in southern England it is thought that common pheasants may be partly responsible for the decline in reptiles and amphibians, including slow worms and common lizards—a surprising conclusion for such a bird.

Pheasant Distribution

After widespread introduction as a bird hunted for sport, the range of the common pheasant stretches across the Canadian–U.S. border region and northern U.S. from the Pacific to the Atlantic, and from Britain and Ireland through the middle of Europe. The range continues eastward in a narrow, broken belt through Central Asia to China, Southeast Asia, and Taiwan. The native range is in this latter part, from Taiwan, China, and Vietnam, westward to the Caucasus Mountains in eastern Europe. The bird was also introduced to parts of Australasia.

There are millions of common pheasants in China—perhaps the densest population of the species anywhere away from localized

concentrations released for shooting in Europe.

Introductions have met with varying success. Even in the core of the European range, including Britain, numbers are constantly being reinforced by newly bred and released stock, most of which have little chance of long-term survival, although a few persist. In areas such as Australia introductions have failed altogether, but in New Zealand and much of the U.S. pheasants thrive.

Many of the wild-living pheasants in Britain are found in and around marshes, often within extensive reed beds provided there is woodland nearby. Most are released into scattered woods within lowland farmland. The marshy habitat, however, reflects the true nature of pheasant habitat in many places further east, since they prefer a mixture of woods, bushy areas, and riversides or more swampy lakeside fens. Common pheasants are also found on extensive plains with intense cultivation and on ranges of hills with scattered woods and farmland in the valleys; ideally, the birds prefer a mixture of terrain.

How Pheasants Live

Outside the spring breeding season common pheasants live in loose groups or sometimes more concentrated family parties. The groups spend the day foraging on the ground, sometimes flying from roosting areas in woodland to the open fields where they feed. In Europe and America they tend to be less mobile, wandering from the edge of a wood into open fields on foot and seldom flying very far. If alarmed, they will usually run, head and tail held high, into cover; they will only resort to flying if absolutely necessary. Released birds are usually very tame. Less tame birds will sometimes remain still until almost stepped on, at which point they will suddenly fly up underfoot with a great clatter of wings and noisy calls—an unwelcome test of an unsuspecting walker's nerves!

At dusk common pheasants move off to roost in trees—in which they are quite at home despite their apparently cumbersome long tails and general lack of mobility. There is usually a chorus of short, crowing calls from birds sorting out their roosting places and social hierarchy. Another call frequently heard is an abrupt, double note—"korr-kok!" It is immediately followed by a short, loud whirring sound made by a few rapid beats of the wings. Pheasants often call in response to loud noises, such as thunder or gunshot, and were frequently noticed calling during the early days of Concorde trials when the supersonic aircraft created sonic booms over land.

Pheasants are almost entirely vegetarian in the natural state, eating large grains and other seeds, as well as berries, fruits, buds, and leaves of many kinds, mostly picked from or close to the ground. Captive birds released into the wild have been found to eat a more varied diet, including reptiles and small mammals such as mice and voles.

Elaborate Mating Display

In the breeding season males become solitary and defend territories against other males. The males call to attract small groups of mature females, and usually from three to five hens gather at a male's territory.

Males then display to females with a ritualized performance designed to show off their glorious upper body colors and tails to best advantage. A male will attempt to corner a hen and head her off each time she tries to move away, by running from side to side and "shepherding" her back into place. At the same time, the male leans over sideways in an

⊕ This study of a calling male common pheasant shows clearly the iridescent colors, the red wattles, and the "horns" that characterize the bird. The "horns" are actually feathers.

extravagant display, slightly spreading his wings and fanning his tail, while tilting over to display the maximum surface area to the hen. Like the female Indian peafowl, the female common pheasant at first appears entirely unimpressed with the male's display, but eventually mating takes place.

Once mated, the female lays her eggs in a shallow, grass-lined nest or almost bare hollow on the ground, well hidden under low vegetation. They are incubated by the hen alone for 22 days, although in many areas where pheasants have been introduced, incubation lasts between 23 and 25 days.

The downy chicks soon leave the nest but stay with their mother while she teaches them how to find food. They grow quickly and, in common with most game birds, develop their wing feathers unusually early, so that they are able to fly before they are fully grown.

Some Concerns

The wild common pheasant needs to be monitored with care; some races are scarce and threatened by habitat loss and excessive hunting. One race found in the Caucasus, for example, may number just two or three

Fast but Short Flights

Like other game birds, pheasants have large flight muscles. They provide the wings with short bursts of great power but quickly lose energy. Pheasants have quite short, broad wings that are ideally suited for maneuvering between trees when flying. The feathers at the tips of the wings are aerodynamically suited to fast acceleration. They can spread apart like the fingers of a hand, helping the wings obtain maximum lift when the bird needs to escape in a hurry. Pheasants take off in a sudden, rapid burst, creating a noisy "explosion" as they call and thrash their wings at the same moment. The birds soon change from powered flight to a long glide, however, and become exhausted quite quickly. A fleeing pheasant will usually fly a short distance, then glide to the ground and land "on the run," dashing off on foot to the nearest thick cover.

The drab plumage of a female pheasant helps her blend into the woodland while she incubates her eggs.

hundred pairs after a drastic decline caused by shooting and could easily become extinct. Other wild populations thrive and remain abundant despite large-scale killing. In areas where pheasants have been introduced for shooting, numbers are boosted every year by millions of young birds bred and released for sport.

Common name Prairie chicken (greater prairie chicken)

Scientific name *Tympanuchus cupido*

Family	Tetraonidae
Order	Galliformes
Size	Length: 16–18.5 in (41–47 cm); wingspan: 31.5 in (80 cm); weight: 1.7–2.2 lb (0.8–1 kg)
Key features	Hump-backed, round-headed, short-legged grouse; yellow wattle over eye; closely mottled and barred plumage with black, white, rufous, and gray, giving an overall pale, marbled effect; some races more closely barred below
Habits	Lives in small groups; males come together to display
Nesting	Shallow scrape on ground, lined with feathers, grass, and leaves; 8–13 eggs; incubation 23–25 days; young fledge after 14–21 days; 1 brood
Voice	Deep, booming "oo-loo-woo" sound in display
Diet	Grains of cereal crops, acorns, leaves, and shoots; some insects
Habitat	Originally open prairies mixed with oak woods—now modified into cereal prairies with patches of original grassland
Distribution	Very local and fragmented in midwestern North America
Status	Much reduced in numbers and range; 1 race perhaps secure through intensive conservation efforts, but even it is still declining in some areas

Prairie Chicken

Tympanuchus cupido

The prairie chicken is noted for its remarkable display. However, this bird is now difficult to see, since it is rare and declining in most of its former North American range.

AT A DISTANCE THE PRAIRIE chicken looks gray-brown, but closeup views reveal a complex and beautiful patterning of stronger colors that merge together into a pale, mottled effect. The underside is broadly and regularly barred with brown and buff. The rare and declining Texas race has a beautifully neat, tighter pattern of fine bars. The male has a big yellow wattle above the eye, and a black-and-white spotted shawl extends down from the back of the head to the base of the neck. In display it is raised in a remarkable upward-pointing spike behind the head, with the yellow wattles expanded and a big, bare, orange-yellow fleshy air sac inflated on each side of the neck.

Vanishing Races

One race of prairie chicken, now extinct in Louisiana, is found in Texas but has declined from 8,000 birds in 1937 to 2,000 in 1970 and to fewer than 1,000 now. Another race, at Martha's Vineyard, Massachusetts, became extinct in 1932. The remaining race is more common and is now found mainly from the Dakotas to Nebraska, Kansas, and Missouri after a long shrinkage of its range. Within the total range only tiny pockets are occupied, mostly because the habitat has become so unsuitable.

The prairie chicken was once the most common and widespread grouse of the great tall-grass prairies, where scattered oak provided patches of shelter, and periodic fires created more open spaces. The Texas race was found on sandy coastal plains that spread through forest clearings to the grass prairies inland and is still concentrated in what remains of such habitat.

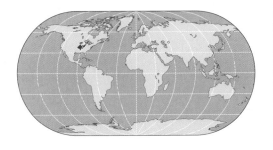

⊕ *During the breeding season male prairie chickens hold small territories within a display arena. Among displaying males there is much mock fighting and ritual. Real fighting often develops, too.*

Nowadays the prairie chicken has to feed on croplands of wheat, sorghum, corn, and rye, but it still needs access to patches of native prairie habitat. The remnant scraps of prairie provide places for prairie chickens to roost at night and for them to nest in; by day they move into fields to feed. They also need open areas in grassland, often on slightly higher ground, for their displays.

Like many other game birds, adults can survive on seeds and shoots, but young birds must eat insects. Grasshoppers are critical to their survival and also form a substantial part of the adult's diet in summer. For the rest of the year prairie chickens in the north now eat cultivated grain. Texas birds eat far fewer cultivated crops, under 10 percent of their diet being cereal grains. The leaves, shoots, buds, and seeds of native prairie plants are also eaten when they can be found.

Prairie chickens satisfy their hunger in quite short bouts of feeding. In winter they may feed for 80 minutes or so in the morning and for a similar period in the evening, resting for the rest of the day. The big cultivated grains provide the birds with plenty of energy, but in winter conserving it is important. At first, the arrival of crops helped the birds, since they now had much more big grain to eat in winter; but this benefit was soon far outweighed by increased hunting and habitat loss.

Making an Impression

Males arrive at the display arenas in the dark and begin to defend their territories. The best territories are in the middle of the arena, for it is here that most females are concentrated. A displaying male enlarges his eye wattles, raises the feathers on the back of his neck, inflates his air sacs, droops his wings to the ground, and raises his tail, which is fanned, rattled, and abruptly snapped shut. He runs to other males and patters with a "foot-stamping" action on the ground. The air sacs on the neck create a deep, booming "oo-loo-woo" sound.

When the hens approach, the males posture and prance and leap into the air, fluttering their wings and striking out with their beak and feet in an effort to rake across their opponent's plumage. The successful males mate with most of the hens. The chicks hatch with some of their wing feathers already partly grown, and they can soon fly a little way.

Sage Grouse

Centrocercus urophasianus

A bird of the American blue sage plains, the sage grouse remains relatively common in much of its range—unlike several of its North American relatives.

Common name Sage grouse

Scientific name *Centrocercus urophasianus*

Family Tetraonidae

Order Galliformes

Size Length: male 26–30 in (66–76 cm), female 19–23 in (48–58 cm); wingspan: 47 in (119 cm); weight: 3–7 lb (1.4–3.2 kg)

Key features Rather long, long-tailed grouse; short, dark bill; yellow wattle over eye; thickset head and neck; redddish-brown plumage with complex pattern; male black-and-white on head and neck, white ruff on breast, black plumage on belly; short legs

Habits Terrestrial; lives in small groups; males mostly separate from hens

Nesting Males display communally at leks; females nest on ground; 7–8 eggs; incubation 25–27 days; young fledge after 14–21 days; 1 brood

Voice Short, chickenlike, clucking calls when flushed

Diet Shoots and leaves of sagebrush, clover, and various herbaceous plants; young chicks require insects

Habitat Low, thick scrub and brush country, and dry grassland in plains and foothills

Distribution Widespread in western U.S and southwest Canada; range shrinking at edges

Status Locally common and secure; declining at fringe of range

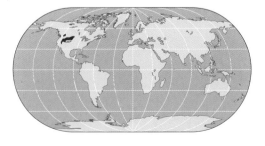

THE WIDESPREAD SAGE GROUSE IS A LONG-TAILED, heavy-looking bird. It is much larger than the other grouse species that can be found nearby—the sharp-tailed (*Tympanuchus phasianellus*), ruffed (*Bonasa umbellus*), spruce (*Dendragapus canadensis*), and blue grouse (*D. obscurus*). They all have short or rounded, fanlike tails, whereas the male sage grouse has a longer, tapered tail with pointed, spiky central feathers normally held in a central point.

The male is eye-catching when seen close up, with a lot of black on the face and a white bib that extends into a densely feathered ruff around the lower breast. European grouse usually have fleshy red wattles above the eyes, but the sage grouse—like other North American species—has a rich, yellow eye wattle. Both males and females are beautifully patterned on the back and wings, with rich, reddish-brown feathers marked with black-edged white streaks. In flight the strikingly white underwing is revealed. The long tail lacks the white sides visible on the sharp-tailed grouse.

Birds of the Plains

Sage grouse are found from Washington and Alberta through southwestern Saskatchewan and North Dakota, to eastern California, Nevada, Utah, and Colorado. This area includes much of the Rockies, although the sage grouse is not really a mountain bird. Nevertheless, higher ground is occupied in summer but vacated in winter as the grouse move to lower ground. Such movements are not the true, seasonal migrations seen in many other species. They only take place when snow covers the topmost shoots of their staple food, sagebrush.

This forces the sage grouse to move on to find food elsewhere.

Previously, there were populations of the sage grouse in British Columbia, New Mexico, and Oklahoma. However, the bird is no longer found there, and some areas of California are also now devoid of the sage grouse.

The sage grouse prefers open plains and rolling hills with broad valleys and whalebacks, rather than steep ridges and sharp peaks. Such areas are generally very dry.

Keeping Out of Sight

Sage grouse are usually fairly unobtrusive, especially in winter and also midsummer, when the small young hatch out. Sage grouse are beautifully camouflaged in the sagebrush and simply "melt away" in the vegetation or crouch and "freeze" motionless if disturbed, avoiding detection just by keeping still. They feed by day—in summer mostly early in the morning and again in the evening, with a lengthy rest during the middle of the day. In winter they have to feed throughout the short daylight

hours. During hot spells they keep under cover.

Males separate from the females in the fall and remain in small groups during the winter. They move to their display grounds in spring, as soon as the snow melts and before the hens arrive. Females and young live in small parties, tending to move farther away from the breeding areas than the larger males, which are more able to cope with severe weather.

Sagebrush is crucial to the sage grouse, as the bird's name might suggest. Sagebrush is a tough, aromatic plant. In winter its leaves make up almost the entire diet of the sage grouse. Other birds such as prairie chickens (*Tympanuchus cupido*) turn to seeds in winter, but they are avoided by sage grouse.

In summer more variety is possible, but sagebrush remains the favored food, although other herbaceous plants are also eaten. Like many young game birds, however, the young chicks require insect food for a fast intake of energy. Insects make up 60 percent of their food in the first week of life, but this gradually declines. By the time they are three months

⊕ *The female sage grouse is less striking than the male, with more uniform gray-brown plumage and a black belly patch. She also has a shorter tail.*

old, 95 percent of their diet is vegetable matter. Insect food (which forms a tiny percentage of the adult diet in summer, too) mostly consists of ants, small beetles, weevils, and grasshoppers.

Food is simply plucked from the growing plants as the grouse wander around on foot, using a chickenlike or pheasantlike quick peck of the stout, curved bill. This action is also ideal for clipping off the tips of shoots and leaves.

Breeding

In the spring males move to their leks—special display areas in open spaces, often on flat ground with rather short grass. When the females arrive, the males begin to display with great vigor. The finest males are selected by the hens for mating, so that their young have the best chance of survival by inheriting the same characteristics as their fathers.

Males are promiscuous, which means they mate with as many females as they can. Sage grouse are mature at one year, but most birds do not breed until they are two years old. Around 10 percent of the cock (male) birds at the display areas succeed in mating with about 90 percent of the hens.

The nest is a small depression in the ground, lined with a little grass and, inevitably, some sage leaves. Each hen lays her eggs, rarely as many as 15, and begins incubation. Hens leave their eggs just two or three times a day for short spells to find food, usually early in the morning and then again in the evening. They feed greedily while they can. Female sage grouse expel their unusually large, spiral-shaped droppings some distance from the nest in order to avoid the attention of predators.

While incubating, the female remains absolutely still; this is essential to make the very best use of the almost perfect camouflage coloration of her plumage. Of course, many predators are able to detect the hen and her eggs by scent, and despite the camouflage, predators take their toll of many clutches of eggs. As few as 25 percent of the clutches may hatch in some areas, but up to 60 percent may hatch in others. The chicks that hatch and survive can fly within just one or two weeks—extraordinarily quickly—in order to get away from ground predators. This defense is little use if they are found by predatory birds, however.

Declining at the Edges

Sage grouse numbers are secure at present in their core range, but in places the population is declining and contracting. In 1952 there were some 150,000 adult birds. This figure had grown in the 1970s, when about 280,000 birds were shot each year by hunters. Hunting does not seem to affect the population overall, since the numbers of birds shot are roughly the same as the numbers that would die naturally through disease, starvation, and predation.

The future of the species is uncertain, however. In many areas sagebrush has been replaced by improved farmland, usually with irrigation or the use of extensive plowing or herbicide application to get rid of the ubiquitous plant. If this continues, the sage grouse will inevitably become more threatened.

⊖ A male sage grouse displays at a lek. The impressive courtship ritual also includes intricate dance movements—all designed to impress females.

Putting on a Show

The sage grouse display is a remarkable sight—one of the most fascinating in a family of expert performers. Now the value of the long tail and heavy white ruff on the males is obvious. In a special display posture the tail is held erect and widely fanned, and the spiky feather tips separated in a broad, spiny-looking dish. The body is held steeply upright and taut, while the head is pulled back, with the thin, pointed black feathers at the back of the neck raised in a spindly ruff. The white neck and ruff are inflated and spread, with the feathers ruffled like the pile of a shaggy carpet. On each side of the breast an oval patch of bare, olive-green skin is exposed, while the wings are pushed forward, half opened, and then pushed backward and forward across the stiffly raised feathers of the ruff. This produces a loud brushing sound, while the bare skin patches are expanded and deflated, forming small air sacs and creating a loud bubbling and popping sound. All this time the male struts around with short, stiff, tiptoe steps in a performance that is spectacular but highly stereotyped and inflexible.

Common Turkey

Meleagris gallopavo

Like the jungle fowl, the common turkey is the ancestor of one of the world's most widespread and abundant domestic animals. It is difficult to believe that this ubiquitous bird was nearly decimated in the wild.

A COMMON TURKEY IS ONE of the easiest birds in the world to recognize because it looks and sounds very much like the turkey of the farmyard. A true wild turkey is, however, a little smaller and slimmer than the domesticated one. Both sexes have an almost bare head and upper neck, although the female's is bluish, with more bristly feathers on the nape. The male has brighter red skin and a bigger, loose, fleshy wattle under the throat. Both sexes have small, red, upright wattles over the bill, big, dark eyes, and prominent ear openings.

The body plumage is essentially blackish with broad, intensely black bands across the feather tips. The rest of the feathers have a purple-brown, copper, and green iridescence. Eastern birds have broad, chestnut tips on the upper tail coverts; in birds of more western areas these feathers are tipped dull white. The wing feathers are browner, with fine, pale buff or whitish bars on the quills. The breast of the male bears a drooping, brushlike tufts. He also has backward-pointing spurs on his shanks.

Fragmented Range

Common turkeys are found in a fragmented range that neatly fills the mainland U.S., with small extensions north and south. Most of the higher Rocky Mountain area is unoccupied, and there are many gaps in the vast cultivated

Common name Common turkey (wild turkey)

Scientific name *Meleagris gallopavo*

Family	Meleagrididae
Order	Galliformes
Size	Length: male 43 in (110 cm), female 36 in (91 cm); weight: 9–22 lb (4–10 kg)
Key features	Massive; fairly long-tailed and long-legged; fairly upright stance; slim, bare neck; small, bare head; glossy, blackish plumage; red coloration on head (females bluish); red legs
Habits	Lives in groups on the ground by day; flies up to roost in trees at night
Nesting	Nest on ground; 10–13 eggs; incubation 28 days by female; young fledge after 14–21 days; 1 brood
Voice	Gobbling sound made by male
Diet	Acorns, seeds, fruits, leaves, shoots, and roots; young eat insects
Habitat	Bushy grassland and cultivated ground near forests; temperate regions south to subtropics
Distribution	Widespread in North America from Pacific to Atlantic coasts, north to Ontario and south to Florida and Mexico
Status	Recent increase after long decline, now numerous; often restocked and reintroduced into parts of range from which it had been lost

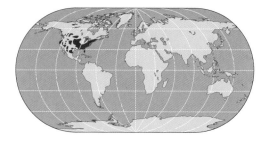

⬅ ⬆ *During display the wattle of the male common turkey (left) becomes expanded (above).*

plains and southwestern deserts; but turkeys can now be found almost everywhere where they traditionally lived before America was colonized by Europeans. They were temporarily lost from many places but have since been transported back and restocked in these areas.

Turkeys need two elements in order to thrive: trees and grass. Trees are vital since they provide most of the bird's food and are also essential for safe roosting at night. Turkeys must roost off the ground so that they do not become victims of mammalian predators. Grass gives cover for nesting and provides more food, but importantly, it is a source of insects, which young turkeys need in their first few weeks.

In North America the ideal turkey habitat is open forest with grassy clearings or glades with sufficient sunlight penetrating the loose canopy to allow a tall, grassy, and herbaceous ground layer to develop. Dense forest bisected with logging tracks and other openings—allowing grass to invade—also provides a habitat for common turkeys.

In summer the young turkeys forage in

⊕ *A turkey preens itself in the snow. In cold conditions turkeys prefer to roost in big, spreading conifers because their wide branches create "pitched roofs" under which the birds can spend nights out of the snow and cold winds.*

The male turkey, known as a tom, is usually found with several females, except in the breeding season, when females are solitary until their chicks hatch. Females (in the background here) have similar plumage, although it is less glossy, and they lack the breast tuft of the male bird.

open places for insect food; hay meadows and some crop fields are ideal for this, and a mixture of woodland and cropland is good turkey habitat, typically replacing the traditional forest with clearings that has mostly been lost. In cold winters forest habitat is more important to the turkey than open spaces; here there is more cover, less exposure to wind, rain, and snow, and usually more food.

Living Together

Turkeys are social birds. For most of the year they live in groups ranging from a few individuals to 20 or so. When nesting, the hen lives a solitary life for a few weeks, and the young family may also remain separate from other turkeys until the early fall. Many families mix together, however, so there are parties of three or four mature females and their broods.

In winter turkeys may be forced to gather wherever food is available. There may be hundreds of birds at exceptionally good feeding sites, but a strong social structure develops, and a good deal of pecking and jousting ensures that a hierarchy is maintained.

By late winter young males will leave the family groups and go off together. They may not become mature early enough to breed in their first year and, in any case, will no doubt be lower in the social hierarchy than older males, so they wait a year before displaying and seeking hens.

Turkeys are true omnivores, eating what they can find. Studies of turkeys have revealed 100 different types of food being taken at one time in a single area. In summer they eat a great deal of foliage—herbaceous leaves and grasses found in the forest glades or along the edges of fields and clearings. Flowers, buds, fruit, and seeds are also taken from plants.

Some seeds and larger items such as acorns and fleshy roots are picked up from the ground or dug from the soil. Turkeys have powerful feet that can dig and scratch through thick leaf litter in a forest with ease. The presence of turkeys in a wood can often be detected by the scratched, scraped, and churned-up ground.

In some places spilled cereal grain in harvested fields is important food for turkeys. And when winter snow cover is too deep even for turkeys to dig through, they feed on buds in the tree canopy. Young turkeys, however, need a high-protein, energy-packed diet of insect food. For six weeks they eat only insects. Initially they survive on remnants of their egg yolk, but then eat 3,000 to 4,000 insects daily.

Calling from Cover

Early in the spring a familiar sound returns to American woods: the gobbling calls of male turkeys trying to attract hens. The vocal performance of the males is important, since the females may not be able to find the males in the dense forest cover without these sounds. Nevertheless, once the female is attracted within visual range, the male then puts on a show. He is determined to prove that he is the best male around, and that the female should choose him as the father of her young.

A displaying male droops his wings and raises his tail in a broad, beautifully banded fan. The pale or rufous tips on his tail feathers and upper tail coverts create a dramatic impression. He holds his head up and slightly back to

Inefficient Flyer

A male common turkey weighs between 9 and 22 pounds (4–10 kg). Turkeys have large, broad wings, but they are quite heavy birds, and their body-weight-to-wing-area ratio is also exceptionally high. This means that turkeys are not efficient flyers, and they use a lot of energy when flying. When disturbed, turkeys usually run away rather than fly. They escape uphill if they can, so that, if necessary, they can take off downhill and glide a considerable distance. They fly up with a sudden, powerful burst, as fast as 60 miles per hour (100 km/h), but must quickly settle into the long, downhill glide that takes them away with the least expenditure of energy. Flight from a treetop perch, going downhill, may last for 0.6 mile (1 km) or more, but much of this is on stiff, motionless wings.

enhance the colors of the blue and red skin against the black feathers of his back. If the female is ready to mate, the display is usually quite short. Females will be ready to nest early in the year if they have wintered well; but if a hen has suffered a bad winter and lost a lot of weight, she may not nest at all that year.

The hen makes a nest in a simple hollow on the ground, hidden under long grasses and herbs. She is isolated now, living away from the social group. She lays her eggs at the rate of

↑ A male common turkey fluffs up his feathers to help retain heat and prepares to ride out a snowstorm.

Vital Brooding

A turkey hen looks after the chicks with no help from the male. The young chicks are at risk from predators and disease, but many also die from exposure if the weather is harsh. The hen often broods her chicks at night under her half-spread wings. For the first two weeks they are brooded on the ground, but later they scramble up into a tree, and the hen remains perched on a branch with her brood safely under her wings. The young soon become too large for this, however, and simply gather together on each side of the mother bird. Young chicks that remain protected beneath the hen's wings may survive cold and heavy rainfall, while those that are not may die. When the chicks are about eight weeks old, they will spread out into several trees at night, able to maintain their own temperature.

one every 25 hours. When the sixth egg is laid, she starts incubation. This is a dangerous time, with foxes, skunks, and raccoons on the prowl. Fewer than half the nests are successful, but older birds fare better than young ones, suggesting that experience helps. Many female turkeys are caught on the nest, too, with eagles, coyotes, and bobcats frequently feasting on fresh turkey meat.

The chicks are able to run around soon after hatching. Although the mother stays with them, many chicks are caught by predators or die by accident or through hypothermia. Only about half the chicks survive the first three weeks of life.

Back from the Brink

Before Europeans reached America, wild turkey populations probably numbered tens of millions. Their forest-grassland habitat was abundant and widespread, and food plentiful. However, turkeys were good to eat and easy to shoot. Hundreds of thousands were killed, and by the late 1600s laws were passed in places in an effort to protect stocks. However, such laws were ignored or impossible to enforce. Turkeys rapidly disappeared from vast areas.

In addition to decimating turkey numbers, humans began to change the land, too. Turkey habitat was lost. Forest and open woodland on low ground was systematically felled—in the same way that the great prairie grasslands were extensively plowed.

This continued for centuries. By the 1940s there were only some 300,000 wild turkeys left. Only in the 1950s were hunting laws enforced and taxes from shooting used to help protect quarry species. Now turkeys were reared in captivity and released on a huge scale. Yet nearly all of these efforts failed to reestablish turkeys in the wild. What had gone wrong?

It seems that turkeys in the wild must be tough and competitive to survive. Yet it was difficult to breed tough and aggressive turkeys in captivity. Instead, captive birds were being released as tame, docile creatures, unable to cope with life in the wild. Young birds had no

The Turkey Story

The curious thing about the turkey for European settlers was that they knew it as a domestic bird before they encountered it in the wild. They had turkeys in their farmyards back home, but presumably had little idea where they originated from. It was the Spanish who first brought turkeys back to Europe from their earliest explorations in Mexico. Turkeys were taken to Spain in 1491 and were common there by 1530. They reached Britain by 1541. In Britain, although other large birds were already called turkeys, the name was applied to the new domestic bird that supplied so much rich meat.

The name was then, naturally, given to the wild bird when it was eventually found living in eastern North America. It was also taken to America as part of the live food supply on ships in 1607. By then, of course, it has been important to native Americans for thousands of years. Along with deer, in the east the turkey was a prime source of food, while feathers were used in a host of ways: spurs made good arrowheads, and bones were useful for making a variety of tools. There is evidence of domestication of the turkey in New Mexico and Arizona as early as A.D. 500–700.

There is debate, however, about whether this was the first area of domestication and that turkeys were traded into Mexico and Central America, or whether the route was the reverse. It is quite likely that such a widespread and extremely useful bird was domesticated in several different places at different times. Domestic turkeys are now often white, and most commercially farmed birds are also white, with just a few farmyard turkey cocks remaining more or less like their wild ancestors. Millions of turkeys are raised every year in countries such as the U.S. and Britain, and in these countries the bird is second in popularity only to the domestic chicken.

chance to learn about survival from their elders, and most soon perished after release.

In the 1960s more effort was made to improve and protect the turkey's traditional forest habitats. At the same time, large areas of marginal farmland were allowed to develop as woodland—ideal for turkeys. Mixed dairy and arable farms made ideal habitats, too, provided the turkeys had some trees nearby.

Now wild turkeys, skilled in the ways of surviving in the natural world, were caught and used to restock the "new" habitats. Thousands of birds were translocated every year by the 1970s. Hunting was banned, and the turkeys were intensively studied so that biologists could learn more about their requirements.

By 1990 turkey numbers were back in excess of the three million mark—a stunning result that turned a mammoth and long-term decline into a great recovery. Although this is good news for the wild turkey, it is sad that many other species, including the closely related ocellated turkey (*Agriocharis ocellata*) of Central America, have been left to suffer and decline through hunting, illegal trade, and habitat loss.

Common name Common moorhen

Scientific name *Gallinula chloropus*

Family   Rallidae

Order   Gruiformes

Size Length: 12–15 in (30–38 cm); wingspan: 19.5–21.5 in (50–55 cm); weight: 7–17 oz (0.2–0.5 kg)

Key features Generally dark plumage except for white streaking on the flanks and white tail panels; beak red, tipped with yellow; legs olive-yellow with long, unwebbed toes

Habits   Territorial and rarely forms flocks; common but shy—quickly slips away from disturbance

Nesting   Nest built in newly emerging vegetation or on solid ground within a wetland in spring and summer; occasionally they make floating nests and will also nest low in bushes, but never more than a few feet from water; usually 6–8 eggs; incubation 21–22 days; young fledge after 50 days; 2 broods, occasionally 3 or 4

Voice   A distinctive "kruuuk"

Diet   A wide range of animal and plant matter, including small invertebrates and carrion

Habitat   Wide range of mainly freshwater habitats

Distribution With 12 separate subspecies stretching across all but one of the world's continents, the common moorhen is the most widely distributed gallinule; the only places it is not found are Australia and New Zealand, where it is replaced by dusky moorhen (*G. tenebrosa*)

Status   Not globally threatened overall, but two island subspecies are listed as Endangered

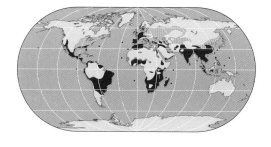

Common Moorhen

Gallinula chloropus

The common moorhen is the most widespread member of the family Rallidae. This attractive bird has adapted to a wide range of habitats and is equally at home in urban settings as it is in wilder places.

THE NOMINATE RACE OF THE common moorhen (*Gallinula chloropus chloropus*) occurs across an extensive range, from western Europe and North Africa through the Middle East to Central and Southeast Asia. In North America a subspecies (*G. c. cachinnans*) breeds from southeastern Canada down to the southern U.S. Other moorhen subspecies also breed in South America and southern Africa, and there are a number of very restricted island races in places such as Hawaii, the Seychelles, and the Mariana Islands.

Versatility Is the Key

With such a wide range, the moorhen is clearly a successful bird that has the ability to exploit a variety of largely freshwater wetland habitats. Along with its need for water, the bird's only other requirement is plant cover in which it can feed and take refuge from potential predators. Although it can be found on larger bodies of water, the moorhen prefers smaller ones. It will often share its habitat with a relative in the family Rallidae, the common coot (*Fulica atra*). In contrast to the coot, however, the moorhen is more reclusive, less frequently swimming out into open water. The moorhen is usually quite easy to spot, however, and is less secretive than its other relatives, the rails and crakes.

Alongside its natural habitats, the moorhen has also made itself at home in manmade habitats like canals and park lakes. Here its loud call can be regularly heard above the hustle and bustle of human activity. While never far from water, the moorhen will nevertheless wander into surrounding habitats and can sometimes be

⊕ Unusually for a bird that spends much of its time swimming in the water, the moorhen's feet are not webbed. Their shape helps the bird walk across surface vegetation, however.

found in fields and even in gardens where they are adjacent to a local pond.

The common moorhen is active largely by day and roosts during the hours of darkness. It is an adept swimmer, nodding its head back and forward as it moves through the water. It is also quite confident on the land; its long, slender toes spread the bird's weight and enable it to walk across surface vegetation as well as clamber about in low trees and bushes.

Characteristically, the common moorhen is frequently observed flicking its tail to reveal white feathering that contrasts starkly with its otherwise dark plumage. It is thought that this is done to startle and deter predators, giving the bird time in which to make an escape.

The moorhen is very much an omnivore, gleaning a wide range of plant and animal matter from both water and surrounding vegetation. The proportions of animal and plant matter in the diet vary considerably, although from studies it appears that a greater volume of plant matter is usually consumed.

In water the common moorhen feeds by dipping its head or alternatively by sifting at the surface. Occasionally it will upend in a mallardlike fashion. The moorhen dives only rarely—unlike its relative the coot, which can regularly be observed diving. When walking on aquatic vegetation or on land, the moorhen picks at whatever food is available. It has also been recorded taking food from other birds, such as great crested grebes (*Podiceps cristatus*).

⬇ *Fighting for territory usually takes place between members of the same sex. These moorhens are attempting to inflict damage on each other with their sharp claws.*

Rare Relatives

The common moorhen is a successful and widely distributed species. In all, it shares its genus with seven other *Gallinula* species. Of them two are extremely rare. First, there is the Tristan moorhen (*Gallinula nesiotis*). This bird is like the common moorhen but a little smaller. It lacks white markings on the flank and is largely flightless. It is only found on Gough Island and Tristan da Cunha in the south Atlantic. Its population is currently stable at between 2,000 and 3,000 pairs (with the majority on Gough Island). However, as with most flightless island species, it is vulnerable to predation by introduced mammals such as rats, cats, and dogs. Indeed, on Tristan da Cunha mammalian pressure caused the bird's disappearance in 1900, although it was successfully reintroduced in 1956.

On San Christobal in the Solomon Islands there is the second species, the San Christobal moorhen (*Gallinula silvestris*). Again superficially like the common moorhen, it lacks white marks on the flank and tail and has red, rather than olive-yellow, legs. Only one specimen of this bird exists, collected in 1929. Since then it has only been seen twice. With the widespread introduction of mammals the worst is feared. It is now listed as Critically Endangered.

On the whole, moorhens are territorial, defending nesting and feeding areas both in and out of the breeding season. In exceptional cases they may feed in flocks of up to 30 birds, for example, in periods of harsh winter weather when food is scarce.

Unusual Breeding Behavior

Moorhens are normally monogamous (in other words, each bird has only one partner). However, there are exceptions; occasionally females may have two male partners (this is called polyandry). Furthermore, mothers and daughters may nest cooperatively—sharing the same male—and a daughter may even lay her eggs in the mother's nest. It is not only daughters that may lay in the mother's nest, however; other females regularly lay eggs in the nests of unrelated neighbors as well as having their own clutches.

If the parasitic eggs are sneaked into a nest when the host has only laid a couple of eggs, all the eggs will be destroyed. However, if the host has laid four or more eggs, the parasitic

In the buildup to nesting male and female moorhens engage in ritualized displays including allopreening, shown here. One bird of either sex adopts a submissive posture, while the other gently preens the back of his or her neck.

eggs will be accepted. It is thought that at this stage the cost of destroying all the eggs (the host's and the parasite's) is too high.

In the Northern Hemisphere the moorhen's breeding season begins in March and is signaled by the pairing of males and females and the establishment of fiercely defended territories. Fights over territory can be quite violent, with the birds squaring up to each other, breast to breast, and using their feet to scratch the opponent. Interestingly, unlike the majority of birds, in the runup to nesting it is females that compete for males. The female chooses her mate on the basis of size; fat birds are preferred to thin ones due to their ability to incubate larger clutches more effectively.

The moorhen nest is made in either newly emerging vegetation or on a solid piece of ground within a wetland. Occasionally they make floating nests and will also nest low in bushes, but never more than a few feet from water. The nest itself is made from twigs and the stems of available water plants within which the birds fashion a deep cup lined with grass and other softer materials.

A discarded chair close to the water's edge makes an ideal platform for a moorhen's nest.

Between laying and the first clutch of eggs it is normal for the birds to make at least two nests. Once one is chosen, the female lays on average between six and eight eggs. Sometimes nests are found with up to 13 eggs, but as mentioned previously, this is most likely due to two females laying in the same nest.

Incubation is shared; after the young hatch, the parents initially share the task of caring for them. If the chicks are from a second brood, they will frequently be looked after by a sibling from the first brood. By 25 days they can feed themselves.

Over most of their range moorhens are largely sedentary. Only at the northern limits of their distribution are they migratory, with birds from northern Europe, Russia, and the U.S. moving from their breeding grounds in the face of freezing winter conditions.

Endangered Subspecies

With their success in a wide range of wetland habitats, the moorhen as a whole is not a threatened species. Harsh winters can temporarily reduce numbers, but not at the expense of threatening the species. However, a couple of the island subspecies are endangered. On Hawaii the race *sandvicensis* is now restricted to only a few hundred individuals on a couple of islands while once it occurred on all five. Likewise, the race *guami* used to occur across the Mariana Islands but is now limited to Tinian, Saipan, and Guam. In both cases habitat loss has caused the decline, but efforts are being made to stop this and recreate suitable wetlands.

Whooping Crane

Grus americana

The rare whooping crane almost became extinct in the 1940s. However, strenuous efforts by conservationists have reversed the bird's fortunes; and while they are still very rare, the future looks brighter for this bird.

Common name Whooping crane

Scientific name *Grus americana*

Family	Gruidae
Order	Gruiformes

Size
Length: 51–63 in (130–160 cm); wingspan: 79–91 in (200–230 cm); weight: 10–18.7 lb (4.5–8.5 kg)

Key features Large, mainly white crane; dark legs, black primary feathers; gray beak and red crown

Habits Territorial during the breeding season; social outside the breeding season

Nesting Nest a mound of vegetation up to 59 in (150 cm) diameter and 18 in (46 cm) above the surface of the water; 2 eggs; incubation 28–31 days; young fledge after 90 days: 1 brood

Voice Loud trumpeting calls

Diet Small aquatic invertebrates, frogs, snakes, and fish; also plant matter such as grain

Habitat Breeds on muskeg and marshy pools; found on prairies during migration; winters on coastal marshes

Distribution Only wild population breeds in Wood Buffalo National Park, Canada, and winters at Aransas on the Texas coast

Status Endangered; 161 adults and 15 chicks at Aransas National Wildlife Refuge in 2001

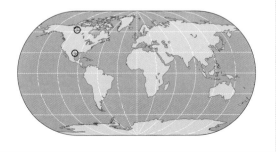

THE WHOOPING CRANE, REACHING 63 INCHES (160 cm) in length, is North America's tallest flying bird. Of the 15 species of crane, the whooping crane is also one of the rarest. It is likely that it has never been particularly common. Prior to European settlement in the nineteenth century various estimates put the population between 500 and 1,400. At this time the bird's breeding range extended across central North America from Alberta through Saskatchewan in Canada to North Dakota, Iowa, and Illinois. Outside the breeding season this population moved south to winter in the southern states and northern Mexico, particularly the coast of Texas and Louisiana. In the latter state there also existed a nonmigratory breeding population.

ⓘ *Whooping cranes are monogamous, usually pairing for life. Soon after arrival at the breeding grounds, territories are established that range in size from roughly 0.4 square mile (1 sq km) to 18,150 square miles (47,000 sq km). Territory size is determined by food availability and the topography of the land.*

Small Populations

During the nineteenth century the traditionally small population began to decline rapidly. The reasons will be described later, but today the only truly wild, self-sustaining population breeds in Wood Buffalo National Park in the Northwest Territories, Canada, and winters in and around the Aransas National Wildlife Refuge in Texas. Alongside this population there are two other groups, both of birds in recovery programs. One is in Idaho, and the other, consisting of nonmigratory birds, is in central Florida.

In the past, during the breeding season migratory whooping cranes nested in the wetlands and aspen parklands of the northern plains and prairies. Today the wild population in Wood Buffalo is found in poorly drained marshland. Of the two recovery program populations, the one at Grays Lake in Idaho is on high marshes, and the one in Florida at Kissimmee prairie is in marshes edging lakes, grassland, and savanna.

Outside the breeding season the Wood Buffalo population migrates south through a large variety of habitats, including farmland and reservoirs, before wintering at Aransas. Here they stay in the brackish bays and marshes that fringe the Gulf of Mexico.

⊕ When foraging, whooping cranes probe the mud with their long bills or pick items from the surface. In summer they eat animals. On migration they also eat waste grain and plant tubers. In winter they eat crabs, clams, shrimp, and plants.

↑ A whooping crane among sandhill cranes (Grus canadensis) at a traditional migration stopover in Colorado. In an attempt to reverse the decline of whooping cranes conservationists placed surplus whooping crane eggs with sandhill cranes nesting in southeast Idaho. The birds were raised successfully, but they failed to pair with other whooping cranes, and so it was decided to abandon the project.

The breeding season starts when the birds return from their wintering grounds in spring. Like all cranes, whooping cranes are fond of dancing! While they will perform throughout the year, the intensity of dancing increases around pair formation and brings the birds together. The dances consist of a variety of leaps and bows, runs, and short flights. Young unpaired birds do the most dancing. Older, more settled birds do much less—the movements only serving to maintain bonds.

Once established, the paired cranes select their nesting site. Here they stand and call in unison. As a species, cranes have remarkably loud voices that can be heard from quite a distance. During the breeding season unison calling is thought, as with dancing, to

Rescued from the Brink

The decline of the whooping crane coincided with the arrival of European settlers, who put pressure on the birds by draining wetlands to turn the land to agriculture. Once the decline had set in, the bird became "collectable," and egg theft put further pressure on a vulnerable population.

By the 1930s only two groups remained. The first consisted of nonmigratory birds at White Lake in Louisiana and the second of other birds wintering in Texas but whose breeding grounds at the time were unknown. They, of course, were later discovered to be the Wood Buffalo birds.

The Louisiana birds last nested in 1939, and a hurricane in 1940 dealt a further blow to this group, reducing their number from 13 to only 6. By 1950 there was only one remaining bird, and it was taken into captivity. The plight of the Wood Buffalo-Aransas, Texas, population was equally perilous, reaching an all-time low of just 15 birds in the winter of 1941–42.

Facing extinction, intensive efforts were initiated in the late 1930s to reverse the bird's fortunes. Through careful research ornithologists discovered the distribution and movements of the Wood Buffalo-Aransas population and established nature reserves to ensure its protection. Alongside this, an education program was started to make sure hunters and farmers realized the bird's importance and acted to safeguard it. The work paid off, and by the 1990s the population had increased to over 150 birds.

The wild Wood Buffalo cranes migrate along a relatively narrow corridor that is only 62 to 186 miles (100–300 km) wide, crossing nine separate provinces and states in Canada and the U.S.

strengthen pair-bonds. The volume of the call is enhanced by a fusing of bony rings in the bird's trachea (throat) with its sternum. These act as a resonator when air passes over them.

The male and female build the nest together. The nest platform is constructed in water from bulrushes and other plant material. When the young cranes first hatch, they have brown plumage to aid camouflage. With only a limited amount of time in the breeding season due to their northerly location, development is rapid. Initially the chicks are tended by their parents, who give them food directly or deposit it in front of them at the nest. As with other waterbirds, the young soon begin to follow their parents to nearby feeding areas.

Fuel for the Journey

With the onset of cooler fall weather the birds gather in premigration flocks, feeding to build up fat reserves to maintain them on their journey south. The movements of whooping cranes have been fully studied. Along their migration route there are a number of crucial stopover points where birds refuel before continuing their journey. Flights of up to 500 miles (800 km) in one day have been recorded, although about 185 miles (300 km) is more common. Within a relatively short time they arrive at Aransas, where they spend the winter before flying north the following spring.

Cranes in Language

In Greek mythology it is said that cranes inspired the Greek alphabet. The hero Palamedes is said to have received his inspiration from watching the V-shaped formations of birds as they flew over his land. Looking at the traditional Greek alphabet, with its many V-shapes, it is easy to see the link. In other stories it is Mercury, the messenger of the gods, who is credited as the observer.

The Romans called cranes *grues*, a word now used in the scientific names of the cranes. (The word *grues* was thought to sound like the birds' calls.) From *grues* the English language has derived two words. First, congruence, which comes from the Latin *congruere*—to agree—and is linked to the cranes' highly synchronized ritual dances and generally social behavior. Second, the word pedigree is derived from the French *pied de grue*, which literally means "foot of the crane." Here the shape of the cranes' feet, with three long branching toes, is reminiscent of branching family trees.

Common name American golden plover

Scientific name *Pluvialis dominica*

Family	Charadriidae
Order	Charadriiformes

Size Length: 9–11 in (23–28 cm); wingspan: 26–28 in (66–71 cm); weight: 4.3–6.9 oz (122–196 g)

Key features Long-winged, with gold-and-black spangled upper parts; black face, breast, and flanks, all edged white; blackish bill and legs; sexes similar, but underparts of breeding male more solid black, female more white; winter juvenile similar

Habits Fast-flying and gregarious, feeding in large flocks while on migration; often tame and approachable

Nesting Shallow scrape in dry moss or lichen; usually 4 eggs; incubation 26–27 days; young fledge after 22–24 days; 1 brood

Voice Variety of whistling calls, including plaintive "klee" and yodeling "tu-ee"; two kinds of song: a clicking "tulick" and a trilling "witt-wee-wyu-witt-witt"

Diet Mainly insects; some berries in breeding season; also worms and mollusks; crustaceans outside breeding season

Habitat Breeds on arctic tundra, on dry, open areas of moss and lichens; winters mainly inland on short grasslands; also plowed land, wetlands, and intertidal flats

Distribution North America from Alaska east to Baffin Island; small numbers from Gulf of Mexico to Venezuela, but mainly from southern Brazil to eastern Argentina

Status Not globally threatened, but recent loss of wintering habitat may be a problem

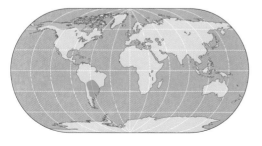

American Golden Plover

Pluvialis dominica

The least studied of all the tundra plovers, the American golden plover was ruthlessly persecuted by hunters in the nineteenth century.

THE AMERICAN GOLDEN PLOVER IS ONE of four closely related, similar-looking tundra plovers; the other three are the Pacific golden plover (*Pluvialis fulva),* Eurasian golden plover (*P. apricaria*), and black-bellied plover (*P. squatarola*). The American and Pacific golden plovers are so similar that until 1993 they were regarded as one species. However, there is no evidence of interbreeding where they overlap in Alaska, so they are now considered separate species.

Of the four the American golden plover is the grayest in nonbreeding and juvenile plumages, but the blackest in its breeding plumage. In the breeding season the adult's upper parts are blackish, spangled with gold. Jet-black plumage spreads from the side of the face down across the center of the breast and fills out the flanks. This black swath is thrown into stark relief by an outline of white that starts across the forehead and extends above and behind the eye and down the sides of the neck to form a brilliant white blaze on either side of the black upper breast. The underwings are a dusky gray.

Long Journey

The American golden plover is a long-winged, powerful flyer, well equipped for its lengthy two-way migration between South America and the Arctic—a return journey totaling up to 16,000 miles (25,750 km). Northward migration begins in late February on a route that strikes through the heart of South America, up through Central America or across the Gulf of Mexico, then into the U.S. By late March passage flocks are common in the Great Plains and the Mississippi Valley, foraging in open fields and grasslands to fuel their onward flight.

⊕ Nonbreeding adult American golden plovers, like the one here, have much less colorful plumage without the striking gold-and-black markings exhibited by breeding birds.

By mid-May they have pushed north into the Canadian prairies, and two weeks later they reach their arctic tundra breeding grounds. They choose to nest in habitat generally similar to that of the Pacific golden plover; but where they overlap, the American golden plover favors the higher, more barren tundra slopes. Even so, observations of the two species chasing each other aggressively at the start of the breeding season suggests some competition for space.

Males First

The males migrate shortly before the females and immediately take up their stations on the breeding grounds. With only a fleeting, three-month arctic summer available for breeding they waste no time and rapidly reoccupy and defend territories, renew pairings, or find new partners as necessary.

Studies show that American golden plovers live to at least eight years old, and like the Pacific golden plover, they may well live twice as long. Since at least some birds probably breed in their first year, and the majority in their second year, the bulk of the population returning to the nesting grounds has previous experience of breeding. Male American golden plovers are especially faithful to their previous breeding territory, returning to claim the same patch year after year. They are also faithfully monogamous to their mates, often for several years if both partners survive. Resorting to the same territory provides a convenient spring rendezvous for partners that lead separate lives outside the breeding season.

⊕ Despite having such bold, strikingly patterned breeding plumage, the nesting birds blend in well against the vegetation of the tundra.

On the spartan tundra of northern Alaska average breeding density is fewer than five pairs per square mile (two pairs per sq km). However, it increases to 16 pairs per square mile (six pairs per sq km) further south on coastal tundra in Churchill, Manitoba, with its relatively luxuriant subarctic mix of sedge bogs, dwarf shrub, lichen-covered gravel ridges, and even a scattering of low conifers.

Eskimo Lore

During 1924–26 Eva Richards, a school teacher at Wainright on the north coast of Alaska, made a list of bird names used by the Inupiat peoples. Their name for the American golden plover was "too-lik," derived from the bird's clicking alarm call. The Caribou Inuit likewise called the bird "tull'iuk tullik," a name observed in 1967 by the ornithologist E.O. Hohn from the west coast of Canada's Hudson Bay. These remarkably similar names, from opposite extremes of the species' breeding range, demonstrate the intimate observation of Arctic birds that was so vital to Inuit survival.

Song Flights

Once the nesting grounds are occupied, the first song flights begin. The displaying male ascends from his territory with increasingly rapid, shallow wingbeats ("fluttering flight") in which all the propulsion is generated by his wingtips alone. Between 50 and 330 feet (15–100 m) the male levels out to enter the main display phase: the "butterfly flight." Singing as he goes, he then cruises back and forth with deep, slow, exaggerated wingbeats, making his body bob up and down. From time to time he breaks into fluttering flight with his wingtips barely flickering above the horizontal.

This territorial signal is enhanced by two kinds of song. Compared with the measured, plaintive "wailing song" of the other tundra plovers, the American golden plover's song during the butterfly flight is a volley of staccato, clicking "tulick" or "p'tulick" sounds similar to its alarm call. When the bird switches to fluttering flight, however, the clicking song changes into a warbling trill.

During the song flight the male describes irregular circles or figure eights over his territory, weaving a cat's cradle of lines that define his aerial domain. The ritualized butterfly and fluttering flights draw maximum attention to the performer, serving both as a keep-away signal to rival males and, if he is unpaired, a cue to potential mates. At the end of his song flight the male descends steeply and rapidly, sometimes skimming low over the ground before landing. When he alights, he may carry

⊕ Resplendent in its breeding plumage, an American golden plover performs a distraction display to divert an intruder's attention from its nest among the short grass and moss of the northern tundra. Pitching forward on the ground, it fans its tail and spreads one or both wings as if broken.

on trilling with wings held aloft above his back, signaling mastery of both his ground space and his air space.

The defensive nature of song flight becomes clear when a neighboring male is displaying nearby. As if playing "chicken," the rivals often fly parallel only a few feet apart along a contested boundary, singing simultaneously. If a male intrudes directly on his neighbor's air space, the owner will likely chase him out before returning in triumphant song flight to proclaim his territorial rights.

Torpedo Runs

The ground courtship of the American golden plover is the least known of any tundra plover. In a display described as the "torpedo run" potential pairs chase each other in a characteristic hunched posture, with their body plumage ruffled. The male initiates most of the chasing, but the female reciprocates in tit-for-tat chasing, the pair sometimes running side by side. The male may also make torpedo runs to chase off rival males, effectively guarding his mate to stop her from mating with intruders.

Berries to the Rescue

American golden plovers often arrive in May to find their nesting grounds blanketed in snow and devoid of insect prey. However, they find a lifesaving substitute in tundra berries. They carpet the hummocks and ridges, which are often the first features to be exposed by the warming sun. When they were fully ripe in the previous fall, the berries were fast frozen, so they are perfectly preserved and nutritious when they thaw out in spring. After a few days' exposure they shrivel and dry up, but the plovers need only a short respite until the insect world begins to stir again. Later in the summer the plovers turn to the fresh crop of fat-rich berries to build up their energy reserves for the southward migration.

⊕ *The short, straight bill of the American golden plover is typical of the family: an adaptable, all-purpose tool for probing and picking up prey.*

Chasing is typically short-lived—lasting for only the first two days and soon giving way to more intimate, domestic behavior as the male reconnoiters potential nest sites. The male takes the initiative in scratching with his feet at likely sites, while the female standing nearby watches his every move: The belly-down, tail-up posture of the scraping male is part of the overall ritual.

Drier areas are chosen for the scrape as a safeguard against flooding, while the short vegetation allows an incubating bird to spot ground predators and raptors such as the hen harrier (*Circus cyaneus*) from a long way off and slip discreetly away from the nest. Once the eggs are laid and incubation gets under way, the male shares the sitting spells almost equally with his mate. The incubation shifts last a marathon 12 hours: The male incubates by day, his mate at night, with changeovers in the early morning and evening.

The incubating male maintains his hostility to neighbors, challenging them by walking parallel as if escorting them off the premises or standing boldly upright with chest puffed out and tail lowered. If such intimidation fails, a vigorous fight can ensue, involving pecking, wing cuffing, and jumping at the opponent.

Protection from Predators

When the eggs hatch, the family quickly moves to moister areas where the young can forage on the summer flush of emerging insect life. In so doing, they often have to encroach on the territories of incubating males, which can provoke violent confrontations. However, the real threat is not from other plovers but from predators. If they see danger in the distance, the adult and young sit tight and rely on their camouflage; but if the predator ventures closer, a parent will fly up and circle it, spitting out alarm calls. In Alaska American golden plovers launch direct attacks on skuas and large gulls. If the threat to nest or eggs is close and extreme, especially from a ground predator, the parent in charge will try to divert its attention by shamming injury.

The female tends to quit the nesting grounds before her brood fledges, leaving her mate in charge. Soon after the young fledge, the flocking of parents on the higher tundra signals that migration south is imminent. Most adults leave in early August, with the females tending to go first, a week or two before the bulk of the juveniles.

Although in spring the population takes the overland route north through South and then North America, most fall migrants appear to head initially southeast to the northern prairies of Canada and then to the Atlantic coast of the northeast U.S. Weather permitting, they then make a nonstop sea crossing, by way of the Lesser Antilles, to South America. The juveniles appear to hug the North American continent more than the adults, as if choosing the safer inland option. A minority of American golden plovers overwinter in the Gulf of Mexico and the Caribbean, but most penetrate deep into South America to winter on the grassy plains of southern Brazil, Uruguay, and Argentina.

Back from the Brink

When the once spectacularly numerous passenger pigeon (*Ectopistes migratorius*) was hunted to extinction in North America in the second half of the nineteenth century, shooting

*⬆ **Newly hatched plover chicks are well camouflaged in the tundra, and both the parents and young rely on melting into the background when danger threatens.***

pressure switched to various shorebirds. They included the American golden plover, which was shot in staggering numbers during spring and fall migration in eastern and central North America. On one spring day alone in 1821, 200 hunters shot some 48,000 American golden plovers near New Orleans. The plover was in serious decline until it was removed from the quarry list at the start of the twentieth century, allowing it to make a recovery. The current population is estimated between 1 million and 2.5 million pairs.

The Protective Umbrella

In Manitoba, in Canada, American golden plovers have been found not to attack aerial predators, possibly because they can rely on their more aggressive whimbrel (*Numenius phaeopus*) neighbors to do the job for them. It is a recognized relationship among various shorebirds, with the whimbrel acting as a "protective umbrella" species for the more passive plovers.

American Black Oystercatcher

Haematopus bachmani

For such a large, noisy, bright-billed wader, the American black oystercatcher is sometimes hard to see. It moves unobtrusively among dark rocks, its voice lost in the sound of crashing waves.

Common name American black oystercatcher (black oystercatcher)

Scientific name *Haematopus bachmani*

Family	Haematopodidae
Order	Charadriiformes
Size	Length: 17–17.7 in (43–45 cm); wingspan: 32.3–34 in (82–86 cm); weight: 1.4–1.7 lb (0.6–0.8 kg)
Key features	Large shorebird; yellow eyes; deep red bill; pinkish legs; all-black plumage; sexes alike
Habits	Forages on rocky shores, looking down intently for food
Nesting	Shallow scrape lined with bits of shell or pebbles; 1–4 eggs; incubation 24–33 days; young fledge after 40 days; 1 brood
Voice	Loud "whee-up" alarm call and soft flight call
Diet	Mollusks, crustaceans, marine worms, and small fish
Habitat	Rocky shores; some winter in estuaries
Distribution	Western seaboard of North America from Aleutian Islands south to Baja California
Status	Not globally threatened

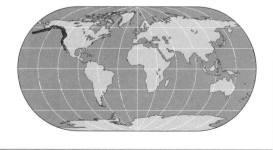

THIS BIRD IS OFTEN KNOWN simply as the black oystercatcher, since it is the only uniformly black species found in the Americas. The related American oystercatcher (*Haematopus palliatus*) has pied plumage. The large blackish-brown body of the American black oystercatcher is offset by a garish, blood-red bill and thick, pinkish legs. Like all of the New World oystercatchers, it has bright yellow eyes and an orange eye ring.

Touch Sensitive

Black oystercatchers throughout the world are birds of rocky coastlines, never venturing inland to breed; the American black is no exception. Its short, thick-toed feet are ideal for clambering over slippery rocks. It bends over frequently, using its long, stout bill to break mussels, barnacles, and limpets off the rock or pounce on crabs or small fish in rock pools. Tough prey is dealt with by being hammered or pried open. The bill is also very sensitive to touch, enabling the bird to feel its prey moving even when its bill is inserted several inches into the mud of an estuary. It has only a short time in which to feed, and it must rush down the shore at low tide to pick off what the sea has left behind.

Defending Their Territory

The birds occupy and defend their breeding territories against intruders in late spring. A study in California showed that breeding pairs defended up to 66 feet (20 m) from the nest. The birds may defend nearby feeding areas too:

⊕ The "nest" consists of a shallow depression just above the high tide mark, lined with pieces of broken shell or pebbles. Although the eggs are laid in the open, they are cryptically colored, often indistinguishable from surrounding pebbles.

The same study found one pair guarding mussel beds 197 feet (60 m) from the nest.

Courtship involves noisy "chase flights" and mutual bowing displays. After mating, both birds share parental duties. They make their nest just above the high-tide level, where it is highly vulnerable to being washed away by storms. It is also wide open to predation; ravens and gulls in particular are able to ignore the harassment of the parent birds to take the eggs. Luckily, the species has a relatively short incubation period—just 24 days in the southern parts of its breeding range.

Once the downy young hatch, they are able to leave the nest at once, even though they rely entirely on their parents for food. Unusually among oystercatchers, the young of the American blacks have a feeding hierarchy. When food is short, the young birds at the bottom of the "pecking order" are denied a share, while the dominant chick maximizes its own chances of survival.

After the breeding season most American black oystercatchers remain close to the rocky shores where they bred and form small, nonterritorial foraging flocks numbering up to 50 birds. Most avoid the fall and winter gales that make rocky shores hazardous by moving up the mouths of estuaries into sheltered areas. Only those birds breeding in northern Canada and Alaska migrate south to escape harsh winter conditions.

A Confusion of Oystercatchers

What happens when two similar species with very similar lifestyles overlap? In Baja California in western Mexico both American black oystercatchers and American oystercatchers bred until the late nineteenth century, apparently without any interbreeding, even though tide-line territories were limited and fiercely contested. Yet after human collectors had wiped them out by the beginning of the twentieth century, replacement birds of both species moved into the area and began to hybridize. Their confusion was possibly not helped by the fact that both species have very similar calls.

Greater Yellowlegs

Tringa melanoleuca

Common name	Greater yellowlegs
Scientific name	*Tringa melanoleuca*
Family	Scolopacidae
Order	Charadriiformes
Size	Length: 11–12 in (28–30 cm); wingspan: 28–29 in (71–74 cm); weight: 3.9–8.4 oz (111–238 g)
Key features	Elegant wader; rakish wings and long, orange-yellow legs; sexes similar, spotted white on dark brown above with white rump, underparts white flecked with brown; in winter gray-brown above, underparts paler; juvenile similar to winter adult
Habits	Rather solitary, but often located by its noisy calls; perches freely on tall treetops
Nesting	Shallow, sparsely lined cup hidden in moss; 4 eggs; incubation 23 days; young fledge after 25 days; 1 brood
Voice	Contact call a loud, ringing "tew," typically repeated three times; incessant, piercing "kip" or "keu" in alarm; song a series of melodious, yodeling "too-whee" sounds
Diet	Mainly insects, small fish; also crustaceans, snails, frogs, worms; sometimes berries
Habitat	Breeds in swampy wooded "muskeg" within northern coniferous forest; also in subarctic tundra and subalpine scrub; outside breeding season on coastal mudflats and beaches, estuaries, marshes, and near lakes and ponds
Distribution	Central Canada and southern Alaska; also southern and east coast U.S. to Central and South America; rarely Europe, Russia, Japan, and South Africa
Status	Not globally threatened

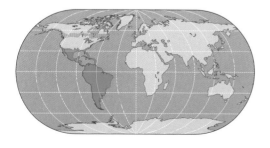

The greater yellowlegs is a regular fish-eater, catching most of its prey by dashing through the shallows on its colorful, rangy legs.

ALTHOUGH THE GREATER YELLOWLEGS IS WIDESPREAD in North America, its preference for nesting deep in mosquito-infested swamps has kept much of its breeding behavior a secret. Many who have braved the inhospitable wilderness have overlooked the bird sitting tight on its nest, its spangled back perfectly camouflaged in the filigree of shrub, moss, lichen, and sedge.

Varied Fishing Methods

Distinguished by its long, trademark legs, the greater yellowlegs also has a long, slightly upturned black bill. It takes most of its food from shallow water, but will wade up to its belly or even swim if the need arises. It gathers shrimp with a sideways sweeping motion of its bill, but its preferred prey is often small fish, which it flushes out by probing into submerged vegetation. As the fish makes a break for freedom, the bird pursues it with a sudden dash through the shallows, then stabs, seizes, and swallows it headfirst. It may toy for several minutes with large or awkward customers—such as sticklebacks—before eating them.

Apart from its highly effective rush-and-lunge approach to fish capture, the greater yellowlegs also has more subtle techniques. When surface ripples betray a fish nearby, the bird may run toward it with bill open, lower mandible submerged, trawling for its prey. Sometimes, a few birds will advance together like this, changing direction in unison, as if cooperating to herd a small shoal.

An Early Bird

The greater yellowlegs is one of the earliest shorebird migrants. Birds that have wintered in South America begin to head north from late

⊕ While one bird sits on the nest, the other stands guard on a nearby high perch watching for any intruders that could threaten the clutch. Alert and cautious, the greater yellowlegs is quick to take alarm and mount a noisy attack.

February. On reaching the breeding grounds, the male sets up a large territory, well separated from his neighbors. Flight displays are common in April and May, both to stake out territories and to attract mates. It is likely that both sexes perform the flight displays; the birds fly an undulating path, flapping at each dip and then gliding through the upward arc. A single display lasts up to 15 minutes and is accompanied throughout by song and other calls.

The greater yellowlegs is presumed to be monogamous, although confirmation is still needed. The detailed repertoire of its ground display also remains to be discovered, but the courting male has been seen running in circles around the female and adopting a heraldic posture with his wings held aloft and quivering.

The nest is often built in or near a mossy hummock, sometimes at the base of a small conifer. It is not known how much each sex contributes to the incubation, but both take part in caring for the young. Their first task once the eggs have hatched is to lead the young to the shelving edge of a pond where there is a guarantee of a good insect supply.

The sitting bird is reluctant to leave the nest when danger threatens and has even been known to allow a human to lift it bodily from the eggs. The sentinel parent, perched on a treetop, quickly detects any approaching intruder and mobs it noisily. If forced to quit the nest, the sitting bird runs clumsily through the vegetation, feigning a broken wing to distract attention.

Early Warning System

The greater yellowlegs used to be a popular game bird up to the early twentieth century. Its vigilance and relentless, scolding calls earned it nicknames like "yelper," "tattler," and "telltale," and hunters would often shoot the birds to stop them from spooking the whole neighborhood. Their frustration is often shared by modern birdwatchers—although with less drastic measures being taken!

Common name Ruddy turnstone

Scientific name *Arenaria interpres*

Family	Scolopacidae
Order	Charadriiformes
Size	Length: 8–9 in (20–23 cm); wingspan: 20–22 in (51–56 cm); weight: 3–6.8 oz (85–193 g)
Key features	Stocky build; short, orange legs; stout, black bill; piebald pattern on head and neck, white belly and tortoiseshell pattern on back; in winter mostly gray-brown above; sexes similar; juvenile like winter adult, but browner
Habits	Busy, quarrelsome forager, typically turning over stones on shore to find food
Nesting	Leaf-lined, shallow cup on ground; usually 4 eggs; incubation 22–24 days; young fledge after 19–21 days; 1 brood
Voice	Main call a rattling, chuckling "kititit"; in alarm a metallic "keu"; also a prolonged rolling chatter; a succession of "pri" sounds when making a scrape
Diet	Mainly insects, but some berries and seeds in breeding season; outside breeding season insects, crustaceans, mollusks, and carrion
Habitat	Breeds on wet tundra and dry rocky ridges in high Arctic; winters mainly on rocky shores, stony beaches, and mudflats
Distribution	Virtually circumpolar; outside breeding season coastal areas farther south throughout much of world
Status	Not globally threatened

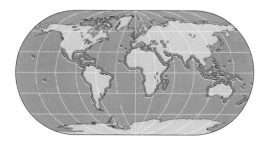

Ruddy Turnstone

Arenaria interpres

The ruddy turnstone is a remarkable success story, likely to turn up on almost any coastline of the world and happy to eat anything from coconuts to carrion.

THE RUDDY TURNSTONE MUST BE ONE of the best-known shorebirds in the world, because the species has made virtually the entire coastline of the world its winter quarters, spanning six continents. Yet in the breeding season the whole population vanishes as it contracts into a remote halo around the high Arctic.

On the shore an active ruddy turnstone invites many comparisons. Its squat build, offbeat harlequin plumage, waddling gait, and staccato alarm calls give it a clownlike personality, and with its bustling bravado it is almost the common starling (*Sturnus vulgaris*) of the shorebird world. The impression is backed up by its omnivorous feeding habits. It is easy to identify, yet not quite unique. It has a close relative, the black turnstone (*Arenaria melanocephala*), with a much more restricted breeding distribution in the northeastern Pacific.

Tortoiseshell Plumage

The ruddy turnstone's plumage almost defies a brief description. In the male, which is the more distinctly marked, the head and the sides of the neck are mostly white, but a black band zigzags from the forehead to below the eye and around the back of the neck before expanding into a broad shield on the chest. Much of the back is blackish-brown with chestnut edges, creating a tortoiseshell effect.

In flight the upper wing pattern is unique among shorebirds in having two white panels on each side, the main one snaking down the wing, while the lower back and upper tail are also white. The bill is short, deep at the base, and although mainly wedge-shaped, can appear slightly uptilted.

Well Named

The powerful neck muscles, strong legs, low center of gravity, and chisel bill of the ruddy turnstone combine to provide exceptional leverage for turning over stones and seaweed to find food: a habit that has earned the bird its name. It can flip over objects weighing up to 3.4 ounces (96 g), only a little less than its own body weight. Like a weightlifter, the bird bends its legs, inserts its bill—and sometimes its forehead—under the obstacle, and flicks it over with a swift, upward jerk. The bird also uses its immensely strong bill for prying limpets from rocks and opening mussels and even barnacles.

No food-finding challenge seems to defeat the ruddy turnstone. Several birds may join forces to overturn something particularly heavy, such as a dead fish. It may also use its bill like a bulldozer to roll up sodden mats of seaweed to expose beach fleas, one of the ruddy turnstone's favorite delicacies. In its quest for food the bird will sometimes disappear right under a raft of seaweed. It is the supreme opportunist among shorebirds and will eat any household scraps it finds on the beach, such as bread and potato peelings. Its boldness in frequenting harbors, marinas, and even rubbish dumps gives it plenty of opportunities.

⊕ The rich colors and patterns of a male in breeding plumage make the ruddy turnstone one of the most attractive shorebirds, although it can be surprisingly difficult to pick out against a background of shingle, empty shells, and other shore debris.

Contrasting black-and-white wing bars and flashes of white on their backs and rumps make ruddy turnstones quite distinctive as they take to the air over their foraging grounds.

Snowbound Breeding Grounds

When ruddy turnstones reach their breeding grounds in late May, the land is still snowbound, so the migratory flocks initially hug the coast, feeding there until the snow line begins to recede. Even when they move inland, insect food is scarce until mid-June, so their fallback diet at this time is seeds.

As soon as conditions improve, the flock structure breaks down, and the birds take up their territories. If they have bred before, they usually choose the same territory and partner. So many established pairs appear together on territory that they probably meet and renew their bond earlier in the flock. Dispensing with the prenuptial preliminaries as quickly as possible helps the birds make maximum use of the fleeting arctic summer.

The Alarm Raiser

The ruddy turnstone's scientific name highlights both its habitat and its noisy alarm call. The generic name *Arenaria* derives from the Latin *arena* or *arenarius,* relating to "sand" or "sandy," although the bird is more attached to rocky than sandy coasts. In Latin *interpres* means a "negotiator" or "messenger," a reference to the ruddy turnstone warning other birds of danger with its alarm call.

Much remains to be discovered about the details of courtship behavior of the ruddy turnstone in the flocking phase, but the male often holds his tail conspicuously up or down in ritual display. On her part the female often responds submissively, to either a suitor or the return of an established mate, by almost squatting on the ground with her wings relaxed. The males also chase females in the air and on the ground; when other males join in, aerial pursuits are feverish affairs.

Competition for the attention of females sparks off numerous confrontations between males in the prebreeding flock. Rival males square up to each other, crouching with their plumage ruffled (to make themselves look big and imposing), vibrating their lowered tails, rushing and bill jabbing at each other, drooping their wings, and occasionally raising them high above their backs. When several males get involved and attempt to intimidate each other with chattering alarm calls, these jousts can get quite hectic and noisy.

Nesting Groups

Inland, ruddy turnstones often nest in well-scattered solitary pairs, but on the coast, especially where food is abundant, they may form loose groups. Six to seven pairs have been found nesting along 330 feet (100 m) of a meadow bordering an island lake in Denmark.

The males advertise ownership of their newly established territories with the same ground display of aggressive behavior rehearsed earlier in the flock. They are especially active when there is an audience of one or more females to impress.

Male ruddy turnstones chase each other off in the air and patrol their boundaries with deep, slow wingbeats, finally alighting on hummocks or other vantage points with volleys of chattering alarm calls. Rivals standing their ground across a territorial border also indulge in bouts of head bobbing—an action that effectively pumps the shield of bold black-and-white markings on the neck and breast up and down in a conspicuous display.

The Enemy Within

Some ruddy turnstones nest habitually among colonies of gulls and terns. They benefit from the way the other birds provide a protective umbrella against predators, but they also have a more sinister motive; they turn predator themselves. The colony supplies them with a fast-food takeout of gull and tern eggs, which they puncture and devour when the breeding adults are off guard. As egg pirates, ruddy turnstones can seriously dent the breeding success of their hosts.

Using a special call, the male ruddy turnstone displays several potential sites to his mate when she is ready to lay. She finally chooses one, makes a shallow scrape, and lays her clutch. Once the females start incubating, neighboring turnstones soon learn to respect each other's boundaries, and skirmishing subsides. Yet in the few days between pairing and egg laying the male guards his mate assiduously to ensure that no stray male sneaks in to mate with her.

Both sexes help rear the young, but the female may quit the nesting grounds before the brood fledges, leaving them in the sole care of her mate. The parents are bold in defense of their young, and neighbors may join forces to mob an Arctic fox. On the ground they flaunt their striking plumage to make their injury-feigning displays even more distracting.

The adults finally migrate south in early August, the juveniles following a month later. Flocks of up to 10,000 gather on migration, which is one of the most far-flung of any shorebird, transporting the ruddy turnstone to nearly every corner of the world.

Beach Vultures

In February 1966 a birdwatcher was walking along a beach in Wales, Britain, when he saw a small flock of ruddy turnstones pecking flesh off what he first took to be a dead pig on the shoreline. However, it turned out to be a badly decomposed human corpse. This is one of the most gruesome of several records of ruddy turnstones feeding on animal carrion, including the carcasses of a sheep, a cat, and even a wolf in arctic Canada. They will also happily eat the maggots that teem in flyblown carcasses.

⊕ The heavy shell of a cockle poses no problem for a ruddy turnstone. Even this immature bird will be able to use its tough bill to lever apart the shells and get at the flesh within.

Common name Short-billed dowitcher

Scientific name *Limnodromus griseus*

Family	Scolopacidae
Order	Charadriiformes

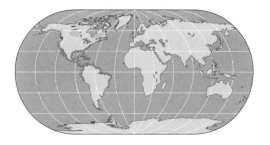

Size Length: 10–11 in (25–28 cm); wingspan: 18–20 in (46–51 cm); weight: 2.3–5.5 oz (65–156 g)

Key features Stocky shorebird; long bill; breeding plumage mostly black, amber, and buff above, pale cinnamon below; in winter gray above and on breast; female larger than male; juvenile dark brown with buff breast

Habits Foraging flocks tame; if disturbed, individuals often stand still with bill tip below surface

Nesting Cup in moss or clump of grass or sedge lined with grass or leaves; 4 eggs; incubation 21 days; young fledge after 16–17 days; 1 brood

Voice Flight call a rapid, mellow "tu-tu-tu"; complex, bubbly melodious song

Diet Mainly insects and their larvae on breeding grounds; also seeds; outside breeding season mollusks, marine worms, and crustaceans

Habitat Breeds in "muskeg," marshes, coastal tundra, wet meadows, and lake edges in northern forests; on tidal mudflats, salt marshes, and mangroves outside breeding season

Distribution Three races with separate breeding grounds in subarctic North America and differing wintering grounds from coastal U.S. to Central and South America

Status Not globally threatened

Short-Billed Dowitcher

Limnodromus griseus

Few North American birds can claim such a long run of anonymity as the short-billed dowitcher, only proved as a separate species in 1950 and still unfolding its breeding secrets to this day.

FEW BIRDS HAVE SUCH A MISLEADING name as the short-billed dowitcher. Its bill is twice as long as its head, so it cannot be described as "short." In fact, "short-billed" only serves to distinguish it from the closely related long-billed dowitcher (*Limnodromus scolopaceus*). But even that name is misleading, since only one long-billed dowitcher in six has an obviously longer bill than any short-billed dowitcher; deciding which species is which can be a real problem.

Controversy also surrounds the origin of the name "dowitcher," which came into

⬇ *Short-billed dowitchers in gray nonbreeding plumage congregate in flocks on tidal flats and marshes on the coasts of the U.S. and tropical America.*

fashion on the Atlantic coast of North America in the nineteenth century. Some claim that the word is of Iroquois origin, but a better clue may lie in Long Island's community of Dutch and German immigrants. "Dowitcher" is just a twist of the tongue away from "Deutscher" or "Duitsch," the name that the immigrants used to distinguish the North American bird from the similar-looking snipe (*Gallinago gallinago*) they had left behind in Europe.

Mystery Bird

Confusion over names is just the tip of the iceberg, for the short-billed dowitcher is one of North America's least understood shorebirds. Mystery long surrounded the location of its chief nesting grounds, now known to be the boggy, mosquito- and black fly-infested Canadian muskegs. In this remote and hostile environment the first short-billed dowitcher's nest and eggs were not discovered until 1906. Even then the significance of the find was overlooked because at the time the bird was

thought to be the same species as the long-billed dowitcher. The suggestion that there might be two species of North American dowitcher was made only in 1932. It was not confirmed until 1950, when Frank Pitelka not only proved there were two species but also showed that the short-billed population was split into three separate races. The revelation stimulated more research, in which a milestone discovery was the first nest and eggs of the eastern race of short-billed dowitcher in Quebec as recently as the late 1970s.

The three races of the short-billed dowitcher look similar in nonbreeding and juvenile plumages. They differ in breeding plumage, but basically all three have a mostly dark-brown crown contrasting with an off-white stripe over the eye. The sides of the head, neck, and breast are a pale cinnamon with rusty spots, gradually becoming whiter toward the belly and undertail. The back feathers are black centered and edged with buff or cinnamon, producing a rich tapestry of color. In flight the

⊕ The cinnamon breast and dark, buff-edged back feathers of the dowitcher's breeding plumage make a colorful contrast with the plain gray of winter.

birds have a conspicuous white oval patch on the back, while the tail is barred brown and white. The lancelike bill is blackish for most of its length, but the base of the bill and the legs are a dull yellow-green.

North to Alaska

In spring the Alaskan and British Columbian race follows the Pacific coast route north, while the other two races mainly hug the Atlantic

coast before heading inland to their ultimate Canadian destinations. Key staging posts on the way may attract large concentrations; in late April there can be tens of thousands in Grays Harbor on the Washington coast before the birds push northward.

At these critical stopovers the dowitchers replenish their reserves by foraging day and night on the mudflats and in the shallows. Each bird probes with a rapid vertical action in soft mud and water, wading belly deep and even swimming. The dowitcher is an opportunist feeder with a bill capable of tackling most invertebrate prey from worms to fiddler crabs.

Most short-billed dowitchers reach their nesting grounds by mid to late May or early June, with the males typically in the vanguard. They may arrive to find their nesting grounds carpeted in snow or inundated by meltwater. Even so, the males immediately carve out and advertise their territories. Because nests are so hard to find and territorial disputes are rarely seen, territory size is virtually impossible to determine, but nests have been found 164 to 1,312 feet (50–400 m) apart.

The Killing Flats

In the nineteenth century the short-billed dowitcher was a popular game bird. It was nearly driven to extinction by hunting, especially on spring migration, when it congregated at stopovers on coastal flats. The massiveness of the pristine flocks merely underlines the scale of the subsequent decimation by shooting. In May 1868 one passage flock in Maine is described as being "12 or 15 miles wide and at least 100 long." There are records of "eighty-five … taken at one discharge of the musket," and the celebrated bird artist J. J. Audubon witnessed 127 birds killed by shots from three gun barrels.

Aerial Extravaganza

Immediately upon arrival, the males sing from the ground and also from a succession of treetops. However, this warmup soon gives way to a full-blown aerial display. At 33 to 50 feet (10–15 m) above ground the male begins flying with deep and even wingbeats. He then switches to rapid, quivering wingbeats and gains some more height, breaking into full song as he does so. Still singing, he then glides down, with wings stretched horizontally or downtilted to expose the white patch on his back and rump. Now partially folding his wings, he suddenly drops, often only to ascend again to repeat the whole extravaganza.

The displaying male is often joined by another male and sometimes a female; an aerial chase follows, with all the participants, including the female, singing. Usually such encounters culminate in the love triangle landing, followed by a melee of singing, chasing, and shoving on the ground until one male concedes defeat. In ground disputes at feeding sites early in the season the rivals charge at each other, head and bill down like jousting knights with tilted lances. If one does not yield, a fight may follow, the combatants fluttering up into the air with their backs arched and legs dangling.

Previous breeders are believed to seek out the same territory and the same mate year after year. One marked male nested within 131 feet (40 m) of the site he used the previous year. The pair investigates several prospective nest sites together, the male making scrapes by molding the ground with his chest. The chosen site is often on a hummock next to a tree stump or shrub. Typically the nest cup is cradled in a tussock of sedge, with a bower of leaves both for concealment and protection against the elements. Short-billed dowitchers are amazingly resilient in this harsh wilderness; and even if eggs are covered with snow during laying, they usually still hatch.

Both parents incubate the clutch of four eggs; but once the chicks hatch, nearly all the brood care falls to the male. Most females

Follow Me, I'm Drowning!

Many dowitcher nests are only found when the incubating bird suddenly bursts up from underfoot. However, once disturbed, the parent may try to lure the intruder away by faking injury. In a hunched posture with head lowered, the bird shuffles along, back ruffled, wings partly open, tail fanned and lowered. The bird accentuates its feigned plight with pathetic bleating calls and may even take to the water, swimming away distractedly to safety.

abandon the nest site just before hatching, although a minority help look after the chicks for the first day or two of their lives. Either way, after a few more days in the area she sets off on her southward migration. Fortunately, the chicks are highly independent almost from birth, self-feeding by pecking at mosquitoes, spiders, and the like. They develop fast on this high protein diet, making their first short-distance flights at 16 to 17 days old.

The male chaperones his offspring for up to two weeks and then, like the female before him, joins the growing postbreeding flock and heads south. The juveniles are the last to leave the nesting grounds, heading for the coast in late July to start the long trek south.

⊕ *Unlike many shorebirds, the short-billed dowitcher is content to wade well into the water to find its prey, probing deeply into the mud with its long bill.*

Snipe

Gallinago gallinago

Equipped with a lance-shaped bill for probing deep into damp ground, the snipe is also remarkable for the male's spectacular aerial display, in which his tail feathers make a unique drumming sound.

Common name Snipe (common snipe)

Scientific name *Gallinago gallinago*

Family Scolopacidae

Order Charadriiformes

Size Length: 10–11 in (25–28 cm); wingspan: 17–19 in (43–48 cm); weight: 2.6–6.4 oz (74–181 g)

Key features Medium-sized body; long, straight bill; dark brown plumage; striped head and back; sexes similar; juvenile has pale feather edges

Habits Zigzagging escape flight; makes characteristic drumming sound during display flight

Nesting Shallow, thinly lined scrape in dense grass or sedge; 4 eggs; incubation 18–20 days; young fledge after 19–20 days; 1 brood

Voice Hoarse "scaap" given when alarmed; male's song a monotonously repeated "chip-per"

Diet Mainly insects, worms, and mollusks; also some seeds

Habitat Mainly marshy ground, often with tussocky grass or sedges with soft, easily probed soil

Distribution Eurasia, Iceland, North America, Central and South America, Africa, Middle East, and Asia

Status Not globally threatened, but has decreased during the twentieth century in regions subject to land improvement and drainage

WITH ITS UNUSUALLY LONG, STRAIGHT bill accounting for a quarter of its entire body length, the snipe is a highly distinctive shorebird. Its upper parts are like a rich, hardwood veneer of dark brown, buff, and rufous tones, with creamy stripes along the head and shoulders. Its underparts are buff, with horizontal brown bars, and a thin white wing bar is visible in flight.

The snipe depends on soft, damp soil for most of its food, inserting its bill up to the hilt in search of earthworms and insect grubs. The sensitive cells at the bill tip can detect prey by touch, and the bird can swallow modest-sized items without extracting its bill from the ground. It feeds mainly at dawn and dusk.

Snipe are not very gregarious, but in winter they may join up in flocks to exploit a generous food supply. When a snipe is alarmed, it flies up explosively from the ground, zigzags, and climbs steeply before descending with closed wings to land some distance away.

Spectacular Displays

In the spring the males arrive on the breeding grounds a week or two before the females and begin their spectacular aerial display to attract a mate. The nearest a male snipe gets to singing is his "chip-per" call, often given before and after the display flight he uses to proclaim ownership of his territory. During the display, however, his signal is not vocal but rather mechanical. He ascends and describes a switchback, circling flight path in which he alternately climbs and plummets with beating wings. During these dives the air rushing past the extended outermost tail feathers vibrates them like the reed in a musical instrument to produce a rapid, bleating "hu-hu-hu-hu,"

① Distinguished by the bold pale stripes on its crown and back, the snipe often wades into shallow water to search the mud for prey, probing deeply with its immensely long bill.

known as "drumming." Exceptionally, snipe have been known to sustain such an aerial display for an hour or more.

When the females arrive on the breeding grounds, each may mate with several males before settling down on a territory with just one. After laying, the female undertakes all the incubation; during this time her mate is the promiscuous one, pursuing any unattached females in the area.

Once the clutch hatches, however, both male and female take responsibility for raising the young. Typically they split the brood between them, the male attending to the first two chicks to hatch, the female to the younger two. If the young in its care are threatened, the snipe has a distinctive display in which it erects and fans its tail to expose the black spot, almost like an eye, in the central tail feathers. Adopting a hunched posture, the bird creeps

low along the ground, repeatedly snapping its tail open and shut to increase the allure of its tail spot. Sometimes the snipe droops and flutters its wings as if injured to draw attention to itself and away from its vulnerable offspring.

Bill to Bill

Because the snipe has quite a specialized feeding method that takes time to learn, the young are at first dependent on their parents for food, being fed bill to bill. The chicks stay with their parents for around six weeks; then they begin to form flocks that can build up to a hundred strong before the fall migration.

The migratory pattern varies, with some populations hardly moving at all, while others undertake long journeys. North American birds winter from the central U.S. to northern South America, and Asian birds winter as far south as Malaysia and India.

Red-Necked Phalarope

Phalaropus lobatus

The red-necked phalarope feeds on the water like a spinning top, churning prey items to the surface. Apart from egg laying, the females are liberated from nesting tasks by the dutiful males.

Common name Red-necked phalarope

Scientific name *Phalaropus lobatus*

Family Phalaropodidae

Order Charadriiformes

Size Length: 7–7.5 in (18–19 cm); wingspan: 13–16 in (33–41 cm); weight: 0.9–1.7 oz (25–48 g)

Key features Breeding female has gray head, white throat, chestnut collar, gray back flecked with gold; male similar, but less bright; both gray above, white below in winter; juvenile's back plumage brown-black bordered with buff

Habits In winter lives on open ocean or near coasts; usual sex roles reversed

Nesting Shallow, thinly lined cup; 4 eggs; incubation 17–21 days by male; young fledge after about 20 days; usually 1 brood unless female finds a second mate

Voice Chirping "chek" contact or alarm call; excited chattering when feeding and in courtship

Diet Mainly insects, crustaceans, mollusks, and worms; in winter takes plankton offshore

Habitat Breeds on open marshy, grassy tundra; winters on open ocean and near coasts

Distribution Circumpolar distribution in the high Arctic from North America through Greenland and Iceland to Siberia; winters at sea off Chile, southern Arabia, and East Indies

Status Not globally threatened, but climate change could damage breeding grounds in the Arctic

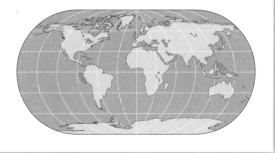

THE RED-NECKED IS THE SMALLEST of the three phalaropes, with a slender body and a delicate, needlelike bill. The female's plumage is more vivid than the male's. Her slate-gray head contrasts with a pure white throat, below which a chestnut collar curves up and narrows to just behind the eye. In winter the plumage of both sexes becomes duller, making them almost indistinguishable. The red-necked phalarope has dark gray legs and half-webbed feet—valuable assets for a bird that spends much of its life swimming buoyantly on the water.

Spinning Up a Meal

Red-necked phalaropes can feed while walking or wading; but when they are swimming, they demonstrate a technique that is unique to the phalaropes: "spinning." Sitting elegantly upright on the surface, the bird spins in circles at nearly 50 revolutions per minute. The action creates a little whirlpool that sucks small prey toward the surface, to be snatched up with rapid pecks of the bill.

⊕ *The red-necked phalarope's whirlpool feeding technique relies on the water being thick with tiny planktonic animals—conditions that occur mainly where ocean water masses mingle to concentrate prey near the surface.*

Female Initiative

The red-necked phalarope nests on open heath or marshy tundra, sometimes deep inland and many hundreds of feet above sea level. In spring the females generally reach the more northern parts of the breeding range at least a week before the males, although farther south the sexes usually arrive simultaneously, many having already paired up on migration.

Females take the initiative in courtship, and there can be intense competition, with rival females jousting with their bills and wings. Unattached females advertise themselves to males by taking off every few minutes with a conspicuous hovering display on whirring wings. They skim low over the water before landing in an alert posture with sleeked plumage and necks extended.

Mating usually occurs on the water—the activity often forcing the female beneath the surface with only her head showing. Both male and female may help choose the nest site, scraping for up to ten minutes at favored spots. However, after laying in the chosen site, the female loses interest immediately and leaves her mate to incubate the clutch and raise the young. In the meantime, if there are still surplus males available, she starts the courtship cycle again and lays a second clutch with a new mate.

Some females may contribute to raising the young, but typically it is an exclusively male task. He leads the chicks away from the nest, and they may forage over a wide area in the next two weeks, after which he leaves them to fend for themselves. Self-feeding from day one, phalarope chicks grow rapidly in the summer flush of insect life and almost triple their weight in the first five days. They become sexually mature in their first year.

Overland Migration

The female phalaropes are the first to leave the breeding grounds, males following a month later, and juveniles later still. Both fall and spring migration are mainly overland via large water bodies and inlets. European and west Siberian birds, for example, migrate through the Caspian Sea and Kazakhstan lakes to winter in the Arabian Sea, while east Siberian birds migrate to the East Indies. Good feeding sites may attract huge concentrations of red-necked phalaropes, with up to a quarter of a million birds feeding in the Bay of Fundy, Nova Scotia. In their winter quarters red-necked phalaropes exist entirely at sea where upwelling currents and other oceanic features concentrate plankton and other suitable prey.

⊕ Wings partly spread, a male red-necked phalarope shelters his brood from the tundra wind. As with all phalaropes, the male bird has duller plumage than the sexually dominant female.

Great Skua

Catharacta skua

Largest of the skuas, the heavily built great skua is a fierce predator and pirate that steals other seabirds' hard-won catches of food; it will even attack humans who trespass on its nesting territory.

Common name Great skua (bonxie)

Scientific name *Catharacta skua*

Family	Stercorariidae
Order	Charadriiformes
Size	Length: 21–23 in (53–58 cm); wingspan: 52–55 in (132–140 cm); weight: 2.5–3.8 lb (1.1–1.7 kg)

Key features Heavy body; broad-based wings; short tail; brown overall except for white, gold, ginger, and black flecks, and white "flashes" near wingtips; heavy, hooked bill; immature birds more uniformly brown with red tinge beneath

Habits Fiercely territorial at breeding grounds; usually seen alone outside breeding season, although gathers at rich feeding sites

Nesting Nests in loose colonies; usually 2 eggs; incubation 26–32 days mainly by female; young fledge after 40–51 days; 1 brood

Voice Soft, nasal alarm calls, and harsh screams or barks when attacking intruders

Diet Mainly sand eels and fish pirated from other birds, but also taken from sea surface; also seabirds, eggs, and young in breeding season

Habitat Breeds on damp, grassy moorland and other treeless habitats, often above sea cliffs; winters at sea, often far from land

Distribution Mainly northeastern Atlantic, north to Arctic; ranges south to Newfoundland, Brazil, and West Africa

Status Increasing in most parts of range; has recently colonized sites in the Arctic

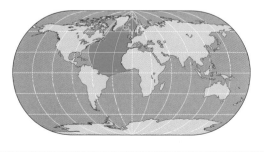

ALTHOUGH IT RANGES WIDELY THROUGH the Atlantic Ocean in winter, the great skua is restricted to Europe during the breeding season. Well over half the total world population, which currently stands at about 14,000 pairs, breeds off Scotland. The great majority of them nest on the Shetland Isles, far to the northeast of the Scottish mainland, with smaller numbers on the more southerly Orkney Isles and Hebrides, as well as a few colonies on the mainland. The only other big breeding population is on Iceland, currently with about 5,500 pairs.

Fossil evidence suggests that the ancestors of the great skua evolved in the Northern Hemisphere; they then colonized the Southern Hemisphere, where they evolved into three other species that remained in the antarctic and subantarctic regions. The great skua then recolonized the Northern Hemisphere, maybe as recently as the fifteenth century, beginning in Iceland and the Faeroe Islands, and not reaching Shetland until the eighteenth century.

Tough Customer

Broad-winged and short-tailed, with a barrel-shaped body and powerful hooked bill, the great skua is a force to be reckoned with. It has much broader, more bluntly tipped wings than the three smaller skuas (or jaegers) of the genus *Stercorarius* and a broader, rounded tail with only slightly protruding central tail feathers. The bold "flashes" at its wingtips are visible at long range and probably serve as a signal to other skuas, especially in connection with finding rich sources of food.

The Shetland islanders know the great skua as the "bonxie." Originally spelled "buncie," the word is apparently derived from the Old

Norse language and means "a heap" or "an unkempt plump woman." It presumably referred to the great skua's stout and rather ungainly appearance on land.

Powerful Predator

The powerful great skua is a formidable adversary of other seabirds, both as a pirate and as a predator on adults, young, and eggs. When hunting, it often soars high in the air, watching for a chance to swoop down in a dramatic headlong dive and surprise a seabird flying home with its crop bulging with food for its young. It can put on a sudden burst of speed thanks to its ability to release energy very rapidly to its large flight muscles and is able to chase its victim relentlessly until the harassed bird succumbs and regurgitates its food for the skua to catch deftly in midair.

When feeding as a predator, a great skua may strike its victim with its broad chest, its powerful, viciously hooked bill, or its sharp-clawed feet, knocking it down to the surface of the sea. There it may deliberately drown the bird if it is not already dead and tear into its body with its bill as it floats upside down.

Great skuas also attack seabirds on the sea and on land, often seizing puffins and other species as they emerge from their breeding burrows. In Iceland they kill ducks and geese, and they are even capable of killing birds as powerful as great black-backed gulls (*Larus marinus*).

Great skuas are highly resourceful birds, and they soon learn to take advantage of new opportunities for gaining an easy meal. They eagerly squabble over discarded fish from fishing vessels, and in places this supplementary food has fueled dramatic increases in skua populations. In turn it has resulted in greater levels of predation by skuas on other seabirds, including storm-petrels and puffins.

On the remote Hebridean island of St. Kilda, for example, the great skua population increased from 145 pairs in 1994 to 271 just three years later, and the skuas were estimated to be killing about 40,000 seabirds each year. On the Shetland Isles the skuas may have killed as many as 200,000 seabirds each year, especially during recent shortages of sand eels, which normally form much of the diet of the skuas and their young during the breeding season.

Great skuas are notorious pirates and predators of other seabirds, but during the breeding season they also catch fish. They are especially fond of the small sand eels that swim in huge shoals and seize them by splashing down onto the water surface or diving just below it.

Food Piracy

When obtaining food by piracy, great skuas concentrate most of their attacks on relatively large seabirds such as murres and various species of gull. They generally ignore the terns, puffins, and other smaller species targeted by their smaller relatives, the jaegers.

A great skua may even chase a northern gannet (*Morus bassanus*), although it is careful to avoid being stabbed by the gannet's formidable daggerlike bill. If its victim does not regurgitate its catch of fish right away, the skua forces it down onto the sea by repeatedly seizing the tip of one of its great wings until the bird loses its balance. Then the gannet often gives up its meal to escape the persistent attentions of the skua.

The female great skua has the task of incubating the eggs. She must also defend the nestlings while her mate hunts for food, and for this reason female skuas are larger and more powerful than males—unlike gulls, in which the males are bigger.

Bad Neighbors

Great skuas are quite exacting in their requirements for breeding habitat, favoring coastal tundra and grassy moorland, and preferring to nest where the vegetation grows around 4 inches (10 cm) high. Many breeding colonies are sited next to large colonies of other seabirds, which the skuas can plunder by taking adults, young, or eggs directly, by pirating food, or scavenging for dead individuals. Even other great skua chicks are not safe—during years when food is scarce, many may be killed and eaten by neighboring adults.

As soon as the birds return to their traditional nesting sites from their ocean wanderings in spring, each pair guards its territory fiercely. The usual clutch is two eggs, but younger, less experienced pairs may lay only one. The female does the greater share of the incubation while her mate guards the nest, perched prominently on a hummock nearby. The first chick hatches a month later, to be followed by a second within two or three days.

The larger female spends more time guarding the brown downy chicks while her mate goes off to find food. When he returns, the chicks beg to be fed by flapping their tiny wings and giving high-pitched whistling calls as they peck at his breast. He regurgitates his catch onto the ground, from which the female extracts morsels to feed to her young. When they are older, they feed from the food pile themselves without her help.

After they have fledged, some immature great skuas spend the next five years or more wandering the Atlantic while they perfect their piratical and predatory skills. They have been seen as far south as the Cape Verde Islands off West Africa and off the north coast of Brazil.

Other youngsters return north after they have molted from their juvenile plumage. When they get back to the breeding sites, these immature birds gather in "clubs," where they practice performing aggressive territorial displays and forming pairs, even though they will not be sexually mature for several years. Some can breed at the age of five, while others may not breed until more than twice this age.

Persecution and Expansion

The great skuas of Shetland and the Faeroes had been driven to virtual extinction by human persecution by the end of the nineteenth century; but protection came just in time, and they have since increased greatly. They are now expanding their range, and over the last 30 years small numbers from the Shetlands have colonized several Arctic islands, including Svalbard, Jan Mayen, and Novaya Zemlya.

Defending the Nest

Great skuas are exciting birds for birdwatchers, especially after they have laid their eggs, when they defend their nests boldly against any intruders. A skua has no hesitation in attacking sheep, dogs, or humans in a spectacular power dive, swooping down silently at great speed with its legs lowered, and usually passing just over the intruder's head with a sudden loud *swoosh* of its wings before shooting up high again and banking for another attack. Sometimes both birds leave the nest to mount an even more unnerving joint attack from opposite directions. Great skuas do not hit people with their feet as often as Arctic terns; but when they do, the impact from such a sizable bird is much more painful.

⊕ *Nesting great skuas are jealous parents, defending their helpless young with terrific ferocity.*

Herring Gull

Larus argentatus

An ability to exploit new food sources and new nesting and roosting sites has made the herring gull one of the most successful of all seabirds, leading to a population explosion over much of its range.

IN EUROPE AND EASTERN NORTH America the herring gull is the commonest of the gulls and one of the most abundant of all coastal birds. In the past it was heavily persecuted for its eggs and feathers, but with increasing protection it has been able to build up its numbers and colonize new habitats. Although most still nest on or near the coast, herring gulls have increasingly invaded farmland, towns, and inland reservoirs.

The herring gull is one of a group of similar large gulls. They include the lesser black-backed gull (*Larus fuscus*), yellow-legged gull (*L. cachinnans*), and Armenian gull (*L. armenicus*). There is considerable variation in size between the different races of herring gull. The back and wings vary from pale, silvery gray to darker bluish-gray. The legs are usually pink, although they are yellowish in one race. Within each race males are distinctly bigger and heavier than females, with larger heads and bills.

Adaptable Opportunists

Originally, the diet of herring gulls consisted chiefly of fish, crabs, worms, mollusks, and other marine creatures. The birds break the shells of mussels and clams by dropping them onto rocks or other hard surfaces from a height.

More recently, herring gulls have discovered a variety of food sources resulting from human activities, and they now eat almost anything they can find, from the carcasses of large fish or seals stranded on beaches to the rich pickings at garbage dumps. Other favorite feeding sites include sewage outfalls and fishing ports, where they eat the offal discarded by fish processors. They are quick to accept food scraps offered by people—or to steal them from unguarded beach picnics.

Common name Herring gull

Scientific name *Larus argentatus*

Family Laridae

Order Charadriiformes

Size Length: 22–25 in (56–63.5 cm); wingspan: 53–57 in (135–145 cm); weight: 1.5–3 lb (0.7–1.4 kg)

Key features Heavily built gull with large head and thick neck; gray back and upper wings; wings have black tips with white spots; rest of plumage white; strong yellow bill with red spot at angle; head has dark streaks in winter

Habits Sociable, noisy, and bold; opportunist feeder at sea and on land; usually breeds in colonies, vigorously defending territory around nest

Nesting Nest of grass, seaweed, or other vegetation on open ground, cliff ledge, or building; 2–3 brown-blotched, pale green eggs; incubation 28–30 days; young fledge after 35–40 days; 1 brood

Voice Wide range of loud, mainly harsh calls

Diet Fish, crabs, worms, mollusks, insects, small mammals, birds, eggs, fish offal, and garbage

Habitat Breeds mainly on or above sea cliffs, on dunes or shingle beaches, and on roofs of coastal buildings; outside breeding season more widespread, including inland

Distribution North America, Europe, Scandinavia, and northern Siberia, ranging south to Central America, Japan, and China

Status Generally widespread and common; increase over past century still continuing in many areas, but some local decreases

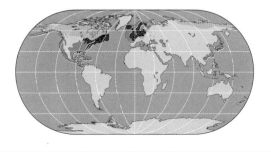

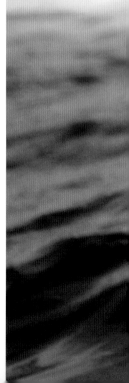

⊕ *Although the herring gull has made a success of exploiting unlikely food sources such as sewage outfalls and garbage dumps, it still catches a lot of fresh prey at sea, such as this flatfish.*

Herring gulls have also learned to follow the plow on farmland, swooping down to seize the worms, insects, and other small creatures that are disturbed as the soil is turned over.

Ringing Call

Herring gulls are very noisy birds, their wide repertoire of calls including low, gruff sounds when anxious at the breeding site, repeated yelps of alarm, and various wailing and squealing calls during social interactions.

Most characteristic is the long call, versions of which are also given by other gulls and skuas. The call forms part of the male's display when attracting a mate, and it is also used in the bonding ritual by pairs at the nest. The bird begins with low-pitched calls while it lowers its head so that its bill almost touches the ground, then raises its head, and stretches out its neck while uttering a series of very loud, ringing laughing notes.

Both sexes incubate the eggs; and when the chicks hatch, they peck instinctively at the red spot on their parents' bills, prompting the adults to regurgitate a meal.

Juveniles fly at about five weeks old, but they look very different from their parents, with streaked brown feathers and dark bills. It takes them four years to acquire the neat plumage and brightly colored bill of an adult.

Noisy Nuisance

In towns where it is common, the herring gull can become a nuisance. The birds are aggressive in defense of their rooftop nest sites, diving on people who pass nearby, and their droppings foul clothes and cars. The most common complaint is the very loud and almost incessant noise as the birds call, which annoys their human neighbors.

Herring gulls that roost on reservoirs have also been implicated in the contamination of drinking water with bacteria that cause disease in humans. The bacteria certainly kill many gulls, and that has contributed to population declines. Measures to control the gulls because of the public health risk, such as improvements in garbage management, have taken their toll on populations, too.

Sometimes, herring gulls nest alongside vulnerable and scarce birds such as roseate terns (*Sterna dougallii*). When this happens, herring gulls are sometimes culled by conservationists to limit their depredations on the eggs and chicks of the other birds. It has also led to local declines in numbers.

Common name Kittiwake (black-legged kittiwake)

Scientific name *Rissa tridactyla*

Family	Laridae
Order	Charadriiformes
Size	Length: 15–16 in (38–41 cm); wingspan: 36–38 in (91–97 cm); weight: 11–18 oz (312–510 g)

Key features Medium-sized, delicately built, round-headed gull; triangular black wingtips; white underparts; yellow bill; short blackish legs; young birds have zigzags across upper wing

Habits Feeds at sea in small flocks or singly; breeds in large, dense, noisy cliff colonies, sometimes with other seabirds

Nesting Bulky nest cup of grass, seaweed, and feathers on narrow cliff ledge; 1–3 eggs; incubation 24–32 days; young fledge after 33–54 days; 1 brood

Voice Very noisy at breeding colonies, uttering loud, nasal "kitti-waaak" calls; also low "uk-uk-uk" of alarm and short, nasal flight calls

Diet Mostly fish and shrimp, plus squid and other invertebrates; also scavenges from carcasses, fish offal, and sewage outfalls

Habitat Breeds mainly on sea cliffs and seaside buildings; otherwise usually well out to sea

Distribution North Pacific, Atlantic, and Arctic Oceans, south to Baja California and West Africa

Status Has increased numbers and expanded range over the last 100 years

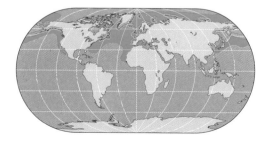

Kittiwake

Rissa tridactyla

Most oceanic and abundant of all the gulls, the delicate, attractive kittiwake is named for its loud, distinctive "kitti-waaak" call.

IF EVER A MEMBER OF THE gull family deserved the name "seagull," this is it. Unlike most other gulls, the kittiwake spends half the year or more out over the oceans, well out of sight of land, feeding on marine creatures, drinking seawater, and coping with winter gales. Instead of joining other gulls at the rich pickings on shores and garbage dumps, it usually stays well out of sight of land. It also stays on the wing unless particularly severe weather forces it to land on the water, or even blows it inshore, when a flock may sit dejectedly on a beach to rest.

In spring it returns to breed in dense, noisy colonies on sheer cliffs. The sight and sound of a huge colony such as those on Scottish islands is unforgettable—as is the powerful fishy smell of the birds' accumulated droppings.

⬇ *The kittiwake has a slender, delicate bill adapted for catching and eating small fish and other prey. Its rounded head and large dark eyes give it a gentler facial "expression" than most other gulls.*

Name Calling

At their breeding cliffs kittiwakes keep up a constant, deafening cacophony of loud, high-pitched nasal calls that sound as if they are repeating their common name over and over again. These rather mournful cries may account for the ancient belief that the souls of dead children pass into kittiwakes.

As well as the common name that imitates the "kitti-waaak" call, there are many other old British names that mimic the kittiwake's calls. They include kittick, keltie, sea kittie, and waeg; others include annet, cackreen, and craa maa. In North America it has been called snow bird and frost bird; in New England, where it appears in winter, it is called the winter gull. It is also known as jack gull because of its relatively small size. On both sides of the Atlantic the distinctively plumaged immature birds were known as tarrocks.

The scientific name of the kittiwake's genus is derived from the Icelandic word *rita* for these birds, while its specific name *tridactyla* is from the Greek for "three-fingered"; at best, kittiwakes have only tiny hind toes without claws and often lack them entirely.

Adult kittiwakes resemble small mew gulls (*Larus canus*), for both have neat, blue-gray upper parts and white heads and underparts. Kittiwakes can be distinguished at long range by their triangular black wingtips, which look as if they have been dipped in ink and do not have the prominent white spots (known as "mirrors") of the mew and many other gulls.

In the breeding season the kittiwake's head is as white as its body; in winter the rear crown is gray, and there is a blackish smudge behind each eye.

The kittiwake has very short legs, but they are adapted for perching upright on tiny cliff ledges—usually the only time the birds are on land—but not for walking around regularly like most other gulls. Its webbed feet enable it to swim well and make shallow dives, and they also bear long, sharp claws to ensure a secure grip on wet, narrow nesting ledges hundreds of feet above the waves.

Easy Action

Kittiwakes have a graceful, buoyant flight action, with easy, springy beats of their long wings. Often, the wings look quite uniform in width for much of their length, tapering to rather blunt ends, but they are angled back when the birds travel at speed, giving them a narrower, more pointed appearance. Immature birds have shorter necks and hunch their heads into their shoulders, and they have broader, more triangular wings.

← *Kittiwake colonies may contain tens or hundreds of thousands of pairs, their nests perched precariously on the tiniest ledges and irregularities in cliff faces rising sheer from the breaking waves below. Inset: while one of the birds builds the nest, the other gathers seaweed and other nesting materials in its bill.*

In light winds kittiwakes beat their wings faster and more often than larger gulls, and groups often fly low over the sea in single file. They are expert at riding gales, dipping up and down as they soar above the ocean surface in long, rising arcs. They use the wind to move great distances with the minimum of effort, slicing into the waves with their wingtips like fulmars (genus *Fulmarus*).

Ocean Riches

Kittiwakes feed mainly on fish such as sand eels, herring, capelin, cod, and pollack, especially in the breeding season. They also eat invertebrates such as shrimp, sea-butterflies, and scale-worms, especially in winter. Increasing numbers of birds take advantage of the fish offal discarded by trawlers.

Kittiwakes have a variety of feeding techniques. They frequently dip down to the sea in flight to snatch prey. Kittiwakes also land on the water to take food from the surface or, by ducking their heads under, from just beneath. They may even plunge from the surface to a depth of up to about 3 feet (1 m). Out at sea kittiwakes may gather to feed where humpback or pilot whales, or even sea lions, disturb prey that they can seize.

Cliff Colonies

Most kittiwake breeding colonies are sited on high, sheer cliffs along stormy, exposed coasts. Kittiwakes often breed together with other colonial seabirds, such as guillemots and other auks, fulmars, and shags. In such mixed colonies the kittiwakes tend to occupy the lower ledges up to about 80 feet (24 m) above the sea, and often with the lower birds almost within the reach of the waves. In Greenland, where the birds are still hunted in large

149

numbers, they nest much higher up the cliffs, at up to 650 feet (198 m) above sea level.

In the more southerly parts of their range kittiwakes may arrive back from their ocean wanderings as early as January to defend their nesting sites, but most colonies do not begin to gather until February or early March. Tightly packed onto long, narrow, winding ledges or the tiniest of projections on precipitous cliffs, kittiwakes display, mate, build their nests, and rear their young. Each pair defends only a very small space around their nest against neighbors, whose nests may touch theirs.

The male chooses the nest site and then sets about attracting a female by performing a "choking" display, jerking his head and neck up and down, and opening his bill to reveal the startling orange-red interior of his mouth.

Soon the pair set to work to build the nest, trampling seaweed, grass, moss, and mud to form a solid cylinder fastened firmly to a projection of rock with a mixture of seaweed and the birds' own droppings.

In mid-May to mid-June, depending on latitude, the females lay their eggs in a snug, secure hollow in the top of the nest. The ground color of the eggs ranges from buff or yellowish to brown, pinkish, or blue-gray, and it is spotted and blotched with dark brown or gray. The female usually lays two eggs, but some lay one and others three. On average, clutches of birds breeding later in the season are smaller than those produced by females who laid early.

After four weeks' incubation by both parents the chicks hatch and immediately start demanding food. A pair of kittiwakes may have to range up to 30 miles (48 km) from the colony to find food to satisfy their appetites. When a parent bird returns to feed them, it does not regurgitate a meal of partially digested food onto the nest site like a ground-nesting gull. It retains the food in its throat, so that the chicks can put their bills into its own and feed from there, reducing the danger of losing the precious catch over the side of the tiny ledge.

The young stay in their nest cup for five to eight weeks after they hatch, until they can fly—unlike those of other gulls, which leave the nest soon after hatching. It ensures that the young kittiwakes do not fall to their deaths.

Until they are about a year old, immature kittiwakes have a bold, M-shaped pattern of

⊕ Kittiwake chicks hatch covered in a snug layer of down. It is mainly bold white, with a grayish back and wings—quite unlike that of almost all other gull chicks, whose down is mottled in grays and browns to camouflage them at their more accessible nest sites.

Adaptable Nesters

Along the east coast of Britain, and at other sites in the North Sea where kittiwakes are fully protected, some birds have learned to take advantage of large buildings on coasts and estuaries, such as warehouses and piers. The windowsills and other projections on these structures provide ideal substitutes for their more usual cliff-ledge nesting sites. Occasionally, kittiwakes will even nest on flat, rocky, or even sandy sites, rarely up to about 12 miles (19 km) inland. In the northernmost parts of their range, in the high Arctic regions of Alaska, northeast Canada, Greenland, and Siberia, they will nest on the face of a snow slope or glacier if it is still covering their nesting cliffs when they return to breed.

Territorial Battles

Kittiwake pairs defend their tiny territory from neighboring pairs if they encroach too close for comfort. Often disputes are settled by the opposing birds adopting a ritual posture with their bills half open, alternately lunging forward and withdrawing. Sometimes the situation becomes more serious, and they grasp each other's bills, pulling and tugging until one backs off or one bird twists the other off the ledge. Occasionally both birds may fall off into the sea, bills still interlocked, and try to duck each other's head underwater.

blackish diagonals on their wings and a black bill, half-collar, and tail band. Most breed for the first time when they are four to six years old, but some do not do so until they reach the age of eight. Kittiwakes have been known to live for up to 21 years.

Target Practice

Kittiwakes have increased dramatically in range and numbers during the twentieth century, largely because of protection. During the nineteenth century kittiwakes were heavily persecuted and were fast disappearing from their colonies in parts of North America and Europe. Huge numbers of immature birds were killed for their patterned wing feathers, which were in great demand for adorning fashionable ladies' hats. The tasty eggs and young birds were also harvested for food. At many colonies the slaughter was multiplied as people shot the birds from boats for target practice.

In Britain the kittiwake became one of the first birds to be given legal protection by the Seabirds Preservation Act of 1869; but since it did not extend outside the breeding season, many kittiwakes were still killed. By the turn of the century few breeding sites remained in England and Wales. Fortunately a small, but enlightened, group of women conservationists formed the Fur, Fin, and Feather Folk to campaign for bird protection, and more legislation was passed. It grew into the Society for the Protection of Birds and eventually became the Royal Society for the Protection of Birds (RSPB), now Europe's largest voluntary wildlife conservation body.

Today the kittiwake is by far the world's most numerous species of gull, with an estimated total population of over 7 million pairs. Around half of them breed in the Old World and half in the New World. The largest population breeds on the huge, mountainous Kamchatka Peninsula in far eastern Siberia, and there are also very large populations in Alaska—although the southern breeders there were seriously affected by the oil spill from the tanker *Exxon Valdez* in 1989.

In other places, such as Shetland, the overfishing of sand eels, one of the kittiwake's main foods, may have caused declines that have been recorded in recent years. Yet despite such setbacks, the overall world population is far greater than it was 50 years ago, and the species faces relatively few threats.

Arctic Tern

Sterna paradisaea

This elegant seabird travels farther than any other bird, flying halfway around the globe and back to migrate between its breeding and nonbreeding habitats near the North and South Poles.

Common name Arctic tern

Scientific name *Sterna paradisaea*

Family Sternidae

Order Charadriiformes

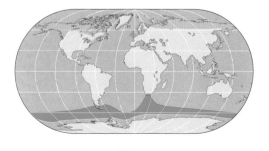

Size Length: 13–14 in (33–36 cm); wingspan: 30–33 in (76–84 cm); weight: 3–4.5 oz (85–128 g)

Key features Mainly gray, with black cap (white at front in nonbreeding season); white cheeks, rump, and tail; narrow black line on trailing edge of wingtips; translucent "window" on hind wing; very long tail streamers; bill and very short legs blood-red, turning black in fall

Habits Feeds at sea by plunge-diving from hovering flight; breeds in small, widely dispersed colonies; exceptionally long migrations

Nesting Nest a shallow scrape; 2–3 eggs; incubation 22–27 days; young fledge after 21–24 days; 1 brood

Voice Very noisy, with loud, high-pitched rasping and clear piping or whistling calls

Diet Mainly small fish; also crustaceans, insects, krill, earthworms, and fish offal

Habitat Breeds mainly along coasts and inshore islands, but also far inland; generally migrates and winters well offshore

Distribution Mainly Arctic, but south to northern Europe, northwest and northeast U.S; winters in Southern Ocean

Status Widespread and common, but many populations have suffered serious declines

WITH ITS LONG WINGS AND tail streamers, its sleek, streamlined body, and buoyant flight style, the Arctic tern is one of the most elegant of the seabirds. As its name suggests, it is the most northerly breeder of all the terns, nesting mainly north of the Arctic Circle, and it is the only member of the tern family that breeds in the high Arctic. Small Arctic tern colonies even survive the bitter cold of Cape Morris Jesup in extreme northern Greenland—the world's most northerly outpost of land, only 439 miles (707 km) from the North Pole.

⊕ *Although they spend much of their lives at sea, Arctic terns like to wash in fresh waters such as this pool in Iceland, sluicing away the salt and preening their feathers with their bills to restore their aerodynamic efficiency.*

The Greatest Migrants

After breeding, adult and young Arctic terns embark on a record-beating journey from their nesting grounds in and around the Arctic to the other end of the Earth, to spend the nonbreeding season in Antarctica.

Each year an Arctic tern may cover as much as 25,000 miles (40,235 km) on its round trip between the Arctic and Antarctica. If it flew there and back in a straight line, the distance would be only about 18,600 miles (29,935 km), but Arctic terns follow complex routes, hugging the irregular coastlines for much of the way. Some may travel overland surprisingly long distances for a seabird, and one was even found at an altitude of 6,500 feet (1,980 m) in the Colombian Andes. Others are forced to strike out over the open ocean.

Arctic terns that breed in Alaska travel south down the Pacific coasts of the Americas and then go around storm-battered Cape Horn to reach the Antarctic Ocean. Those that nest in eastern Canada and Greenland might be expected to follow the eastern coastlines of North America, the Caribbean, and South America; but instead, they cross the Atlantic, flying southeast toward Europe until they meet other migrant Arctic terns heading south from their breeding grounds in Europe and Siberia. After passing Spain and northwest Africa, some birds diverge to fly down the Atlantic coast of South America, while most continue to follow the African coast, past the Cape of Good Hope, and on to Antarctica.

When they reach Antarctica, the terns gather along the edge of the pack ice surrounding the Antarctic continent, where there is plenty of food. As the southern summer progresses and the ice retreats, the terns follow it southward. This takes them into a zone of westerly winds that help carry them east to a position to the south of the Atlantic, so they are ideally placed when they need to fly back north to breed again.

Some Arctic terns can reach an age of 25 or more (the record is 34). During their lifetimes these birds will have traveled a distance at least equivalent to flying to the Moon and back—over 620,000 miles (1 million km).

Since the Arctic tern spends its breeding season in the Arctic and much of the rest of each year in Antarctica, it enjoys the perpetual Sun of the polar summer in both regions and probably experiences more daylight each year than any other animal.

The stronghold of the species is in the subarctic zone, with by far the largest numbers breeding in Iceland. The Arctic tern population here fluctuates between about a quarter of a million and half a million breeding pairs, accounting for about 60 percent of the total population in Europe. The next largest concentration is in northern Britain, where almost 70 percent of the British breeding population of about 44,000 pairs is found on the island groups of Orkney and Shetland off northeast Scotland. In North America the greatest numbers occur in remote parts of Alaska and the Canadian Arctic.

Hover and Plunge

Throughout the year Arctic terns feed mainly on small fish, although they also include insects, crustaceans, and other animals in their diet. The proportions of these different foods vary from one area to another and throughout the year. In some breeding colonies, such as on the Arctic island of Spitsbergen, Arctic terns catch many krill to feed their young. In Antarctica they gorge themselves on the huge concentrations of these shrimplike crustaceans that build up in the southern summer. It is at this time that the terns molt and become flightless for a short period, but they can still feed because they can gather the krill from just beneath the surface as they swim around on the water with their small webbed feet.

An Arctic tern uses a variety of methods for obtaining its prey. Like other sea terns, it catches fish mainly by hovering against the wind until it spots a victim, then plunging down to enter the water with a splash and catch the fish just below the surface. However, its technique has some distinctive features. An Arctic tern typically

descends in stages by hovering, then dropping down a few feet before hovering once more; it then either repeats the process or slips away to one side until it has a more precise fix on its target and makes its final dive.

On occasion an Arctic tern may also behave like its more distant relative the black tern (*Chlidonias niger*), dipping down low in flight to pick off insects and their larvae, taking crustaceans from the surface of the water, or even snatching caterpillars from low vegetation on land. It also alights to feed on earthworms.

Arctic terns sometimes steal food caught by other birds. In Iceland, for instance, they have been seen taking fish dropped by puffins being chased by jaegers; but they are far more likely to be victims themselves of these aerial pirates.

Fascinating Rituals

Most Arctic terns nest along coasts and on small, low, sparsely vegetated rocky or sandy inshore islands or sea stacks, around the fringes of the Arctic Ocean. The birds' favorite nesting sites are on rocky shores or on shingle or sandy beaches and among the sandy pockets that build up along ridges of gravel such as those that form beneath glaciers. There are also many breeding colonies far inland on tundra, heathland, rough pasture, sedge grassland, and islets in lakes or large rivers.

Arctic terns usually pair for life and return to the same nest site every spring. Their courtship and pair-bonding rituals are fascinating to watch.

⊕ *The Arctic tern is an exceptionally noisy seabird, especially at its northern breeding colonies; although when danger threatens, the whole colony can fall silent in a "dread."*

⊖ *A remote, rocky, largely barren shore makes a perfect nesting site for Arctic terns, which are more than capable of defending their nests against ground predators such as foxes, weasels, and even people.*

nests, and soon settle down. This odd behavior, known as a "dread," occurs most often in dense colonies where the nests are close together. Usually there seems to be no obvious reason for it, but researchers think that it may be linked to the presence of aerial predators, such as gulls, skuas, crows, ravens, or falcons.

Arctic terns also suffer from ground predators such as Arctic foxes, but they are extremely aggressive in defense of their eggs and young. Working together, the birds dive at any intruder, including a human one, rising into the air and then swooping down at the trespasser's head. They often strike with their sharp bills, which can easily draw blood from an unprotected scalp.

Initially the male flies around higher and higher with a fish grasped in his bill, hotly pursued by his mate. Then both birds glide down with a curious, swaying flight action, to land close together on the ground. The female then begs for food like a chick, and the male feeds her with his trophy. This courtship feeding not only serves as an indication of the male's prowess at fishing, but also provides his mate with the nutrients she needs to produce her large, protein-rich eggs.

The beautifully camouflaged downy chicks leave the nest within a day or two, but they hide among vegetation or stones if danger threatens, prompted by alarm calls from their parents. At intervals the usual clamor of harsh calls from a busy colony abruptly ceases as almost all the birds suddenly take silently to the air and circle over the sea. After about half a minute they start calling again, return to their

⊖ *While their parents are away fishing, Arctic tern chicks stay hidden, but they rush out to beg for food as soon as an adult bird appears. Sometimes the parent bird feeds its chicks from the air.*

Delayed Molt

The Arctic tern delays the molt of its flight feathers until late in the year, after it has made its marathon migratory journey to Antarctica. It contrasts with most terns that breed in the north, including its close relative the common tern (*Sterna hirundo*), which has two partial molts in a year. It also helps birdwatchers distinguish these very similar-looking birds when they see them passing along coasts on their southward migrations—the Arctic tern's wings are neat and complete, while those of its cousin often show gaps where the primary flight feathers of the wings have been lost during molt.

Black Skimmer *Rynchops niger*

The black skimmer and its two close relatives are uniquely equipped with an unusual, elongated lower bill—an adaptation for a distinctive and highly successful inflight fishing technique.

WITH THEIR BIG, BRIGHTLY COLORED, extraordinarily shaped bills and their striking black-and-white plumage, black skimmers are unmistakable whether resting on a sandbank or patroling the shallows low over the water. Males are distinctly larger than females. In winter both sexes have a white collar that separates the black crown from the black plumage of the back.

The eyes of skimmers have very large pupils to help the birds see in poor light conditions, for they fish mainly at night. Therefore

Common name Black skimmer

Scientific name *Rynchops niger*

Family   Rynchopidae

Order   Charadriiformes

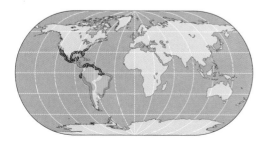

Size Length: 16–18 in (41–46 cm); wingspan: 42–50 in (107–127 cm); weight: 8–10 oz (227–283 g)

Key features Large head; huge bill with elongated, knifelike lower mandible; slender body; very long, pointed wings and short tail; pied plumage contrasts with half-red, half-black bill and red feet

Habits   Feeds in flight by "skimming" water surface, mainly at dusk and during night; breeds in small colonies and roosts in dense groups, often with terns and other seabirds

Nesting   Nest a shallow depression in sand or shells; 3–4 eggs; incubation 21–26 days; young fledge after 28–30 days; 1 brood

Voice   Barking calls, especially at breeding colonies

Diet   Fish, plus shrimp and other crustaceans

Habitat   Sheltered coastal waters; also large rivers and even high-altitude lakes in South America

Distribution Coastal U.S. to Central and South America, ranging south to southern Chile

Status   Locally common in parts of its range, but very vulnerable to disturbance, habitat alteration, pollutants in fish prey, and predators

skimmers do not feed in competition with other fish-eating birds. The surface of the sea is also calmer at night, which helps skimmers catch their surface-swimming prey.

Because they have such large pupils, skimmers might be dazzled by intense sunlight during the day, especially when it is reflected off white sand and a sparkling sea. To prevent being dazzled, skimmers' pupils close to vertical slits, like those of a cat, an adaptation found in no other bird. The slits permit less light to pass than circular contracted pupils of similar size.

Air Attack

A skimmer searches for food on the wing, flying along only a couple of inches above the water's surface. It has a distinctive, easy graceful flight with rather shallow, slow flaps of its long, pointed stiffly held wings. The skimmer avoids wetting its wingtips in the water by never allowing its wingbeats to extend below the horizontal.

Despite the skimmer's bizarre appearance, its oversized bill is a perfect adaptation to its very precise method of feeding. Its mandibles (top and bottom parts of the bill) are flattened sideways, like a knife, and the lower mandible extends well beyond the upper one. As it flies along, the bird holds the longer lower mandible so it shears the water surface. The instant it strikes suitable prey—mainly small fish such as silversides, killifish, anchovies, and minnows—the skimmer jerks its head down so that the upper mandible can contact the fish. The skimmer then snaps its bill shut to trap the prey.

The horny covering of the lower mandible grows faster than the upper one. To keep it trimmed, the skimmer flies over very shallow water and submerges its bill so that the lower mandible touches the sandy or muddy bottom, wearing away its surface. The tip of the bill may also break if it hits a rock or other submerged object. Because of this, the length of a skimmer's lower mandible varies throughout its lifetime, and each individual's bill is different.

Sociable Breeders

Black skimmers usually feed alone, but they roost in tightly packed groups and breed in colonies, sometimes of 1,000 pairs or more. They prefer coastal islands and isolated beaches for nesting. Their bills are not suited to gathering nesting material, so they build no nest, but simply kick sand away and slowly turn around to fashion a shallow basin about 1 foot (0.3 m) wide in which they can lay their boldly marked brown-and-purple blotched eggs.

The chicks leave the nest at around a week old and are brooded and fed by both parents. At this stage a chick's bill has a knifelike shape like that of an adult, but the two mandibles are more or less equal. By the time the young black skimmer is about a month old, its lower mandible is noticeably longer, and within a further three months the bird develops the extraordinary bill shape that it will use to catch fish during the rest of its life.

⊕ Dwarfed by the unusual, knifelike bill of its parent, a tiny black skimmer chick is barely visible against the sand of its nesting hollow. Its coat of gray down provides almost perfect camouflage until it fledges at the age of around four weeks.

Dovekie

Alle alle

The hardy little dovekie breeds in vast colonies on remote, rock-strewn arctic coasts, but most people see it only when the birds are driven ashore by severe storms during their southward migrations in fall.

Common name Dovekie (little auk)

Scientific name *Alle alle*

Family Alcidae

Order Charadriiformes

Size Length: 7–7.5 in (18–19 cm); wingspan: 16–19 in (41–48 cm); weight: 5–7 oz (142–198 g)

Key features Very small, compact, black-and-white auk with small, stubby bill; almost entirely blackish underwing; fast, agile flight

Habits Very sociable, breeding in huge colonies and migrating and wintering in loose aggregations made up of small flocks; feeds by deep diving from sea surface

Nesting Nest of pebbles among rocks or in crevice in sea cliff; 1 egg; incubation 28–31 days by both sexes; young fledge after 23–30 days; 1 brood

Voice Short rippling or chattering, trilling "song"; also short, sharp harsh calls of alarm; usually silent away from breeding colonies

Diet Almost entirely planktonic crustaceans; occasionally tiny worms or other marine animals, including fish larvae

Habitat Breeds on sea cliffs and mountains, among boulders or smaller-sized scree; spends most of nonbreeding season well out to sea

Distribution Mainly high Arctic, on islands and oceans; ranges south to eastern U.S. and North Sea

Status The most abundant of all auks, so not currently in any danger

THE DOVEKIE IS ONE OF THE smallest of the auks and the most arctic in its distribution—indeed, few other birds breed so far north. It is also one of the world's most numerous seabirds, with a total population rivaling that of species such as the chinstrap penguin, which breeds in huge numbers in the Southern Hemisphere. The birds are extremely difficult to census accurately, so estimates of their numbers vary from 8 to 18 million pairs, but a likely figure for the total population is around 12 million pairs.

Neckless and Froglike

The dovekie is about the size of a thrush, but much plumper. With its disproportionately big, rounded head, tiny, broad-based bill, often bulging throat pouch, and normally almost completely neckless shape, it can have a rather froglike appearance.

On shore dovekies often perch more or less upright; and unlike most auks, they move quite easily on land, sometimes running. They often swim low in the water with their wings trailing; at other times they bob up and down like corks on the waves, their tails cocked.

In flight dovekies resemble overgrown, pied bumblebees as they speed along low over the water, their stubby little wings reduced to a blur as they whir furiously up and down. Because their wing area is small in relation to their body weight, dovekies have to expend considerable effort to stay aloft. By skimming the water where the wind is slowed by friction with the waves, the birds have less work to do and save precious energy.

⊕ *The little dovekie makes a tasty snack for predatory seabirds like the glaucous gull, so the auks have to keep a wary eye on the sky. The gulls may even snatch breeding dovekies as they enter or leave their nest holes.*

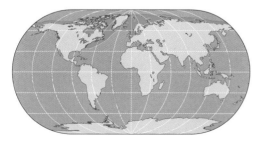

Plankton Haul

Dovekies are specialized feeders, since their diet and that of their chicks consists almost completely of swarming planktonic crustaceans, especially copepods, and the shrimplike amphipods and krill. A dovekie may dive from the surface to depths of 65 feet (20 m) or more to trap masses of prey in its bill. It uses its soft, flexible tongue to hold the plankton firmly against the roof of its mouth, which has many tiny, toothlike projections.

Arctic Colonies

The dovekie's stronghold is Greenland; the huge colonies in the Thule region of the northwest coast contain an estimated total of 10 million pairs. Another million pairs at least breed on the islands of Svalbard far to the north of Norway. There are smaller colonies on Jan Mayen Island, Bear Island, and off the north coast of Siberia on the islands of Novaya Zemlya, Severnaya Zemlya, and the New Siberian Islands. Small numbers also breed on Grimsey Island off Iceland and also on the other side of the world in the north Pacific, on islands in the Bering Sea between Siberia and Alaska.

Like penguins, dovekies establish their dense colonies in places where they can find relative safety from predators, notably Arctic foxes and glaucous gulls. They must also be reasonably near rich sources of food for themselves and their young. They find such sites along the edge of the arctic pack ice, where convection currents provide abundant nutrients to support their tiny prey.

A large dovekie colony can contain over a million birds. Huge flocks indulge in mass aerobatic performances before they return to their nests, which are hidden from predators beneath boulders. At such times dovekies demonstrate that they are more maneuverable in the air than the larger auks. They have a light, buoyant flight; and unlike their larger relatives, they often wheel and turn like flocks of sandpipers or other shorebirds, or even make steep dives. During courtship the pairs give their attractive trilling "songs" in chorus.

The single chick is covered in very warm, dense blackish down to keep out the arctic chill. Its parents are kept busy making journeys out to sea to satisfy its growing appetite. When they return, their throat pouches bulging with plankton, they deliver each meal in the form of a mucus-covered package that contains a mass of up to 600 tiny marine crustaceans. The chick grows fast on this diet, but it does not leave the colony until it is able to fly well.

Black Guillemot

Cepphus grylle

The handsome black plumage and white wing patches of the black guillemot make it quite unmistakable in summer; but after the breeding season is over, it molts these feathers and becomes pale and mottled.

Common name Black guillemot

Scientific name *Cepphus grylle*

Family Alcidae

Order Charadriiformes

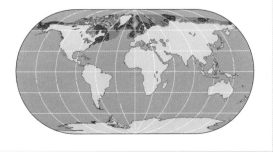

Size Length: 12–12.5 in (30–32 cm); wingspan: 20–23 in (51–58 cm); weight: 1–1.2 lb (0.45–0.5 kg)

Key features Breeding plumage wholly sooty-black with large white wing patches; retains white wing patches in nonbreeding (and juvenile) plumage, but has pale, dark-mottled upper parts and white underparts; bill black, but with bright red mouth; legs brilliant red

Habits Much less gregarious than typical auks; feeds underwater, making long dives to seabed

Nesting Nests among boulders on shore or in crevices usually low down in cliffs; usually 2 eggs; incubation 23–40 days; young fledge after 31–51 days; 1 brood

Voice Variety of shrill, high-pitched whistling and squeaking calls; sometimes trills during breeding season

Diet Mainly fish; also some marine invertebrates

Habitat Breeds along rocky and boulder-strewn shores; feeds only in shallow waters; winters near breeding areas except where ice prevents it in Arctic

Distribution Scattered around Arctic and north Atlantic coasts

Status Most populations fairly stable, but increases at some colonies and declines at others

UNLIKE MOST OTHER MEMBERS OF THE auk family, the black guillemot has two dramatically different plumages, being a mainly black bird in the breeding season and a mainly pale one for the rest of the year. Nonbreeding birds look pale gray above and white below. They are often mistaken for small grebes, although they have smaller heads and plumper, more rounded bodies. But before long a black guillemot will raise its forebody out of the water and flap its wings, revealing its distinctive, large white wing panels. They flicker when the bird takes to the air, emphasizing its fluttering flight style. At close range the brilliant red feet can be seen underwater as the bird swims or dives.

Underwater Search

Unlike most auks, black guillemots feed mainly on animals living on or near the seabed. For this reason they feed in relatively shallow, mostly coastal waters. Black guillemots do not dive deeply, but they submerge every seven to fifteen seconds or so and then travel up to 246 feet (75 m) over the seabed in dives lasting up to a minute.

In the southern parts of their range black guillemots eat many fish and their young, but they also catch a great variety of invertebrates such as crustaceans, marine worms, sponges, and jellyfish, particularly during the winter. In the Arctic they often feed along the edge of the pack ice, searching for food in cracks in the ice and even beneath stones. Birds breeding in the high Arctic catch more crustaceans to take back to the nest than other populations, which feed their young mainly on fish.

Arctic Refuges

Black guillemots breed mainly in the Arctic, on the coasts and islands of northeast Canada, Greenland, Iceland, Jan Mayen and other European arctic islands, northern Scandinavia, parts of Siberia, and Alaska. Smaller numbers are found further south on both sides of the Atlantic, extending as far as Maine in the northeastern U.S. and northern Britain and southern Ireland in Europe.

Many black guillemots breed on mainland coasts and larger islands that are also home to predatory mammals such as mink, ermine, rats, or feral cats. In such situations the birds usually choose crevices and caves in sheer cliffs that are inaccessible to their enemies. Along coasts where there are no such mammalian predators, guillemots use a wide variety of natural and artificial holes, nesting among boulders or scree slopes, under piles of driftwood or fish boxes, in abandoned rabbit burrows, holes in harbor walls, or even in buildings and nestboxes.

When the birds return to their breeding coasts, they spend a great deal of time in courtship and territorial displays. They include swimming across the water in straight lines or V-formations, uttering thin, high-pitched whistling, piping, or twittering calls. During courtship, and at other times when they want to signal to each other, black guillemots open their black bills to reveal their dramatically contrasting bright red mouths. After swimming for a while, the birds dive and chase each other underwater, when their equally bright red feet provide the visual signals.

The female lays her eggs right onto the surface of the rock crevice or other nest site, where they are incubated by both parents. When the young are ready to leave, they launch themselves from the breeding cliff or scramble across a rocky shore to reach the sea, even though they are still incapable of flight at this stage. In contrast to young murres and razorbills, they make this momentous journey without any help from a parent and lead a completely independent life from then on.

The black guillemots' scattered distribution helps reduce the impact of human threats, but locally the birds may suffer from predators that have been introduced to their island breeding sites, as well as from oil pollution and accidental drowning in fishing nets.

⊕ *Since black guillemots catch most of their prey on or near the seabed, they are able to feed alongside other auk species that fish nearer the surface without threatening their survival by competing for the same food supply.*

Common name Atlantic puffin

Scientific name Fratercula arctica

Family	Alcidae
Order	Charadriiformes

Size Length: 10–14 in (25.4–36 cm); wingspan: 18.5–25 in (47–63.5 cm); weight: 12–19 oz (340–539 g)

Key features Plump body; short wings with broad tips; neat black-and-white plumage; large white patch on head (grayish in winter); huge, triangular multicolored bill (duller in winter); bright orange legs (yellowish in winter)

Habits Feeds at sea by "flying" underwater to catch fish; breeds in colonies, often large and dense, defending nest area fiercely against rivals; usually solitary or in small, widely scattered groups in winter

Nesting Chamber, lined with grass and feathers, at end of a tunnel or in a crevice among rocks; 1 egg; incubation 36–45 days by both sexes; young fledge after 34–60 days; 1 brood

Voice Various growling calls at breeding colonies

Diet Mainly fish; adults also eat crustaceans and other marine invertebrates

Habitat Sea cliffs—on tops and terraces with low vegetation, in rock crevices, and among boulders; winters at sea

Distribution Coasts, islands, and open ocean throughout northern Atlantic, from Arctic to New England and Canary Islands

Status Despite many large breeding populations, fluctuations in numbers give cause for concern; threats include rats, foxes, and other predators at breeding colonies, overfishing, being caught in fishing nets, and oil pollution

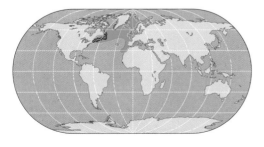

Atlantic Puffin   *Fratercula arctica*

With its dapper black-and-white plumage, brightly patterned, oversized bill, and clownlike face, the portly little Atlantic puffin is one of the most colorful and attractive of all seabirds.

FEW SEABIRDS ARE SO RECOGNIZABLE as the Atlantic puffin thanks to its dominating feature—its huge, gaudy near-triangular bill. The bill looks clumsy, but it is a versatile instrument with several functions. As well as being an efficient tool for catching fish, it makes an excellent implement for digging the birds' nest-burrows. It also serves as an important visual signal during courtship and other interactions, as do various decorations on its face and its bright orange legs.

At the end of the breeding season the puffin loses these bright beacons, having no more need for them. It sheds the multicolored, horny plates decorating its bill, which becomes smaller and much duller as a consequence. It also loses the small, blue-gray horny ornaments above and below its red-rimmed eyes. The crinkled egg-yellow "rosette" of skin at the base of its bill on each side fades to a dull cream, and the bird's legs become a duller yellowish color.

Juvenile puffins are easily distinguished from their parents. Their bills, although already deepening, are not nearly as large as those of the adults and much duller than those of a wintering adult. It takes five years for a youngster's bill to acquire its full adult glory.

Icelandic Stronghold

As its name suggests, the Atlantic puffin is restricted to the north Atlantic, although two other species of puffin are found in the north Pacific. On the western side of the ocean it breeds from northeast Canada south to Maine. Its breeding range extends east through Greenland and Iceland to the coasts and islands of Britain and Scandinavia, and across to

⊙ *Its bill stuffed with fish, an Atlantic puffin comes in to land at its crowded nesting colony. Its short wings make the puffin a rather clumsy, labored flyer, but they are well adapted for driving the bird along underwater when it is pursuing its prey.*

Full of Fish

The puffin's extraordinary bill is beautifully adapted for catching fish. Inside the upper mandible the roof of the mouth is lined with a series of sharp spines. Together with the bill's sharp edges, they afford the puffin a sharp grip on its slippery, struggling prey.

Normally a puffin swallows its catch of fish underwater one by one. During the breeding season, however, the structure of the bill allows it to carry more than one fish at a time to take back to its hungry chick. It minimizes the time the adult needs to forage. When it catches a fish, the puffin pushes it up with its strong tongue to clamp it securely onto the spines. The back of the tongue has a rough covering that ensures the prey cannot wriggle forward. It leaves room for the puffin to catch several more small fish, such as sand eels, and store them in its bill in a crosswise arrangement.

Puffins breeding at colonies in Britain regularly bring 12 or more fish back to their chicks in this fashion, although at some colonies in northern Norway many birds carry up to 40 tiny fish at a time. The world fish-carrying record is shared by a Scottish puffin, which managed to transport an amazing 61 sand eels, and a Norwegian bird that carried over 60 unidentified small fry.

western Russia. Over 90 percent of the world population, estimated at around six million breeding pairs, breed on European shores. Iceland is the core of its distribution, with two to three million pairs, while Norway (with about two million pairs) and the Faeroe Islands and Britain (each with about half a million pairs) are also important breeding sites.

After breeding, Atlantic puffins disperse from their nesting colonies and normally winter well out to sea, flying as far south as the waters off New Jersey, northwest Africa, and the western Mediterranean.

Seasonal Diet

Atlantic puffins feed mainly on small schooling fish such as sand eels, sprats, and capelin. The type of fish they catch depends on where the birds live. The diet varies seasonally and from year to year, reflecting changes in the relative abundance of different prey.

⊕ *With their enameled bills, clownlike faces, whirring wings, and bright webbed feet, Atlantic puffins are among the most popular of seabirds—both in the flesh and as symbols of wildlife conservation.*

Adults, especially those that winter in arctic regions, supplement their main diet of fish with planktonic crustaceans, marine worms, small squid, and other invertebrates. The real importance of these other animals in the diet of adult puffins is little known, since researchers can find out only by killing the birds to examine their stomach contents—something they are usually reluctant to do. It is known, however, that the adults feed their young almost entirely on fish, because the birds can be trapped in fine mist nets without causing them too much distress, enabling their catches of fish to be identified, measured, and weighed.

Borrowed Burrows

In the more temperate parts of their range, Atlantic puffins prefer to breed on places such as the grassy slopes above sea cliffs or on vegetated cliff terraces. They favor offshore islands. Birds that breed in the low Arctic nest mainly among boulders or rock crevices at the base of cliffs, while in the high Arctic they tend to choose higher sites, often in crevices on sheer, inaccessible cliffs.

Puffins sometimes take over the old burrows of rabbits or Manx shearwaters (*Puffinus puffinus*). They may even move into burrows that are in use, ousting their rightful owners. They seem adept at evicting rabbits, but they have less success with shearwaters— although slimmer and lighter than puffins, shearwaters have long, sharp-edged bills with viciously hooked tips that command respect.

More commonly, a pair will dig out their own burrow. Both male and female share in the task, hacking vigorously at the soil with their huge bills and kicking the spoil away behind them with their large, powerful webbed feet, whose sharp claws help in excavating the passage. They also use their bills to carry away clods of turf or small stones. This strenuous work usually takes a pair of puffins more than one breeding season to complete—up to three years is typical.

sometimes grab an adult puffin by the scruff of the neck as it leaves or enters its burrow. More often, however, a great black-backed gull will launch its attack in midair, since it is a greatly superior flyer. It usually seizes the puffin by the neck, then spirals down to the ground, striking its victim repeatedly on the back or chest with its bill until it has killed it.

Some gulls are adept at plucking puffin chicks from their burrows as they wait near the entrances for their parents to return with fish. Unwittingly, the chicks betray themselves to the gulls by their piercing hunger cries.

Heavy Weather

If a young puffin survives to fledge, it must make its first flight out to sea totally alone in the middle of the night to reduce the risk of being killed by a predator. It launches itself from the cliff top, splashes down on the waves, and swims and dives out to sea as fast as possible. By daybreak it may be several miles offshore. The adult puffins follow a few weeks later.

Many youngsters, and adults, too, may die due to savage weather out at sea. Most sink without trace, but sometimes large numbers are washed ashore in mass "wrecks." Severe storms can even blow the birds far inland. Many years ago one bewildered puffin was encountered by astonished passersby walking along the Strand, a bustling major road in the heart of London, England's capital city!

At breeding sites where the soil is deep and reasonably soft, the burrows may be several yards long. In locations where the soil is hard and compacted, or there is only a thin layer of topsoil above the bedrock, the burrows are usually much shorter. Sometimes the birds are forced to use a natural hollow among rocks or beneath boulders instead.

At the end of the tunnel the birds dig a nest chamber where the female lays her single egg in a scrape that is often insulated with a snug lining of dry grass and feathers.

Big puffin colonies can contain many tens of thousands of pairs. The maze of burrows, the trampling of countless webbed feet, and the huge amount of accumulated droppings cause significant and long-lasting alterations to the habitat. The whole area becomes a jumble of pits where the birds have dug out their burrows, alternating with hummocks where they have heaped the waste soil, adorned with a natural garden of thrift, sea campion, and other maritime wildflowers that flourish in the soil fertilized by the birds' droppings.

At their breeding colonies puffins are attacked by a variety of predatory birds, from gulls to peregrine falcons (*Falco peregrinus*). Great black-backed gulls (*Larus marinus*) are major predators of puffins, and on some islands such as St. Kilda off northwest Scotland, the gulls depend on killing puffins for their own survival. One of these big, powerful gulls will

An Atlantic puffin chick is a drab creature compared with its gaudy parent, but its dull upper parts and dark bill help conceal it from predators in the gloom of its nesting burrow.

Bill Wrestling

Puffin courtship involves bowing and billing—the ritual in which the two birds of a pair rapidly clatter their bills together, making a sound like the clicking of castanets. Disputes over burrows and mates may escalate from ritualized displays, such as opening their great bills to reveal their bright orange mouth linings, into real fighting. If it happens, the birds lock bills and twist them from side to side, and batter their opponents with their wings. The combatants may tumble down a slope, their bills locked together, and may even fall off the cliff edge before releasing their powerful grip.

Mourning Dove

Zenaida macroura

Common name	Mourning dove
Scientific name	*Zenaida macroura*
Family	Columbidae
Order	Columbiformes
Size	Length: 12 in (30 cm); wingspan: 18 in (46 cm); weight: 4.2 oz (120 g)
Key features	Small, slim dove with long, graduated tail; mostly soft brown, grayer toward head, with large button-shaped black spots on the wing; some tail feathers tipped black-and-white; red legs; sexes alike
Habits	Perches on wires, aerials, trees, and bushes; feeds mostly on ground; forms flocks in winter; male has spiraling aerial display
Nesting	February–October; flimsy-looking cup nest of sticks in a tree fork; 2 white eggs; incubation 14–15 days; young fledge after 12–14 days; regularly 3 broods, occasionally up to 6
Voice	A low mournful "oo-AAH coo coo coo"
Diet	Mostly seeds
Habitat	Highly adaptable, anywhere from cities and towns to dry scrub and semidesert
Distribution	North America as far north as southern Canada, and ranging south to Central America
Status	Widespread and often very common, despite large-scale hunting

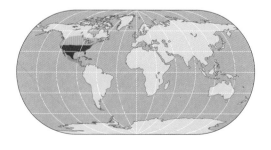

Fed by some, hunted by others, the mourning dove is one of North America's commonest birds. Originally from wild, arid places, it has adapted to all kinds of artificial habitats from farms to city centers.

THE AMERICAN MOURNING DOVE IS NAMED after its sad-sounding song: a series of gentle coos with a wistful, regretful tone. Its lamentations are a familiar sound throughout the farmlands and settlements of North America. It is an attractive bird, with the slender, slightly fragile look typical of small doves. Its plumage is unremarkably brownish-pink, with a few button-shaped black spots on its wings, but its tail is distinctive and unusual: long with a very sharp tip. The shape is described as graduated—broad at the base but gradually getting narrower toward the end. The edge of the tail is decorated with white spots, so that when the tail is spread, it looks like a necklace of pearls.

The mourning dove is so common in many North American cities that it is hard to believe that it was originally a bird of dry savanna and semidesert. It still occurs there and shows typical desert toughness. Mourning doves have been known to survive without water for four days and have been found incubating eggs in outside temperatures of 110° F (43° C). Birds that still live in the desert often nest in large cacti, using the plants' imposing thorns as protection for the nest. Although some need to commute long distances to find water at the beginning and end of the day, that does not prevent them thriving in such a harsh habitat.

Seed Specialists

Mourning doves are typical seed-eating members of the pigeon family. In fact, they have been recorded feeding on no fewer than 200 species of seeds even in one small area. Most of these seeds come from grasses that the

⊕ The mourning dove's nest is a slapdash affair, little more than a few sticks loosely woven into a flimsy platform; but in desert habitats it is often sited in a large cactus such as a saguaro, where the brood is protected by the plant's formidable defensive spines.

doves can pluck from the stems while they are feeding on the ground, as is their custom.

The seed-eating habits of mourning doves have caused problems ever since people began growing crops in North America. These adaptable doves can devour all sorts of wild and cultivated grain, including corn and wheat. In some areas they are a serious pest and are shot in enormous numbers. In fact, it has been estimated that in the course of any one year in the U.S. no fewer than 45 million mourning doves are shot for pest control or recreational hunting. The populations of many species would buckle under the strain of such a slaughter, yet the ever-resilient mourning dove somehow manages to survive and thrive.

Multiple Broods

One reason for the mourning dove's resilience lies in its high breeding potential. Although the female lays the characteristic pigeon clutch of two eggs, mourning doves have a very long breeding season. They often attempt at least three successive broods and occasionally up to

six. The high brood rate is more than any other North American bird, giving the mourning dove the ability to recover quickly from any setback.

The nest consists of a bare minimum of sticks interwoven to form a fragile-looking platform. The young are quickly "weaned," so although they depend on the adults' crop milk for their first three days of life, they are feeding entirely on seeds by the time they are a week or so old. With nest building typically taking just a single day, incubation taking 15 days, and the hatched young taking just 30 more days to achieve independence, the mourning dove "production line" is fast and efficient.

It seems, therefore, that the population of mourning doves is balanced, and those that are shot are quickly replaced. Yet there is no room for complacency, as the case of the passenger pigeon (*Ectopistes migratorius*) shows. Once North America's most abundant bird, with a population of up to 3 billion, the passenger pigeon was eliminated in fewer than 100 years, mainly by hunting. So no bird, not even the mourning dove, is ever completely safe.

Rock Dove

Columba livia

The feral pigeon is a familiar sight in cities throughout the world, yet in its original, wild form as the rock dove, this same bird is a shy inhabitant of remote cliffs and sheer rock faces.

Common name Rock dove (rock pigeon, feral pigeon, town pigeon)

Scientific name *Columba livia*

Family Columbidae

Order Columbiformes

Size Length: 12 in (30 cm); wingspan: 18 in (46 cm); weight: 9 oz (255 g)

Key features Medium-sized pigeon; wild-type birds dark gray on head and tail, paler on wings and lower body, with iridescent green and pink neck patch; feral-type birds very variable, often with checkered or reddish plumage; red eyes and coral-red legs; sexes alike

Habits Highly sociable; wild birds shy, swift-flying; feral birds tame; courting male displays on ground, bowing and ruffling head feathers; also has circular display flight

Nesting All year, in loose colonies; cup nest of stems, leaves, and roots, with no lining, on a ledge; 2 white eggs; incubation 16–19 days, by female only; young fledge after 35–37 days; usually 3 broods in wild

Voice Throaty coo with slight stammer

Diet Wild birds eat mostly grain; feral birds eat all kinds of scraps

Habitat Sea cliffs and inland rock faces; also towns and cities

Distribution Almost worldwide apart from the far north, but scarce in South America

Status Abundant

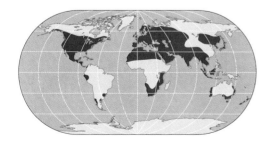

THIS IS THE BEST-KNOWN OF ALL pigeons; indeed, many people seem unaware that there are any other species at all. It is the pigeon of many colors and forms that you see in city centers, from Times Square in New York City to Trafalgar Square in London. It is a bird so far removed from any natural habitat that it seems to have abandoned any pretension of being a "true" species at all.

And yet this same species is still found in the wild, far from human dwellings. Under its correct name of rock dove it lives along sea cliffs and among inland mountains in Europe and Asia, nesting on rock faces and in caves. Many wild rock doves never come into contact with humans at all, and any that do are shy and wary. But they are the ancestors of all "feral" pigeons, from city scavengers to ornate fancy pigeons and prize-winning racing birds.

Fattened for Food

The beginning of the transformation from cliff dweller to city dweller took place between 5,000 and 10,000 years ago, when the rock dove became the first bird in history to be domesticated. The young birds (or squabs) were probably originally collected for meat and fattened in makeshift cages. From there it was a short step to keeping the adult birds in captivity and breeding squabs from them. In time this led to true domestication.

Two aspects of the rock dove's natural behavior helped the domestication process along: the birds' habit of building simple nests on ledges, and their diet of grain and other seeds. The first people to breed rock doves were probably grain-growing farmers, with plenty of food at their disposal.

⬇ *Feral pigeons have become a common sight in cities and parks all around the world and have spread into many wilder habitats. This flock is roosting in the trees of Jericho Park in Vancouver, Canada.*

From this point of domestication, over many centuries the paths of wild rock doves and domestic rock doves diverged, so that they even began to look different. Wild rock doves continued to nest in wild places (as they still do today), and they remained basically unchanged, keeping their stocky shape and gray plumage. But under the care of people the domesticated rock dove was transformed by selective breeding into many different forms and colors, with many different names, showing all kinds of different attributes. Today there are over 350 varieties of domestic pigeon, including fantail pigeons, white doves, pigeons with feathered feet and strange head adornments, and racing pigeons. Yet they are all the same species—just as there are many varieties of dog, of different shapes, colors, and attributes, which are all breeds or varieties of the same species.

Inevitably, during centuries of domestication many birds of different forms escaped from cages and pigeon lofts. Although some had the opportunity to rejoin the wild population, the majority did not. Instead, the escapees settled into a half-wild lifestyle, in which they lived in close association with people but were neither pets nor captives.

Homers and Racers

The homing ability of rock doves is extraordinary. In 1986 a pigeon called Charlie managed to find its way from the coast of France to a pigeon loft in Brazil. In so doing it crossed the Atlantic and traveled, in all, 4,715 miles (7,590 km). It is an extreme example of an innate ability that enables pigeons to fly from almost any point of release to their home loft with almost unerring accuracy. They do it quickly, too: A good racing pigeon can travel up to 600 miles (965 km) a day, flying at a steady 40 miles per hour (64 km/h).

But how do they find their way? The key to their success is being able to determine where they are in relation to their home loft. One way they do this is by sensing how the magnetic field of the release site differs from that at home. Substances sensitive to magnetic fields have been found in a pigeon's skull, and pigeons fitted with devices that affect magnetic fields lose their ability to home effectively. They also have an innate sense of the time of day; they can use it to compare the position of the sun at the release site with its position at home and fly in a direction that reduces the difference.

But perhaps the most surprising aspect of pigeon navigation relates to the birds' sense of smell. Research has shown that they use subtle smells carried on the breeze in short-distance orientation. Since the sense of smell is poorly developed in most birds, the discovery of this ability was very surprising.

⊖ *A courting male rock dove tries to win favors from a female by bowing and ruffling up his head and neck feathers, a display that has become a familiar sight in cities worldwide.*

Drinking

When pigeons drink, they suck up water, as people can. This is an unusual habit among birds, most of which scoop up billfulls of water and then lift their heads to allow the water to drain down their throats by gravity. Only a few other families of birds (such as mousebirds and waxbills) can match the ability of pigeons and doves to keep their bills immersed in the water for as long as they need to keep drinking.

Recent studies have shown that sucking is no more efficient than the more common sip-and-tilt method of drinking. It neither allows pigeons to drink more water at a time than other birds, nor does it enable them to drink more quickly. So why do they do it?

The answer lies in the nature of their water sources. For the sip-and-tilt method to work efficiently, a bird needs to drink at a reasonably substantial body of water, such as a stream or pool. Yet birds that suck up their water can utilize almost any water supply, including small temporary puddles and raindrops on leaves. The ability to use almost any water source gives pigeons and doves a competitive advantage in arid regions where large bodies of water are hard to find.

They exchanged rock ledges for the ledges of buildings and swapped the seeds of wild plants for farmyard grain or city scraps. With their many backgrounds and color varieties, these birds are the ones with which we are so familiar today. They are best described as "feral pigeons": domesticated pigeons that have escaped from captivity and are living wild.

Miraculous Navigators

The selective breeding of domesticated rock doves focuses on three special attributes of these birds: their ability to fly fast, their capacity for breeding quickly, and their extraordinary aptitude for finding their way back home when released from a far-off place. How this last talent was developed is a mystery, but it has led to pigeons being used as messengers and more recently in the pastime of pigeon racing. Some birds are faster flyers and better at homing (finding their way home) than others, and increasingly efficient navigators have been produced by selective breeding.

One of the extraordinary aspects about homing pigeons is that these miraculous navigators belong to a species that is essentially sedentary. Most town pigeons hardly move from one set of streets to another, while wild birds on rock faces barely range much further

⊕ *By sucking up water with its bill, rather than using the sip-and-tilt technique of most birds, a pigeon can drink from the smallest, most temporary water source.*

than a few dozen miles between their breeding and feeding sites. The migration of many species of birds is remarkable for its extent and precision, but in the pigeon it is remarkable for even existing.

Production Line

The rock dove's ability to breed fast was of special interest to those who nurtured them for food. Although the birds only ever lay two eggs at a time, brood can follow brood almost continuously throughout the year in wild rock doves. Nourished on the highly nutritious crop milk, the young grow quickly and can themselves begin breeding when only six months old.

Such inborn abilities are easily refined into the profitable production of squabs. Wild birds may rear six or eight squabs in one year, but specially bred varieties can produce between 12 and 22. At the same time, the age at which the birds can begin breeding has been reduced in domestic varieties to less than four months.

Pests and Heroes

Interbreeding with feral pigeons has made pure, wild-type rock doves relatively scarce except on remote coasts and mountain ranges. However, feral birds are so abundant in some cities that the authorities, and some citizens, regard them as pests. Yet their positive contribution to human history has been significant. During wartime life-or-death communications have been carried on the backs of homing pigeons as recently as during World War II (1939–45). Individual message-carrying pigeons have saved dozens of human lives and have even been awarded official military honors.

From cliff top to battleground, the rock dove has undergone a remarkable journey.

⊕ The "crop milk" produced by an adult pigeon is the only food taken by the nestling for its first few days of life. Rich in protein, it ensures that the chick grows unusually fast, enabling rock doves to rear several broods of young each year.

Greater Roadrunner
Geococcyx californianus

Common name Greater roadrunner

Scientific name *Geococcyx californianus*

Family	Cuculidae
Order	Cuculiformes

Size Length: 23 in (58 cm); wingspan: 22 in (56 cm); weight: 13 oz (369 g)

Key features Very long tail; long, powerful legs; long, thick bill; short, ragged crest that can be raised; blue-and-red patch of bare skin behind eye; plumage mostly streaky brown, straw-colored, with fewer streaks on belly

Habits Forages on ground; prefers to walk and run, rarely flies

Nesting Any time of year, depending on rains and range; nest of sticks in low tree, bush, or cactus, lined with leaves, feathers, dung, and snake skins; 2–6 eggs; incubation 17–18 days; young fledge after 17–25 days; 1–2 broods

Voice Series of low pitched "coo" notes descending in scale; also bill rattling

Diet Wide range of animal foods, from insects to small mammals and birds; a few seeds and fruits, such as prickly pear

Habitat Arid, open country

Distribution Southwestern U.S. and northern Mexico

Status Not threatened

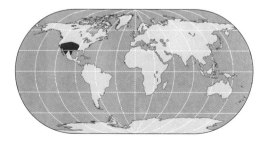

Perhaps best known as a cartoon character, the roadrunner lives in the deserts of the southern U.S. and Mexico. True to its name, it really does run along roads, but it is also famous as a fearless predator that kills and eats small rattlesnakes.

THERE IS NOT A SMALL creature in the deserts of the southwestern U.S. and Mexico that does not cower at the approach of a greater roadrunner. This highly modified cuckoo lives up to its name with its athletic behavior, and it is equipped with specially adapted long legs for speed. Using its long tail to help it steer, the roadrunner careers across the desert floor, a match for anything that tries to flee from its multipurpose bill. Nothing, not even the most fleet-footed lizards, can outrun it.

Its prey may fear the roadrunner, but many people see it differently, recognizing the perky creature immortalized in children's cartoons. It is relatively big and tame, and is popular among humans who share its desert home.

Desert Survivor

There is no doubt that the roadrunner is a highly effective survivor. It could not thrive in the desert without a range of adaptations, both behavioral and physiological, to the unique stresses of its environment: extreme heat by day, extreme cold by night, and constant aridity. It has several solutions to these problems.

Its adaptations to a lack of water include an ability to reabsorb liquid from its lower intestine and a system for removing water-sapping salt through its nasal glands. The bird rarely needs to drink because it obtains most of its liquid requirements from the body fluids of its prey. To combat extreme heat, it can cool itself down by evaporating water from its skin. It can pant like a dog, and it can expose the pale feathers below its wings to reflect heat.

⊕ The deserts of the Southwest are not the easiest places to make a living, but the greater roadrunner is adapted to make the best of its harsh habitat.

It can also lose heat through the blood vessels in the head. To combat the cold desert nights, the bird can reduce its body temperature to use less energy, then warm itself up again in the morning sun. It is the definitive, resourceful desert dweller.

Morning Patrol

A typical day starts when the birds bask in the morning sun. Having lowered their temperature overnight, they work to raise it again by ruffling their back feathers and drooping their wings to expose their black dorsal skin directly to the sun. The sun warms the skin like a solar panel, and the birds are soon ready to be active. By using the sun like this, roadrunners can save up to 60 percent of the energy they would need to heat themselves internally.

⊕ Although the greater roadrunner gets most of the water it needs from its food, it drinks when it can. Roadrunners are opportunists and always make the most of the available resources.

The morning is the best time to go on patrol in search of food before it becomes too hot. The roadrunner walks to a suitable hunting area, stopping to look around and maybe running after something that it has spotted before looking around again. It is also proficient at flushing out prey: Sometimes it will simply brush past an herb or bush and disturb something; at other times it will jump around and flap its wings.

When a roadrunner is running flat out, it can attain a speed of 18 miles per hour (29 km/h)—almost as fast as a human—but its stamina is far greater. When running fast, the roadrunner holds its head and tail in a straight line, horizontal to the ground to improve its streamlining. To cope with the uneven surface of the desert, its toes are mobile and flexible, so they can change in shape as the bird runs. It can also fly, although it seldom does.

A Varied Diet

The roadrunner eats an enormous variety of different animals, including venomous tarantulas, scorpions, and snakes. It regularly takes lizards, frogs, toads, small mammals (including young ground squirrels and rabbits), and all kinds of insects. Roadrunners even catch birds, snatching them in midair as they sweep low over a dry riverbed or visit favorite feeding sites on or near the ground. Hummingbirds drinking nectar from low-growing flowers are particular favorites. Adventurous roadrunners may also visit caves to pick up bats that have fallen from the ceiling. Ten percent of its diet also consists of fruit, such as prickly pear.

From time to time pairs of roadrunners cooperate in hunting, especially when faced with large snakes and other potentially dangerous animals. One bird distracts the prey, while the other strikes at the back of its head

Snake Dance

A rattlesnake is a formidable creature, but it is just another item on the roadrunner's menu. When a roadrunner encounters a rattler, it is an absorbing contest. If the roadrunner makes a mistake, the result will be fatal, so it has to move with extreme caution. The bird crouches, watching the snake intently, then it begins to circle around it. The snake follows it with its gaze. The roadrunner feigns a strike, then retreats, still circling. During the next few minutes the combatants follow each other's moves in a kind of gruesome dance—a dance to the death. But the battle is an uneven one, and before long the far more mobile roadrunner gets the chance it needs.

It dashes in and catches the snake by the back of its neck, effectively finishing the spectacle apart from the writhing of its victim. The rattlesnake now suffers the indignity of a slow death, being beaten against a hard surface for up to 15 minutes until it is unconscious. The beating breaks many of the bones in its body, making it easier for the roadrunner to swallow the snake whole.

The ability of the roadrunner to kill snakes has made it greatly respected among desert people, and several legends have grown up concerning its almost supernatural powers. One folklore tale suggests an alternative snake-catching scenario. Instead of killing it directly, the roadrunner finds a sleeping serpent and stealthily builds a ring of cactus around it. Woken up by a cactus thrown at it by the bird, the snake angrily begins crawling toward its tormentor, spearing itself to death on the corral of spines.

with its long, sharp bill. Once the victim is subdued, they beat it to death.

The roadrunner's long, sharp bill is a multipurpose tool, able to deal effectively with a wide range of prey from insects and mice to venomous rattlesnakes.

Mating for Life

Pairs of greater roadrunners live together in their own territory and probably mate for life. The male defends his borders each breeding season, using a low-pitched cooing like that of a dove or an owl, which carries for a great distance. If an intruder crosses into his territory, the male approaches with his head lowered, the bare red skin on his face fully exposed, his tail raised and wagging feverishly. This display is usually enough to drive away the stranger.

Nesting depends on the prevailing temperature and, especially, on the amount of recent rainfall. Stimulated by suitable conditions, the male begins to bring substantial food items—mainly mice, lizards, snakes, or small birds—as offerings for the female, helping her get into condition.

The pair begin building, but they are fickle househunters, happy with a site at one moment and uncertain the next; they have been known to abandon work just minutes after starting. It may be several days before they finally begin to put a few thorny twigs together. The male finds the materials, and the female assembles the nest, piling up sticks to make an open platform about 12 inches (30 cm) in diameter and up to 4 inches (10 cm) deep. The site is usually 3–10 feet (1–3 m) above ground in a bush or cactus clump, preferably in the shade. The nest is often lined with leaves, feathers, dung, and appropriately for a roadrunner, snake skins. Fussy as ever, they may continue adding bits to the nest even when the female is incubating.

In common with many species of birds adapted to a habitat with an unpredictable food supply, greater roadrunners leave several days between laying each egg, but start the incubation with the first. The result is that chicks hatch on different days, and some nestlings are as much as seven days older than others. Better at begging for food, the older chicks have the best chance of survival. The survival of younger chicks is a bonus. Sometimes the issue is settled by the nestlings themselves, the older chicks evicting the younger ones in an eerie reminder of their cuckoo heritage.

Growing Up

Nestling roadrunners are feisty survivors, like their parents. Their skin is black, so they can warm themselves effectively in the sun. If they are disturbed on the nest, they can expel a disgusting, smelly black liquid at any intruder. The adults also defend their offspring by performing several distraction techniques, such as making themselves obvious by running around and fanning their tails or pretending to have broken wings.

↑ This male has caught a lizard as a wedding gift for the female, but he will not present it to her until after they have mated.

Sometimes a disturbance can lead to young roadrunners leaving the nest early, although they usually fledge between 17 and 24 days. When they leave, the youngsters are only half as heavy as their parents and still greatly dependent on a constant provision of food.

Roadrunner Courtship

Roadrunners form long-term pair-bonds and live in a territory all year around, but that does not stop them from performing some entertaining courtship displays prior to breeding. The first sign of mating is a series of chases around the territory. Either bird can lead, and they may rush around in this way for hours. At intervals each bird may jump toward the other, spreading its wings and tail, then calling. The courtship becomes more serious when the stick presentation begins. In this display either bird will collect a stick and place it at the other's feet. It is an obvious prelude to nest building.

The "prance display" leads to copulation. At this time the two sexes have definite roles to play. The male approaches the female with a food offering in his bill. Wagging his tail, he runs back and forth, toward and away from the female, every so often lifting his wings. He may also wag his tail from side to side. After doing this for some time, he calls and jumps on the female's back, still holding the food offering, which she takes from the male following mating.

Over the next few days the young move further from the nest site, following their parents toward the best feeding areas. They learn how to catch food for themselves, and by 40 days old they are more or less independent.

If the weather has been good, the female parent is less generous with her time toward her fledglings because she is preparing to lay a second clutch of eggs. Then the male will take over the whole task of looking after the first brood. It is a demanding time for him because besides feeding his young he also has to provide for the female on the nest. Yet making two or even three nesting attempts is well worth the effort since ideal conditions are always at a premium in the desert.

Although losses from nests are high—73 percent in some cases—the greater roadrunner has a built-in capacity to withstand difficult circumstances. It has a stable population throughout most of its range, although in California it has been shown to disappear when its habitat is fragmented. For now this tough bird is doing well enough to be under no risk.

A roadrunner uses its long tail like a rudder to help it steer as it hurtles over the desert on its powerful legs. The bird rarely flies, although it can do so perfectly well if it needs to escape danger.

Sitting in Partnership

There is a very definite division of labor to be seen among parent roadrunners when they are incubating their clutch of eggs. The male takes the night shift, while the female incubates for two long sessions during the day.

There is a good reason for this arrangement. Once she has reached the incubation stage, a female roadrunner's energy reserves are depleted by the effort required to produce the eggs and build the nest. In contrast, the less stretched male should be in peak condition. When it comes to incubation, the night shift is by far the harder task, since the sitting bird must expend much energy in keeping the eggs adequately warm, but the fit male should be able to cope well.

Freed from this task, the female can get a proper rest at night. She can lower her body temperature and metabolic rate, and save some 36 percent of the energy she would normally use up. What food she has eaten can then be used in getting her body back into good condition and in better readiness for the tasks ahead.

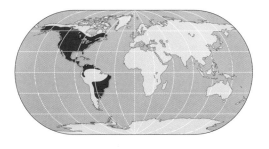

Common name Great horned owl

Scientific name Bubo virginianus

Family   Strigidae

Order   Strigiformes

Size Length: 17–24 in (43–61 cm); wingspan: 53–56 in (135–142 cm); weight: 1.6–5.5 lb (0.7–2.5 kg); female bigger than male; northern races biggest

Key features Large, powerful owl with big ear tufts; yellow eyes; very variable mottled gray-brown above, dark-barred below; pale or orange-buff facial disk and breast; desert races paler than forest races; sexes similar; juvenile duller, more orange, with shorter ear tufts

Habits   Hunts at twilight and night, usually from a perch

Nesting   Often uses old nest of crow or hawk, or tree hollow; 2–3 eggs, rarely up to 6; incubation 28–35 days; young fledge after 50–60 days; usually 1 brood

Voice   Male gives a series of booming hoots; other calls include screams, growls, and barks

Diet   Mainly small mammals and birds, plus carrion

Habitat   Anywhere with trees, from extensive forests to wooded farmland and suburban parks, even sparsely wooded semideserts and mountains

Distribution North and South America from Canadian conifer forests south to central Argentina

Status   Naturally scarce throughout range, but numbers fairly stable

Great Horned Owl

Bubo virginianus

The great horned owl is the night-flying equivalent of an eagle—a formidable hunter that swoops out of the dark to carry off animals as large as jack rabbits.

APART FROM THE SNOWY OWL of the arctic tundra, the largest hunters among the owls are the 18 species in the genus *Bubo*: the eagle owls. Found on every continent except Australia, they live up to their name by regularly killing animals far larger than they are able to swallow whole.

The American representative of the group is the great horned owl, which thrives in a huge range of habitats in North, Central, and South America. In the north it lives in the conifer forests that extend to the fringes of the Arctic and may occasionally stray onto the semifrozen tundra. Further south it ranges over the farmlands of the Midwest to the mountain forests of the Rockies and south into the deserts of Arizona, California, and Mexico. In South America it hunts both high in the Andes and down among the mangrove swamps bordering the Caribbean. The bird is extremely adaptable.

The great horned owl can exploit all these habitats because it will take such a wide variety of prey. It favors cottontails and jack rabbits but willingly eats all kinds of creatures, including porcupines, skunks, squirrels, voles, monkeys, crabs, beetles, spiders, and scorpions. Mammals account for about three-quarters of its prey, but it also takes birds up to the size of swans.

Variable Hunting Methods

The bird's hunting technique is tailored to the terrain. On open grassland it flies low over the ground, watching and listening. If there are trees, it hunts from a perch, often near a clearing that gives it room to maneuver. When it detects a victim, it swoops down in a steep dive, leveling out just above the ground to seize it with immensely powerful talons. The owl

⊕ *The female normally lays two eggs but may lay more, especially in the north. Like other owls, the female stays with the eggs and young while the male keeps the whole family supplied with food.*

swallows small prey whole but uses its bill to rip apart bigger victims, like a bird of prey. The owl may eat only part of the carcass, and in the far north individuals often store the surplus in frozen caches and then thaw it when needed by "incubating" it beneath their warm bodies.

A great horned owl needs a lot of food. It makes sure it gets it by driving other owls from its territory and even attacking day-flying hawks and falcons. It frequently catches and eats other species of owl, effectively dealing with two problems at once.

Nest Borrowers

Each pair usually occupies the same territory for many years, but not necessarily the same nest site. They often take over nests built high in the trees by day-flying raptors such as the red-tailed hawk (*Buteo jamaicensis*), but then they allow the hawks to reclaim their property the following season. They may also adopt disused heron nests in active heron colonies.

In years when large prey is easy to find, the male may bring too much to the nest, and it becomes littered with discarded fragments of meat. In lean years the last chicks to hatch usually die; and in northern and prairie regions

⬆ With its earlike feathers flattened against its head to improve aerodynamics, a great horned owl quarters the ground in the Northwest Territories, Canada.

where prey numbers regularly rise and fall, the numbers of great horned owls rise and fall, too. Most young first breed when three years old.

Legally Protected

Although the great horned owl is adaptable, it suffered from the destruction of temperate forest in the early years of U.S. colonization, and more recently it was persecuted because it took valuable game birds. Today it is legally protected, but large prey has become so scarce in many areas that the owls must feed on smaller animals such as voles, which affects their breeding success. In the wilder parts of their range, like the taiga forests of the north, great horned owls are still common, however.

179

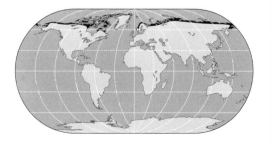

Common name Snowy owl

Scientific name *Nyctea scandiaca*

Family	Strigidae
Order	Strigiformes
Size	Length: 21–26 in (53.5–66 cm); wingspan: 56–65 in (142–165 cm); weight: 1.6–6.5 lb (0.7–2.9 kg); female bigger than male
Key features	Large and thickset, with massive, heavily feathered feet; golden-yellow eyes; male white with dark spots and bars; female has dark-brown bars; juvenile gray-brown with white face and brown-barred wings and tail
Habits	Nomadic; typically hunts from perch at dusk and dawn, but active all hours in daylight of arctic summer; winter activity uncertain
Nesting	Nests in shallow scrape on ground, usually on hummock, in northern summer; usually 3–9 eggs, rarely up to 14; incubation 31–33 days; young fledge after 43–50 days; 1 brood
Voice	Male has loud, booming territorial hoot; female has hooting, whistling, or mewing notes; alarm call a repeated, cackling "kre-kre-kre-kre"
Diet	Lemmings, voles; also rabbits, hares, game birds, wildfowl, occasional fish, and insects
Habitat	Mainly open, low tundra; also mountains and moorland, meadows, and saltmarsh
Distribution	Found throughout the arctic tundra zones of North America, Scandinavia, and Asia; often moves south in winter or if prey populations crash
Status	Scarce but widespread throughout range; numbers probably slightly reduced by some loss of wild habitat

Snowy Owl

Nyctea scandiaca

Adapted for life in one of the most desolate habitats on Earth, the snowy owl finds its prey where it can, often ranging far away from its breeding grounds on the arctic tundra.

BIG, POWERFUL, AND ALMOST PURE white apart from its glaring yellow eyes, an adult male snowy owl is one of the most strikingly beautiful of all hunting birds. It is like a white cat with wings, an impression reinforced by its habit of crouching with its breast on the ground. The female is bigger than the male and, uniquely for an owl, has different plumage. She has dark brown bars and spots contrasting with the white. Both sexes have broad white faces with thick feathering that almost hides their dark, hooked bills. They also have heavily feathered legs and toes, but that cannot conceal their long, wickedly sharp talons.

Life on the Arctic Edge

The dense feathering on the snowy owl's face and legs is insulation against the numbing cold of its home on the tundra—the bleak, treeless, half-frozen land that fringes the polar ice caps. Throughout the long, dark winter the tundra is shrouded in snow, and the ground is frozen solid. But for a few months each year the summer sun defrosts the top few inches of soil and melts the snow to reveal a swampy carpet of plants such as sedges, mosses, and saxifrage.

The whole landscape now bursts into life, with swarms of mosquitoes and other flies attracting vast breeding flocks of waders, wildfowl, and other migrant birds. The plants attract migrant reindeer and caribou in summer, but throughout the year they support small rodents called lemmings that feed beneath the blanketing snow, protected from the freezing wind. The lemmings are the staple prey of Arctic foxes, weasels, ermines, and snowy owls.

In the arctic summer the lemmings are forced to feed in the open, so they make easy targets for predators on the tundra. The snowy owl takes its share, hunting nonstop in the constant daylight to feed its hungry young. But in winter the lemmings are invisible as they forage in their runs under the snow, and they are much harder to find. The snowy owl's acute hearing helps in the task, since it can detect the lemmings' squeaking and scurrying beneath the snow cover. Hunting from a low perch, and homing in with the deadly precision perfected by owls the world over, the snowy owl punches through the snow with its powerful feet and seizes its prey.

Every four years or so lemmings multiply to plague proportions in summer and exhaust their food supply. Then they embark on reckless cross-country journeys in search of new food supplies. Snowy owls and other predators enjoy a feast at such times and raise unusually large numbers of young. But high lemming numbers are usually followed by population crashes, especially in the harsh winter months. By now the birds that breed in the arctic summer have flown south, so the lemming shortages mean that resident predators such as snowy owls have virtually nothing to eat.

Snowy owls are therefore forced to fly off to look for alternative prey. It happens so regularly that snowy owls have become accustomed to a nomadic lifestyle. They roam widely over the tundra searching for food; and if the hunting is particularly poor, they head south to the moorlands and pastures of regions like northern Europe and the U.S. The sudden irruptions (movements of birds in areas outside their usual range) are most frequent in North America because the large area of tundra in Arctic Canada and Alaska is home to many of the world's snowy owls. When lemmings are very hard to find, snowy owls may fly south as far as North Carolina, and strays have even been seen in Bermuda.

Normally these wanderers return north in spring to breed, along with the migrant wildfowl and waders. Even if lemmings are scarce in early summer, they breed so fast that

numbers soon build up, and the flocks of breeding birds provide plenty of alternative prey. Snowy owls also take ducks and even medium-sized geese, as well as willow grouse (*Lagopus lagopus*) and snowshoe hares.

⊕ *Thick feathers conceal the snowy owl's big, curved beak—a feature it shares with other owls.*

Ground Nesters

Since there are no trees on the tundra, the owls nest on the ground, although they try to select places that provide a good view over their hunting territories. The male defends the territory with deep hoots that may carry for 7 miles (11 km) or more, and in the perpetual daylight of the arctic summer he performs swooping display flights over the nest site. When he has attracted a female, he courts her with gifts of lemmings to demonstrate his hunting efficiency, since once the female has laid her eggs, she depends on the male to keep her fed while she incubates them. When the eggs hatch, she also needs him to deliver a steady supply of lemmings and other prey to the nest so she can feed the young.

Like the other birds nesting on the tundra, snowy owls must defend their brood against predators such as Arctic foxes. They may try to lure foxes away from the nest with distraction displays—sprawling on the ground

Camouflage

Most owls are superbly camouflaged—for their own protection. Small owls in particular are targets for raptors such as northern goshawks (*Accipiter gentilis*) and may even be killed by bigger relatives such as eagle owls (genus *Bubo*), so camouflage is vital for concealment on their daytime roosts. During the arctic winter the white plumage of a snowy owl performs the same role, concealing the bird from both its enemies and its prey on the snowbound tundra.

However, the tundra is not always snowbound. In milder regions the snow melts in summer, and then the male snowy owl in particular can be highly visible. This coincides with the owls' breeding period, and it is likely that the male uses his conspicuousness to attract females for mating in the same way that the males of many other birds use bright colors. Females, by contrast, have barred dark-brown markings, giving them a grayish appearance that helps them blend in with the rocks around the nest scrape and therefore conceal them from predators.

⬆ Female snowy owls, like the one above, have darker plumage than males. The coloration is an adaptation to help the nesting females remain concealed on the ground during the arctic summer when much of the snow temporarily melts.

and flopping around with wings spread, apparently injured and easy to catch. A fox is usually fooled by the hoax and follows the birds as they move away from the defenseless nestlings. At a safe distance from the nest the owls suddenly "recover" and fly off, leaving the fox with nothing.

Variable Numbers

The "boom-and-bust" natural economy of the tundra means that snowy owl numbers have always fluctuated wildly. The owls' nomadic habits also make them seem common one year and scarce the next regardless of the real situation. In fact, it is likely that the owls are losing ground slightly as the tundra is exploited for oil and other resources, but the region is such a vast and inhospitable wilderness—covering some 5 million square miles (13 million sq km)—that the snowy owl will probably always have a future there.

⊕ *A snowy owl adopts a threatening posture, sheltering the chicks beneath its body. Natural predators of snowy owls include Arctic foxes and other birds.*

Family Planning

Owls that live in the cold north often lay more eggs than owls that live in the tropics. The snowy owl may lay up to 14 eggs, while Pel's fishing owl (*Scotopelia peli*) of the African forests rarely lays more than two. Why?

Life is relatively easy in the tropical forests. There are no harsh winters, and local populations of adult owls stay fairly stable throughout the year. Most hunting territories remain occupied, and there are few new territories available to young owls. So if each pair raises just one or two chicks a year, the young birds stand a reasonable chance of inheriting territories and breeding in their turn.

In the Arctic life is very different. Scarce prey in winter may lead to the death of many adult snowy owls, yet in summer the explosive breeding of lemmings and other small animals creates a huge surplus of food. So the surviving adults can often raise large families, and the new chicks make up for the winter losses. The owls vary the number of eggs they lay depending on the prey supply: the more prey, the bigger the clutch. They also lay the eggs at two-day intervals and start incubating the first one right away. This means that the last chicks to hatch are the smallest. So if prey runs short, they get less food than the bigger chicks, die, and leave fewer mouths to feed.

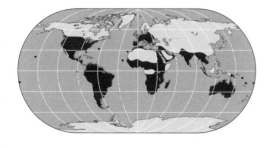

Common name Barn owl

Scientific name *Tyto alba*

Family	Tytonidae
Order	Strigiformes
Size	Length: 12–17 in (30.5–43 cm); wingspan: 33–37 in (84–95 cm); weight: 7–25 oz (198–709 g); female larger than male
Key features	Medium-sized owl; heart-shaped face; dark eyes; long, densely feathered legs; plumage very variable, typically golden-buff and gray with dark spots above, dark-spotted white to buff below; many races darker above, with orange-buff underparts; juveniles similar
Habits	Normally hunts alone at night, patrolling open ground with low, slow buoyant flight; also hunts from perch; occasionally active by day
Nesting	Typically uses hole in tree or cliff, ruin, or farm building, sometimes abandoned bird nest; usually 4–7 eggs, but up to 16; incubation 29–34 days, young fledge after 55–65 days; 1–2 broods, rarely 3
Voice	Shrill, eerie shriek; also snoring, wheezing, hissing, and yapping sounds at nest
Diet	Small mammals such as mice and voles; also small birds, reptiles, frogs, fish, and insects
Habitat	Favors farmland, grassland, or marshes; needs hollow trees, rock crevices, barns, or ruined buildings for nesting
Distribution	America south of Great Lakes, western Europe, Africa except Sahara Desert, southwest and southern Asia, Southeast Asia, and Australia
Status	Not globally threatened; declining in North America and Europe through pesticide use and loss of grassland habitat and nest sites

Barn Owl

Tyto alba

The spine-chilling shriek of the barn owl pierces the night over fields and pastures throughout much of the world, but it is becoming a rare sound in the intensively farmed landscapes of the West.

FOR MOST PEOPLE A BARN owl is a ghostly white vision caught in the car headlights. For a second or two it seems held in the glare, its black eyes framed by the pristine white of its heart-shaped face. Then it is gone, floating away over the fields and into the night.

A Special Owl

A barn owl has unusual anatomical features that indicate a different ancestry from most other owls. They include a heart-shaped facial disk, relatively small eyes, and curiously serrated middle claws. So zoologists classify it in a different family from the "typical owls," along with 11 more species of barn owl and the two bay owls (genus *Phodilus*) of Asia and Africa.

The eyes of a barn owl give a clue to its nature. Like most other owls, it hunts by night, often when there is very little light. The eyes of typical night-hunting owls are extremely large, enabling them to gather as much light as possible when flying in woodland. But the barn owl's eyes are smaller. Although they are sensitive enough to enable the bird to navigate over its preferred hunting grounds of open grassland, they are probably not so important for hunting, when the bird relies on its ears.

A barn owl has supersensitive ears. They are linked to a specialized array of nerve cells in its brain. Each cell responds to audible signals received from a small part of the bird's environment. The sounds are then mapped on the cell array to create a sonic image, just as light creates a visual image on the retina of the eye. Furthermore, one of the barn owl's ears is set higher on its head than the other, so it can locate sounds in the vertical as well as horizontal dimension. And since the movable

⊙ *A barn owl can locate the rustle of a mouse in absolute darkness, making an attack that is unerringly accurate. It makes the barn owl one of the most efficient night hunters on Earth and probably accounts for the way it has spread over much of the globe.*

⊙ *Barns and other farm buildings are favorite roosting and nesting sites for barn owls. Hay bales make comfortable and secure hiding places.*

Flying Hunter

Owls normally hunt from perches, but the barn owl habitually hunts on the wing. It flies slowly and silently a few feet above ground level, methodically quartering the terrain to check for prey. It may glide, hover, or sideslip, all the while keeping its face pointing down to pick up any telltale squeaks or rustles. When it locates something, it usually hovers and then swoops down in a glide, throwing its long legs forward to seize its victim with outspread talons.

In complete darkness the owl uses a slightly different tactic, plunging headfirst to keep the target directly aligned with its ears and only throwing its head back and swinging its feet forward at the last moment. This maneuver has only been studied using infrared imaging equipment because the owl employs it when it is far too dark for human observers to see.

A barn owl swallows nearly all its prey whole, even animals as large as rats. A roosting owl will sometimes sit for hours with the tail of a rat hanging from its mouth while the rest is in its stomach being digested. Eventually it ejects

flaps on its ears allow the owl to direct them toward sound sources, this may enable it to pinpoint distance as well, adding a third dimension. Other owls have similar abilities, but the barn owl seems to rely on them heavily.

Owl Pellets

Like most owls, the barn owl normally preys on small animals and swallows them whole. In the process it gulps down a lot of material that it cannot digest: fur, feathers, teeth, bones, claws, beaks, and the hard external skeletons of insects such as beetles. The owl's digestive system processes all the different prey items, digesting what is useful and getting rid of the rest. It does so by compressing the waste matter into a compacted lump enclosed in a feltlike mass of fur or feathers known as a pellet and ejecting it through the mouth. Birds of prey also eject pellets, but only to discard indigestible material that they have swallowed by mistake.

Many owls cast up their pellets at random, but some, like the barn owl, habitually produce them at their favored roosting sites. That enables a particular owl's pellets to be collected and taken apart to discover what the owl has been eating. In practice it is not as easy as it might seem because some bones are difficult to identify, and soft-bodied creatures like earthworms—which may be a significant part of an owl's diet—are almost completely digested. But by studying its pellets, zoologists now know more about the diet of the barn owl than that of any other hunting bird.

⊕ *A male barn owl brings a mouse to his young brood. As with other owl species, the male hunts for the family while the female guards the eggs and chicks.*

the skin and bones as a compact pellet. Barn owls generally use the same sheltered roosts for months or even years, and the pellets can accumulate in deep layers.

The roosts are often in church towers, abandoned buildings, or barns—the latter accounting for the owl's name. Originally the birds used hollow trees and similar cavities near areas of open country that suited their hunting style; but when people started clearing the landscape for farming, they provided more hunting opportunities for barn owls as well as warm, dry roosts in their farm buildings.

Providing accommodation was not entirely accidental. Barns were once used for storing grain, so they attracted vermin such as rats and mice. The barn owl is a very efficient rat catcher, with rats forming up to 60 percent of its diet by weight, so it makes a useful ally for the farmer. In some countries, such as the

Netherlands, farmers traditionally built their barns with special access doors for barn owls, which were only too eager to take up residence. The easy pickings on farms allow the owls to raise large families, so unusually the barn owl has actually benefited from the transformation of its natural habitat into farmland. It is another reason for the barn owl's worldwide success.

As well as rats and mice, barn owls also eat a lot of voles. These small rodents are related to lemmings and, like lemmings, voles periodically undergo population explosion cycles. When vole numbers increase, barn owl numbers also increase because the more voles there are, the more owl chicks each pair can feed. When the local vole population collapses, there are too many barn owls for the food available. Many owls starve, particularly in winter, but others become nomads. Nomadic birds are generally young adults with no territories of their own. They wander far and wide. Although many die of exhaustion, a few manage to claim territories, mate, and have young, spreading the species even further.

Quick Breeders

Barn owls can breed when less than a year old, the male courting the female with a variety of strange postures in the gloom of their chosen nest site. The nest is often in the same old building or hollow tree as the daytime roost used throughout the year, although nests have been recorded in unlikely places—including 33 feet (10 m) down an abandoned well.

The female usually lays about six eggs, but she may lay many more if prey is abundant. The first chicks to hatch get a head start on the others and are generally the first to feed when prey is brought to the nest. If there are plenty of voles, it makes little difference, because the eldest chicks cannot eat it all. But if prey becomes harder to find, the younger chicks go hungry and may starve. The female sometimes feed these casualties to the surviving chicks. It may seem like a callous act, but it can make the difference between raising at least one

chick or none at all. If all the chicks die, the birds often lay another clutch.

Barn owls normally manage to rear most of their chicks, and one pair in South Africa reared 12 chicks from a single nesting attempt. The ability to exploit abundant food has given the barn owl an advantage over some slower-breeding species, and over most of its range the species is flourishing. In North America and Europe it is doing less well, however, and in some areas it has declined steeply.

Declining Populations

One reason for the decline is the very feature that made the owl successful in the first place: its ability to exploit farmland and farm buildings. It served the bird well for 1,000 years or more, but the past 50 years have seen a revolution in agriculture. Machines have taken over from horses, and old-style mixed farming is far less common. Instead of being stored in barns and stacks, grain is swept off the field with combine harvesters and sealed in special rat-proof metal silos. As a result, the rough

Mobbing

Owls are secretive creatures. They mostly hunt by night and spend the day concealed in sheltered roosts. Barn owls in particular often hide from view in the shadowy recesses of old buildings, and most tree-roosting owls choose perches where their camouflage makes them virtually invisible. Despite trying to hide, roosting owls are frequently discovered by small birds. The birds may be part of the owl's regular prey; but instead of escaping while they can, they harass the owl by fluttering around it, calling excitedly. They do the same to perched birds of prey—even bird killers like the peregrine (Falco peregrinus)—and may pursue them through the air.

Such activity is known as "mobbing." Mobbing looks risky; but since most hunters rely on surprise, it is not as dangerous as it seems. Yet why do birds do it? Mobbing is most common in areas where the mobbing birds breed, so they may be trying to drive the predators away from their nesting sites. They may also be alerting others to danger or teaching young birds to recognize their enemy. Or they may simply be attempting to drive an intruder out of their territory.

Enemy Alien

Over most of the world barn owls are highly beneficial to humans. They kill vermin, particularly rats. In some areas where rats are a major problem the owls are encouraged to nest in specially provided nestboxes. This proved very successful in Malaysia in the late 1980s, when 200 nestboxes built on a rat-infested plantation attracted some 190 pairs of barn owls.

Yet sometimes the barn owl itself becomes a pest. In the 1950s it was introduced for rat control on the Seychelles, a group of islands in the Indian Ocean that had no native barn owls. The owls found the rats more elusive than the local birds, and within 12 years they had wiped out two populations of terns and were threatening the survival of other rare species such as the Seychelles kestrel (*Falco araea*). Now the barn owl itself is classed as vermin on the Seychelles.

pasture that the owls prefer to hunt over is becoming scarce, the places that they use as roosting and nesting sites are disappearing, and so is part of their food supply.

Rats and mice are also routinely controlled with poisons, but many farm rats have become resistant to standard rat poisons. So farmers now use chemicals that are up to 600 times more lethal. A barn owl can die after eating just a couple of mice poisoned with one of these substances. In the 1990s a chemical rat-control program in northeastern Australia also killed 80 percent of the local barn owl population.

Barn owls also suffered from poisoning by DDT and similar pesticides in the 1950s and 1960s, since these substances were widely used on farmland. When farmers stopped using DDT-type pesticides in North America and Europe in the 1970s, barn owl numbers recovered a little, but the other problems remain. Many barn owls also get killed colliding with cars while flying low across roads at night. After centuries of profitable partnership with humans it appears the barn owl no longer benefits in some places.

⊖ *The four well-grown barn owl chicks seen here still reflect the differences in size caused by the fact that the eggs are laid two or three days apart and hatch in order.*

Common name Whippoorwill

Scientific name *Caprimulgus vociferus*

Family	Caprimulgidae
Order	Caprimulgiformes

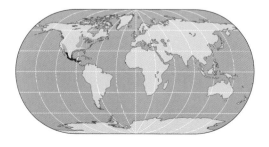

Size Length: 8.5–10.5 in (21.5–27 cm); wingspan: 18–19.5 in (46–49.5 cm); weight: 1.5–2.5 oz (43–71 g)

Key features Medium-sized nightjar with short legs; small bill; big, dark eyes; cryptic plumage grayish brown above; buff cheeks; underparts brown, spotted and barred pale gray-and-buff; male has pale-gray breast band and broad white tips to outer tail feathers; female has narrow buff tips; immature similar but with more buff

Habits Aerial insect hunter; active at night and twilight

Nesting On ground in clearing, in leaf litter, often beneath undergrowth; 1–2 eggs; incubation 19–21 days; young fledge after 15 days; often 2 broods

Voice Male gives repeated, whistling "whip, poor-will"; also short, sharp "quit" and variety of coos, chuckles, and hisses

Diet Mainly flying insects

Habitat Forest, woodland, suburban gardens, scrub

Distribution Central and southeastern Canada, central, eastern, and southwestern U.S., Mexico, and Central America south to Nicaragua

Status Common over much of range, but declining in eastern U.S. owing to loss of wild habitat, pesticide pollution, roadkill, and predation by domestic cats

Whippoorwill

Caprimulgus vociferus

Although well known for the way it repeats its name over and over again during the warm summer nights, the whippoorwill is an elusive hunter, usually seen as a flitting shadow as it pursues its insect prey through the dusk.

SUPERBLY CAMOUFLAGED TO THE POINT of virtual invisibility by day, yet relentlessly noisy by night, the whippoorwill can be a frustrating target for a birdwatcher. Like all nightjars, it spends most of the day asleep, either on the ground or perched with its body lying along a low branch, its cryptic plumage allowing it to sit in full view without being noticed. At dusk it stirs itself to hunt and often to call with apparently endless repetitions of the same three notes: "whip, poor-will…whip, poor-will…whip, poor-will…"

The whippoorwill winters in Central America, flying north in spring to the woods and forests of North America. Most nightjars choose more open habitats, but the whippoorwill is always found among the trees. It lives in all types of forest, although it favors oak or mixed oak and pine.

Insect Hunter

In typical nightjar fashion the whippoorwill preys mainly on flying insects, especially moths, pursuing them with great agility on near-silent wings and scooping them up in its gaping mouth. It often hunts from a perch at the edge of a forest clearing, launching itself in short sallies to intercept passing insects, flying low over the ground, and often returning to the same perch. Sometimes it may stay on the wing for quite a while, hawking back and forth over the same patch of ground. Occasionally, it pounces on beetles or worms on the ground.

Repeated Caller

As soon as males arrive in the north in spring, they start singing to claim breeding territories

① Large eyes enable the whippoorwill to see in low light conditions. Long bristles around the mouth help trap insect prey.

and attract females. A male whippoorwill may repeat his three-note call 100 times in succession and sometimes more; the record is 1,088 calls in a row, so the bird certainly earns its scientific name _vociferus_. The tone of the call varies from region to region: Eastern birds have a clear, warbling note, while southwestern whippoorwills sound more guttural.

Pairs nest on the ground among fallen leaves, often in the shelter of a rock or fallen tree. They display to each other by strutting with fanned tails, the male purring seductively to his mate while she responds with soft chuckling notes. Egg laying seems to be timed so that the eggs hatch toward full moon, allowing two weeks of easy hunting throughout much of the night to keep the chicks supplied with food. By then the young are almost ready

to fly, but it is another two weeks before they are ready to take off on their own.

Forest Recolonizers

For thousands of years the whippoorwill inhabited the vast, mixed forest extending from the prairies to the Atlantic and from the subtropical swamps of the Gulf coast to the southern fringes of Canada. Most of the forest was swept away during the eighteenth and nineteenth centuries; but when the colonists discovered the fertile lands to the west of the Ohio River, they abandoned much of the farmland on the stony Appalachian Mountains, allowing the forest to grow again. This means that in the eastern states at least, the whippoorwill can still find plenty of woodland where it can hunt and breed.

Ruby-Throated Hummingbird

Archilochus colubris

Perhaps the best-known hummingbird in North America, the tiny ruby-throat is remarkable for its long-distance migration, often traveling 1,000 miles (1,610 km) or more to reach its winter quarters.

Common name Ruby-throated hummingbird

Scientific name *Archilochus colubris*

Family	Trochilidae
Order	Apodiformes
Size	Length: 3.75 in (9.5 cm); wingspan: 4.5 in (11.5 cm); weight: 0.1 oz (2.8 g)

Key features Minute, with long, pointed wings typical of hummingbirds and making soft hum; short, forked tail with spiky tip; long, slender needlelike bill; small head and thin neck; plumage mainly iridescent green, with whitish underparts; male has glittering red throat

Habits	Active and pugnacious, usually seen hovering at flowers
Nesting	Cup nest of bud scales and lichen, bound with spider silk, usually on horizontal or downward inclining branch of deciduous tree; 2 white eggs; incubation 16 days by female; young fledge after 15–28 days; 1 brood
Voice	Male's song is high-pitched rattle; also "tsip" call during chases
Diet	Nectar and insects
Habitat	Deciduous and mixed woodland and gardens
Distribution	Eastern North America and Central America
Status	Common, but may be in decline

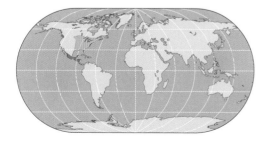

AT CERTAIN TIMES THE RUBY-THROATED hummingbird can look completely out of place on its northern breeding grounds, especially if caught by a late flurry of snow when it arrives in spring. But this pioneer among hummingbirds is a tough and resilient bird. It is one of the few hummingbird species to have ventured out of the tropics or subtropics to breed, and it is the only one that has conquered most of the eastern half of North America. By doing so, it has found a new opportunity unnoticed by its competitors and made the most of it. The ruby-throated hummingbird has a wide distribution and is probably one of the most numerous of all the hummingbirds.

The ruby-throated hummingbird is a small hummingbird, and by the standards of its relatives it is not very brightly colored. But the male does have a brilliant scarlet throat, which he shows off to advantage during display. The bird's tail is short and forked, and each tail feather has a spiky tip. Its bill is long, straight, and needle-thin for sipping nectar from inside narrow-throated flowers.

Possessive Owner

The ruby-throated hummingbird is a territorial species, defending a concentrated patch of nectar sources against competitors, including insects and other birds. When another hummingbird intrudes on its territory, a male ruby-throat attacks it unhesitatingly, driving it off using its claws and bill. Sometimes birds in combat hold onto each other and may even fall to the ground still locked together. Such fights

⊖ *Only the male ruby-throated hummingbird has the glittering red throat, which he shows off to a succession of females in a stylized aerial "pendulum" display.*

Taking a Break

When hummingbirds are feeding, they do not satisfy their hunger in one burst. Instead, they hover and feed in front of flowers for short bursts, then return to a perch for a "rest" before hovering again. Each feeding burst lasts less than a minute, and a hummingbird can manage about 15 bursts every hour. For the rest of the time it perches motionless.

Researchers have found the reason for this unusual feeding pattern. When hummingbirds drink nectar, the liquid passes immediately into a storage organ called the crop, from where it is transferred to the rest of the digestive system. But the crop only has a limited capacity. When a hummingbird feeds, its crop takes less than a minute to fill, but rather longer to empty. So a point is reached when the hummingbird cannot take in any more food until the crop has emptied some of its store of already-eaten food. That is when the hummingbird takes its rest. In fact, hummingbirds resume foraging when their crops are half-empty, not completely empty. This stage is reached after about four minutes into the resting period.

between rival birds look vicious, but they rarely result in any injury.

Red and orange flowers are the food sources most favored by the ruby-throat. They include the red blooms of columbine, trumpet creeper, and bee balm, and orange touch-me-not flowers. The bird also visits members of the horse chestnut tree family, especially the dwarf buckeye. The importance of a particular species in the diet varies from place to place. Studies have also shown that the ruby-throat exploits comparatively few native plants (only about 30) throughout North America. The bird visits more varieties in gardens, but for its general welfare it requires a comparatively small number of plants growing in abundance in the wild.

When the birds migrate north in spring, they are sometimes faced with a lack of available blossoms. It is then that they look for a most unusual resource for a hummingbird: tree sap. Rich in sugar, sap is nutritious enough to nourish them until things improve. To find it, they search the trees for holes drilled by a species of woodpecker: the yellow-bellied sapsucker (*Sphyrapicus varius*). It is likely that the northern distribution of the ruby-throated hummingbird is directly related to the activities and distribution of the yellow-bellied sapsucker.

Insects form yet another part of the ruby-throated hummingbird's diet. It captures most of them during short aerial chases, but it may also glean some from flowers. The importance of insects as food items varies, but it has been reported that they can account for up to 70 percent of a ruby-throated hummingbird's diet during the winter, apparently while suitable nectar is still available.

Aerial Displays

The males form the vanguard of the spring migration, arriving on the breeding grounds a week or so before any females. During this time the males settle disputes among themselves and set up territories. By the time the females arrive, the males have spread out and are ready to perform their impressive aerial display routines, each starting from his own set of perches.

When a male has attracted a female's attention, he displays before her in a swinging, side-to-side flight, whose course mimics the motion of a pendulum. At its height the male's flight arc takes him 10 feet (3 m) above the female and 6 feet (2 m) to the side of her. If this considerable effort pays off, more intimate displays follow, involving the male and female flying face-to-face. The birds eventually drop to the ground and mate.

Separate Roles

Once he has mated with a female, the male plays little further part in any of the breeding tasks except a little nest building. Having invested so much effort in obtaining a territory and refining his display, he puts most of his skills to use by trying to attract further females.

Meanwhile, the female sets about finding the materials to build a nest, including bud scales and other items for the main structure, lichens for the outside, and plant down for the

The Incredible Journey

It seems amazing that a bird as small as a hummingbird could make a journey of 1,000 miles (1,610 km) or more, but that is what ruby-throats routinely do on their migration between eastern North America and Central America every spring and fall. Even more surprising is the fact that, according to available evidence, at least some make a 620-mile (1,000-km) nonstop crossing of the Gulf of Mexico to get there. There are well-authenticated records of birds seen flying some 25 feet (7.6 m) above these waters far from land.

A ruby-throated hummingbird has to double its body weight before attempting to cross the gulf, or it will not have enough reserves to make the flight. Once it sets off, it must continue at a speed of some 25 miles per hour (40 km/h) to make the crossing in about 25 hours. It is an extraordinary feat.

nest lining. The nest is bound with cobwebs to ensure strength and flexibility.

The female follows the typical hummingbird pattern by laying two white eggs, one a day. She incubates them for a standard 16-day period, but the young may leave the nest any time between 15 and 28 days after hatching. The considerable variation is probably caused by fluctuating weather and food supplies. The female also feeds the young after they leave the nest, but for how long is uncertain. Much is still to be learned about this part of the ruby-throat's breeding cycle.

Very occasionally a female will attempt to nest twice, extending the breeding season until July or even August. But that is a gamble, since it will not be long before these tiny birds must embark on their long migration southward. The males, unfettered by the tasks of parenthood, take no such chances and leave early on their travels, well before the females and their young.

In recent years the ruby-throat appeared to be declining in many areas, leading to it being placed on the Blue List of birds of conservation concern. Yet the latest breeding surveys show no clear national change in population between 1966 and 1994. That is good news because it suggests that the future of one of the toughest and most resilient of hummingbirds is secure.

↑ *Nectar-rich feeding territories are vital to the survival of ruby-throated hummingbirds, and males in particular regularly fight each other for possession of suitable flowers.*

← *While a male ruby-throat concentrates on mating with as many females as possible, the female tries to maximize her breeding success by ensuring the survival of her young. She takes on most of the job alone, from building the nest to feeding the nestlings.*

Common name Belted kingfisher

Scientific name *Megaceryle alcyon*

Family   Alcedinidae

Order   Coraciiformes

Size Length: 11–13 in (28–33 cm); wingspan: 20–27 in (51–68 cm); weight: 4–6.3 oz (113–178 g)

Key features Thickset with large head and ragged crest; huge, daggerlike beak; gray with white underparts; both sexes have gray chest belt, but female has red band on belly

Habits   Spends most time perching, waiting for prey; dives into water for fish

Nesting   Digs tunnel holes in banks; usually 6–7 eggs; incubation 24 days; young fledge after 42 days; 1 brood

Voice   Loud, rattling calls given by both sexes

Diet   Mainly fish, but also opportunistic—feeding on amphibians, insects, small mammals, and birds

Habitat   Common around lakes, ponds, rivers, streams, and estuaries

Distribution Found throughout North America; also in Central America, Caribbean, and northern Colombia

Status   Not globally threatened; widespread and common in many areas

Belted Kingfisher

Megaceryle alcyon

Perched almost motionless for hours at a time on a branch overhanging water, the belted kingfisher gets its reward with a quick and usually successful dive when a fish swims past. Its efficiency in hunting, coupled with an ability to colonize almost any fish-supporting water, mean that this bird is common throughout North America.

THE BELTED KINGFISHER IS DEFINITELY a heavyweight in the kingfisher world. Its big, shaggy crest gives it a somewhat disreputable appearance. The bird's large head is set on top of a thick neck, and the body is bulky, too. Its legs are short, but thick and fairly powerful. However, the tail is a surprise in a bird of this shape—it is relatively thin, barred, and pointed.

At rest the male and female are easy to tell apart. Both have a gray head and upper parts and a white collar and belly; but while the male has a gray band across the breast, the female has, in addition, a thin red band just below that runs down the flanks. This is one of the few bird species in which the female is more colorful

↪ *A male belted kingfisher about to enter the nest hole. The breeding distribution of the bird seems to be limited only by the availability of nest sites. Birds become sexually mature in their first year.*

↓ *A pair of belted kingfishers in customary pose over water. The female, on the left, is distinguished by the red band of plumage just below her breast.*

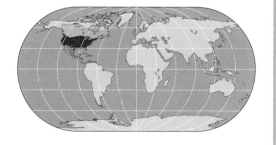

than the male. It is possible to differentiate juvenile birds, too; young of both sexes have a tawny brown-spotted band instead of gray, but the female also has, on either side, the first signs of the red band underneath that will eventually meet in the middle.

Wide Choice of Habitats

Belted kingfishers can take advantage of most waters. They are found everywhere from sea level to 6,560 feet (2,500 m) up in the Rockies; they live in mangrove swamps, fast mountain streams, large, slow rivers—they even fish in backyard ponds! They can hunt up to 0.6 miles (1 km) off the shores of lakes or the sea. Such an ability enables belted kingfishers to occupy far more coastal waters than if they were restricted to hunting from a perch. And in the dry, sandy riverbeds of Arizona they are adept at catching lizards and spiders.

Fishy Offerings

In spring the male establishes his territory along a river or around a lake. At the sight or sound of an intruder he raises his crest, rocks his body, and gives a loud, rattling call of warning. He chases rivals away; and once he has formed a pair

with a female, she will join him in harrying away intruders, too.

Courtship of the female involves the presentation of a fishy gift. The female flies into the male's territory; and when the male returns to his perch with a fish, the female flies up to him and sits on the same branch. They shuffle toward each other until they are close enough for the male to offer the fish. She takes it unhesitatingly and promptly swallows it.

Once the birds have mated, they indulge in an aerial display, with the female flying close behind the male as he flies up into the sky. Even after the female has returned to her perch, the male continues his aerobatics, spiraling high, plummeting down, and then banking into a glide.

A well-drained earth bank beside a river is an ideal nest site, but belted kingfishers are remarkably unfussy. They willingly use human-excavated road cuttings, banks in gravel, or sandpits. Even a beaver mud slide will do. The male pecks at the "cliff face," and the female responds by calling from a perch nearby.

How to Catch Fish

Kingfishers rely on good eyesight to spot their prey. Belted kingfishers have good color vision and can see near-ultraviolet light. This probably enables them to avoid glare on the surface of the water. They also need clear water for good visibility. If the water is muddy or turbulent after rain, they may leave the area altogether.

The bird has two hunting strategies. It usually perches on a branch over water and remains there motionless but for slight movements as it turns its head to focus on any fish moving around. It can be a long wait. One study found that belted kingfishers spent 98 percent of their time perching. Alternatively, birds hover over water, sometimes as much as 50 feet (15 m) above, beating their wings rapidly to maintain position. At the moment the bird dives, it pulls the wings into the body, making it streamlined. When the kingfisher hits the water, the wings spread out to act as a brake. Most fish are caught near the surface. If the bird goes underwater, it pulls down a transparent third eyelid to protect the eyes and improve visibility.

The prey is held firmly in the beak, but not swallowed, as the kingfisher flies back to its perch. Usually, the fish is still alive, so the kingfisher juggles it until it is holding the tail, then it smashes the fish's head repeatedly against its perch. Not only does this stun or kill the fish, but it also breaks the bones and protective scales that might otherwise harm the kingfisher when it swallows the prey. Having done this, the kingfisher eats the fish headfirst.

⬅ A belted kingfisher and prey. The kingfisher aims to catch the fish about a third of the way down its body before returning to a perch to eat it.

Eventually she helps with the digging, although the male does about twice as much work. The bill is used like a pickax; and once they start excavating the tunnel, they use their feet to kick out the soil behind them. They dig a tunnel over 3 feet (1 m) long, with a lip in front of the egg chamber to keep the eggs from rolling out.

The nest is usually about 1 foot (0.3 m) from the top of the bank. That reduces the threat of flooding and lessens the risk of the young being taken by predators such as skunks. The pair take turns incubating the eggs, which are pure white, like those of all kingfishers. There is very little light in the nest chamber, and white eggs are easier to see and therefore less likely to get stepped on. The adults need to fish almost continuously once the eggs hatch, for in time the young will need up to ten fish a day.

After 20 days the young have developed all their adult feathers and reached their adult body weight. For the next three or four days their parents feed them less and less. Eventually the adults sit outside the nest with fish in their beaks, calling the young to leave the nest.

At first the adults teach them to catch food by dropping dead fish onto the surface of the water. Within a week the young have learned to catch their first fish, although their parents continue to feed them for a couple of weeks.

Heading for the sun

In the fall millions of kingfishers from Alaska, Canada, and the northern U.S. escape the freezing winter by flying south to the warmer lands of Texas, Florida, and other U.S. states, and further still to Central America and the West Indies. Migrating kingfishers move from wetland to wetland, so it is not unusual to see large numbers along the shores of big lakes and along the ocean seaboards. On Lake Michigan alone, 12 kingfishers per hour have been counted heading south in the fall.

Kingfishers and Humans

The modern world has treated the belted kingfisher comparatively well. The persecution the birds faced at fish farms in the early twentieth century has virtually disappeared, partly as a result of protective legislation and partly because scientific evidence has shown that the birds caused much smaller losses of fish than originally thought. The risks to kingfishers from water pollution are largely unknown, however. A study of industrial chemical pollution in Wisconsin found that kingfishers were building up high levels of toxins in their bodies, but the results were inconclusive as to whether the birds were adversely affected. The excavation of sand and gravel for the construction industry has affected kingfishers significantly, however. It has resulted in a proliferation of lakes that have boosted kingfishers in terms of both range and population.

⬇ As the kingfishers approach fledging, the parents leave food at the entrance hole. The young race down the tunnel to be first to the feast.

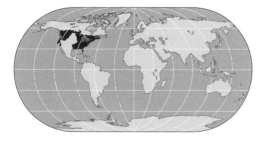

Pileated Woodpecker

Dryocopus pileatus

One of the biggest and most spectacular of its family, the pileated woodpecker is a much admired, successful bird that has extended its habitat from its stronghold in mature old-growth forests to parks and even suburban gardens.

Common name Pileated woodpecker

Scientific name *Dryocopus pileatus*

Family	Picidae
Order	Piciformes
Size	Length: 16–19 in (41–48 cm); wingspan: 16.5–18 in (42–46 cm); weight: 8.8–12 oz (249–340 g)
Key features	Big, long-billed woodpecker; black plumage with white streaks along head and neck; red crown with crest; female has black forehead, male has red forehead and red "mustache" stripe; juvenile browner, with paler crown
Habits	Largely solitary; feeds both in trees and on ground; not particularly shy around people
Nesting	Excavates hole in large tree at a height of 20–40 ft (6–12 m); 2–4 eggs; incubation 18 days; young fledge after 26–28 days; 1 brood
Voice	Loud "wuk" or "cac," either singly or repeated; drums with two-second rolls once or twice a minute
Diet	Invertebrates, especially ants; also nuts, fruits, and berries
Habitat	Old-growth forests and woodlands with large, old trees; also some secondary woodlands and town parks with older trees
Distribution	From British Columbia across southern Canada and through eastern U.S. to Florida
Status	Increasing in east of range

INSTANTLY RECOGNIZABLE BOTH BY ITS size and its bold black, red, and white coloration, the pileated woodpecker makes a dramatic sight. Both sexes have a crest of red feathers that can be erected to a point ("pileated" simply means "crested"), but a male can be distinguished from a female by his red "mustache." Young birds are browner than adults and have a hint of orange in their crest. The adult's call is a distinctive, loud staccato note, often repeated. It carefully selects a resonant piece of dead timber to hammer with its bill, producing rolls of drumming that carry a long way across the forest. Sadly, the only species with which the pileated woodpecker could be confused was the ivory-billed woodpecker (*Campephilus principalis*), which is now feared extinct.

⊖ Although well equipped for hacking wood-boring insect grubs from their tunnels, the pileated woodpecker also takes a lot of its prey from the ground, especially ants such as the big, heavy-jawed carpenter ant.

Essential Trees

The pileated woodpecker has a large range across southern Canada and down through the eastern U.S. Throughout this range the woodpeckers mainly inhabit old-growth forests and woodlands where large old trees provide a great many opportunities for roosting and nesting. They may nest in "second growth" woodlands or even in town parks, but older trees are essential. Within these places the birds often favor areas near rivers or other bodies of water.

Like all the larger woodpeckers, the pileated woodpecker uses its feet, legs, and tail to support itself on the trunks of trees as it hammers at the timber. In one of the various woodpecker "design variations" all four of its toes can point forward; that allows the lower part of its leg—the tarsus—to sit on the timber and help grip the surface. In smaller woodpeckers one or two toes point backward, preventing the bird from using the tarsus to provide grip. The bird uses its tail for extra support, wedging its strengthened tail feathers into the bark when it is at rest.

Chiseling for a Meal

Like many of its relatives, the pileated woodpecker eats a lot of ants. It is particularly fond of carpenter ants. It also preys on the larvae of wood-boring beetles, exposing them by persistently chiseling away at the timber. It eats caterpillars and termites when available. When invertebrates are less plentiful during the cold winter months, the woodpecker increases the proportion of nuts, berries, and seeds in its diet. And like its relatives in other parts of the world, it may be attracted to gardens by bird foods containing suet.

A Great Excavator

Pairs hold territory year-round; but as the nesting season approaches in mid to late winter, the territorial and pair displays begin in earnest. Each pair indicates the boundaries of their territory by calling and drumming. Meanwhile, they display to each other with ritualized movements, including mutual head swinging, bobbing, and raising their red crests. They accompany these displays with exaggerated flights that show off their white wing patches. All of this helps establish a strong pair-bond.

Work on nest construction begins once the pair are established. In most cases a new nest is constructed each year, probably because the construction process is integral to maintaining the pair-bond. In over half the cases the chosen tree will be dead or dying. Obviously, the timber of a dead tree is weakened and easier to hack away, so the birds save energy in excavation. Even when an apparently healthy tree is chosen, it may have been weakened internally through the action of fungi. There has been speculation that with many woodpecker species abortive excavation attempts in hard live wood actually initiate attacks by fungus that are later utilized by other woodpeckers.

The nest hole itself is often at some height above the forest floor. Both sexes share the work of excavation, but the male does more work than the female. The job itself starts with the birds chiseling a conical entrance hole running horizontally into the tree trunk. Chiseling can last for several minutes without a break, apart from pauses while the birds fling wood shavings away from the nest site. As the

⊖ *The bright red crest of the pileated woodpecker forms part of a colorful pair-bonding display in the breeding season. This bird's red "mustache" stripe indicates that it is a male.*

Woody Woodpecker

Perhaps the most famous woodpecker—and one that shares the pileated woodpecker's proud red crest—is the mischievous cartoon character Woody Woodpecker. A hit for Universal, Woody was created by Walter Lantz in the early 1940s and first appeared in an Andy Panda cartoon called *Knock, Knock*. Lantz declared that the inspiration for Woody came to him when on honeymoon. He and his new wife were both irritated and amused by a woodpecker that regularly visited and drummed on the wooden cabin in which they were staying. But amusement and irritation turned to frustration when, after a storm, they discovered rain pouring in through the freshly excavated holes in the walls!

hole gets deeper, the birds start to dig down to create a vertical nest chamber.

At first, the birds perch outside while excavating; but as the job progresses, they disappear inside the tree. The only signs of their presence are occasional puffs of shavings from the entrance hole. When completed, the nest cavity can measure up to 26 inches (66 cm)

⊖ *As the woodpeckers excavate their nest chamber, they toss the wood chippings out of the entrance hole.*

Best Foot Forward

Nearly all birds have four toes, but they are arranged in a variety of ways and have evolved into numerous shapes to help the bird make the most of its habitat and lifestyle.

By far the most common layout is three toes to the front and one—the "hallux"—to the rear. This standard arrangement is called "anisodactyl." In many waterbirds the three forward-pointing toes have developed webbing or lobes to help movement in water. Birds of prey have developed sharp, powerful talons, and the feet of the osprey (*Pandion haliaetus*) have evolved special barbed nodes to help grip slippery fish. In the passerines, or "perching birds," the arrangement of tendons in the feet provides an automatic grip when the bird perches on a branch.

A slight variation on the anisodactyl arrangement has two of the forward toes fused together. It is called "syndactyl" and is typical of the rollers and their allies in the order Coraciiformes.

A different arrangement has two toes to the front and two to the rear. Called "zygodactyl," this layout has developed independently in birds such as the cuckoos, parrots, and in some woodpeckers. In the trogons the position of the fourth toe is slightly different and is called "heterodactyl."

Last, some groups, such as the African mousebirds, have "pamprodactyl" feet in which the hallux and fourth toe can be placed either forward or backward.

⊕ *Different types of bird feet: anisodactyl foot of a perching bird (1); webbed foot of a typical waterbird (2); powerful, strong-clawed talon of a bird of prey (3); zygodactyl foot of a small woodpecker (4).*

deep and 6.5 inches (16.5 cm) across. The last of the shavings are left to line the base of the nest chamber. Here they provide a soft surface for nesting and a suitable medium to soak up waste material from the chicks. The whole construction process takes around 25 days.

Buzzing Youngsters

Once the nest is complete, the female lays her clutch of white, almost translucent eggs. One egg is laid each day until the clutch is complete, but incubation may start before the final egg is produced. Both sexes share incubation duties; but as with nest construction, the male is in attendance more than the female and always incubates at night. During this sensitive period at least one bird attends 99 percent of the time. As is the case with other woodpeckers, the incubation period is relatively short, and the young appear after some 18 days. At first, they are blind, naked, and completely helpless.

For the first seven to ten days both parents brood the offspring, the male again doing more work than the female. Indeed, the male's role is vital. In a couple of observed cases the death of the male led to the female abandoning the nest, while on the death of a female the male continued to raise his offspring.

When in the nest, the young are fed a diet consisting mainly of insects and other small invertebrates. Food is regurgitated on demand, the young birds taking turns to receive the food directly from their parents' bills. Initially food is brought at least hourly; but as the chicks grow, the parents visit once every two hours.

At first, the newly hatched chicks can do very little apart from call for their food. These calls have been described as sounding like a "buzzing beehive." As the young grow, their confidence develops, and they begin to scale the walls of their nest chamber. By 15 to 18 days they are able to reach the nest entrance, where they wait for their parents to return.

Between 24 and 30 days they leave their nests, but their first flights are short and rather speculative. Initially, they remain within easy reach of their natal home, only gradually exploring new areas. As their confidence develops, they accompany their parents around the forest on feeding flights and remain together in family flocks. But with the onset of winter the family group splits up. By the following spring the first-year birds are able to nest themselves and begin to set up territories.

Doing Well

Pileated woodpeckers suffered quite a range contraction in the face of extensive logging in the nineteenth and early twentieth centuries. However, they have recovered and are not of global conservation concern. In the east of their range their population is actually increasing.

⊕ When they are old enough to climb up to the nest entrance, the young woodpeckers perch there and wait for their parents to return with food.

Yellow-Throated Vireo

Vireo flavifrons

Unusually confiding in the presence of people, this green-and-yellow vireo is often to be seen foraging in leafy treetops in suburban residential areas and even in town centers.

NEAT, BRIGHT, AND CLEAN-CUT, THE yellow-throated vireo is one of the most attractive birds in its family. It has a short, thick, slightly hooked bill, with a yellow line extending back from the bill to join a yellow eye ring in a striking spectacle pattern. Its throat and breast are clear yellow, but its flanks are grayer and its belly white. The crown and back are olive-green, and the grayish and black wings have two white bars. The rump is gray, giving way to a dark tail with pale sides.

Summer Visitor

From southern Manitoba and Minnesota east to Maine, the range of the yellow-throated vireo extends south to eastern Texas and east to Florida, encompassing roughly all of the eastern half of the U.S. A few winter on the Gulf coast, but most migrate to the Bahamas, Central Mexico, Venezuela, and Colombia. Most arrivals in the U.S. appear in the second half of May, and they leave in August and September.

It is a bird of deciduous woodland in summer, preferring tall woods and mature oaks and maples beside streams or along roadsides, or even in towns. It avoids woods with dense undergrowth and is not found in mixed or coniferous woods, where it is replaced by the solitary vireo (*Vireo solitarius*). It often frequents orchards close to farms. In winter it occupies rain forest and scrub in lowlands and foothills.

Canopy Feeder

Although the yellow-throated is a rather colorful vireo, it is still secretive and hard to see, especially since it usually feeds well up in the leafy canopy of tall trees. Nevertheless, the male

⊙ *Although a colorful vireo, the yellow-throated vireo can be elusive as it feeds high in the trees. The male sings persistently and loudly, however, and he often betrays his location.*

Common name Yellow-throated vireo

Scientific name *Vireo flavifrons*

Family Vireonidae

Order Passeriformes

Size Length: 4.5 in (11.4 cm); wingspan: 8.5–9.5 in (21.6–24 cm); weight: 0.5–0.7 oz (14–19.8 g)

Key features Thick-billed vireo with a yellow eye ring; green upper parts; gray rump; two white wingbars; yellow breast; sexes alike

Habits Quiet and tame; gleans insects from foliage of tall trees

Nesting Shallow cup nest, built high in tree; 3–5 eggs; incubation 14–15 days by both adults; young fledge after 14–15 days; 1–2 broods

Voice Slowly repeated song of harsh two- or three-note phrase: "come here" or "de-ar-ie"

Diet Insects and berries

Habitat Forests of oak and other tall, leafy deciduous trees

Distribution Eastern U.S. and southern Canada; also from Bahamas and Mexico south to Venezuela and Colombia

Status Stable overall, but local declines in northeast of range

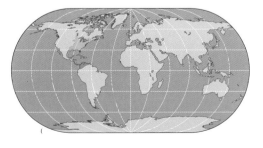

sings right through the summer until August or September, and the loud, rich song is a familiar sound in its breeding areas.

The bird has the usual vireo foraging action—moving slowly and carefully through the leaves with occasional heavy jumps, interspersed with long periods of inactivity. It eats mainly insects in summer, with more than a third of its diet consisting of caterpillars, moths, and butterflies. Various bugs, beetles, sawflies, and cicadas make up the rest. At other times it supplements its insect food with berries.

Beautiful Nest

The nest is from 3 to 66 feet (1–20 m) above ground, built around a horizontal fork in typical vireo fashion, with the cup slung beneath and the rim woven around the twigs with cobwebs and fibrous plant material. The birds then add cobwebs, lichens, and mosses to the outside to help camouflage the structure. It takes about a week to build. The nest is said to be one of the most beautiful of all eastern U.S birds.

Both parents incubate the eggs, and the male may sing from the nest while taking his shift. When the chicks are ready to fly, each parent cares for half of the brood until they become independent. They often move a little way from the nesting territory as family groups, feeding eagerly on berries until they migrate.

Cowbirds (*Molothrus* species) often parasitize the nests, and the vireos readily rear cowbird chicks instead of their own. The activity may have affected vireo numbers in some areas, and loss of winter habitat and climate change could also pose long-term threats.

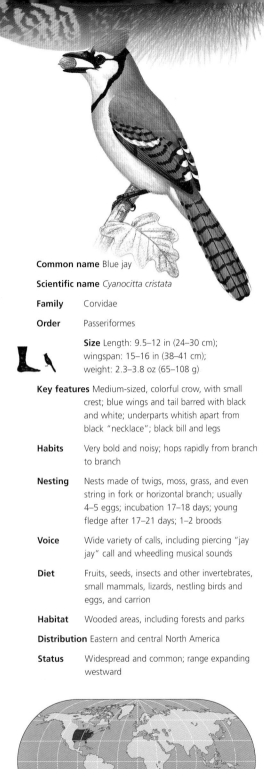

Blue Jay

Cyanocitta cristata

It is hard to ignore a noisy, confident neighbor, and the vociferous character and audacious habits of the blue jay have earned it an almost iconic status in its native North America.

EVEN THOUGH IT IS ABSENT from the western side of the continent, the blue jay is known throughout North America. Its appearance is certainly memorable. It is strikingly light blue on the top of its head, its wings, back, and tail, with a blue crest at the back of its head. A black eyeline runs into a thick "necklace" that loops around its upper breast. There are fine black bars on its wings, as well as white patches that are highly visible in flight, and it has a long, black-barred tail. It has a voice to match its vivid colors, with an extensive vocabulary ranging from piercing calls to musical whistles.

Essentially, it is a bird of the woodland edge rather than deep forest. In Illinois, for example, its population is higher in towns than in the forests outside. Human settlements offer an attractive alternative to the forests, provided there are enough nut-producing trees available.

⊕ In winter blue jays rely heavily on nuts and seeds, and they are quick to visit garden bird feeders to gather what they can. Out in the forests they survive by making food caches to see them through the winter.

Common name Blue jay

Scientific name *Cyanocitta cristata*

Family Corvidae

Order Passeriformes

Size Length: 9.5–12 in (24–30 cm); wingspan: 15–16 in (38–41 cm); weight: 2.3–3.8 oz (65–108 g)

Key features Medium-sized, colorful crow, with small crest; blue wings and tail barred with black and white; underparts whitish apart from black "necklace"; black bill and legs

Habits Very bold and noisy; hops rapidly from branch to branch

Nesting Nests made of twigs, moss, grass, and even string in fork or horizontal branch; usually 4–5 eggs; incubation 17–18 days; young fledge after 17–21 days; 1–2 broods

Voice Wide variety of calls, including piercing "jay jay" call and wheedling musical sounds

Diet Fruits, seeds, insects and other invertebrates, small mammals, lizards, nestling birds and eggs, and carrion

Habitat Wooded areas, including forests and parks

Distribution Eastern and central North America

Status Widespread and common; range expanding westward

In late summer and fall the annual berry crop provides a feast for blue jays intent on building up their energy reserves before winter closes in.

There are a wide variety of backyard microhabitats in town, with many offering bird feeders, potential nesting material, and open areas for hiding supplies of food. Blue jays have learned to thrive in close proximity to humans.

Only a very small proportion of blue jays migrate, and those that do tend to be birds spending the summer in northern states of the U.S. and Canada. Many jays are resident even in northernmost areas. The travelers seek company, with day-flying flocks of 20–30 birds flying in a southerly or southwesterly direction.

Exaggerated Notoriety

A painting by the famous nineteenth-century naturalist Audubon shows three jays stealing the eggs from another bird's nest. In reality its reputation as a nest raider is greatly exaggerated, for the eggs and young of other birds make up only a tiny part of its diet. Fruit, insects, and other invertebrates are much more important, and the birds regularly take rodents and carrion, as well as scavenging scraps. But the blue jay is primarily a seed-eater, favoring the nuts of oak, beech, chestnut, hickory, and

⟲ *The jaunty crest, colorful plumage, and bold character of the blue jay have made it a backyard favorite over much of its range, although it also has an ill-deserved reputation for raiding the nests of other songbirds.*

hazel. In every month of the year, apart from July and August, these nuts alone make up nearly half of its diet.

Like the Eurasian jay (*Garrulus glandarius*), the blue jay is a prodigious collector of acorns, with each individual collecting between 3,000 and 5,000 acorns each fall. By choice the jay plucks them from the tree, although it will also take nuts from the ground as long as they are not infested with weevils or other insects. Unlike its transatlantic cousin, the blue jay does not travel far for its acorns: 2.5 miles (4 km) is about as far as it will go. It also carries fewer in its bill, with no more than five acorns at a time. It returns to an open patch of land, perhaps a plowed field or a recently mowed meadow, and

Go West, Young Jay

Historically, North America has been divided between two species of blue jay, with the Great Plains acting as a huge wild frontier. To the east the blue jay has occupied the land as far as the Atlantic coast. On the other side of the Plains Steller's jay (*Cyanocitta stelleri*) has traditionally had western North America to itself. Since the late 1940s scientists have noticed a westward expansion of the blue jay's range. It continues today, with nesting recorded in British Columbia, Oregon, Montana, Wyoming, and New Mexico among others.

Why should this have happened? The most likely reasons have to do with how humans have altered the Great Plains. Until comparatively recently, the open, treeless prairies would have offered little for a tree-dwelling species, and so this area remained jayless. But modern settlement has brought more tree cover to these areas. Farm shelter belts have been planted, and new residential areas have brought new woodland and a plethora of backyard bird feeders. The opportunistic blue jay has taken advantage.

As the blue jay has spread, it has moved into areas that are already occupied by Steller's jays. These very closely related species share a number of physical and behavioral characteristics. For example, they both feed primarily on nuts and seeds, take food readily from humans, and nest in trees. In some places they have even begun to breed with each other, although at the moment such hybridization is rare. It is too early to know whether North America's two blue jay species will become competitors in the future, but ornithologists are watching very closely.

Highly Adaptable

During the winter months blue jays are especially dependent on acorns for food. One difficulty they face is that acorns are high in tannin, a chemical that interferes with the digestion of protein. If jays ate nothing but acorns during this period, they would probably die, but the birds are able to supplement their diet by searching out small numbers of spiders and insects. Invertebrate food seems to counteract the protein-inhibiting properties of tannin, ensuring that the jays survive.

In spring and summer insects and other invertebrates become a significant source of food for this highly adaptable species. It hunts both in trees and on the ground for creatures such as caterpillars, grasshoppers, cicadas, and ground beetles, and occasionally takes to the air to snatch a dragonfly in flight. On finding a wasp's nest, it may break the nest off from where it is attached and carry it to a perch before deftly tearing it open with its bill and pulling out the larvae one by one.

Bobbing Blue Jays

In early spring blue jays get unusually and loudly sociable. Small flocks, which can number more than 20 birds, work their way through a woodland, calling loudly and engaging in a conspicuous bobbing action. The "bob" involves the bird sinking onto a branch, then extending its legs quickly, pointing its bill skyward, and raising its crest at the same time. At tense moments a bobbing bird may bob up so fast that it loses its footing on the branch and springs into the air.

Ornithologists used to think that this bobbing display formed part of courtship, but close observation suggests that the apparently random groups consist of several pairs of mated birds and a few unattached individuals. Blue jays are thought to mate for life; but although most pairs stay roughly within the same area all year around, they are not really territorial. It is likely that these loose gatherings evolve so that individual pairs can establish their own breeding space, as the groups patrol a larger area.

makes a pile of acorns. Once it has a sizable collection, it buries the acorns close together, topping off each cache with a stone or a leaf.

Studies of captive blue jays suggest that they have a good memory for hidden food supplies. Once a jay has retrieved an acorn, it holds it against a branch or other hard object with one foot and batters it open with its bill. Like other New World jays, it has a specially strengthened lower jaw to cope with the twists and stresses of repeated battering.

⊕ Many blue jays stay on their breeding ranges all year despite freezing winter temperatures. They can fluff up their plumage to keep out the cold, and their caches of stored food ensure they never go hungry.

Another Bluer Bird

People from the western states and provinces of North America are often puzzled when they first learn to identify birds. They see an almost completely blue bird with a black crest that should be a blue jay. Except that it is not. The settlers on the eastern side of the continent had already named the bird now called the blue jay by the time eighteenth-century ornithologist Georg Steller discovered another, slightly bigger blue jay in Alaska. The much bluer bird that he found was named Steller's jay. Today, the blue and Steller's jay are recognized as the only species within the genus *Cyanocitta*. So, in one respect, they do share the same name, albeit a scientific one.

When the birds do engage in courtship behavior, their display has a touching quality. The birds nudge each other on a branch, pass twigs, and even "kiss" bills. The male cements the pair-bond by bringing food to the female shortly before nesting. Such offerings are a prelude to more serious feeding once the female is incubating eggs.

Enterprising Nesters

Once the birds find a suitable nesting tree, the sexes tend to fall into specific roles. The male collects most of the material, while the female builds the nest. Gathering up the twigs that the male has thrust at her, she constructs an outer shell and then begins to slot in other materials. In wild areas they use bark, moss, grasses, and leaves, but around human settlements blue jays are quick to use paper, string, wool, and pieces of plastic. The nest is then lined with roots and fallen leaves, which are often held together with mud. In North America the use of mud in nest construction is unique to both the blue jay and the Steller's jay.

Some nests are never finished. Scientists once thought that the abandonment of "false nests" was part of courtship behavior. It is more likely that disturbance by a human or a predator is the main cause.

During incubation, and for the first few days after hatching, the male provides all the food for his growing family, while the female broods the young. After about 12 days the chicks have gained their first feathers and opened their eyes, and the female begins to forage, too. By the time the chicks are ready to fledge, they have already made sorties into the outside world, perching on the edge of the nest or venturing just beyond. Within two days of fledging they are able to fly erratically between trees and climb up them to relative safety.

Some young blue jays leave their parents in midsummer. Others stay with their parents for the rest of the summer, fall, and part of the winter. Their parents, meanwhile, begin their molt. By the end of the summer they are restored to full plumage, ready for the winter.

⊕ *Nesting blue jays take advantage of any building materials they can find, including artificial ones such as paper, string, plastic, and other garbage. Yet despite this, the nest itself is very well built.*

Early Warning System

The blue jay's vocal skills are legendary. Not only does it have a range of loud, instantly recognizable calls, it also has a huge talent for mimicry.

The specific function of each of the jay's calls is not well understood, partly because individual jays defy categorization. Birds will give forth a random selection of calls in different situations; and since a bird's syrinx—its voicebox—can make two sounds at once, it is quite possible for a bird to produce elements of two different calls at the same time. Yet some of the jay's calls are distinctive. Its harsh, so-called jeering call carries far and seems to be used most when danger threatens or when the birds want to keep in touch. More melodious is the bell-like musical whistle that sounds from cover. We tend to hear this call a lot—perhaps because it is an early warning alarm call that says "humans are approaching."

The blue jay can imitate the calls of a number of raptors, including the red-tailed hawk (*Buteo jamaicensis*) and red-shouldered hawk (*B. lineatus*), as well as crows, cats, and fragments of human speech. Yet the reason why the blue jay mimics other species is something of a mystery. By imitating a predator, it may be warning other birds that danger is present. Or it may simply gather interesting sounds to add to its musical repertoire.

Common Raven

Corvus corax

Common name Common raven

Scientific name *Corvus corax*

Family Corvidae

Order Passeriformes

Size Length: 23–27 in (58–69 cm); wingspan: 47–59 in (119–150 cm); weight: 2–3.4 lb (0.9–1.6 kg)

Key features Huge, bulky, heavy-billed crow with wedge-shaped tail in flight; all-black plumage, shaggy throat and "trousers"; sexes alike

Habits Glides and soars over open ground or flies with slow, powerful wingbeats

Nesting Builds big stick nest lined with fur and grass on cliff ledge, tree, or building; 3–7 pale bluish-green eggs; incubation 18–21 days by female; young fledge after 6–7 weeks; 1 brood

Voice Harsh croaking calls given by both sexes

Diet Omnivorous, but mainly carrion

Habitat Mainly open wild country remote from centers of human population, including sea cliffs, mountains, steppe, and semidesert

Distribution North America, except southeast; Europe; Asia, except India and Southeast Asia; North Africa

Status Thinly distributed, but very widespread.

Any bird that can live in habitats ranging from the Arctic Circle to the cactus deserts of the southwestern U.S. has to be tough and adaptable. The common raven is unquestionably both.

THE COMMON RAVEN IS BIG. Just occasionally, as it flaps slowly on huge wings displaying deeply indented primary feathers and tilts its great wedge-shaped tail, it can be mistaken for a raptor. It does not have a raptor's hooked bill, yet its enormous, thick black bill is just as formidable. The shaggy feathers around its throat and at the top of its legs help distinguish it from other glossy black crows. So too does its size, for it is one and a half times the size of an American crow (*Corvus brachyrhynchos*).

Constant Watch

Always alert, the raven patrols its territory looking for food. Sometimes it sits on a good vantage point such as a tree or a cliff ledge. Other times it glides slowly or soars on rising air currents, ever watchful. Unlike some vultures, the raven does not have a good sense of smell, so it relies on sight to locate food. By maintaining constant watch, it keeps track of injured or dying animals, sees where they fall, and marks them out as its next meal. The soldiers who gathered on the battlefields of medieval Europe thought that the arrival of ravens was an ominous foretelling of slaughter and even credited it with supernatural powers. But in reality the birds were simply acting on their experience that a big crowd of large animals could often supply an easy meal.

Opportunistic feeding is the key to the raven's success. Its huge bill makes an effective tool for ripping flesh apart, and the bird's main source of food in most habitats is carrion. On the coast it picks pieces from the carcasses of stranded whales and dolphins, as well as fish that have been washed onshore. Dead domestic animals, especially sheep, are a common meal in open country. Deer, rabbits, hares, and other mammals are taken too, sometimes as roadkill.

Despite its formidable appearance, the raven is a cautious bird, landing some distance from its victim and appearing to pay no attention to it. Only gradually does it edge closer. This careful approach may be designed to assess the risk posed by even a dying animal. A large carcass is more than a single meal, so the raven frequently hides food under stones or grass for later consumption.

This "vulture of the Northern Hemisphere" supplements its diet with a wide range of food. It can be a proficient egg thief: One study in Saskatchewan, Canada, found that more than 80 percent of common loon nests had been predated by ravens. It also eats a great many insects such as beetles and grasshoppers. Locusts are staple fare for North African ravens. Coastal birds eat crabs, limpets, and mollusks, and ravens everywhere take advantage of the seasonal glut of nuts and berries, and crops such as barley.

Wandering Nomads

Finding a territory is a defining moment in a raven's life, for the birds stay on their territories until they die or until they are driven out by usurpers. Until they breed, the birds undergo

⊕ *Raven pairs stay together for life and occupy the same territory for life. Young ravens may have to wait for some years before they can move into a vacant territory, nest, and start breeding.*

an apprenticeship in loose flocks of young and unpaired birds. Feeding and roosting together, they wander from territory to territory, often chased off by resident pairs. Eventually, a bird may find a widowed raven, or a new pair may be able to move into a vacant territory. In a late-winter courtship the male feeds the female, and the birds fly together in a tumbling, rolling

⤒ The heavy bill of a raven makes an effective butcher's tool, allowing these birds in Finland to feast on the remains of a dead cow.

A Literary Legend

The raven has a starring role in some of the world's most famous literature. In the Koran a raven shows Cain how to bury his dead brother. In the Bible the bird fails to return to Noah's Ark when it is sent to seek land. The mythology that linked the raven with prophecy and doom gave the bird a literary resonance. Shakespeare exploited this in a number of plays. In *Othello* he wrote:

> It comes o'er my memory,
> As doth the raven o'er the infectious house
> Boding to all.

The horror story writer Edgar Allen Poe tapped into the mystery surrounding the bird in his famous poem of 1845, *The Raven*. And Charles Dickens made use of the bird's humanlike qualities when describing Grip, the pet raven of Barnaby Rudge in the novel also called *Barnaby Rudge*.

display flight. Once mated, each raven pair remains together for life.

Early Nesters

Most raven nest sites are carefully selected for their inaccessibility to predators. The same cliff ledge or tall conifer is used repeatedly; the large number of places with names such as Raven Crag testify to their continued use. Some birds use artificial sites such as deserted buildings. As a last resort, they nest on the ground, even though there they are more likely to have their young eaten by predators.

The large stick nest is lined with softer materials such as animal fur and fine grasses. Ravens are comparatively early nesters: In many places the female lays her eggs when there is still deep snow on the ground. But the timing depends on temperature and the availability of food; ravens nest in January in northern India, but wait until April north of the Arctic Circle.

Parental Care

While the female incubates the eggs, the male feeds her and brings water in his throat pouch. He also defends the nest against predators and other ravens. Although the territory is occupied all year, it is defended only during the breeding season. Even then, only the area around the nest is actively contested. Otherwise, the birds move freely with other ravens to find food either within their territory or farther afield.

Once the naked, blind chicks hatch, they are treated with great care by both parents. The adults break up food and drink water to moisten it before presenting the young with regurgitated food parcels. In a few days the chicks acquire a thick, brown down, and within three weeks the female ceases brooding them.

Gradually, the amount of parental care diminishes. The young leave the nest at six to seven weeks, flying clumsily and often crash-landing, but they remain with their parents for much of the summer. The family party leaves the nest site, but remains largely within the territory. Adult ravens continue to feed the fledged youngsters or put out food for them to

⬅ A ledge on a sheer coastal cliff makes an ideal nesting site for ravens, since it is inaccessible to predators and close to rich sources of food, which may include the breeding colonies of other birds.

find. The youngsters develop their foraging skills by searching out invertebrates.

When the young birds are finally driven from their parents' territory, they gather with others in loose flocks. The distinctive "krok" calls, which paired birds use as contact calls, are used by young birds to alert other ravens to sources of food. When one juvenile finds a carcass, it calls loudly to attract other ravens. It is unlikely that they intend to help each other by this; they are probably seeking assistance, so that the group can defend its find from other predators, including resident raven pairs.

Under Fire

Ravens have endured centuries of human persecution, at one time only held in check by superstition and their usefulness to humans. Many early cultures believed it was unlucky to kill a raven. In Scandinavia the raven was seen as the messenger of Odin, so it escaped the punishment routinely meted out to crows. The towns of medieval England welcomed the bird as a garbage collector, and in Elizabethan times killing a raven could incur a fine of a crown. But as towns became cleaner, superstition lost its hold, firearms became more effective, and ravens suffered. Threats to livestock, often unfounded, and the ravens' taste for some agricultural crops meant that they were largely eradicated from Central Europe and widely persecuted elsewhere in the nineteenth and early twentieth centuries.

Thanks to its adaptability, the raven has reoccupied some, but not all, of its former range and is not considered threatened. A greater problem comes from the threat that it poses to other species. In the southwestern deserts of the U.S. ravens have had to be controlled because of their attacks on young desert tortoises, a species that is listed as endangered by the U.S. Fish and Wildlife Service.

Birds at Play

Many people have watched ravens indulging in what can only be described as play. Just like children, they fool around in the snow, kicking it up in the air or sliding down snow slopes on their backs, sometimes performing somersaults for extra effect. They have been seen springing up and down on branches or hanging upside down for no apparent reason. They even drop sticks or pieces of dung, then fly down and catch them before they reach the ground. Scientists are largely baffled by this behavior, but one explanation is that it is usually carried out by males in a bid to impress females.

Common name Horned lark (shore lark)

Scientific name *Eremophila alpestris*

Family	Alaudidae
Order	Passeriformes

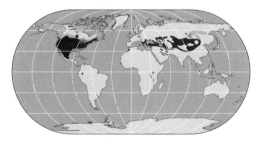

Size Length: 6–8 in (15–20 cm); wingspan: 12–14 in (30–35 cm); weight: 1–1.5 oz (28–42.5 g)

Key features Sleek, long-bodied lark; brownish above, with pale underparts; black band around front of neck; bold facial pattern of black, white, and pale yellow; breeding male has small, black feather tufts (horns) on head; female paler with smaller "horns"

Habits Feeds unobtrusively on ground; forms flocks in winter, often with other species

Nesting Female builds nest from grasses and roots, lined with fur, feathers, and rootlets; 2–5 eggs; incubation 11 days by female; young fledge after 9–12 days; 1–3 broods

Voice Call a short, piping "tseeep"; song a tinkling warble, usually from ground, sometimes in song flight

Diet Adults eat weed and grass seeds; young eat mostly insects

Habitat Tundra, steppes, shortgrass prairies, deserts, farmland, and grasslands from sea level to 13,125 ft (4,000 m)

Distribution From high latitudes around most of the Arctic to northern Mexico, Turkey, the Middle East, Central Asia, China, and Mongolia; also Morocco and Colombia

Status Possibly one of the world's commonest birds

Horned Lark *Eremophila alpestris*

The distinctive horned lark is North America's only native lark, with a range that includes virtually all of Canada and the mainland U.S. Each local population is adapted to its habitat, which may vary from cactus desert to arctic tundra.

THE HORNED LARK IS USUALLY instantly recognizable, especially a male in breeding plumage, but it is a very variable species. Birds in the southern and western U.S. tend to be smaller and paler than those in the east and north. The pale facial areas can be anything from white to yellow, and the color of the upper parts varies to match local soil color. Females are typically a little smaller than males and not as brightly marked.

Over 20 races of horned lark have been described, and there is much confusion over which is which. Horned larks can exhibit a range of plumages at one locality, and there is a gradation from one race to another.

The differences can be structural. Horned larks that migrate have longer wings than those that do not to enable them to complete their long journeys more easily. Birds that live in hotter habitats also have longer legs, perhaps to help with heat loss.

Wide Range

Horned larks can live in a wide range of open landscapes, but individual birds or populations tend to be restricted to certain habitats; some are coastal specialists, others thrive in mountain areas, others in deserts, and so on.

This trait has enabled the horned lark to colonize a wide variety of habitats and even climatic zones. In the Americas it has a range that is almost continuous from the Arctic to Central Mexico. However, one look at the distribution map shows that the situation is different outside the Americas, with a large gap between the northern and southern distributions. That is due to competition with the skylark (*Alauda arvensis*), which occupies

⊙ *The "horns" of the male are unique adornments, making the horned lark instantly identifiable despite many local variations over its wide range.*

Shuffling Flocks

Horned larks feed mostly on seeds, particularly grass seeds, which they gather from the ground. Feeding flocks are often difficult to see as they walk, hop, or shuffle along, keeping a very low profile until they suddenly take flight and move to new feeding sites. During the breeding season they feed their young on a protein-rich diet of insects such as beetles, caterpillars, and grasshoppers, plus spiders and other invertebrates.

⊕ The cryptic plumage of the birds provides excellent camouflage for the female as she incubates her clutch of eggs. Ground-nesting horned larks are very vulnerable to predators, so concealment is vital.

many of the habitats in the middle latitudes that might otherwise be home to horned larks.

Horned larks are resident over much of their breeding range. However, the birds that breed in the far north—both in the Americas and elsewhere—migrate south for the winter. The migration flight takes place during daylight and in flocks. Horned larks that breed at high altitudes also migrate down the mountains to lower elevations for the winter.

Paved Areas

Horned larks seem to be monogamous, for one season at least. Males sing from rocks, posts, and mounds to defend their territory, and in flight at up to 820 feet (250 m) to attract mates. Many of their nests have "pavings" beside them formed from pebbles, cow dung, corncobs, and clods of soil collected by the female and laid down in and around the nest. Those in the nest may simply keep lighter nest material from blowing away.

The birds leave their nest very carefully to avoid betraying its location to predators, which include skunks, raccoons, domestic cats, and crows. In the Central Plains area especially, horned lark nests are often parasitized by brown-headed cowbirds (*Molothrus ater*).

Declining Numbers

In the 1800s and 1900s the horned lark expanded its range as forests were cleared and grasslands and farmland created. More recently, many farms have been abandoned and are reverting to forest. Coupled with changes in the crops planted on farms, this appears to be causing a decline in horned lark numbers.

Barn Swallow

Hirundo rustica

Throughout the northern lands of the world, the annual appearance of the forktailed barn swallow is an eagerly awaited sign that the warm days of summer have finally arrived.

FAST, GRACEFUL, AND SUPREMELY AGILE in the air, with long wings and tail streamers, the barn swallow is one of the most elegant of all hunting birds. It is also one of the most successful, with a range that extends virtually worldwide apart from Australasia, the icebound polar regions, and a few oceanic islands.

Insect Diet

The barn swallow feeds almost entirely on flying insects, and like other insect-hunters, it retreats to the tropics to find prey in winter. Barn swallows from northern Europe fly 6,000 miles (9,656 km) or more to southern Africa, while North American birds make similar journeys to Latin America. In spring they return north to breed and take advantage of the seasonal flush of hatching insects to rear their young.

In the tropics the barn swallow eats a wide variety of small insects, including flying ants and aphids, but in the north the bird prefers big, burly flies such as blowflies, dung flies, and bloodsucking horseflies. These insects are particularly common on open grassland, where they feed on grazing animals and their dung, so the felling of forests and expansion of farming and ranching over the past 2,000 years or so have suited the barn swallow very well.

The barn swallow is often to be seen hunting at low level over pastures and stockyards, swooping among the cattle and sheep with a relaxed, fluid flight action, using its long tail to steer as it pursues its insect prey. Lakes and rivers are also good places to find prey, especially when bad weather drives most insects from the skies. At such times the barn swallow frequently hunts low over the water and even hovers over marginal plants looking

⊖ *The barn swallow thrives in climates ranging from the dusty prairies of North America to the damp Atlantic coasts of Europe and from the southern fringes of the arctic tundra to the plains of Africa.*

Common name Barn swallow (swallow)

Scientific name *Hirundo rustica*

Family Hirundinidae

Order Passeriformes

Size Length: 6.7–7.5 in (17–19 cm); wingspan: 12.5–13.7 in (32–35 cm); weight: 0.6–0.8 oz (17–23 g)

Key features Slim, medium-sized swallow; small bill; long wings and forked tail, with outer tail feathers elongated into streamers; shiny metallic blue-black above, pale to reddish buff below with blue-black chest band and chestnut forehead and throat; sexes similar; female has shorter tail streamers; juvenile duller, with paler forehead and throat, and short tail streamers

Habits Hunts in the air by day, mostly at low level, often over water, with graceful swooping flight; often perches on overhead wires

Nesting Open, featherlined cup of mud and dry grass on ledge, usually in outbuilding or beneath bridge, sometimes in cave or tree; 4–6 eggs; incubation 11–19 days; chicks fledge in 18–23 days; 2–3 broods

Voice Song a melodious, twittering warble; call a sharp "tswit tswit"

Diet Flying insects, particularly large flies such as blowflies, horseflies, and hoverflies

Habitat Open country, especially grassland, pasture, and marsh grazed by large animals, with suitable buildings for nesting

Distribution Temperate Eurasia and North America, Africa, Central and South America

Status Common but declining in north due to loss of breeding sites, feeding habitat, and prey

Broad-front Flyers

Many migrant birds follow well-defined routes as they travel from their breeding grounds to their winter quarters and back again. Birds of prey, in particular, often soar on thermal upcurrents to gain height for gliding, so they follow routes where such updrafts are common and avoid broad stretches of cool water. They are "narrow-front" migrants, all passing through the same air corridors.

By contrast, barn swallows migrate on a broad front. In Europe, for example, they work their way south in the early fall until they gather all along the northern shores of the Mediterranean. Then they set off across the water to north Africa in a great wave. After a break they carry on across the Sahara Desert without attempting to skirt the vast expanse of inhospitable sand. Swallows from Central Asia fly straight across the wastes of Arabia in the same way. Eventually they all arrive on the savanna grassland, where they can rest before carrying on south of the equator.

for flies and beetles that have settled on the leaves. When it needs a drink, the barn swallow darts across the surface of a pool and skims a mouthful of water from the surface with its lower bill. In early summer it also forages along woodland edges looking for caterpillars dangling from the trees on silken threads and seizes them on the wing.

⊕ It takes a week to build a new nest, and over 1,000 mud pellets like the ones this barn swallow has gathered in its beak are used in the construction.

Many Nest Sites

Barn swallows breed in early summer, and the caterpillars provide vital protein for nesting birds and their young. The birds pair up as soon as they return from the tropics, and any that have bred before usually return to the same site and renew their pair-bond. The male arrives first, checks out the old nest, and may start repairing or rebuilding it. When the female arrives, she often takes over most of the task of nest building, while the male defends the site against rival swallows.

Originally barn swallows nested in tree cavities and rock crevices, but for centuries they have favored ledges and beams in outbuildings and roof spaces or under bridges and culverts. An ideal site is among the roof beams of an open-fronted cattle shelter in a traditional farmyard, offering protection from the weather, easy access, and a plentiful supply of flies. But barn swallows will also often nest in garages, porches, verandas, and other such places.

The nest is built from pellets of mud gathered by the birds in their bills, reinforced with dried grasses or straw, and lined with feathers. When the eggs hatch, the parent birds feed the hungry chicks on insects that they carry to the nest in their throats, like swifts. Swallows often raise a second or even third brood, although they may get some assistance

⊕ Barn swallows are well adapted to a life in the air and even feed each other on the wing.

Fine Feathers

To humans one of the most attractive features of the dashing barn swallow is its forked tail, in which each of the outer feathers is extended into a long, tapering streamer. It appears that humans are not the only ones to appreciate the tail. Males have longer streamers than females, and there is evidence that the males with the longest tail streamers get the opportunity to mate earlier and enjoy more breeding success. The females clearly prefer their mates with fine feathers and compete for the favors of the most eligible long-tailed suitors. Long streamers may indicate health, strength, and strong genes.

from one of the first brood, which stays on at the nest to help out with the food supply. Barn swallows can breed in their second year.

Heading South

At the end of the breeding season barn swallows leave their nests to perch in restless, noisy groups on overhead wires and to form mass night roosts as they prepare for migration. They often roost in reed beds, along with related species of swallows and martins. Such gatherings are frequently targeted by birds of prey such as the hobby, a fast-flying falcon that specializes in hunting swifts and swallows.

Older birds migrate first, blazing a trail for the younger birds that follow afterward. Swallows take long breaks as they move south, usually roosting in reed beds, and the young birds may stop off in an area for up to two weeks before resuming a journey that may last two months or more.

Decreasing Insect Prey

Barn swallows are still widespread, but they are less common than they once were, especially in regions where traditional mixed farming has been abandoned in favor of intensive, chemically assisted agriculture. Chemical pesticides kill off the birds' insect prey, and flies in particular have become harder to find. Many flies breed in animal dung, and it has become

less common as farmers have turned to artificial fertilizers and plowed up their pasture to grow crops. Suitable nesting sites are also becoming scarce as outbuildings are demolished and roof spaces are sealed up. So while the barn swallow will probably never disappear from northern skies, its appearance every spring will no longer be something that can be taken for granted.

⊕ Each nestling may eat more than 150,000 insects between hatching and fledging, so a pair with a brood of five chicks is kept very busy indeed.

Black-Capped Chickadee

Parus atricapillus

Often tame and confident around people, this small, lively, neat bird of woodlands, parks, and gardens is the most widely distributed tit in North America and one of the most familiar of all backyard birds.

Common name Black-capped chickadee

Scientific name *Parus atricapillus*

Family Paridae

Order Passeriformes

Size Length: 5 in (12.7 cm); wingspan: 7–8 in (18–20 cm); weight: 0.4 oz (11 g)

Key features Black crown and nape, chin, and throat; broad white cheek patch; upper parts gray-brown with paler panel along closed wing; underside rusty-buff; short black bill and gray-black legs; sexes alike

Habits Active, acrobatic, often in mixed flocks; frequently visits garden feeders

Nesting Nests in hole in tree; 6–8 eggs; incubation 12–13 days by female; young fledge after 16 days; 1 brood

Voice Typically a buzzy, gurgling "chick-a-dee-dee-dee"; also "day-day-day" and high, clear whistled "phe-be" or "phe-be-be"

Diet Insects, seeds, berries, spiders, and snails

Habitat Mixed woods, thickets, woodland edges, and suburban gardens

Distribution North America from Alaska to California and east to Newfoundland

Status Widespread and common, stable or increasing

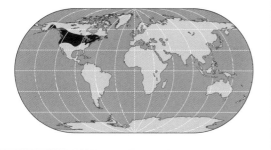

IN WINTER SMALL PARTIES OF BLACK-CAPPED chickadees descend on gardens throughout much of North America to exploit the food that people leave out for them. As a result, this adaptable, acrobatic little tit is one the most recognizable of all suburban songbirds. It gets its name from the black cap that, together with the wide black bib over its chin and throat, outlines its strikingly white cheeks. The lower edge of the black bib is slightly ragged in fresh plumage, compared with the sharper edge on the very similar Carolina chickadee (*Parus carolinensis*). Apart from this it is mainly gray-brown above, with pale edges to some of the wing feathers that create a band of pale gray along the closed wing. That is less obvious in late summer, when the feathers are worn, and the pale feather edges are much reduced. Its underside is a quite rich, bright tawny-buff, whiter beneath the bib.

Winter Survivor

The black-capped chickadee is a common bird across a broad band of North America from western Alaska and the southern half of Canada south to extreme northern California in the west and eastward in a narrowing belt to the Atlantic coast. In the north it is found across southern Manitoba, Ontario, and Quebec, and through Nova Scotia to Virginia. The southern limit of its range runs through Kansas, Missouri, Indiana, and Ohio, with a southward spur along the Appalachians. The bird is a resident within this area, able to survive severe winter weather, but occasional food shortages sometimes force it south in winter. Its breeding range may then be extended south for a season or two.

The bird lives in a variety of mixed and deciduous wooded habitats in and around the edges of forest and in open woodland and parkland. It also feeds in gardens and in thickets and scrub. Its frequency in gardens depends largely on the food supply in winter and the availability of nest sites in summer. The black-capped chickadee is commonest in open birch and alder woodland, often close to clearings, and avoids pure stands of conifers.

Where other chickadees occur, reducing its feeding options, the bird is mostly found in clumps of deciduous trees. In the Appalachians, where both black-capped and Carolina chickadees live, black-caps prefer higher areas, and Carolinas favor valleys and low foothills.

Broad Diet

Although mostly insectivorous, the chickadee eats a wide range of food, taking whatever is available. In summer it eats mostly caterpillars and other small insects, spiders, and various other invertebrates. Vegetable food then forms only about ten percent of its diet. But in winter seeds, fruits, and berries may make up as much as half its diet, and it also eats more insect eggs and pupae.

It searches for food among small twigs and branches and their foliage, picking prey from the bark and often hanging underneath to scour the whole surface. A chickadee has specially developed leg muscles that enable it to take food from the undersides of branches that is missed by many other birds. Its feet and toes are short, but strong, with an excellent grip. Its feeding technique involves careful examination of the bark, with much pecking and probing. It may also hover occasionally to reach particularly difficult places, and it can catch flying insects in midair like a flycatcher.

⊕ Throughout much of North America the black-capped chickadee is a familiar visitor to garden bird feeders in winter, when food may be hard to find elsewhere. In spring they disappear into the forests to breed, reappearing when the weather deteriorates again in the fall.

Courtship Feeding

Beginning in late winter, the male chickadee starts to feed the female—an activity called courtship feeding. It is seen in many species of birds, including warblers, chats, and tits, and has two obvious functions. One is to reinforce the pair-bond. It is essential in birds that spend most of their lives repelling others but that must now work together to mate, nest, and rear a brood of young. Courtship feeding helps break down the birds' desire to "keep their distance," allowing close contact and trust between the pair. The female must also produce a clutch of eggs, laying one egg a day. It is a huge drain on her body resources, and any extra high-nutrition food supplied by the male helps the female greatly at this time.

In winter a chickadee must spend around 80 percent of its day searching for food. It is typical of the many small birds that must maintain a continual intake of energy in the short daylight hours of winter if it is to survive the low temperatures and the long, dark nights when it is unable to feed. Studies in England of the very similar willow tit (*Parus montanus*)— once regarded as the same species—revealed that each bird must find one average-sized insect every 2.5 seconds to ensure its winter survival. To achieve this goal, it might have to examine more than 1,000 trees in a day.

The black-capped chickadee visits feeders in gardens especially in winter, where it seeks out food items such as seeds and suet in particular. It eats any kind of fatty material such as bacon rind or pork fat, as well as split squash or pumpkin seeds and sunflower seeds.

Food Stores

When feeding, a black-capped chickadee may take a big food item up to a large branch and then clamp it securely with the front toes of one or both feet, while it pecks it to pieces. The use of the feet when feeding is limited to this activity, however. Food is always located with and then grabbed by the bill. Indeed, only one family of passerines, the drongos, are known to catch and lift food using their feet.

Chickadees store food in bark crevices or similar places and usually recover it later in the course of normal foraging. They store insects as well as seeds, usually killing them first, but sometimes squeezing them into a tight space while still alive. Related European species may store up to 4,700 items per day in spring, but only 200 or so per day in winter. A single bird may store up to half a million items in a year.

⊕ *Chickadees often spend most of the daylight hours searching for food, especially in winter, when they need extra energy to keep warm during the long, dark, cold nights. At this time they eat a lot of seeds, but in summer they take mainly insects.*

Winter Flocks

Black-capped chickadees are active and lively birds, always adding life and movement to the winter woods when they join the small mixed bands of nomadic birds that roam in search of food. They call frequently with the contact note that gives them their name, and that allows them to be picked out from the various nuthatches, kinglets, and other birds with which they associate. At this time many woods seem empty until one of these feeding flocks appears, and the chickadee's call is often the first clue to the flock's approach.

Sociable feeding in winter appears to be a way of maximizing feeding efficiency, since concentrations of food are more likely to be found by a wandering group moving through on a broad front than by single birds. When one bird stops to feed, the others notice and concentrate on the area, too, moving on only when the food is exhausted.

Furthermore, many pairs of eyes are better than one pair at spotting potential predators, and chickadees are quick to raise the alarm at the approach of a predator. They may also feel more secure in a flock: A single bird is the sole target of a predator, but in a flock the chances of being singled out for attack are reduced.

Despite their generally sociable nature, these little birds are aggressive in close encounters and very possessive when it comes to food or nest sites. In confrontations with other chickadees they try to avoid actual fighting when possible. Instead, they stretch upward, ruffle their body feathers, or raise their head feathers in display—all in an attempt to appear bigger and more threatening. That may be enough to discourage an intruder, but sometimes an open bill or even a quick peck has to reinforce the meaning of such postures.

The black-capped chickadee is no great songster, but its frequent, familiar calls are welcome in the winter woodland. It shares a basic pattern of vocabulary with several other tits, such as the European willow tit and marsh tit (*Parus palustris*). Chickadees respond to imitations of their calls or even to squeaking sounds. They seem to be confident when approaching people and may come to within arm's length of someone keeping still.

A chickadee often bathes, and it preens regularly to keep its plumage in top condition. It will sunbathe, too, pressing itself flat with its wings extended, and the feathers of its back and rump raised to allow the heat of the sun to warm its exposed skin.

⊙ *A cavity in a birch tree makes an ideal nest site for a pair of black-capped chickadees. The pair works together to enlarge it with their bills and shape it to their requirements, but the female alone is responsible for building the hair-lined nest inside the hole.*

⊕ *When other birds fly south for the winter, the black-capped chickadee stays on. It is partly sustained by the food that it has stored in crevices scattered over its home range, but it also joins other birds in winter feeding flocks.*

Pairing Up

Chickadee pairs form in the fall and remain together within the winter flocks. Their courtship is simple and does not involve complex postures or displays. In spring the paired birds begin to feed on their own on nice days but may return to the flock if the weather deteriorates. Eventually the flock splits up, and each pair defends a territory together. The male calls with sweet "phe-be" or "phe-be-be," the first note longer and higher than the others.

The pair finds a suitable site, usually a natural cavity in rotten wood that can be enlarged or reshaped with their bills. Old woodpecker holes are sometimes used, as are artificial nestboxes. Sometimes a shallow cavity made by a woodpecker digging for larvae under the bark is chipped away to make a larger nest hole. They never excavate holes in sound wood. The hole is usually 6 to 20 feet

Varied Chickadees

In the southeastern states the black-capped chickadee is replaced by the similar Carolina chickadee, which sometimes learns to imitate the black-cap's song and occasionally interbreeds with it. They look alike and occupy similar habitats, but the Carolina chickadee, living in milder areas, is less likely to visit garden feeders. In the west it is also found with the mountain chickadee (*P. gambeli*), a mountain conifer forest specialist, and locally the chestnut-backed chickadee (*P. rufescens*); in the north it overlaps with the browner boreal chickadee (*P. hudsonicus*), also a conifer forest species.

(1.8–6 m) above the ground. Both sexes enlarge the nest hole if necessary, but the nest itself is built only by the female, using moss or other soft vegetable matter with a lining of hair.

Like other tits, the female black-capped chickadee covers her eggs with nest material when she leaves an incomplete clutch. She incubates the eggs herself, with the male often bringing her food. When the chicks have just hatched, the male brings food while the female remains with them in the nest; but as they grow and become more demanding, both parents find food. The chicks typically leave the nest early in the morning and need constant attention, calling greedily to be fed. Many are taken by predators, or starve if food (especially caterpillars) is scarce, or succumb to cold, wet weather in poor springs. But populations are able to recover quickly from such setbacks in warm, dry seasons with plentiful caterpillars.

Winter Supplies

The black-capped chickadee can often be seen eagerly taking sunflower seeds from feeders, flying off with them one at a time, and pushing them into crevices in rough bark. It recovers and eats these seeds later in the course of normal foraging. This habit of storing food and returning to it later is important, since it enables the chickadee to survive the winter without migrating. It does, however, depend on periods when food is superabundant, enabling the hard-working chickadee to find much more than it can eat and store the surplus for leaner times. Provided it has enough food, the chickadee can survive the winter cold well enough; but freezing days when frost coats the trees in thick glazed ice hit it hard, because it is then unable to penetrate the ice to reach its food supplies.

Common name Red-breasted nuthatch

Scientific name *Sitta canadensis*

Family   Sittidae

Order   Passeriformes

Size Length: 4.5 in (11.4 cm); wingspan: 7.5–8.5 in (19–21 cm); weight: 0.3 oz (8.5 g)

Key features Small, short-tailed bird; male blue-gray above, orange-brown below; black cap and eye stripe; female similar, but with dark gray-blue cap, paler below

Habits   Climbs tree trunks and branches

Nesting   Nest of bark, grass, and pine needles in tree hole, normally excavated by female; 5–8 eggs; incubation 12–13 days; young fledge after 18–21 days; 1 brood

Voice   Distinctive "yank yank," often compared to toy tin horn

Diet   Mainly insects, spiders, and similar animals in breeding season; conifer seeds, flies, even fruit outside breeding season

Habitat   Mainly coniferous forest from sea level to high altitude; also mixed forest

Distribution West and north of North America, except far north; ranges south to Florida and Mexico

Status   Common to very common in suitable habitat; some population increase over last 30 years

Red-Breasted Nuthatch

Sitta canadensis

Although there are four nuthatch species in North America, the red-breasted nuthatch differs from all of the others in its preference for coniferous forests with plenty of spruce and fir trees.

THE COMPACT, SHORT-TAILED RED-BREASTED NUTHATCH is typical of its family: a lively, agile little bird that is specialized for feeding on large trees—climbing up, over, and under their trunks and branches with a jerky motion, clinging on with strong, sharp claws. Its claws are flattened laterally so that they can fit into smaller cracks in the bark—a useful adaptation for clinging and climbing as it searches for food.

Nuthatch Irruptions

Red-breasted nuthatches are resident over most of their breeding range through the north and west of North America. But those that breed in the northernmost parts head south in most winters, and many more birds join them in years when there is a poor crop of conifer seeds. These "irruptions" occur roughly every other year. When they happen, red-breasted nuthatches can be found as far south as northern Florida and even northern Mexico. They have even been seen in Iceland and England, although it is possible that the transatlantic nuthatches have hitched rides on ships rather than flying the full distance.

Poke and Probe

The red-breasted nuthatch uses its bill to poke around in crevices in the bark, seeking out beetles, ants, spiders, and caterpillars. Such invertebrates make up most of its diet in the breeding season and are the nestlings' main food. They have also been seen flycatching and even eating fruit in summer and fall.

Conifer seeds are their staple winter diet, and some are hidden away for eating later.

⊖ *Given the choice, red-breasted nuthatches look for food on live trees rather than dead trees, although they are also known to search among leaves on the ground. During the winter they eat mainly conifer seeds, switching to insects and other small animals in summer.*

They are concealed beneath bark, in holes made by sapsuckers (a type of woodpecker), and sometimes in the ground, and the hiding place is often covered with lichen, bark, or stones. But the system is not impenetrable. A hairy woodpecker (*Picoides villosus*) may be watching; and when the nuthatch has disappeared, the woodpecker moves in and makes off with its hoarded food.

Aggressive Males

Red-breasted nuthatches are monogamous, and the males can be highly aggressive. They chase off other males that approach their territorial boundary; and when the female is nest building, they chase off any birds that come too near the nest hole. They prefer to create their own nest hole rather than use an existing one, but are less fussy about their nesting materials; they sometimes steal materials from the nests of pygmy nuthatches (*Sitta pygmaea*) and mountain chickadees (*Parus gambeli*).

They have a habit of collecting conifer resin to spread around the nest hole, using their bills or occasionally pieces of bark, which they use as "resin applicators." The sticky resin probably protects the nest from predators, and the birds are adept at getting in and out of their hole without getting stuck in the resin themselves.

In the right habitat the red-breasted nuthatch is a common bird, and population increases have been noted over the last 30 years. Sadly, some are killed when they fly into buildings or into windows near backyard feeders, but this is unlikely to have a significant effect on their population levels.

Winter Wren *Troglodytes troglodytes*

A tiny, quarrelsome, loud-voiced bird of dense undergrowth, the winter wren is more often heard than seen as it scolds an intruder or defends its patch with a powerful burst of song.

ALTHOUGH IT IS USUALLY SEEN only fleetingly as it darts across an open space into cover, the winter wren is easy to identify by its jaunty manner, stumpy body, and short, cocked tail. It is warm brown, almost russet, with a darker cap and eye stripe, and gray-buff underparts. Obscurely barred above, it is more distinctly barred across its wings, tail, and flanks.

Versatile Birds

Winter wrens are typically lowland birds, but they are very versatile, breeding above the tree line at 7,900 feet (2,400 m) in the Alps. They flourish in dense woodland of all kinds, on remote, windswept islands, in rich, varied gardens, and in scrubby thickets along stony streams in high, otherwise arid areas.

They breed across most of northern North America from Alaska east across the Great Lakes to Newfoundland and Nova Scotia, with outposts in the west, south to California. Most of Europe except the far north has breeding wrens in summer, and they occur in a band across Central Asia to Japan, with an isolated population in Kamchatka in far eastern Siberia.

Common name Winter wren (northern wren, common wren, wren)

Scientific name *Troglodytes troglodytes*

Family Troglodytidae

Order Passeriformes

Size Length: 3.5 in (9 cm); wingspan: 5–7 in (13–18 cm); weight: 0.3–0.5 oz (8.5–14 g)

Key features Tiny, rotund, with short, thin tail, often cocked; fine bill; warm brown above, buff below, with long pale stripe over eye; wings barred rufous buff and brown, flanks barred dark brown; pale pink-brown legs; sexes alike

Habits Hops and skips through low, dense vegetation and over rocks; may sing from high in tree

Nesting Builds rounded nest with side entrance under overhang; 5–6 eggs; incubation 14–15 days; young fledge after 16–17 days; 2 broods

Voice Dry, rasping, or chattering "chit," "chiti," and "churrr"; very fast, loud, vibrant musical song includes low, flat trill

Diet Insects and spiders and their eggs and larvae; also some aquatic animals and berries

Habitat Undergrowth in woods, gardens, cliff tops, rocky islands

Distribution North America; Asia from Japan and China westward to Europe and south to northwest India; North Africa

Status Generally common and stable; suffers occasional big declines after severe winters

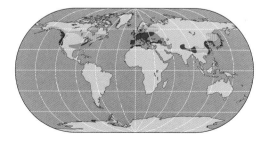

⤵ *The roofed nest of the winter wren not only makes a sheltered nursery for the chicks; it may also provide a snug refuge for the older birds throughout the hard winter months.*

Although some local island races are resident, most northern populations migrate southward in winter. In America the birds appear in many U.S. states only in winter, which accounts for their name. In severe winters they can become locally rare, but their high breeding rate allows them to bounce back to normal numbers within a few years.

Whirring Flights

The winter wren is a tiny but aggressive, restless bird, often scolding intruders from the top of a twig before diving out of sight into a thorny thicket. It makes short, low whirring flights and creeps around like a mouse in the bottoms of hedges or ditches, sometimes slowly, sometimes flicking about quickly and erratically. By day it is solitary, but at night many may come together in hard weather to roost, with as many as 50 in one small nestbox.

Spiders, beetles, and other insects are the bird's favored food. It also picks woodlice, bristletails, springtails, and various other small, ground-living creatures from the ground or vegetation and from dank, cobwebby places in deep shade. It may also take dragonflies, tiny fish, tadpoles, minute frogs, and a few berries.

Cock's Nests

Males sing loudly to defend territories. They may pair with more than one female and may build several nests, sometimes as many as eight, even if they have only one mate. The female selects one of the male's nests and lines it herself. She then undertakes all the incubation. Chicks are independent within nine to eighteen days of leaving the nest.

Males with two or three mates may have overlapping broods, but many males fail to attract more than one female, and some island races seem to be typically monogamous. In such cases the male takes a share in feeding the chicks, but many mainland males play little or no part in rearing the young until they are fledged, when they may take over while the female begins incubating a new clutch of eggs.

⊕ Breeding adults keep the nest clean by picking up the chicks' fecal pellets in their bills and carrying them away for disposal. This also helps reduce the number of insects and other scavengers in the nest.

American Dipper

Cinclus mexicanus

It was once called the water ouzel. Now it has been renamed the American dipper—a suitably descriptive name for this remarkable bobbing bird of western mountains, rivers, and streams.

Common name American dipper

Scientific name *Cinclus mexicanus*

Family Cinclidae

Order Passeriformes

Size Length: 7.5 in (19 cm); wingspan: 10 in (26 cm); weight: 2–3 oz (58–84 g)

Key features Sooty-gray bird; short, dark bill; bulky body with short wings and tail; longish legs for its size; juvenile has lighter bill and underparts

Habits Perches on rocks by mountain streams and rivers, bending legs in "dipping" motion; dives in for food

Nesting Dome-shaped, mossy nest built in early spring, usually on rocky ledge, in tree roots, or under bridges; usually 4–5 eggs; incubation 16 days; young fledge after 23–28 days; sometimes 2 broods

Voice High-pitched, wrenlike song made by both sexes

Diet Mainly aquatic invertebrates and fish

Habitat Mountain streams and rivers; some move to lower altitude waters in winter

Distribution Mountains of western North America, Mexico, and Central America

Status Not globally threatened

THE AMERICAN DIPPER IS FAIRLY nondescript in appearance, being grayish and stocky with short wings and tail. Yet watch it bobbing vigorously on a rock over a stream, its eyes blinking furiously, and it becomes one of the most entrancing of birds. Dippers are found by rocky mountain streams and small rivers in western North America. They can only live where there is clear, unpolluted water. Clean water contains small fish, as well as the mayflies, caddisflies, and stone flies and their larvae that make up the bulk of their diet. The birds are specially adapted to diving or wading into the water after their prey.

➔ *By the time the nestlings are well grown, a parent bird— most often the female— returns to feed them up to 18 times an hour. The adults save some time and effort by collecting more than one prey item at a time and regularly come back with their beaks stuffed with six or seven insect larvae.*

← *An American dipper dives to the pebbly bottom in its search for aquatic invertebrates and other small animals.*

Large Nests

The birds build a soccer ball-sized nest with moss on the outside and lined with dry grasses and roots. Increasingly, they nest under bridges, perhaps one reason why more dippers now nest downstream, where rock overhangs are in short supply. The nest must be safe from predators such as mink, wolverines, and martens. It must also be very close to water, but not so close that it is liable to be washed away.

When the young hatch, they stay in the nest for twice as long as other closely related birds because the dippers' feeding techniques require greater strength and stamina. Once the juveniles leave the nest, they stay close to their parents for another two weeks, hiding at the edge of the stream or sitting quietly on rocks until a parent returns with food. Once independent, the young may stay in their parents' territory while they molt. After molting, they leave to find a territory of their own. Most juveniles fly upstream, but sadly, few survive until the following spring.

In June and July, when the young leave, the adults cease singing, a noticeable break for a bird that trills loudly for ten months of the year. The birds then begin a rapid molt, and for a while they are virtually flightless and vulnerable to predators. Hiding in tree roots and rocks and foraging at the water's edge, they are able to shed and replace all of their feathers over a two-month period.

At the onset of cold weather most adult dippers remain on the stream or river where they bred. Only in the high mountains of states such as Alaska is there a significant fall migration downstream to escape freezing over.

Numbers Unknown

Nobody is sure whether the dipper is under any serious threat—too many nest in inaccessible locations for nationwide censuses to take place. The birds are vulnerable to water pollution by industry, agriculture, and river engineering. But they have also benefited from the construction of bridges, walls, and buildings near water as artificial nest sites.

Eastern Bluebird

Sialia sialis

Despite its popularity—it is the state bird of both New York and Missouri—the eastern bluebird suffered huge population declines through the twentieth century. But thanks to the efforts of local bird conservationists, it is now making a comeback.

THE EASTERN BLUEBIRD IS A WELL-KNOWN species throughout much of North America east of the Rockies. Striking and easily recognized, it lives up to its name with bright blue upper parts that contrast markedly with its red breast and white underparts. It has two close relatives in North America: the western (*Sialia mexicana*) and mountain (*S. currucoides*) bluebirds.

Pest Controller

Like other members of the thrush family, the eastern bluebird is most at home in places that offer a mixture of open grassland and shrubs where it can feed and scattered trees where it can roost and nest.

Two-thirds of its diet consists of small invertebrate animals, including earthworms, spiders, snails, and many insects such as katydids, crickets, and grasshoppers. It also eats many species that are agricultural pests, such as cutworms, making it a beneficial species in farming areas. When invertebrates become scarce in the colder months of the year, it switches to eating the fruits and berries of plants such as hawthorn and dogwood.

Like the European robin (*Erithacus rubecula*), the eastern bluebird's favored hunting method is to fly from a low perch to snatch food from the ground, then fly back again—a technique called "ground sallying." If a suitable low branch is not available, it may hover briefly above the ground in the manner of some birds of prey. Occasionally bluebirds fly up from perches on branches to catch flying insects on the wing, rather like flycatchers.

Common name Eastern bluebird

Scientific name *Sialia sialis*

Family Turdidae

Order Passeriformes

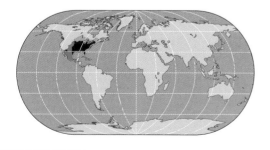

Size Length: 5.5–7 in (14–18 cm); wingspan: 11–13 in (28–33 cm); weight: 1–1.2 oz (28–34 g)

Key features Medium-sized thrush; bright-blue upper parts, red breast, white underparts; male has blue or black wings and tail; female duller and grayer; juvenile brown with blue on wings; brown legs and bill

Habits Often feeds by flying from perch to ground and back

Habitat Grassland with scattered trees and shrubs

Nesting In tree cavity such as a woodpecker hole; 3–6 pale blue eggs; incubation 12–14 days mainly by female; young fledge after 15–20 days; 2 broods

Voice Call described as "chur-lee"; song a development of call, "chur chur chur-lee"

Diet Insects, spiders, and other invertebrates; fruits, berries, and other plant matter

Distribution North America east of the Rocky Mountains from southern Canada south to the Gulf States and northern Central America

Status Not globally threatened

Natural Cavities

The bluebird's nesting season begins with the male occupying territory and choosing a nest site. Bluebirds nest in cavities, and once back on his territory, the male searches for a suitable hole at between 10 feet (3 m) and 66 feet (20 m) from the ground. Natural cavities (the bluebird does no excavation work itself) include old woodpecker holes and rotting tree stumps. If natural sites are not available, they will readily take to nestboxes.

Once he has chosen a site, the male has to attract a partner by singing. Bluebird song is not particularly loud,

⊕ A fat grasshopper provides a protein-rich meal for a colorful male eastern bluebird. In summer such animals make up most of the bluebird's diet.

more a gentle warble, but it is enough to advertise his availability to potential partners. Courtship may last anything from a few hours to a few days, but when ready, the female signals her willingness to mate by entering and inspecting the chosen nest site. After this, in a burst of enthusiasm, the male circles the female in short courtship flights, singing and quivering his wings before sealing the bond between them.

During this period other birds may intrude, at which point fights may ensue between occupier and usurper. Although normally monogamous, bluebird males may accept two females; sometimes a female mates with two males. Research with other species, such as the European dunnock, has demonstrated that songbird relationships can be extremely complex, with polygamy and even communal breeding occurring in the same population.

Local Materials

Following mating, the burden of work falls to the female in the usual manner of thrushes. She constructs the nest using local materials such as grasses or pine needles, but unlike other passerines, she only rarely lines it with softer materials such as feathers and plant down. It can take up to six days to complete.

She lays up to five blue eggs and starts incubating them after laying the final egg, to ensure the young hatch at the same time—and therefore have equal chances of survival. As with construction of the nest, incubation is carried out entirely by the female; but her partner remains on duty nearby, occasionally bringing food. On warm days she may be able to leave the nest to preen or feed, but in colder weather she sits tight.

The young birds hatch naked and blind, and are closely cared for by their parents. Soon after they hatch, the female removes the egg shells. Food is brought at regular intervals and initially consists of soft, easily digestible small invertebrates such as caterpillars. The adults

Blue Names

Blue is not uncommon in bird plumages and appears in many bird names. There are the American eastern bluebird described here, two species of fairy bluebird from Asia (*Irena puella* and *I. cyanogaster*), and the blue-tailed hummingbird (*Amazilia cyanura*). There are the Eurasian bluethroat (*Luscinia svecica*) and the red flanked bluetail (*Tarsiger cyanurus*), both in the thrush family. There is also the blue-footed booby (*Sula nebouxii*), a seabird in the Sulidae family from the coasts of Mexico south to Peru. It is one of the few birds with blue feet; another is the pied avocet (*Recurvirostra avosetta*), found increasingly on European coastal wetlands.

keep the nest clean by regularly removing the chicks' fecal sacs. The young develop rapidly, and after a little while they can be fed on more challenging items such as beetles and crickets.

At between 12 and 18 days the young have grown sufficiently to leave the nest. It has been suggested that the young of hole-nesting species such as bluebirds are better able to fly on leaving the nest than their counterparts from open nests—no doubt because the hole may not have a convenient branch nearby! In the case of young bluebirds their first flight may take them 100 feet (30 m) from the nest to find shelter in a neighboring bush or tree.

After landing, the young make their way

⊙ Once a male bluebird has attracted a female, he brings her food to demonstrate his ability as a provider. Depending on the quality of the food, the female may or may not decide to mate.

up into the canopy, where they find food and keep in regular contact with each other by calls. For a short while a parent—or even a young adult from a previous brood—may feed them, but eventually they are left to make their own way in the world. If time and conditions allow, the adults may start a second brood.

Foreign Competition

Eastern bluebirds have not fared well since the turn of the twentieth century. The population has suffered declines across its range, in some places by up to 90 percent. There are a number of reasons for this.

First, and perhaps most importantly, the bluebird has faced enormous pressure from introduced species. In the nineteenth century homesick immigrants imported many European birds to North America. In 1851 the European house sparrow (*Passer domesticus*) made a transatlantic crossing, followed in 1896 by the European starling (*Sturnus vulgaris*).

Both were highly successful. Within 50 years both the house sparrow and starling had spread widely across the continent and in many places had become the predominant passerines. Both sparrows and starlings nest in holes. They are also nonmigratory and aggressive. So they simply started to out-compete the native bluebirds, either occupying nest sites before the bluebirds returned from migration, or ousting them when they attempted to set up territories.

This competitive problem for the bluebird was compounded when suitable nesting sites started to become even more scarce as modern farming methods demanded the removal of dead wood. As if this was not enough, the generic problem of pesticides and the loss of invertebrates made it difficult for the birds to feed both themselves and their young.

Arresting the Decline

Without either nest sites or food the bluebird population began to dwindle. However, wildlife conservationists soon understood the bird's problems, and they were able to enlist the public in efforts to reverse its decline.

The strategy revolved around the provision of nestboxes and their management by teams of local birdwatchers. With careful design, the nestboxes were made secure against starlings, and the vigilance of the birdwatchers kept away the sparrows.

This gave the competitive advantage back to the bluebird, and across its range the bird's population began to increase. The plan is also popular with people, with many miles of "bluebird trail" laid alongside strings of nestboxes providing interest for local people involved in their monitoring. So along with habitat management to ensure the bluebird's food supply, it is hoped that the scheme will secure the future of this much loved species.

Nestboxes and Bird Conservation

Nestboxes are familiar sights around homes and gardens. In most cases they simply provide an extra nesting space for otherwise common species and much enjoyment for the observer. They also help gardeners by providing "on-site" insect pest control owing to the needs of hungry nestlings and their attentive parents.

In some places, however, they can actively assist in the conservation of scarce and declining species. The eastern bluebird is one good example. Another example is found in Britain where conservationists have been successfully reversing the declines of tree sparrows by targeted provision of boxes in key areas. The nestboxes are cleverly placed on farm buildings and in tall trees, in clusters to suit the tree sparrow's colonial habits.

Nestboxes need not be limited to small perching birds. Barn owls (*Tyto alba*) are among the birds to have benefited from manmade homes. Even the normally tree-nesting goldeneye duck (*Bucephala clangula*) has used nestboxes alongside rivers in its breeding grounds.

American Robin

Turdus migratorius

Happy to feed and even breed in urban and suburban gardens, the American robin has profited from human impact on the environment, significantly increasing its range and population throughout the last 200 years.

Common name American robin

Scientific name *Turdus migratorius*

Family Turdidae

Order Passeriformes

Size Length: 8–9 in (20–23 cm); wingspan: 17 in (43 cm); weight: 2.6 oz (74 g)

Key features Large, long-winged thrush; male has red breast contrasting with gray back and black head; white eye ring; yellow bill; female similar, but paler and duller

Habits Familiar around human habitation, often seen hopping on lawns in search of food

Nesting Cup-shaped nest of coarse grass and mud in fork of tree, manmade sites also used; 3–4 blue eggs; incubation 11–14 days mostly by female; young fledge after 16 days; 2 or 3 broods

Voice Spring song rich sequence of rising and falling notes, described as "cheer-up, cheerily, cheer-up, cheerily"

Diet Invertebrates, fruits, and berries

Habitat Open forest, farmland with scattered trees and bushes, gardens, and parks

Distribution Across North America from Alaska and northern Canada to the southern U.S. and Mexico

Status Increasing

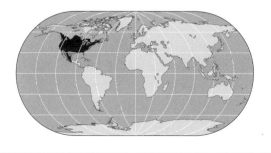

In the eighteenth century the conspicuous red breast of the American robin reminded English settlers of the equally red-breasted European robin (*Erithacus rubecula*); so although it is much bigger and only distantly related, they gave the American bird the same name.

American robins can be found across the North American continent from northern Canada right down to Mexico. The southern races of the eastern U.S. and Mexico are resident, but the northern races fly south for the winter in small flocks to avoid falling temperatures and scarcity of food.

Welcome in Gardens

American robins are naturally birds of open forest. Before the arrival of humans they would have lived near natural woodland glades. Here a combination of grassland and wooded cover proved ideal for both feeding and nesting. With the expansion of human settlement and the creation of much more open space by forest clearance, the birds' population dramatically increased. Farmland, parks, and increasingly gardens clearly proved excellent substitutes for woodland glades.

For many, American robins are a welcome and popular sight. They often search lawns for food, stopping at intervals to wrestle a stubborn earthworm from its lair. This frequently observed behavior may give the impression that earthworms form most of their food, but careful study has revealed that American robins eat a mix of both animal and plant matter, with the proportions varying according to season.

Song Posts

For migrant American robins the return journey north starts as early as February, with birds appearing back in their summer neighborhoods through March, April, and May. The first birds back are invariably the males, who select their territories in readiness for the arrival of females a few days later. Each male marks his territory by singing from a series of prominent boundary markers or song posts. The territories can be mapped by observation of the singing males, and they range from 0.3 acres (0.1 hectares) down to as little as 0.05 acres (0.02 hectares) in dense vegetation.

The birds favor maple or spruce trees as nest sites, but they use many other locations, including artificial structures. They may also reuse their own nest from the previous year—a remarkable navigation achievement for this long-distance migrant—or the nest of another species. Their nest is normally supported in the fork of a tree and often quite exposed, for the birds do not seem worried about elaborate concealment. In typical thrush fashion the female does the work, weaving the final cup from coarse grass bound together with mud. She molds the lining with her body, then completes it with softer materials.

The female lays her clutch at the rate of one egg a day early in the morning. Incubation starts with completion of the clutch; the female does most of the sitting, guarded by the male on duty nearby.

On hatching, the chicks are naked and blind, but they develop rapidly. Observers have recorded the parent bringing an incredible 100 meals a day to the nest, mainly in the morning. By 16 days old the young are ready to leave the nest; and if time and conditions allow, the pair may attempt to raise a second brood. On departure, the fledglings initially stay close to the nest. They are often taken care of for a while by the male alone, especially if the female has started a second clutch.

Male Roosts

One of the many interesting aspects of American robin behavior concerns their roosting pattern. In the fall and winter both males and females share communal roosts away from their breeding territories. They may be quite sizable, and one was found to cover an area of 2.6 square miles (6.7 sq km). Yet such winter roosts are not unusual among birds. What is unusual is that otherwise territorial males will roost together in the evening during the breeding season, often after a hard day defending their space against each other.

Having profited from the conversion of forest to agriculture and settlement, the American robin is flourishing. Today, it is a familiar and popular species, immortalized as the "bob bob bobbin'" bird in Harry Woods' 1926 song, originally written for Al Jolson.

⊕ *In the cold winter months American robins eat more berries and other fruits, owing to the relative scarcity of insects, earthworms, and similar invertebrates.*

Common name Northern mockingbird

Scientific name *Mimus polyglottos*

Family	Mimidae
Order	Passeriformes
Size	Length: 8.5–10 in (22–25.4 cm); wingspan: 12.5–14 in (32–36 cm); weight: 1.6–1.8 oz (45–51 g)

Key features Medium-sized, long-tailed bird; gray above, paler below; long, black tail with white outer feathers; wings mostly black with white wing flash; sexes alike; juvenile speckled below

Habits Often feeds on lawns; vigorous defender of territory and food sources

Nesting Builds twig cup nest with lining of finer material; 3–5 blue-gray or green-white eggs, spotted and blotched with brown; incubation 12–13 days by female; young fledge after 12 days; 2–3, sometimes 4, overlapping broods

Voice Complex song includes original phrases and much mimicry of other species; repertoire may include 45–200 song types

Diet Fruit, insects, worms, occasionally small lizards

Habitat Parks, thickets, woodland edges, suburbs

Distribution Southern Canada; whole of mainland U.S.; most of Mexico except south; Caribbean

Status Common; numbers declining at south of U.S. range, but range expanding to north

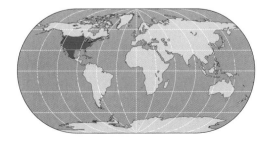

Northern Mockingbird

Mimus polyglottos

Well known as an excellent mimic, the northern mockingbird has been adopted as the emblem of five U.S. states. Yet for over 100 years it was caught and sold as a cage bird, and its population has only recently recovered.

THE REMARKABLE VOCAL SKILL OF THE northern mockingbird is the main reason for its popularity throughout the U.S. Like the European nightingale (*Luscinia megarhynchos*)—which has the same habit of singing at night—it is a rather drab, inconspicuous bird, likely to go unnoticed until it opens its bill and bursts into song. Perhaps its most obvious features are its striking white wing flashes and outer tail feathers, which are easy to see when it flies. The mockingbird also uses its wing flashes in courtship displays and territorial encounters.

Male and female northern mockingbirds look similar, although males are typically a little heavier. But it is very difficult to reliably sex northern mockingbirds on either appearance or weight. Other mockingbirds in the *Mimus* genus such as the tropical mockingbird (*M. gilvus*) and Bahama mockingbird (*M. gundlachii*) are also very similar in appearance to the northern mockingbird.

It lives throughout much of North America and the Caribbean islands, and seems to be sedentary over most of its range. But the northern mockingbird's migratory behavior is poorly understood, and birds at the northern end of the species' range may be partial migrants, flying south to avoid hard winters.

Bee-eater

The northern mockingbird is essentially a ground-feeding species, with a diet of fruit and invertebrate animals. During the breeding season invertebrates form a more substantial part of its diet than in the winter, and prey

⊙ *Like most of its relatives, the northern mockingbird has a long tail, which it often flicks. Apart from this, it is a rather unremarkable bird—until it opens its bill to sing.*

items include bees, wasps, ants, grasshoppers, and beetles. It feeds on ground with short vegetation or even on bare earth. It forages mostly on foot, walking or running after its next meal, but it sometimes flies up a little way to snap up a flying insect.

It may employ other feeding techniques from time to time. It uses perches as vantage points, dropping to the ground like a shrike to catch unsuspecting prey. When hunting cicadas, the bird often flies directly at an insect, hitting it with its wings and chest and knocking it to the ground, where its fate is sealed. Occasionally, northern mockingbirds do a reasonable woodpecker impression, clinging to tree trunks and searching for invertebrates.

Northern mockingbirds may eat fruit straight off the tree or bush, or after it has fallen. The multiflora rose is one of their favorites. They can also be fruit thieves, stealing fruit from the breeding territories of other mockingbirds to take back to their nests and feed to their own young.

As food themselves, their bold and aggressive behavior may make them less vulnerable to predators than might be expected. But they are still eaten by sharp-shinned hawks (*Accipiter striatus*) and screech owls (*Otus asio*). Mockingbird eggs and nestlings are often taken by blue jays (*Cyanocitta cristata*) and American crows (*Corvus brachyrhynchos*), as well as snakes and squirrels.

Exceptional Song

Most northern mockingbirds are monogamous, although bigamy is not unknown, and some females mate with more than one male. Song plays an important role in attracting and keeping a female, and the northern mockingbird's song is exceptional.

It supplements its "own" song with much that is copied from other birds—both mockingbirds and other species—and sometimes from artificial sources too. The song changes as the bird gets older, and its repertoire may increase with age; there seems to be no

Birds in a Cage

The singing abilities of the northern mockingbird once made it a highly sought-after cage bird. The trade was at its peak from the late eighteenth century to the early twentieth century, with the traders satisfying demand for mockingbirds in both the U.S. and Europe. Large sums of money were paid, especially for older birds, which were regarded as better songsters.

In 1828 the famous ornithologist Wilson realized that there were very few mockingbirds left around Philadelphia. But there was still plenty of demand for mockingbirds, and they were being imported from other parts of the U.S. Some birds were selling for as much as $50. The cage-bird trade left gaps in the species' range where local populations had been virtually wiped out. It was not until the 1940s that these areas were repopulated by mockingbirds from farther south. The cage-bird trade also resulted in the introduction of mockingbirds to many new areas, including Hawaii.

Today, most cage birds are bred in captivity, and the trade in these captive-bred birds is no threat to wild bird populations. But there is still a trade in wild-caught birds; this can be a serious conservation issue, particularly for species that are already in decline.

limit to its "song memory," which keeps on increasing until it dies. The song may vary with locality too, because mockingbirds generally mimic local species, and they may vary from one place to the next.

Singing starts as early as February or even earlier at the southern end of the mockingbird's range. Females do not normally sing during the spring and summer, but both sexes sing in the fall to claim feeding territories. Yet even then females sing less than males and more quietly. In the breeding season males start singing before sunrise, waking many a light sleeper! Unmated males start singing earliest, and one study has revealed that between midnight and 4:00 a.m. only unmated males sing.

Overlapping Broods

Aerial chases and in-flight displays complete the courtship, helping form a secure pair-bond. The

⊖ *By taking over the rearing of a brood of chicks, the male releases the female to incubate another clutch of eggs. That enables the pair to raise up to four broods of young in a single season.*

male builds the twiggy outer part of the nest, and the female adds the softer lining, although the male may have to make several nests before any of them are used. One pair may make use of up to eight nests in one breeding season. Mockingbird broods overlap; while the female is sitting on the one clutch of eggs, the male is looking after the young from the previous clutch. This unusual arrangement makes two or three broods common, and even four is possible.

Northern mockingbirds are highly territorial. Males defend the breeding territory against other male mockingbirds, and females against females. Some people think that mockingbirds drive other species out of their breeding territory too, but there is no convincing scientific evidence to support this. Mockingbirds do evict cedar waxwings (*Bombycilla cedrorum*) from fruit trees, which represent a highly desirable feeding area. This eviction is sometimes so aggressive that the waxwings are killed as a result.

Fights between northern mockingbirds do occur. The so-called "boundary dance," a confrontation between the males of two neighboring territories, was once thought to be a courtship display. It is now known to be an act of aggression and normally one that ends only when one of the males retreats.

Northern Expansion

Although it suffered badly from the cage-bird trade in the past, the northern mockingbird is not currently of conservation concern. Its population is densest around the Gulf Coast, becoming sparser to the north and west. Numbers have declined at the southern end of the range, but the range has expanded at the northern end and, indeed, continues to do so, aided perhaps by the planting of multiflora roses, a favorite food source.

Mimicry

The ability of some birds to copy the sounds made by other birds, by people, and even by artificial objects is truly remarkable. Yet only a small number of bird species are good mimics. European starlings (*Sturnus vulgaris*) and northern mockingbirds are well-known mimics. Less well known is the marsh warbler (*Acrocephalus palustris*), an Old World warbler. The average male marsh warbler can mimic 76 other bird species. Half of them are from its European breeding grounds, and the remainder are African species that it encounters on its tropical winter range. So it is possible to hear bird sounds from tropical Africa in a European landscape.

Domesticated birds can be excellent mimics, especially parrots (family Psittacidae) and mynas (*Acridotheres* species). Many can mimic the human voice with great accuracy, probably as a learned response: The birds discover that they enjoy more social interaction with their owners if they copy their voices.

Yet Australia's superb lyrebird (*Menura novaehollandiae*) may win the prize for best mimic. The repertoires of some lyrebirds are said to include the sound of camera motordrives—and, poignantly, the sounds of chainsaws and trees crashing to the ground.

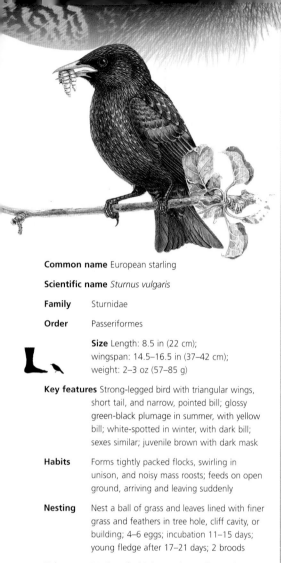

European Starling

Sturnus vulgaris

Common name European starling

Scientific name *Sturnus vulgaris*

Family Sturnidae

Order Passeriformes

Size Length: 8.5 in (22 cm); wingspan: 14.5–16.5 in (37–42 cm); weight: 2–3 oz (57–85 g)

Key features Strong-legged bird with triangular wings, short tail, and narrow, pointed bill; glossy green-black plumage in summer, with yellow bill; white-spotted in winter, with dark bill; sexes similar; juvenile brown with dark mask

Habits Forms tightly packed flocks, swirling in unison, and noisy mass roosts; feeds on open ground, arriving and leaving suddenly

Nesting Nest a ball of grass and leaves lined with finer grass and feathers in tree hole, cliff cavity, or building; 4–6 eggs; incubation 11–15 days; young fledge after 17–21 days; 2 broods

Voice Medley of whistles, rattles, and screeches

Diet Soil invertebrates, insects, fruits, and seeds

Habitat Open areas and light woodland

Distribution Europe and western Asia; introduced to North America, Australasia, and South Africa.

Status Widespread and common, although declining in western Europe

Bold, noisy, and enterprising, European starlings are also highly sociable, roosting and traveling in huge flocks. If you see one starling, you can almost guarantee that there will be more nearby.

ONE OF THE MOST COMMON birds in both Europe and North America, the European starling is so familiar that few people take the trouble to really look at it. If they do, then a close view in winter reveals a glossy, blackish bird, flecked with white spots. By the spring it takes on a range of vivid colors as the light tips of its feathers wear away to reveal an iridescent sheen of greens, blues, and bronzes, depending on how the light reflects from its plumage. Its bill turns yellow, and it is possible to distinguish the sexes: The male has a bluish bill base and dark brown eyes, while the female's bill is pink at the base and her eyes have a pale rim.

In flight these fast-flying birds can resemble tiny jet aircraft, their thin, pointed bills and long, pointed wings giving them a triangular shape. A flock of starlings could easily be a miniature squadron, twisting and turning in close formation.

Powerful Jaw Muscles

The omnivorous starlings divide their year between an insect-dominated winter diet and a seed and fruit menu in the warmer months. In particular, they have evolved into very effective ground-feeders. Their strong jaw muscles enable them to probe the ground and pry their beaks open under the soil to obtain seeds or insect larvae. But they can also hop around on trees to take fruit, pick caterpillars off leaves, or snatch flies and other airborne insects out of the air. They are bold, if wary, opportunists, quick to take advantage of food put out in backyards and just as quick to fly off at the first sign of danger.

⊕ *At sundown European starlings gather in vast flocks before retiring to their night roosts. The flocks may contain thousands of birds, which often perform spectacular aerobatic maneuvers before swirling down to settle for the night.*

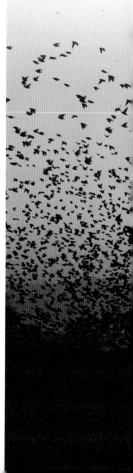

⊕ Strong jaw muscles and a sharp, all-purpose bill enable the starling to exploit a huge range of food sources. The pale feather tips of this winter bird will wear off to leave its plumage glossy black with an iridescent sheen.

Part of the Crowd

Starlings are compulsively social. Juvenile birds have no sooner left their parents than they gather in great numbers with others of the same age to form huge flocks. If they are part of a migrant population—starlings in the north and northeastern parts of the species' range tend to migrate to the milder south and west for the winter—then they will migrate in company in late summer.

Throughout the fall and winter starlings gather in ever-increasing numbers. During the day they move through the skies in small groups, with each bird in the flock alert to feeding possibilities. If one small group spots food, it begins foraging—and is soon joined by another and another. Interestingly, a group of starlings on the ground does not always attract the attention of other starlings; it is only when the birds are seen to be foraging actively that other birds join them at the feast.

Sheltered Roosts

The biggest starling gatherings take place at night roosts. The locations are chosen carefully to maximize protection from predators and the elements. Islands, reedbeds, swamps, and high buildings are all relatively safe from predators. A roost in a wood will invariably be sited where it is sheltered from the wind, and a city center is often a warmer place to spend the night than the surrounding countryside. The birds assemble cumulatively as one small flock is joined by another. As they head toward the roost, other flocks add to the increasing multitude. Just before they reach their final destination, the whole flock may descend on a field to eat one last meal at a preroost staging point, before rising and heading off in a huge, swirling flock.

As they land at their night roost, the birds chatter and jostle for space and a place close to the center, where they are at least risk from predators. Usually, the older males get these prime spots, while younger females are pushed to the edges, making them more vulnerable to being snatched by a passing owl in the night.

At dawn the chattering reaches a crescendo before suddenly the starlings fall silent, and the first wave of birds leaves the roost. This pattern is repeated several times, with a hush preceding each departure.

A Welcome with Flowers

Resident male starlings begin the breeding year in the fall, when they seek out potential nest holes for the following spring and use song to defend them against other males. As winter approaches, however, the hole-defense phase peters out, although both males and females sing throughout the winter.

Courtship begins in earnest in early spring. The resident males reestablish their claims to several nest holes. As migrant males return and other males compete for nest sites, the sitting tenants realize the impracticality of guarding more than one hole and select just one. Each male fills his chosen nest hole with grasses, creating a cup-shaped space at the back, and places green leaves or flower petals inside to welcome any potential mates.

The Great Colonist

European starlings are found across nearly a third of the world's land surface. They have been such successful colonists that it is easy to forget that they are native only to the Old World. In numerical terms North America remains their biggest triumph. The entire population of about 200 million birds is descended from about 60 birds released into Central Park, New York, in 1890. The birds quickly colonized the relatively new city and spread out rapidly. They reached California in 1942, and today they occupy virtually the entire continent from northern Canada to subtropical Mexico.

One of the reasons for their phenomenal success may be that they were among the first birds to exploit relatively new habitats. The fields and towns created by the European settlers through much of North America were ideally suited to a species that is adept at feeding on cultivated land and nesting in artificial structures. And the released birds had retained the ability to migrate, enabling them to spread much more quickly and take advantage of seasonal opportunities. In fewer than 100 years the starling's spread through North America replicated the colonization of Europe and northern Asia thousands of years before, when people began clearing the primeval forests and creating settlements.

Clearly, such an invasion was bound to have some negative effects on the native wildlife. Starlings often occupy nest holes at the expense of other hole-nesting species, with the eastern bluebird (*Sialia sialis*) perhaps worst affected.

Most starling introductions were accidental or made for whimsical reasons. In New Zealand, however, they were released in an effort to control a grassland insect pest. Whether that aim was achieved is debatable; nevertheless, the starling has gone on to become New Zealand's most numerous bird.

When a female arrives, the male perches close to his favored nest, adopts a hunched-back posture by lowering his tail, and begins whirling his wings and singing. If the female lands nearby, the male leaps into his nest hole and resumes singing in a bid to entice her inside. Once the birds have mated, the male stays close to his female until she begins incubating her eggs, to ensure that no other males are able to fertilize the eggs.

Starlings retain their colonial nesting habits even if their nest holes are spread all around a town. Invariably, all the birds within a particular area will lay their eggs within four to ten days of each other. The coincidental timing of egg laying is probably guaranteed throughout the dispersed population by song.

⊖ *Although this adult starling has already molted into its pale-flecked winter plumage in late summer, it is still feeding a chick from a late second brood. Within the week the chick will be fending for itself.*

Despite such coordination, breeding irregularities creep in, and timings become more erratic as spring goes on. Up to one-third of males mate with other females—often year-old birds—while their mates are incubating eggs. The offspring of such extrapair liaisons receive a tough upbringing, for the males play no part in raising these young. Instead, they focus all their attention on their first progeny. Once the first brood is fledged, the pair may raise a second brood, but many choose other mates.

Fueled by a high-protein diet of invertebrates, starling chicks grow very quickly. They leave the nest in about three weeks, although the parents continue to feed them for around a week. But once the brown-colored juveniles depart for good, they do what starlings do best and gather in flocks of their own.

Friend or Foe?

The European starling is seen as both beneficial and harmful to human interests. Every year the people of northern Russia welcome the return of the starling as a sign of spring. Its popularity is not hard to fathom, since throughout the spring and summer it feeds on "harmful" soil invertebrates. When Russia was part of the former Soviet Union, a massive nest-box scheme was launched. Twenty-five million boxes were made and tended by schoolchildren in an effort to encourage the birds to breed and protect their crops.

Yet when the same birds fly south and west to their wintering grounds, they get a different welcome because they cause damage by feeding on winter cereals and cattle fodder. They also raid cherry orchards, olive groves, and blueberry and strawberry crops.

Common name American redstart

Scientific name *Setophaga ruticilla*

Family	Parulidae
Order	Passeriformes

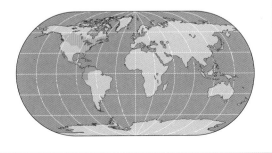

Size Length: 5–5.5 in (12.7–14 cm); wingspan: 8–9 in (20–23 cm); weight: 0.2–0.4 oz (5.7–11 g)

Key features Male black, paler below, with orange-red on side of breast, in wing, and at side of tail; female greenish on back and bright yellow where male is red; short black bill; black legs

Habits Flits lightly through foliage; catches flies in the air; restless and active

Nesting Male sometimes polygamous; female builds cup nest in tree fork; 3–5 eggs; incubation 11–12 days by female; young fledge after 9 days; 1 brood

Voice Thin "tseet"; wheezy song with slurred, rising flourish

Diet Insects and spiders of many kinds; some seeds and berries

Habitat Scrubby or open woodland; streamside and roadside trees

Distribution North America from southeast Alaska east to Newfoundland, south to Washington, Oregon, Colorado, northeast Texas, coastal Louisiana, and Florida; ranges to West Indies, Central America, and northern South America

Status Widespread and common, but showing recent signs of decline

American Redstart

Setophaga ruticilla

A vividly patterned gem of open woodland, the beautiful American redstart combines striking plumage with great delicacy of movement as it searches for food in the trees.

IMMEDIATELY STRIKING BECAUSE OF ITS boldly patterned plumage, the American redstart is a slim, long-tailed warbler with a marked difference between the sexes. An adult male is largely smoky-black with a whitish belly, but on each side of the bird's chest is a patch of bright reddish-orange extending back as a paler orange flush on the flanks. A broad bar of similar color crosses its wings, making a vivid band across the perched bird. Its tail, which is often fanned and flicked, has broad panels of the same bright color. The intensity of the color varies, and some faded birds look more yellow-orange on their wing bars and tail panels.

The female has a similar pattern but is paler; her head is grayish, with a white eye ring and line from eye to bill. Her back is greener, her underside silky white. Both wings and tail are dark brown, and the broad wing panel and tail sides are pale lemon yellow. Her chest has yellow patches on each side.

⤼ The female American redstart is quite unlike her mate, with gray and yellow where he has black and orange, and a distinctive white ring around her dark eye. Her more subdued coloration makes her harder to see while incubating her eggs on the nest.

⤳ Dazzling in flaming orange and smoky-black, a male American redstart makes a dramatic sight as he defends his territory and displays to potential mates.

Winter Migrant

The breeding range of the American redstart covers much of North America from Alaska to Newfoundland and south to Florida. In winter it migrates to the West Indies and to Central America from Mexico south as far as northern Peru and northern Brazil. A few stray migrants turn up outside the regular range, and some spend the winter in southern California. Exhausted birds on migration often settle on ships in the Caribbean.

The American redstart favors clearings and open, swampy places within lowland deciduous woods, but it also occupies the edges of woodland near pastures and even beside large gardens and orchards. On the Great Plains it is a bird of mixed or even coniferous woodland, either in bushy, mixed growth or at the edges of open clearings within more mature or extensive forest.

Although it is found within areas of tall trees in the breeding season, it typically feeds quite low down in the saplings. On migration and in its winter range it tends to feed lower down in trees than other North American warblers and in more open areas.

Active Feeder

Mainly insectivorous, the American redstart eats beetles, caterpillars, leafhoppers, aphids, adult moths and butterflies, crane flies, and midges. It takes many of them from the air, but picks others directly from foliage. It sometimes supplements this diet of insects with some

A Colorful Array

New World warblers fall into several recognizable groups, of which those in the genus *Dendroica* are the most colorful in spring. Typically *Dendroica* warblers have white tail spots, and the males are brighter than females. Several species are boldly patterned in black, white, and gray, but many have vivid yellow, green, chestnut, and orange in their plumage. The most strikingly black-and-white bird is the black-and-white warbler (*Mniotilta varia*), a creeping bird resembling a nuthatch (genus *Sitta*) in zebra stripes. In the genus *Wilsonia* there are green birds with varied black-and-yellow head markings: Wilson's warbler (*W. pusilla*) has a simple black cap, while the hooded warbler (*W. citrina*) has a yellow face surrounded by a wide black band. The American redstart, however, is unique among this colorful array in being patterned in orange and black.

⊙ *The female American redstart builds the nest of grass, roots, and bark—birch bark in this case—in the vertical fork of a tree. She often disguises it with lichen, bark, and feathers to make it less conspicuous to potential enemies.*

seeds and berries, especially in the fall. As with many other insect-eating migratory birds, these sugary foods help it build up a store of energy-rich fat before its long flights.

It is an active little bird, foraging through foliage and frequently making short flights or little darts from twig to twig to catch flying insects. During these sallies it often fans and twists its tail for balance, which shows off the side panels of bright color. The bird also hovers well, a skill that it often uses to take insects from the air or from the undersides of leaves. Males are usually more likely to hover or dash out to catch flies than females.

It has a rather broad bill with stiff bristles around the mouth, like those of a flycatcher, which it also resembles in behavior. Yet despite having more aerial habits than most warblers, it is less acrobatic when feeding in the trees. It rarely clings to twigs or hangs upside down to reach food that is otherwise inaccessible: It prefers to hover instead. It often beats big prey such as fat caterpillars against branches to subdue them and make them limp before attempting to swallow them.

Confusing Fall Warblers

Some New World warblers are as easy to identify in the fall and winter as they are in the summer because their plumage colors do not vary very much from season to season. But other New World warbler species can be exceptionally difficult to identify after spring and summer because they molt into dull winter colors that all look much the same as those of their relatives. Juveniles too young to breed also have similar obscure, drab colors known as immature plumage. That is because they have no reason to look bright and conspicuous until they are ready to attract a mate; they are safer hiding away in the foliage with their subtle green feathering.

So while American redstarts remain easy to pick out in the fall, identifying species such as the Tennessee warbler (*Vermivora peregrina*), orange-crowned warbler (*V. celata*), blackpoll (*Dendroica striata*), pine warbler (*D. pinus*), bay-breasted warbler (*D. castanea*), Wilson's warbler (*Wilsonia pusilla*), and hooded warbler (*W. citrina*) takes concentration and good views, but it can still be confusing.

Winter Wanderers

In winter the American redstart is often found loosely associating with other warblers, such as the magnolia warbler (*Dendroica magnolia*), prairie warbler (*D. discolor*), Cape May warbler (*D. tigrina*), and northern parula warbler (*Parula americana*). These groups wander through woodland and swampy thickets together, staying in contact with frequent calls, including a clicking "tsip" or a more drawn-out "tseet" from the redstart. They are often quite tame and easy to approach, although elusive. The American redstarts in these groups are especially excitable and restless, drooping and flicking their wings, and raising and fanning their tails. In Cuba, where many spend the winter, this habit has earned them the name *mariposas*, or butterflies.

Multiple Families

Some male American redstarts pair with more than one female at the same time and are involved in rearing two or three families. Males defend their territories against other males in summer, using a stiff-winged, gliding display flight to patrol their territorial boundaries. Their song is variable and resembles that of a yellow warbler (*Dendroica petechia*). They display to females by spreading their wings and tails to show their colors, and bowing in front of them.

The female selects a nest site, quite low in an upright fork of a tree, sometimes 65 feet (20 m) or more from the ground. She incubates the eggs alone, but is often duped into raising the chick of a parasitic cowbird (*Molothrus* species), which destroys her own brood.

If she avoids this disaster, her young fly when they are only nine days old. The female cares for half the brood, the male the other half. She has only one brood to look after, but polygamous males are kept busy trying to care for two or even three sets of hungry fledglings.

Young males begin to sing in their first fall, although at this stage they still look much like females. They return to breed the following summer if they survive the rigors of migration to Central America and back.

Common name Cardinal (red cardinal, northern cardinal)

Scientific name *Cardinalis cardinalis*

Family Emberizidae

Order Passeriformes

Size Length: 8.75 in (22 cm); wingspan 12 in (30 cm); weight: 1.6 oz (45 g)

Key features Medium-sized; fairly long, broad wings; long tail; obvious head crest that can be raised or lowered; male bright crimson all over, except for black around eye and on throat, and hint of gray on back and wings; female washed-out brown version of the same; both sexes have thick, waxy red bill; juvenile brown with black bill

Habits Often moves around in groups; mostly feeds on ground; flicks tail; flight has unsteady look

Nesting Cup nest of grass, twigs, stems, bark strips, and rootlets interwoven with leaves and often paper, lined with hair; 3–4 eggs; incubation 12–13 days; young fledge after 9–10 days; 3–4 broods, occasionally 5

Voice Both sexes give very variable series of loud, melodic whistles with distinctive slurred tone; contact call is modest "tip"

Diet Seeds, fruit, and insects

Habitat Dense, scrubby habitats with open areas for feeding; gardens often ideal

Distribution Southern and eastern U.S. to Central America

Status Not threatened; very common

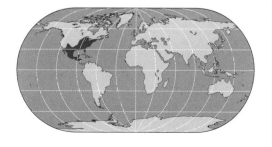

Cardinal

Cardinalis cardinalis

The cardinal is one of America's most attractive birds, with its brilliant red plumage and tuneful song. It has recently expanded its range north thanks to the regular provision of bird food in gardens.

IT IS RARE TO FIND the twin attributes of striking plumage and pleasing song in a single bird. The most musical songs usually resonate from small, soberly clad introverts hidden in the undergrowth, and most of the great beauties of the bird world sing with discordant voices. But the cardinal, one of North America's most popular birds, presents both qualities in abundance. Its striking red plumage brightens up the pale hues of winter, and at the same time its tropical-sounding song, tuneful and varied, promises the arrival of spring.

The bird is named after the cardinals of the Roman Catholic church, who wear scarlet ceremonial robes as a mark of their high office. Actually it is only the male that merits the comparison, being red all over but for a black face and throat. A female cardinal is mainly brown, with red on her crest, wings, and tail. But both sexes have the same shape: quite slim,

⊕ The dazzling crimson plumage of the male cardinal is a stunning sight at any time of year, but particularly welcome in midwinter, when the branches are bare of leaves, and natural color of any kind is muted.

Female Song

Small birds sing songs for a variety of reasons, but primarily to proclaim territorial boundaries or to attract mates. In the vast majority of species these tasks are essentially male preserves, so during the breeding season the females tend to be silent except for short calls of one or two syllables, usually directed at their mates or young. For a short part of the breeding season, however, female cardinals burst into full song, performing at least as loudly and with the same quality as the males. This unusual behavior poses a question—why do the females sing?

Recent studies have shown that the song of the female cardinal is heard at a very specific part of the breeding cycle, just before nesting begins. At this stage pair-bonding is not yet complete, although territorial boundaries have been set up. Playing recorded male songs to females does not make them sing, so it is unlikely that the singing females are defending territory. But playing the song of a female to her mate may lure him into joining in a duet, the two singers interweaving their songs.

There are several possible reasons for the behavior. One is that female song helps ensure pair-bonding. Another is that it helps the two members of the pair prepare for mating. And a third possibility is that a female's song could command the attention of neighboring males, giving her a chance to mate with other males as well as the male in her established pair-bond.

with a long tail, a thick bill, and an exotic-looking crest that can be raised and lowered.

The cardinal is a common and familiar bird across most of the eastern half of North America. Although its original habitat would have been woodland edge and dense thickets, such as those found along the edges of streams and swamps, today it is common in field borders, parks, villages, and suburban gardens. With their patches of greenery and open ground, gardens are very like woodland edges, so it is not surprising that the cardinal has adapted to them so well. A pair will often occupy a garden all year around, using it for nesting, feeding, and roosting. They are less fond of tall trees and tend to avoid gardens with a closed canopy.

Vegetarian Bias

The cardinal eats both plant and animal foods, but it is mainly vegetarian. A study carried out in the early 1900s listed 33 kinds of wild fruit and 39 types of weed seeds, and concluded that about three-quarters of the entire diet consisted of plant material. The cardinal has a large, thick bill adapted to eating seeds, so this bias is to be expected. It also takes flower blossoms and elm buds, and occasionally drinks sap from the holes made in maple trees by the yellow-bellied sapsucker (*Sphyrapicus varius*), a type of woodpecker.

In the breeding season it feeds mainly on invertebrate animals such as insects and spiders, and the young are fed 95 percent animal food and 5 percent vegetable matter.

↑ *The female cardinal is an attractive bird in her own right, although she cannot compete with the crimson glory of the male. Both sexes have crests that they erect at the slightest provocation.*

The animals are caught mostly on the ground, the birds hopping around under the shrubbery and locating their prey by sight. Studies have shown that the cardinal consumes an amazing variety of insects: no fewer than 51 species of beetles, ten species of bugs (including cicadas), four species of grasshoppers and crickets, and the caterpillars of eight species of butterflies and moths. The birds also take centipedes, snails, slugs, and spiders.

It is not difficult to entice cardinals to bird feeders in a garden, since they find corn and sunflower seeds impossible to resist, especially in winter. In places some individuals have become so tame that they will perch on the hand to feed. Their social behavior at bird feeders seems to vary from place to place. While some birds seem placid, others have given cardinals a reputation for being aggressive at feeding stations, driving away other, smaller species and even members of their own kind.

Red Flush

Although some cardinals stay as a pair in the same territory all year around, most join up in winter flocks that may number as many as 60 or 70 birds. These groups move around the neighborhood widely, often visiting bird feeders en masse in a spectacular flush of red. The male-to-female ratio in these flocks is about even, and it suggests that many of the birds are pairs. On the whole, group members are mildly aggressive to each other, keeping their distance, but some males object to others feeding anywhere near them and may even drive away their own mates.

A change of behavior among cardinals can signal the arrival of spring long before it becomes noticeable in the landscape. Aggressive males suddenly allow females to approach much closer, so that they feed amicably side by side. As early as January the

⊖ *Male birds with spectacular plumage often try to attract several mates, but male cardinals are an exception, forming monogamous pairs and gathering their share of food for the growing young.*

Duelists in Song

Male cardinals usually sort out their territorial disputes by means of song duels instead of resorting to actual fighting. During these duels one male utters a song phrase, and the rival male responds to him immediately. Quick responses like this are known as countersinging. In most bird species in which song duels occur, countersinging males stick to their own song phrases and do not mimic exactly what they are hearing. In the cardinal, however, the rival's response is usually the same as the preceding song phrase, as if he were copying the insult and hurling it back. Such vocal performances are known as "matched countersinging" because the echoing singer matches the song phrases of the first singer.

Matched countersinging occurs in a number of songbirds. It may seem an unusual way to confront rivals, but perhaps some birds find that hearing their own territorial proclamations matched note for note is more intimidating than hearing a rival's own notes.

⊕ Like all seed-eating birds, cardinals such as this female must drink regularly due to the high proportion of dry material in their diet.

cold air fills with the cardinal's superb singing.

The song is highly variable, but is always characterized by liquid trills and almost slurred whistles. It is sung with vigor and confidence, dominating the local bird chorus, and is as ear-catching as the bird is eye-catching.

The cardinal is one of the few birds to sing energetically almost year round, and it is clear that song plays an extremely important role in the social life of the species. Nearly 30 distinct song types have been described, but each singer has only eight to twelve songs in its repertoire, which is quite small for such a vocal species. However, territorial males sing all through the day, with hardly a letup, and some have been heard singing in the dead of night.

Defensive Tangle

While the male defends the territory by song, the female sets about building a nest. She nearly always selects a site in low shrubbery rather than in a tree. In gardens honeysuckle bushes, privet hedges, and roses are greatly favored, and in the wild the birds resort to clumps of vines, saplings, and blackberry bushes, although almost anywhere with enough dense, tangled foliage will suffice. The maze of vegetation protects the nest well, and it is safer here than if it were placed high up in a tree. Occupied cardinal nests, with females sitting on eggs, have been found in the hedges along busy walkways in urban parks. The safety of a nest depends on its privacy, not its elevation above the ground.

The nest is a well-built cup. Although it looks simple, its construction is quite intricate, with four separate layers built on top of each other. The bottom layer consists of a platform of stems. Leaves and bark follow on top, with grass and thin plant stems above them. The upper layer (the lining) consists of fine grass stems and small rootlets. Collecting all these materials requires considerable effort. Despite this, the male very rarely helps the female, although he will give "moral support" while accompanying her on a collecting expedition.

Cardinals display a sense of great urgency during their breeding activities, doing everything with great haste. For example, they may build the nest in as little as three days, and both the incubation period and the nestling period are short for the size of bird. A pair may even start a new brood before the last has flown the nest. At such times it is possible to see a male cardinal feeding the recently fledged young while his mate is already on the nest

incubating the next clutch of eggs. By working at such a pace, and starting early in the year, it is quite common for a pair of cardinals to raise three or four broods each season. Occasionally, five broods have been recorded.

Insidious Enemies

Various disasters can break this chain of production. Cats may catch adults and young, squirrels raid the nests for eggs, and blue jays (*Cyanocitta cristata*) are a danger to eggs, nestlings, and even quite large fledglings. More insidiously, the house wren (*Troglodytes aedon*) will sometimes steal inside the nest and prick the eggs with its bill. This diminutive destroyer attacks the eggs of many species besides its own, for reasons that are not fully understood.

Of all the enemies that cardinals face, potentially the worst is the brown-headed cowbird (*Molothrus ater*). It is a parasite on many smaller North American birds, since it makes no effort to raise its own young and instead lays its eggs in the nest of a "host" in the same way as the common cuckoo (*Cuculus canorus*). Although the cowbird chick does not evict the young of its host, it hatches earlier than they do, grows faster, and therefore out-competes them for food. As a result, the host young often starve and ultimately die. In some parts of its range the cardinal is one of the cowbird's main targets, and many broods may fail as their food supplies are diverted into the ever-hungry mouths of cowbird chicks.

For the most part, however, the cardinal is a success story. It has embraced the switch from woodland undergrowth to suburbia with enthusiasm, benefiting in both population growth and range expansion. The ready availability of food at garden feeding stations has enabled the species to spread northward, so it is occupying areas such as the state of Michigan, where once the harsh climate and consequent lack of food would have prevented it from surviving. It has now reached southern Canada. There seems little doubt that its spread will continue for some time at least, and that it will be welcome wherever it goes.

The Cardinal's Courtship

It is enjoyable and fairly easy to watch the growing courtship of a pair of cardinals. At the first sign of spring a male and female begin to feed side by side on a bird-feeding station, with no bickering. Singing follows, with both members of the pair taking part, one following the phrases of the other.

After they have performed their song, the next stage is an attractive ritual known as mate feeding. Quite simply, the male picks up an edible item and passes it to the female, bill to bill. This is endlessly repeated and may carry on intermittently for several weeks.

A much more private ceremony follows, which is not often seen. Each member of the pair leans from one side, then the other, in a swaying motion often accompanied by quiet sounds. It is called the "lopsided" pose and signals intense courtship between the pair.

⊕ *Gaping to display its colored mouth lining, a nestling cardinal begs for food. Its parents feed it almost exclusively on insects and other small animals, which have a higher protein content than seeds.*

Snow Bunting

Plectrophenax nivalis

Common name Snow bunting

Scientific name *Plectrophenax nivalis*

Family	Emberizidae
Order	Passeriformes
Size	Length: 6.8 in (17 cm); wingspan: 13 in (33–38 cm); weight: 1.5 oz (42.5 g)
Key features	Plump songbird with long, broad wings and medium-length tail; typical seed-eater's conical bill; breeding male has all-white head and underparts, black back, and pied (blotches of two or more colors) wings and tail; females and nonbreeding birds are curry-brown and white, with black streaking
Habits	Quite tame; often travels in flocks, especially in winter; flocks move forward in "leapfrog" style, birds at the back flying over and in front of lead birds
Nesting	On ground; large open cup nest of moss and grass, lined with feathers; 3–5 eggs, sometimes more, pale blue with red spots; incubation 10–15 days by female only; young fledge after 8 days; 1 brood
Voice	Song is short, crystal-clear "turee-turee-turee-turitui"; flight/contact call is short trill
Diet	Seeds and some insects
Habitat	Barren areas of high Arctic, often near snow and ice; also open ground, including fields
Distribution	Many parts of Northern Hemisphere
Status	Not threatened; often common

Breeding further north than any other small bird, the snow bunting thrives in windswept, snowy conditions throughout the year, thanks to a variety of adaptations to its hostile habitat.

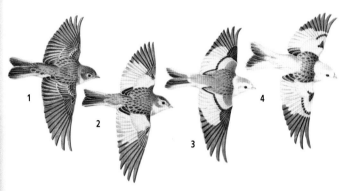

YOU NEED ONLY LOOK AT A MALE snow bunting in breeding plumage to guess where it lives. The bold black-and-white pattern is perfect for living in ice and snow, providing camouflage where rocks interrupt the smooth white surface. It is an adaptation for breeding in the high Arctic—further north than any other bird of its type—as far as the edge of the permanent ice in Alaska, Arctic Canada, Greenland, Europe, and Russia. Even in winter it retains its taste for extreme conditions, with some birds not migrating, and others going south to wind-blasted coasts and mountains

Arctic Survivor

The snow bunting is equipped for arctic survival by being larger than most buntings, with quite a heavy body. That gives it more bulk relative to its surface area, so it loses heat less readily than smaller birds. The bird's plumage is unusually fluffy and thick, to provide insulation. The snow bunting has a shuffling gait, accentuated by its habit of crouching, to keep its legs under the fluffed-out plumage of its belly and protect it from the cold.

⊕ *Snow buntings in their various plumage: an immature female (1); an adult female (2); an immature male (3); and an adult male (4). The winter plumage is browner than the bold black-and white plumage of an adult male in summer.*

Snow buntings eat seeds and insects gathered from the ground or from very low-growing plants. What they take varies from place to place and from season to season. In the winter flocks of snow buntings forage on shorelines and take sandhoppers, a favorite food item, from the heaps of seaweed dumped by the tide. Snowfields on mountains and tundra also make excellent foraging grounds. Insects are blown here by the wind, and in the very cold conditions they are immediately immobilized, making them easy to catch. In the breeding season young snow buntings are fed on an exclusive diet of protein-rich insects, but throughout the year the adults feed mainly on seeds, including spilled grain and weed seeds gleaned from stubble in fields.

Early Birds

Male snow buntings arrive on their breeding grounds as much as a month before the females. They use the time to establish territories, which they defend by singing and the occasional skirmish.

When the females eventually arrive, the males initially treat them aggressively, as if they were rival males. But the females remain calm in the face of this hostile reception, and eventually the males recognize them as potential mates. Aggression is replaced by the "mannequin display," in which each male struts to and fro on a boulder, alternately spreading and closing his wings and tail.

Harsh Strategy

The nest is placed on the ground, often among boulders or on a scree slope. Other nests are placed in crevices, especially in rock faces, and often among large colonies of seabirds. The nest is bulky and often lined with the white feathers of a ptarmigan (*Lagopus mutus*).

Snow buntings practice a system known as "brood reduction." Instead of beginning incubation when the clutch of eggs is complete, like most small birds, the female starts incubating before she lays the last egg. As a result, some eggs hatch earlier than others. The older chicks are usually stronger and out-compete their siblings for food. The apparently unfair system ensures that at least the older chicks survive in times of food shortage, because a fairer share would put the whole brood at risk. It is a severe strategy, yet a necessary one in the bird's harsh environment.

⊕ *In winter many snow buntings fly south from their arctic breeding grounds and can often be found feeding in flocks on shorelines, looking for seeds and small invertebrates such as sandhoppers. This winter flock is foraging on the coast of Norfolk in eastern England.*

Common name Common grackle

Scientific name *Quiscalus quiscula*

Family	Icteridae
Order	Passeriformes
Size	Length: 11–13.5 in (28–34 cm); wingspan: 14–17.5 in (36–44.5 cm); weight: 3–4 oz (85–113 g)
Key features	Large bird with long, wedge-shaped tail; iridescent black plumage; obvious pale eyes; females smaller and slightly duller than males
Habits	Often on suburban lawns; flocks with other icterids and starlings
Nesting	Bulky nest of stems and leaves, lined with mud covered by grass or hair; 1–7 pale blue to gray eggs with dark markings; incubation 11–15 days by female; young fledge after 12–15 days; 1 brood, occasionally 2
Voice	Song brief, variable, harsh, and squeaky, like a rusty gate; also loud "chuck" call
Diet	Grain and invertebrates in breeding season; grain, fruit, and acorns at other times; rarely eggs and chicks of other birds
Habitat	Open areas with scattered trees, including woods, swamps, and parks; roosts in patches of trees, marshes, and street trees during migration and winter
Distribution	Most of the eastern U.S., expanding north and west in breeding season to southern edge of the Canadian Northwest Territories
Status	One of the commonest birds in North America

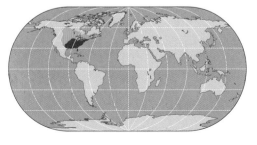

Common Grackle

Quiscalus quiscula

In the eighteenth and nineteenth centuries the common grackle benefited from forest clearance in the east, since it provided new places to breed and new sources of food. It is still making a good living in many American suburbs.

VERSATILE AND SUCCESSFUL, THE COMMON grackle is a common and familiar bird throughout most of its large range. Yet despite being instantly recognizable, it varies a lot in color and structure. There are currently thought to be three races. In most areas common grackles are of the "bronzed" race, with a shiny bronze body. The "purple grackle" is found east of the Appalachian Mountains from southwest Connecticut down to Alabama and Georgia, with some birds wintering in Florida. The purple grackle has a shiny purple body rather than shiny bronze. Finally, the "Florida grackle" has a green back. This southeastern race occurs from Louisiana to North Carolina and as far south as the Florida Keys.

Bill size and wing length also vary. Northern common grackles have longer wings and smaller bills than southern grackles. Their wings get shorter and their bills get larger the farther south you go.

Most, although not all, common grackles are migratory and head toward the Gulf of Mexico in the fall. But they may not get there. The distances between their breeding areas and wintering areas are not great, and birds from the northern part of the species' range may travel just a few hundred miles to reach suitable wintering sites. Common grackles that breed around the Gulf coast do not migrate at all. For some reason female grackles tend to migrate a little further than male grackles—perhaps about 60 miles (100 km), and birds migrating for the first time travel 150–200 miles (240–320 km) farther than older birds.

⊖ *Big, bold, and very adaptable, the common grackle has become almost too successful for its own good. This female of the bronze race has duller black plumage than a male, but has the same conspicuous pale eyes.*

They travel in mixed-species flocks with red-winged blackbirds (*Agelaius phoeniceus*), brown-headed cowbirds (*Molothrus ater*), and European starlings (*Sturnus vulgaris*), stopping to spend the night at roost sites with hundreds of thousands of other birds.

Secret of Success

Common grackles are adaptable feeders, a quality that has helped make them a very successful species. They follow plows to find insect larvae, search for food around the tide line in coastal areas, and have even been known to wade into shallow water to catch fish! They will take bread, soaking it in water before eating it, and steal worms from American robins (*Turdus migratorius*). The grackle even has a special blade sticking down from its palate, which it uses to score around an acorn before cracking it open.

Some of the common grackle's feeding habits do little to enhance its reputation. Large mixed-species flocks of common grackles and red-winged blackbirds descend on grain and fruit crops to feed, and losses caused by these flocks can amount to tens of millions of dollars a year. As a result, common grackles are regarded as pests and may be legally culled.

They also have a reputation for eating the eggs and nestlings of other birds, and even for occasionally killing and eating adult birds. Yet roughly three-quarters

⊖ *The iridescent effects on the body of this male bronze-race common grackle are caused by the way light is reflected from its feather structure, rather than by the actual color of the feathers.*

of their diet is plant material, and insects form most of the remainder. Overall, birds account for less than one percent of their diet. But they have the reputation anyway, and that does little to improve their image.

Early Nesters

Common grackles start nesting at the end of March in the central part of their range, making them some of North America's earliest nesters. Normally they are monogamous and semi-colonial, although occasionally males mate with more than one female. The males return to their breeding grounds about a week before the females. Once the females arrive, courtship can begin, with several males trying to impress a single female. When the pair is formed, the female chooses a nest site, normally high up in a conifer. She builds the nest as well, either resting it on a roughly horizontal branch or hanging it between branches. Occasionally, she may move to the nest of another bird, for common grackles are adaptable breeders as well as adaptable feeders. They have nested in occupied osprey (*Pandion haliaetus*) nests and the nests of great blue herons (*Ardea herodias*).

Both sexes defend the nest site against other pairs of common grackles, red-winged blackbirds, and yellow-headed blackbirds (*Xanthocephalus xanthocephalus*). Yet interestingly, they do not drive away unpaired common grackles. When the eggs are laid and incubation is underway, roughly half of all male common grackles abandon the females, leaving them to complete the incubation and defend the nest against mammal and reptile predators.

Grackle Deterrents

It is a common bird—so common that its appetite for grain, sunflowers, and fruit has turned it into a serious agricultural pest. To reduce its impact, crops are sprayed with

Striking Effects of Iridescence

Iridescence produces some stunning plumage effects on a range of bird species, including starlings, hummingbirds, and American blackbirds. Most plumage colors are created by pigments in the feathers, but iridescence is a type of "structural coloration."

The main shaft of a feather is known as the "rachis." Many barbs branch off each side of the rachis to form the vane of the feather. Barbules branch off each barb, hooking into barbules from adjacent barbs and joining the vane of the feather together. Iridescence is the result of light interference created when a barbule is twisted and flattened along some of its length. Twisted, iridescent barbules do not have hooks or flanges to join to neighboring barbules, so iridescent feathers are not as strong as noniridescent feathers. This means that iridescence is not normally found in flight feathers, because a flight feather needs to be as strong as possible.

Bird Pests

O f nearly 10,000 bird species in the world only a very small proportion truly qualify as pests. Most of them get into trouble for the same reason as the common grackle—because they eat seeds or agricultural produce. Seeds are an energy-rich food; and when we plant huge numbers of seeds to produce crops or grow crops that produce lots of seeds, it is not surprising that some birds make the most of the wonderful feeding opportunity. Seed-eating bird "culprits" include grackles and other American blackbirds, starlings, weavers, and parakeets. Some birds target the leaves and stems of crops as well. Pigeons and geese are among the guilty parties here. Commercial fruit production is also an irresistible temptation for some birds. Starlings, thrushes, finches, and parrots are all on the list of convicted frugivores. Even fish farming attracts birds such as herons, gulls, and ospreys, and in some areas mute swans (*Cygnus olor*) have been blamed for eating fish eggs.

Young plantations may be damaged by roosting birds when the sheer weight of the birds breaks off branches. Where large numbers of birds are involved, the buildup of guano can kill trees. Big roosts can also cause problems where birds have adapted to living in towns. The droppings of European starlings and feral pigeons (*Columba livia*) can create slippery and dangerous sidewalks, and some large roosts may harbor serious human diseases.

methiocarb, a taste repellent that reduces the damage caused by birds. The birds are also controlled at their roost sites, because the roosts are thought to harbor the fungus that causes histoplasmosis, a respiratory disease that can kill people. A chemical called PA-14 is used to kill the birds at their roost sites by destroying their natural waterproofing. Their feathers get wet, and the birds eventually die of exposure. So although the grackle population grew following the forest clearances of past centuries, the bird is now declining east of the Rockies. Yet its range is still expanding to the west, where common grackles are taking advantage of planted shelter belts.

⊕ *It may be a problem to farmers and even public health authorities, but there is no denying that the common grackle is a handsome bird.*

Baltimore Oriole

Icterus galbula

In 1731 this species was known as the Baltimore bird. It was named after the Baltimores, Maryland's colonial administrators, because its vivid orange-and-black plumage echoed their family colors.

WITH ITS STRIKING PLUMAGE AND powerful song, this vivid orange-and-black vocalist brings color and music to suburbs and riversides throughout much of the eastern U.S. It is quite distinctive, but in 1983 the American Ornithologists' Union regarded it and Bullock's oriole (*Icterus bullockii*) as the same species: the northern oriole. In 1995 opinions changed, and Bullock's oriole and the Baltimore oriole were split into two separate species. In fact, scientists now think that the Altamira oriole (*I. gularis*) or the black-backed oriole (*I. abeillei*) may be closer relatives of the Baltimore oriole than Bullock's oriole.

Baltimore orioles are found throughout much of North America east of the Rockies in the breeding season. After breeding, they head south; most spend the northern winter in the Caribbean and the tropics, although some winter in Florida and California. A few stay in the north for the winter, making the most of well-stocked bird feeders, but it is unlikely that they survive for another breeding season.

Versatile Feeders

Baltimore orioles are versatile feeders. They will take food out of spiders' webs, and in some areas they help control plagues of orchard tent caterpillars. They use "gaping" to good effect, too; an oriole will stick its bill into a fruit and then open it so it can extract the flesh with its tongue or use a similar action to search out insects tucked away in rolled-up leaves.

In their wintering areas they supplement their fruit and insect diet with nectar. They take the nectar from trees and epiphytes (plants that grow on trees). They use gaping for this, too.

Common name Baltimore oriole

Scientific name *Icterus galbula*

Family Icteridae

Order Passeriformes

Size Length: 6.5–7.5 in (16.5–19 cm); wingspan: 11–12.5 in (28–32 cm); weight: 1–1.5 oz (28–42.5 g)

Key features Medium-sized, sharp-billed bird; male has black head, neck, and upper back; mostly black wings; orange "shoulders"; black-and-orange tail, orange underparts and rump; female duller, browny-green above, pale orange below

Habits Often lives close to people

Nesting Sacklike nest in outermost branch of tree; 3–6 off-white eggs marked with brown, black, and bluish purple; incubation 11–14 days; young fledge after 11–14 days; 1 brood

Voice Male has loud, melodic song; female has simpler song; "chatter call" used to deter intruders and predators

Diet Insects (especially caterpillars), fruit, and spiders; also nectar in wintering areas

Habitat Deciduous woodland edges, especially near rivers, parkland, shade trees; winter habitats include damp woodlands and plantations

Distribution Most of U.S. east of Rocky Mountains, some of southern Canada, ranging south to Central America and northern South America

Status Apparently stable

An oriole may hold a plucked flower in one foot, insert its bill, and open it to gain access to the energy-rich nectar within. Not surprisingly, Baltimore orioles often act as plant pollinators. They also take sugar solution from oriole and hummingbird feeders and, occasionally, defend the feeders as private food supplies.

Pendulous Nest

Baltimore orioles are mainly monogamous, although some males do mate with additional females. The males arrive on the breeding grounds ahead of the females. Once the pairs are formed, the female chooses the nest site and builds the pendulous nest, crafting it from grasses, milkweed stems, hair, string, and wool. Cottonwood, willow cotton, and feathers help form the soft lining. Building the nest takes

around a week. Both birds defend the area near the nest against intruders, but in areas shared with other Baltimore orioles they may have to go a little farther away to feed.

On the Great Plains the Baltimore oriole often hybridizes with the Bullock's oriole. The two species are different sizes, behave differently, sound different, and look different, but they still interbreed.

Stable Population

The Baltimore oriole population seems to have stabilized after an increase between 1966 and 1979 and a decrease from 1980 to 1994. The species has moved into areas where woodland has been cleared or trees planted and does well even in areas near man, so its future is likely to be secure.

⊕ Adaptable and quick to learn, the Baltimore oriole is quick to exploit feeding opportunities in surburban backyards —a trait that promises well for its future in a changing world.

Common name Pine grosbeak

Scientific name *Pinicola enucleator*

Family	Fringillidae
Order	Passeriformes

Size Length: 9 in (23 cm); wingspan: 14.5 in (37 cm); weight: 2 oz (57 g)

Key features Medium-sized, very plump songbird; long tail; soft-looking plumage; large, stumpy bill; adult males faded red; females and immatures gray-green, russet patches on head and rump; white edges to wing feathers form double white bar

Habits Quiet and unobtrusive, especially when breeding; powerful, undulating flight; forms flocks outside breeding season; feeds mainly above ground among branches

Nesting Bulky cup nest of moss, twigs, grass, and lichens, lined with finer materials; usually low in shrub or tree; usually 4 eggs, blue-green with some spotting; incubation 13–14 days by female only; young fledge after 13–20 days; 1 brood

Voice Song is high-pitched, descending phrase; call is repeated "pew"

Diet Buds, shoots, seeds, and berries, with insects in breeding season

Habitat Coniferous forest; also gardens in winter

Distribution Taiga forest belt of Northern Hemisphere

Status Not threatened; very widespread

Pine Grosbeak

Pinicola enucleator

With its thick, soft plumage the pine grosbeak is well adapted to the extreme climates of the far north and high mountaintops, where it is perfectly at home even when there is thick snow on the ground.

THERE ARE FEW MORE HARDY birds than the pine grosbeak. It is perfectly capable of living well north of the Arctic Circle even at the height of winter, so long as food is readily available. It seems quite immune to the harsh climate and has often been seen taking baths in fresh snow.

The pine grosbeak is large for its family, with an unusually long tail. Adult males are particularly handsome, and their plumage is dominated by strawberry crimson. They have dark wings with two bold white bars and a large, stumpy bill. Birds in the extreme north and west of North America are the most colorful, with crimson all over; those that live in the southern Rocky Mountains have much more gray on their underparts.

Polar Distribution

The pine grosbeak occurs all around the North Pole in the arctic and subarctic zones of both North America and Eurasia. An offshoot of the North American population occurs in the high Rocky Mountains south to New Mexico, and there is an isolated population in California.

Pine grosbeaks are fussy about where they live, even among the vast subarctic coniferous forests, or taiga. For example, they prefer sloping ground and gullies. Some favor wooded areas surrounded by extensive marshes or swamps. In Eurasia they have a fondness for birch woods with an undergrowth of juniper, especially since juniper berries are a favorite food. But the populations of these birds tend to be scattered and hard to locate. They leave vast tracts of terrain unoccupied, even though it appears to be perfectly suitable habitat.

⊖ *Like many birds of the far north, the pine grosbeak is equipped with thick, insulating plumage, which gives it a distinctive, soft appearance. This male has fluffed up his feathers for extra warmth in the winter snow.*

Grosbeak Irruptions

The pine grosbeak is a seldom-seen bird, confined to the vast, far-northern forests of North America and Eurasia. But every so often, and always in the winter, it unexpectedly arrives in large numbers in places far to the south of its normal range. Such arrivals, or "irruptions," are irregular, unpredictable events. Flocks descend on gardens and towns, the birds eagerly feeding on berries in suburban streets or taking seeds from bird feeders. Arriving from nowhere, they are hard to miss. But what causes these sudden arrivals of visitors from the extreme north?

Research on several irruptive species—others include the red crossbill (*Loxia curvirostra*) and the Bohemian waxwing (*Bombycilla garrulus*)—has shown that these movements are caused by irregular food supplies. Many trees and shrubs have cycles of productivity, with a year of plentiful fruit production often followed by a poor one. In a year when a key food source is in short supply, birds can be forced to move southward to look for alternative nourishment.

However, that does not always happen, because even in poor years there may still be enough food to feed the current population of pine grosbeaks; it depends on the numbers. Most bird populations are also cyclical, varying according to factors such as summer food supply and resulting breeding success. Every so often there will be a boom year for pine grosbeaks, leading to greater than usual numbers of young birds swelling the early winter population.

When a booming population of birds coincides with a failure in the fall food supply, the conditions are right for an irruption to occur. In the case of the grosbeak it is often a shortage of rowan berries that triggers the irruption. The food shortage encourages a mass movement south, and suddenly pine grosbeaks are everywhere.

Fastidious Feeder

The pine grosbeak's bill is stubby, with a slightly hooked tip. It is adapted for dealing with buds and berries, which the bird takes in large quantities along with shoots and seeds. When dealing with a bud, a bird grips it firmly, then tilts its head to one side to slice it away. Pine grosbeaks do not like the sticky scales on buds, so they take them off and eat only the kernel beneath. When tackling berries, pine grosbeaks are equally fastidious, carefully removing the skin before swallowing the pulp and seed. To deal with spruce cones, a favorite food, they peel away the outer parts of the cone to reach the core.

A flock will often stay at a feeding site for hours on end, carefully stripping a tree of all its produce. The birds can be surprisingly agile, clambering to all parts of a tree to reach every berry. They also use their hooked bills as "third

When the berry crop is good, pine grosbeaks like this immature male can stay in the far north all winter; but if a poor crop follows a highly successful breeding season, the lack of food may force grosbeak flocks to move south in random "irruptions."

The "Silly Idiot"

The silly idiot seems an unlikely label for a bird, but one of the old Swedish names for the pine grosbeak, *dumsnut*, means just that. The name arises from the extremely confiding nature of this bird, which, in the light of what some people have done to it in the past, could indeed be described as idiotic.

Pine grosbeaks show virtually no fear of humans. In the heart of their range there is little human activity, even less persecution. Most pine grosbeaks never see a person in their whole lives. When lack of food drives them southward, they have no experience of people and no reason for caution. However, their trusting nature also extends to the breeding season, when birds incubating eggs allow a very close approach. There are records of people actually touching female pine grosbeaks sitting tight on their nests.

In the past people have sadly abused this trusting nature. Many birds were caught for food during irruptions even in the twentieth century. Longer ago, pine grosbeaks were also regularly kept as cage birds. There are stories of wandering minstrels visiting Scandinavian towns and performing stage acts using grosbeaks as "assistants." The birds were trained to fly to and fro from the audience, carrying written messages.

Today, a visiting flock of these northern wanderers is more likely to inspire people to reach for a pair of binoculars to get a close view. As a result, the birds can be admired, rather than ridiculed, for their magnificent indifference to humans.

limbs" for climbing in the same way that parrots use their bills.

The breeding season brings about a major change in foraging behavior, as adult grosbeaks start eating invertebrates and feeding them to their young. They capture moths, flies, beetles, and grasshoppers, sometimes during brief, cumbersome airborne sallies. The birds also eat snails, perhaps to provide calcium for eggshell formation. They subdue larger insects by biting repeatedly with their hooked bills; other large-billed finches like the hawfinch (*Coccothraustes coccothraustes*) crush their prey instead.

In late summer the birds alter their feeding patterns slightly, from seeking insects and buds up in the trees to taking berries in the shrubby undergrowth of the northern forests. The supply of berries will dictate their lives for many months to come. If there is a good berry supply, the birds will remain in the north for much of the winter; but if the supply shows signs of running out, they will have to head south. Such movements occur between August and October, and most of the wanderers—if they survive—return in February.

Territorial Pairs

The onset of spring triggers pair formation. There is evidence that the pairs get together in the winter flocks; but since these flocks have a tendency to travel to their breeding grounds intact and then split up, the pairing process may be more protracted. However, the woodlands soon fill with pine grosbeak song as each pair settles into its own territory.

The pine grosbeak is unusual among cardueline finches for being territorial, with each pair well separated from the next; no aggregations of pairs, or "neighborhood groups," have been found. Perhaps that is because there is plenty of food available close by, since a secure local food supply makes defending a territory worthwhile.

Pine grosbeaks sing from exposed perches. The song consists of high-pitched, descending notes. It is fairly prolonged and has a distinctly fast, muttering quality to it. Unusually, both sexes regularly sing, which suggests that there is a definite courtship element to their song as well as a territorial one. In most small, territory-holding bird species, especially in temperate regions, song is largely the male's duty.

Nesting duties in pine grosbeaks follow the pattern of the rest of the finch family. The female takes on the bulk of the physical work but is fed by the male. Thus the female collects the twigs, grass, and other plant matter used to build the bulky nest; it is also she that incubates the eggs (although there are some claims that the male helps occasionally), and it is she that broods the resulting chicks, at least during the first few days.

Meanwhile, the male keeps her supplied with food, collecting what she needs and delivering it to her mouth in much the same way that he will later provide for the young. The male varies in his delivery style: Sometimes he brings food straight to the nest, but at other times he gives a summoning call to his mate and feeds her a little distance away.

Short Season

By the time the eggs have been laid, in late May or early June, the northern summer is close to its height. If the first clutch is lost, pine grosbeaks will occasionally re-lay as late as the middle of July; but the season is short, and time is not on their side. Most related finches pack several broods into a season, but not pine grosbeaks; there are no definite records of more than one brood being raised.

Once the young have hatched, both parents become fully committed to the task of collecting food for their offspring. Their feeding trips are cooperative occasions: They set out together and return together. There seems no obvious reason for this close association, but it may be a way of ensuring that all the young in the nest get fed at once.

The more food the adults can gather, the quicker the young birds grow; some broods leave the nest after two weeks, others after three. About a third of pine grosbeak nests successfully produce fledged young. Those that

Food in Pouches

The pine grosbeak has developed a most unusual way of carrying food to its young. Inside the mouth cavity are two special food pouches, one on each side of the tongue, that develop early in the breeding season. When the parents are on a foraging trip, they stuff a mixture of seeds and insects into their pouches and carry it back to the waiting nestlings. This normally ensures that the young birds are well catered for at each feed.

Such pouches are very unusual in birds, although both the rosy finch (*Leucosticte tephrocotis*) and the Eurasian bullfinch (*Pyrrhula pyrrhula*) have similar structures. Most birds carry food in the bill, in the floor of the mouth, in the crop, or in the gullet.

fail are usually robbed by crows. Apart from this, pine grosbeaks have few enemies.

Although it is extremely choosy in regard to its breeding habitat, the pine grosbeak is a born survivor. With such a large range there is no obvious threat to its future, and pine grosbeaks will probably be flying around the northern woods for many years to come.

⊕ Female pine grosbeaks have generally gray-green plumage but may also have patches of russet on their heads and rumps. That makes them very hard to distinguish from first-year males.

American Goldfinch

Carduelis tristis

Specially equipped for feeding on the seeds of thistles and similar plants, and using their soft down for its nest, the American goldfinch breeds unusually late in the year to make the most of the annual weed harvest.

Common name American goldfinch

Scientific name *Carduelis tristis*

Family Fringillidae

Order Passeriformes

Size Length: 5 in (13 cm); wingspan: 9 in (23 cm); weight: 0.5 oz (14 g)

Key features Small songbird with small conical bill; fairly long wings and short tail; male colorful in breeding season, mainly bright yellow with black forehead, wings, and tail; females, immatures, and nonbreeding males mainly gray-brown with yellow wash and black wings with pale wing bars

Habits Highly active, with distinctive light, airy flight; feeds acrobatically on seed heads; forms twittering flocks

Nesting Cup nest lined with plant down woven tightly to fork in branch of tree; 4–6 pale blue eggs; incubation 10–12 days; young fledge after 11–17 days; 1–2 broods

Voice Song is lively musical repetition of trills and twitters; call is very thin "twee"

Diet Seeds; some fruit

Habitat Weedy fields and open woodland

Distribution North America north to southern Canada and south to Mexico

Status Not threatened; common, although some declines in east of range

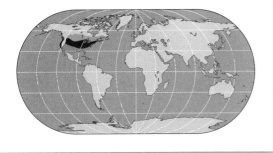

THE AMERICAN GOLDFINCH IS A COLORFUL, popular bird. The male is especially attractive, with buttery yellow plumage that can gleam golden in the sunlight. The song is also pleasing, with light, airy notes. Yet the bright plumage is seen only during the spring and summer because after breeding, the male molts to an undistinguished yellow-green.

American goldfinches are highly sociable, living in groups throughout the year. Winter flocks often number 300 or more and frequently intermix with other small finches, including Eurasian siskins (*Carduelis pinus*). On many days it does not take long to acquire enough seeds to satisfy a bird's requirements, so the members of a flock can spend time resting, preening, and often singing together.

Thistle Probe

The bill of the American goldfinch is fairly thin, allowing it to indulge in its speciality: probing between the sharp spikes of thistle heads to retrieve the tiny seeds within. The taste for thistle seeds means that parties of feeding American goldfinches are a common sight on weedy fields and untended gardens throughout much of North America.

The American goldfinch's small size and relatively strong legs make it a nimble feeder. It balances effortlessly on the seed heads of thistles and similar plants, maneuvering with a few flutters of its wings and clinging on even when the stems bend over. It can also feed up in the trees, where it performs acrobatic routines such as clinging to catkins. The flocks often feed in the same places for long periods,

↪ *Although the American goldfinch has a specialized diet, it can be attracted to backyard feeding stations by providing thistle seed in specially designed bird feeders. The seed is particularly welcome in winter, when the adult males lose their bright breeding colors.*

working away at clumps of suitable plants until the supply of food is almost exhausted.

Late Breeder

As a thistle specialist, the American goldfinch enjoys a glut of food in the late summer and fall. As a result, it has one of the latest breeding seasons of any North American bird, often producing young in July or even later. In common with other cardueline finches, the young are fed mainly on regurgitated seeds, plus a few insects.

Pairs meet and form within the feeding flocks, often quite gradually. As the pairs become better acquainted, the male performs a song flight, flying along a level course with rapidly fluttering wings, singing all the time.

The female nearly always returns to the nest site that she used in previous years. It is usually in the outer fork of a low shrub or tree, often not much more than 6 feet (1.8 m) above the ground. Some nests are built much higher than this, up to 60 feet (18 m) above ground, where wind can be a problem.

Goldfinch nests are amazing structures. They are cup shaped and made up of various plant fibers, including rootlets and stems; the lining is mainly thistledown, and the outer walls of the nest are often strengthened with cobwebs and caterpillar silk. The fibers are so intricately interwoven that the nests can actually hold water.

All the incubation is done by the female, who is fed all the while by the male. In contrast to most small birds, goldfinches often begin incubating before their clutch is complete, with the result that some of the eggs hatch sooner than others. This is an adaptation to an unpredictable food supply. If there are plenty of seeds and small insects around, all the chicks will be well fed. But if food is scarce, the adults can feed only the older, more aggressively begging youngsters, and the younger ones starve. Although harsh, it is an inevitable result of the American goldfinch's specialized diet.

House Sparrow

Passer domesticus

Tame but not trusting, the house sparrow lives on the coattails of humans. Where people thrive, so do house sparrows—a talent that has enabled them to spread throughout much of the world.

Common name House sparrow

Scientific name *Passer domesticus*

Family Ploceidae

Order Passeriformes

Size Length: 6.25 in (16 cm); wingspan: 9.5 in (24 cm); weight: 1 oz (28 g)

Key features Small songbird with thick, conical seed-eater's bill; streaky-brown above, plain below; male has bold black markings around eye, on chin, and on breast; also has gray crown, chestnut nape; female lacks all bold coloration; juveniles similar

Habits Bold, noisy, and sociable throughout year; young birds form large roosts

Nesting Season varies; in small colonies, often in thick bush; dome-shaped nest formed of grass lined with feathers; 3–6 eggs, whitish with speckles; incubation 11–14 days; young fledge after 14–16 days; 2–3 broods

Voice Variety of perky chirps; song of male is a series of single chirps in sequence

Diet Mainly seeds, but takes insects in breeding season; urban birds take household scraps

Habitat Essentially wherever there are people: cities, towns, villages, and farms

Distribution Europe and Asia; introduced to many other parts of the world, including North America

Status Not threatened, but recent decline; still abundant in many places

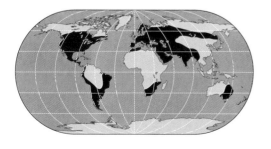

THE TERM "LITTLE BROWN BIRD" could have been coined with the house sparrow in mind, for it is such an accurate description. The house sparrow is instantly visible and recognizable wherever it occurs; indeed, as a familiar part of our artificial environments, it makes itself hard to miss. The bird is sociable, noisy, perky, and impudent in its use of our buildings and discarded food. However, the house sparrow also keeps its distance: near us but not part of us, dependent yet independent.

The house sparrow certainly owes its success to humans. About 12,000 years ago it was probably restricted to the Middle East, where it learned to feed on grain from agriculture and perhaps made the transition to nesting near human settlements. It soon became so dependent on the activities of people and their livestock that it followed them around, spreading quickly to new areas. From then on the fortunes of humans and birds ran side by side, leading to its vastly increased population and its spread and settlement over the whole world.

The house sparrow is so ubiquitous that it is often hard to appreciate the handsome pattern of the male. In spring it sports a black throat, gray cap and cheek, and a line of chestnut from the eye to the back. The wings, too, are attractively patterned with chestnut. It can be a rather slouching, horizontal bird, frequently drooping its wings, but it often holds up both its head and tail. Its flight is fast and unusually

⊙ *Adaptable and opportunistic, the house sparrow has learned that human settlements are rich sources of food, from spilled grain and kitchen scraps to the seeds of garden exotica like this red-hot poker.*

⊙ *Although both the male (1) and female (2) house sparrow are basically "little brown birds," the adult male develops boldly patterned plumage in the breeding season.*

1

2

direct for a small bird, without the characteristic swooping undulations of, for example, finches.

Bold Opportunists

It is not hard to see why house sparrows were attracted by agriculture, for both arable farming and the raising of livestock provide them with endless feeding opportunities.

Essentially they are seed-eaters, with the typical conical, seed-cracking bill, and there is a a great deal of seed around farms and fields. But what has always set them apart from other seed-eating birds is their audacity, which enables them to take grain left out for domestic animals or spilled on barn floors and farmyards a few feet away from working people. They are bold and highly opportunistic.

This resourcefulness has led the house sparrow in many directions. The more urban birds eat little grain, but take kitchen scraps, including bread, oats, cooked potatoes, and meat. In England sparrows have been recorded opening the tops of milk bottles. They have adapted to using all kinds of bird feeders, learning to cling on upside down and to hover so they can take peanuts from hanging bird feeders. They can feed outdoors, indoors, in greenhouses, and even down mineshafts. Sparrows searching for insects—a regular summer food—have been seen picking dead or trapped flies from car radiators.

In New York City they have been seen 80 stories up the Empire State Building, catching mayflies attracted to the floodlights. There seem to be few places that a house sparrow will not exploit.

Resourceful Breeders

It seems unlikely that the house sparrow would have achieved its success without showing the same kind of resourcefulness when nesting that it does when finding food. Above all, the bird has developed a tolerance of human disturbance that few other species possess. House sparrows have been recorded raising their young in rooms continually occupied by

277

⊖ *The house sparrow's cooperative breeding habit may enable a pair to raise several broods each season. Blind, naked, and helpless when they hatch, the nestlings soon grow their first feathers and emerge from the nest, although they do not travel far.*

people; they have been found nesting in parked vehicles, on streetlights, and in every kind of building. Their young may hatch only yards from roaring traffic, heavy industry, or the noise of commuters. Essentially, all that a house sparrow requires to raise its brood is a suitable hole into which to stuff its untidy nest, just out of reach of human hands.

In common with its human neighbors the house sparrow is an extremely sociable animal. Although isolated pairs do exist, most sparrows live in small colonies with a stable membership. New members usually join in the late summer, when recently fledged birds leave flocks of the young to become members of the breeding population. There are always vacancies to fill, since an individual adult house sparrow has a life expectancy of only about 18 months.

Pair formation takes place within a colony. It is the young male's responsibility to find a vacant or new nest site and take possession of it. Then, by perching conspicuously and uttering the series of loud chirps that make up his song, he will attract the attention of an unpaired female. Once he is successful, he can, in theory, look forward to keeping the same mate for life. But it seldom works out that way, for mortality among sparrows is quite high, especially in the breeding season, and they are not always monogamous. Female sparrows regularly mate with neighboring males, and polygamy is a common occurrence.

Productive Teamwork

However, male and female sparrows are extremely cooperative in the breeding season, undertaking most major tasks together. They build or refurbish the nest together, feed and brood the young together, and more unusually, incubate the eggs together. In most small birds incubation is the sole duty of the female.

Alien Invader

Although the house sparrow is one of North America's most familiar birds, it has not always been so. In 1800 there were no sparrows on the continent at all. It was brought to America in the midnineteenth century by European settlers who appreciated the bird as a reminder of home, and who mistakenly supposed that it might help control insect pests. The first successful introduction was make in Brooklyn, New York City, in 1850.

That introduction led to an explosion in house sparrow numbers. The bird found North America to its liking, and the population expanded with astonishing speed. By 1873 it had spread as far west as Ohio. Ten years later it covered the Great Lakes region, south to the Carolinas, followed by Florida and the Gulf Coast. By 1888 it reached the Midwest, and the first house sparrows reached the Pacific Coast soon after. By the early 1900s the house sparrow was North America's most abundant bird. It had spread over the whole continent in under 50 years.

Stay-at-homes

House sparrows live in colonies of ten to twenty pairs, inhabiting a home range that they defend against others for their exclusive use. Once an individual is accepted into a colony, defections are unusual. So a house sparrow remains in the company of the same group of individuals all its life and shares many activities with them, including feeding and dust bathing.

The nests are an important part of colony life because the same ones are used year after year by the same pair. Nests are usually built close together and are sometimes attached to each other, as if forming a row. In common with other colonial birds, breeding activities tend to be synchronized, with all members of the colony building nests, laying, and feeding young at the same time.

Only in late summer do sparrows regularly leave their own patch, when they gather in fields with other sparrows to molt and take advantage of the crop harvest. But this "vacation" does not last long, and very soon they are back within their familiar borders.

⊕ When they leave the nest, young sparrows still rely on their parents for food. The male supplies most of their needs, while the female often concentrates on laying and incubating her next clutch of eggs.

Working as a team, a pair of sparrows in an area with regular, varied food supplies can be very productive, raising three or more broods in the course of a season.

A house sparrow nest can be a messy structure. Essentially it is a bundle of hay and straw made into a dome, with an entrance in the side. The inner cup is lined with soft material, including feathers and finer strands of plant material.

⊜ In many cities the house sparrow has become so bold that it will feed from the hand. But cities are becoming less attractive to nesting sparrows, and in some parts of their range they are getting scarce.

In many major cities, especially in the developed world, nest materials can be quite hard to find. The house sparrow has never really adapted to making use of more artificial material, and here its fortunes have been adversely affected. The true heyday of the house sparrow in North America was at the start of the twentieth century, when livestock, and especially horses, were an integral part of city life. From then on, as motorized transport increased, house sparrows declined, retreating to more agricultural areas.

Sharp Declines

In some parts of Europe, especially Britain, there have been recent sharp declines in some sparrow populations. Although the cause is unknown, air pollution may be the reason. So perhaps the house sparrow's reign as man's most successful "bird partner" will come to an end as modernization increases. For now, however, such a possibility seems a long way in the future.

Glossary

Words in SMALL CAPITALS refer to other entries in the glossary.

A

Adaptation features of an animal that adjust it to its environment. NATURAL SELECTION favors the survival of individuals whose adaptations fit them to their surroundings better than other individuals

Adaptive radiation when a group of closely related animals (e.g., members of a FAMILY) have evolved differences from each other so that they occupy different NICHES

Adult a fully grown animal that has reached breeding age

Air sac thin-walled structure connected to the lungs of birds that aids respiration

Alarm call call given to warn others of the presence of a PREDATOR

Albinism abnormally white PLUMAGE (whole or partial) caused by lack of PIGMENT; true albinos also have red eyes, pink legs, and a pink beak

Allopreening the act of one bird PREENING another

Allospecies one of the SPECIES within a SUPERSPECIES

Allula group of several small, strong FEATHERS on leading edge of WING; used in flight to reduce turbulence and prevent stalling

Altricial refers to young that stay in the NEST until they are more or less full grown (as opposed to PRECOCIAL). See also NIDICOLOUS

Anisodactyl feet with three toes pointing forward and one pointing backward

Aquatic associated with or living in water

Arboreal associated with or living in trees

Arctic the polar region north of 66° 33' N

Avian pertaining to birds

Axillary the bird's "armpit"; FEATHERS in this region are called axillaries

B

Barb side branch from the central shaft of a FEATHER

Barbicel one of the tiny, hooklike structures on BARBULES

Barbule side branch from the BARB of a FEATHER

Beak see BILL

Bill the two MANDIBLES with which birds gather their food

Binocular vision the ability to look at an object with both eyes simultaneously, which greatly improves the ability to judge its distance, for example

Brackish slightly salty water (e.g., as found in estuaries where fresh water and seawater mix)

Breastbone bone separating the ribs, often deeply keeled to hold the strong flight muscles; also called the STERNUM

Breeding season entire cycle of reproductive activity from courtship and pair formation (and often establishment of TERRITORY) through nesting to independence of young

Brood group of young raised simultaneously by a pair (or several) birds: single-brooded (birds make only one nesting attempt each year, although they may have a replacement CLUTCH if the first is lost); double-brooded (birds breed twice or more each year); also triple-, multiple-brooded

Brood parasitism condition in which one SPECIES lays its eggs in the NEST of another, so that the young are raised by "parents" of a different species

Brood patch featherless area on the breast, with many blood vessels close to surface allowing more effective egg INCUBATION

Burrow tunnel excavated in soil where eggs and young are kept safely

C

Call short sounds made by birds to indicate danger, threaten intruders, or keep a group of birds together. See also SONG

Camouflage markings on PLUMAGE that aid concealment

Canopy fairly continuous (closed) or broken (open) layer in forests produced by the intermingling of branches of trees; the crowns of some trees project above the canopy and are known as emergents

Cap area of single color on top of head, sometimes extending to neck

Carrion dead animal matter used as food by scavengers

Casque bony extension of the upper MANDIBLE

Cere fleshy covering on BILL where the upper MANDIBLE meets the face

Chick term applied to a bird from HATCHING to either FLEDGING or reaching sexual maturity

CITES Convention on International Trade in Endangered Species; an agreement between nations that restricts international trade to permitted levels through licensing and administrative controls; rare animals and plants are assigned to categories

Class a taxonomic level; all birds belong to the class Aves; the main levels of taxonomic hierarchy (in descending order) are: phylum, class, ORDER, FAMILY, GENUS, SPECIES

Claw sharp, pointed growth at the end of a bird's toes

Clutch the eggs laid in one breeding attempt

Colony group of animals gathered together for breeding

Comb fleshy protuberance on the top of a bird's head

Communal breeder SPECIES in which more than the two birds of a pair help in raising the young. See also COOPERATIVE BREEDING

Community all the plants and animals that live together in a HABITAT

Conservation preservation of the world's biological diversity through research, HABITAT and SPECIES management, and education

Contour feather FEATHER with largely firm and flat VANES; contrasts with DOWN, which is soft and loose

Cooperative breeding breeding system in which parents of young are assisted in the care of young by other ADULT or SUBADULT birds

Countershading form of protective CAMOUFLAGE in which areas exposed to light (upper parts) are dark, and areas normally shaded (underparts) are light

Coverts smaller FEATHERS that cover the WINGS and overlie the base of the large FLIGHT FEATHERS

Covey collective name for groups of birds, usually game birds

Crèche gathering of young birds

Crepuscular active at twilight

Crest tuft of FEATHERS on top of a bird's head that can often be raised and flattened, especially during courtship DISPLAYS

Crop a thin-walled extension of the foregut used to store food; often used to carry food to the nest

Cryptic CAMOUFLAGED and difficult to see

D

Dabbling picking food from near the surface of water without diving, submerging, or UPENDING

Dawn chorus the peak of bird SONG around sunrise

Deforestation process of cutting down and removing trees for timber or to create open space for activities such as growing crops and grazing animals

Dimorphic literally "two forms"; usually used as "sexually dimorphic" (i.e., the two sexes differ in color or size)

Dispersal movements of animals, often as they reach maturity, away from their previous HOME RANGE

Displacement activity animal behavior in a particular situation, often during times of frustration, anxiety, or indecision; examples in birds include pulling at grass, BEAK wiping, or food pecking

Display any fairly conspicuous pattern of behavior that conveys specific information to others, usually to members of the same species; often associated with "courtship," but also in other activities (e.g., "distraction," "ecstatic," or "threat" displays)

Diurnal active during the day. See NOCTURNAL

DNA (deoxyribonucleic acid) the substance that makes up the main part of the chromosomes of all living things; contains the genetic code that is handed down from generation to generation

Domestication process of taming and breeding animals to provide help and useful products for humans

Down insulating FEATHERS with or without a small shaft and with long, fluffy BARBS; the first feather coat of CHICKS; in ADULTS down forms a layer beneath the main feathers

Duetting coordinated bouts of singing or calling by a mated pair or family group of birds

Dust-bathing squatting on the ground and using the WINGS, BILL, and feet to work "dust" (sand or fine, dry soil) into the FEATHERS to help condition PLUMAGE and remove external PARASITES; also known as dusting

E

Ear tuft bunch of long FEATHERS on the head, especially in owls, that the bird erects when excited or alarmed, but have nothing to do with the ears or hearing

Echolocation method of navigation and food capture that uses echoes from emitted sounds to warn of objects in the animal's path

Eclipse plumage drab, CAMOUFLAGING femalelike PLUMAGE acquired by males after a MOLT in the fall, when they lose their FLIGHT FEATHERS and become flightless and vulnerable for several weeks

Ecosystem the COMMUNITY of living organisms and their environment

Endangered species a SPECIES whose POPULATION has fallen to such a low level that it is at risk of EXTINCTION

Endemic found only in one small geographical area

Extinction complete dying out of a SPECIES

Eye patch large area of contrastingly colored PLUMAGE surrounding each eye of some birds

Eye ring ring of contrastingly colored FEATHERS around each eye

Eye spot an eyelike pattern on PLUMAGE (e.g., the eye spots on the long tail COVERTS of male peacocks); also known as ocellus (pl: ocelli)

Eye stripe stripe of contrastingly colored FEATHERS running through each eye of a bird; one above the eye is called a supercilium

F

Family either a group of closely related SPECIES (e.g., loons) or a pair of birds and their offspring. See also CLASS

Feather unique structure found only in the PLUMAGE of birds; a typical body (CONTOUR), wing, or tail feather consists of a central shaft, or rachis, and a VANE, or web, bearing many horizontal branches, or BARBS, each bearing many BARBULES arranged so that they are linked together by tiny hooks (BARBICELS) forming a smooth surface; the lower, bare end of the shaft, inserted in the skin, is called the quill

Filoplume hairlike feather with a shaft but few or no BARBS

Fledge to grow feathers; also refers to the moment of flying at the end of the NESTING PERIOD, when young birds are more or less completely feathered

Fledging period time from HATCHING to FLEDGING

Fledgling recently fledged young bird

Flight feathers large WING FEATHERS composed of PRIMARY FEATHERS and SECONDARY FEATHERS

Flock assemblage of birds, often involved in a coordinated activity

Food chain sequence in which one organism becomes food for another, which in turn is eaten by another

Frugivore an animal that eats mostly or entirely fruit

G

Gape width of an animal's open mouth

Gene basic unit of heredity enabling one generation to pass on characteristics to its offspring

Genus (pl. **genera**) group of closely related SPECIES. See CLASS

Gizzard muscular forepart of the stomach; often used for grinding food

Gonys bulge toward tip of the lower MANDIBLE; most visible in gulls

Grassland terrain with vegetation that is dominated by grasses, with few or no trees

Gregarious tendency to congregate into groups

Gular pouch extension of the fleshy area of the lower jaw and throat

H

Habitat place where an animal or plant lives

Hatching emergence of a CHICK from its egg

Hatchling young bird recently emerged from the egg

Heterodactyl toe arrangement in which the first and second toes point backward, and the third and fourth toes point forward

Hibernation becoming inactive in winter, with lowered body temperature to save energy

Hierarchy establishment of superiority and rank among groups of animals, with dominant individuals at the top and subordinates lower down; subordinates often give way to higher ranking birds when feeding; among POLYGAMOUS SPECIES dominant males may mate with all available females; also called PECKING ORDER

Home range area in which an animal normally lives

Homing ability of some birds to find their way back to a regular ROOST from great distances; most familiar in pigeons

Hybrid offspring of a mating between animals of different SPECIES

I

Immature a bird that has not acquired its mature PLUMAGE

Incubation the act of incubating the egg or eggs (i.e., keeping them warm so that development is possible)

Incubation period time taken for eggs to develop from the start of INCUBATION to HATCHING

Indigenous living naturally in a region; NATIVE (not an introduced SPECIES)

Insectivore an animal that feeds on insects

Introduced describes a SPECIES that has been brought from places where it occurs naturally to places where it has not previously occurred

Iridescence a glittering "rainbow" effect of green, blue, or bronze caused by the scattering of light from microscopic ridges on a bird's FEATHERS

Irruption sudden or irregular spread of birds from their normal RANGE; usually as a consequence of a food shortage

IUCN International Union for the Conservation of Nature, responsible for assigning animals and plants to internationally agreed categories of rarity (see table following page)

J

Juvenile young bird that has not reached breeding age

K

Keel deep extension to the BREASTBONE or STERNUM of a bird to which flight muscles are anchored

Kleptoparasitism stealing food gathered from other birds; a speciality of skuas and frigatebirds

L

Lamellae comblike structures used for filtering organisms out of water

Lek display ground where two or more male birds gather to attract females. See DISPLAY.

Life cycle cycle from egg, through CHICK and IMMATURE to ADULT, and then to egg again

M

Mandible one of the jaws of a bird that make up the BILL

Mantling threat DISPLAY, usually seen in birds of prey, in which a bird stands over prey, ruffles the mantle (neck) FEATHERS, and droops its WINGS slightly; the display is intended to ward off potential food pirates

Marine associated with or living in the sea

Mating act of copulation in which the cloacae of the two sexes touch, and sperm is released from the male; "mating" is also used as a general term for pair-formation

Melanism an excess of black PIGMENT (melanin) in the PLUMAGE

Migration the movement of animals from one part of the world to another at different times of year to reach food or find a place to breed

Mimicry imitation of one or more characteristics of a SPECIES by another for the gain of the imitator—e.g., vocal mimicry, PLUMAGE mimicry, or egg-coloration mimicry

Mobbing aggressive and often noisy demonstration by one bird against another in order to harass it; often refers to a collective demonstration of small birds against a PREDATOR

Molt replacement of old FEATHERS by new ones

Monogamous taking only a single mate at a time

Monotypic the sole member of a SPECIES, GENUS, FAMILY, ORDER, etc.

Morph a form, usually used to describe a color form when more than one exists

Mutation random changes in genetic material

Mutualism close association between two different organisms from which both benefit

N

Native belonging to an area; not introduced by humans

Natural selection process whereby individuals with the most appropriate ADAPTATIONS survive to produce offspring

Nest structure built or excavated by a bird or a preexisting site where eggs are laid and remain until they HATCH

Nesting period time from HATCHING to flying. See FLEDGE

Nestling a young bird in the nest

New World the Americas. See OLD WORLD

Niche part of a HABITAT occupied by a SPECIES, defined in terms of all aspects of its lifestyle (e.g., food, competitors, PREDATORS, and other resource requirements)

Nictitating membrane fold of skin, often translucent, which can be drawn across the eye to form a "third eyelid" for protection, lubrication, or cleaning

Nidicolous young birds that remain in the NEST until they can fly. See ALTRICIAL

Nidifugous young birds that leave the NEST soon after HATCHING. See PRECOCIAL

Nocturnal active at night. See DIURNAL

Nomadic wandering; having no fixed home

O

Oil gland organ located in the rump that secretes an oily substance used in FEATHER care during PREENING; also called uropygial gland or preen gland

Old World non-American continents. See New WORLD

Omnivore animal that eats a wide variety of foods from meat to plants

Opportunistic animal that varies its diet according to what is available

Order level of taxonomic ranking. See CLASS

Ornithologist scientist who specifically studies birds

P

Pair-bond behavior that keeps a MATED pair together

Pamprodactyl having all four toes directed forward or having the capability of being so directed

Parallel evolution development of similarities in separate, but related, evolutionary lineages through the operation of similar selective factors

Parasite bird laying its eggs in the nests of other SPECIES and leaving the foster parents to raise the young. See BROOD PARASITISM

Passerine strictly "sparrowlike," but normally used as a shortened form of Passeriformes, the largest ORDER of birds

Pecking order See HIERARCHY

Pellet compact mass of indigestible portions of a bird's food, such as FEATHERS, hair, bone, and scales, that is ejected through the mouth rather than as feces

Pigment substance that gives color to eggs and FEATHERS

Plankton layer of (usually) minute organisms that float near the surface of the ocean or in the air at a certain level above ground

Plumage all the FEATHERS and DOWN that cover a bird

Polyandry when a female mates with several males

Polygamy when a male mates with several females

Polygynous when a male mates with several females in one BREEDING SEASON

Polymorphic when a SPECIES occurs in two or more different forms (usually relating to color). See DIMORPHIC, MORPH

Population distinct group of animals of the same SPECIES or all the animals of that species

Prairie North American STEPPE grassland between 30° N and 55° N

Precocial young birds that leave the NEST after HATCHING. See ALTRICIAL

Predation the act of taking animals by a PREDATOR

Predator animal that kills live prey for food

Preening the act of arranging, cleaning, and otherwise maintaining the PLUMAGE using the BILL; often oil from the OIL GLAND is smeared over the plumage during this process

Prenuptial prior to breeding

Primary feather one of the large FEATHERS of the outer WING. See SECONDARY FEATHER

Promiscuous describes SPECIES in which the sexes come together for mating only and do not form lasting PAIR-BONDS

Q

Quartering the act of flying back and forth over an area, searching it thoroughly

R

Race See SUBSPECIES

Range geographical area over which an organism is distributed

Raptor a bird of prey, usually one belonging to the ORDER Falconiformes

Regurgitation ejection of partly digested food (or the indigestible remains of food in a PELLET) from a bird's GIZZARD

Resident animal that stays in one area all the year around

Roost place where birds sleep

S

Salt gland part of the excretory system, helping eliminate excess salt, especially in seabirds

Scrape (or hollow) NEST without any nesting material where a shallow depression has been formed to hold the eggs

Scrub vegetation dominated by shrubs (woody plants usually with more than one stem); naturally occurs most often on the arid side of forest or grassland, but often artificially created by humans as a result of DEFORESTATION

Secondary feather one of the large FLIGHT FEATHERS on the inner WING

Sedentary nonmigrating. See RESIDENT

Semiarid describes a region or HABITAT that suffers from lack of water for much of the year, but less dry than a desert

Sequential molt situation in which FEATHERS (usually the WING FEATHERS) are molted in order, as opposed to all at once

Siblings brothers and sisters

Soaring gliding flight without wingbeats, typically with WINGS widespread, on currents of rising air or on wind currents sweeping upward over steep slopes or waves

Solitary living alone or undertaking tasks alone

Song series of sounds (vocalization), often composed of several or many phrases constructed of repeated elements; normally used by a male to claim a TERRITORY and attract a mate

Song flight special flight performance during which TERRITORIAL SONG is produced; typical of birds occupying open HABITATS with few perches

Specialist animal whose lifestyle involves highly specialized strategems—e.g., feeding with one technique on a particular food

Species a POPULATION or series of populations that interbreed freely, but not with those of other species. See CLASS

Speculum distinctively colored group of FLIGHT FEATHERS

Spur sharp projection on the leg of some game birds; often more developed in males and used in fighting; also found on the carpal joint of some other birds

Steppe open, grassy plains, with few trees or bushes, of the central temperate zone of Eurasia or North America (PRAIRIES), characterized by low and sporadic rainfall and a wide annual temperature variation

Sternum See BREASTBONE

Stooping dropping rapidly from the air (usually by a RAPTOR in pursuit of prey)

Subadult no longer JUVENILE but not yet fully ADULT

Subarctic region close to the ARCTIC circle, or at high altitude, sharing many of the characteristics of an arctic environment

Suborder subdivision of an ORDER. See CLASS

Subspecies subdivision of a SPECIES that is distinguishable from the rest of that species; often called a RACE

Sunbathing spreading WINGS and tail and ruffling FEATHERS to expose skin and DOWN feathers to the sun; probably to assist the production of vitamins or to help remove PARASITES

Superspecies two or more species, geographically separated, of such close relationship that they form a single entity across their combined ranges

Symbiosis when two or more SPECIES live together for their mutual benefit more successfully than either could live on its own

Syndactyl foot having two toes joined for part of their length

Syrinx vocal organ unique to birds at the division of the TRACHEA

T

Tactolocation method of sensing, often to locate prey, by using touch

Taiga belt of coniferous forests (evergreen conifers such as firs, pines, and spruces) lying below the latitude of TUNDRA

Tail streamer specially elongated tail FEATHER (e.g., as seen on a swallow, tern, or tropicbird)

Talon sharp, hooked CLAWS used for grabbing, holding, and killing prey (usually refers to those of PREDATORS such as birds of prey and owls)

Temperate zone zones between latitudes 40° and 60° where the climate is variable or seasonal

Terrestrial living on land

Territorial defending an area; in birds usually refers to a bird or birds that exclude others of the same SPECIES from their living area and in which they will usually nest

Territory area that an animal or animals consider their own and defend against intruders

Thermal an area of (warm) air that rises by convection

Trachea See WINDPIPE

Tree hole any crevice or hollow in the trunk or limbs of a tree that can be used by birds for ROOSTING or NESTING

Tribe term sometimes used to group certain SPECIES or GENERA within a FAMILY. See CLASS

Tundra open grassy or shrub-covered lands of the far north

U

Upending swiveling motion used by swimming WILDFOWL, immersing the head and foreparts of the body to reach submerged food

V

Vagrant individual bird blown off course or having migrated abnormally to reach a geographical area where its SPECIES is not normally found

Vane the web or flat expanded part of a FEATHER

Variety occasional variation in a SPECIES, not sufficiently persistent or geographically separated to form a SUBSPECIES

Vertebrate animal with a backbone (e.g., fish, amphibian, bird, or mammal)

W

Wader term sometimes used for "shorebird," including sandpipers, plovers, and related SPECIES; neither term is strictly accurate, since some species live neither on the shore nor by water

Wattle fleshy protuberance, usually near the base of the BILL

Wetland freshwater or saltwater marshes

Wildfowl inclusive term for geese, ducks, and swans

Windpipe tube that takes air from the mouth and nostrils to the lungs; also called the TRACHEA

Wing the forelimb; the primary means of flight in flying birds, carrying the SECONDARY and PRIMARY FEATHERS (quills) and their smaller COVERTS

Wing patch well-defined area of color or pattern on the WING (usually the upper wing) of a bird

Wingspan measurement from tip to tip of the spread WINGS

Wing spur sharp projection at or near the bend of the WING. See SPUR

Wintering ground area where a migrant spends the nonbreeding season

Wishbone the furcula, formed by the two clavicles, or collar bones, joining the shoulders across the forepart of the STERNUM

Z

Zygodactyl having two toes directed forward and two backward

Further Reading

Attenborough, D. *The Life of Birds*. London: BBC Books, 1998.

Birkhead, T. *The Magpies: The Ecology and Behavior of Black-Billed and Yellow-Billed Magpies*. New York: Academic Press, 1991.

Brooke, M., and T. Birkhead. *The Cambridge Encyclopedia of Ornithology*. Cambridge, UK: Cambridge University Press, 1991.

Byrkjedal, I., and D. Thompson. *Tundra Plovers: The Eurasian, Pacific and American Golden Plovers and Grey Plover*. London: T. & A. D. Poyser Ltd., 1998.

Chatterjee, S. *The Rise of Birds: 225 Million Years of Evolution*. Baltimore: Johns Hopkins University Press, 1997.

Clements, J. F. *Birds of the World: A Checklist*. Vista, CA: Ibis, 2000.

Curson, J., D. Quinn, and D. Beadle. *New World Warblers*. London: Christopher Helm, 1994.

del Hoyo, J., A. Elliott, and J. Sargatal, eds. *The Handbook of the Birds of the World*. Vols. 1–7. Barcelona: Lynx Edicions, 1992–2002.

Ehrlich, P. R., D. S. Dobkin, and D. Wheye. *The Birder's Handbook*. New York: Simon & Schuster, 1988.

Elphick, C., J. B. Dunning Jr., and D. Sibley. *The Sibley Guide to Bird Life and Behavior*. New York: Alfred A. Knopf, 2001.

Elphick, J., ed. *The Random House Atlas of Bird Migration*. New York: Random House, 1995.

Farrand, J. *National Audubon Society Field Guide to North American Birds; 1 Western Region; 2 Eastern Region*. New York: Alfred A. Knopf, 1994.

Feduccia, A., *The Origin and Evolution of Birds*. New Haven, CT: Yale University Press, 1996.

Gaston, A. J., and I. L. Jones. *The Auks*. Oxford, UK: Oxford University Press, 1998.

Gill, F., and A. Poole eds. *The Birds of North America: Species Accounts*. Washington, DC: American Ornithologists' Union, 1992.

Goodwin, D., *Crows of the World*. London: British Museum,1986.

———. *Pigeons and Doves of the World*. 3rd ed. Ithaca, NY: Cornell University Press, 1983.

Goss-Custard, J. D. *The Oystercatcher: From Individuals to Populations*. New York: Oxford University Press, 1996.

Hancock, J. A., J. A. Kushlan, and M. P. Kahl. *The Heron's Handbook*. New York: HarperTrade, 1984.

———. *Storks, Ibises, and Spoonbills of the World*. New York: Academic Press, 1992.

Harrison, P. *Seabirds: An Identification Guide*. Boston: Houghton Mifflin, 1991

Hayman, P., J. Marchant, and T. Prater. *Shorebirds: An Identification Guide to the Waders of the World*. London: Croom Helm, 1986.

Hientzelman, D. S. *Guide to Owl Watching in North America*. New York: Dover, 1992.

Howard, R., and A. Moore. *A Complete Checklist of the Birds of the World*. 2nd ed. New York: Academic Press, 1980.

Johnsgard, P. A. *Cormorants, Darters, and Pelicans of the World*. Washington, DC: Smithsonian Institution Press, 1993.

———. *Hawks, Eagles, and Falcons of North America*. Washington, DC: Smithsonian Institution Press, 1990.

———. *The Hummingbirds of North America*. Washington, DC: Smithsonian Institution Press, 1997.

———. *North American Owls*. Washington, DC: Smithsonian Institution Press, 2003.

———. *The Pheasants of the World*. Washington, DC: Smithsonian Institution Press, 1999.

Johnston, R. F., and M. Janiga. *Feral Pigeons*. New York: Oxford University Press, 1996.

Kaplan, G., and L. J. Rogers. *Birds: Their Habits and Skills*. New South Wales, Australia: Allen & Unwin, Crows Nest, 2001.

Madge, S., and P. McGowan. *Pheasants, Partridges, and Grouse*. Princeton, NJ: Princeton University Press, 2002.

Marchant, S., and P. J. Higgins. *Handbook of Australian, New Zealand and Antarctic Birds*. Melbourne: Oxford University Press, 1990.

Monroe, B. L., and C. G. Sibley. *A World Checklist of Birds*. New Haven, CT: Yale University Press, 1993.

Page, J., and E. S. Morton. *Lords of the Air: The Smithsonian Book of Birds*. Washington, DC: Smithsonian Institution Press, 1989.

Perrins, C. M., ed. *Firefly Encyclopedia of Birds*. Buffalo, NY: Firefly Books, 2003.

Poole, A. F., P. Stettenheim, and F. B. Gill. *The Birds of North America*. Philadelphia: American Ornithologists' Union/Academy of Natural Sciences, 1992–present.

Ryden, H. *America's Bald Eagle*. Guildford, CT: Lyons Press, 1985.

Savage, C. *Eagles of North America*. Vancouver: Greystone Books, 2000.

Scholz, F. *Birds of Prey*. Mechanicsburg, PA: Stackpole Books, 1993.

Short, L. L. *Woodpeckers of the World*. Wilmington, DE: Delaware Museum of Natural History Museum, 1984.

Sibley, D. *North American Bird Guide*. New York: Alfred A. Knopf, 2000.

————. *The Sibley Guide to Bird Life and Behavior*. New York: Alfred A. Knopf, 2001.

Skutch, A. *Life of the Flycatcher*. Norman, OK: Oklahoma University Press, 1997.

————. *The Life of the Hummingbird*. New York: Crown Publishers, 1973.

Smith, D. G. *Great Horned Owl*. Mechanicsburg, PA: Stackpole Books, 2002.

Smith, S. M. *The Black-Capped Chickadee: Behavioral Ecology and Natural History*. Ithaca, NY: Cornell University Press, 1992.

Snow, D. W., and C. M. Perrins. *Birds of the Western Palearctic*. Concise ed. New York: Oxford University Press, 1998.

Sziij, L. *Welty's Life of Birds*. 5th ed. St. Louis: Academic Press, 2003.

Taylor, B., and B. van Perlo. *Rails: A Guide to the Rails, Crakes, Gallinules and Coots of the World*. London: Pica Press, 1998.

Turner, A. *A Handbook to the Swallows and Martins of the World*. London: Christopher Helm, 1989.

Walkinshaw, L. H. *Cranes of the World*. New York: Winchester Press, 1973.

Wauer, Roland H. *The American Robin*. Austin, TX: University of Texas Press, 1999.

Useful Websites

General

http://www.aou.org
Founded in 1883, the American Ornithologists' Union is the oldest and largest organization in the New World devoted to the scientific study of birds

http://www.audubon.org
The website of the National Audubon Society includes news, avian science, product reports, and conservation work throughout America

http://www.birdlife.net
Website of the worldwide BirdLife International partnership, leading to partner organizations around the globe and to information about species

http://www.birds.cornell/edu
Cornell Laboratory of Ornithology website, leading to information about North American birds and actions you can take to study and conserve them

http://www.bsc-eoc.org/links
"Bird links to the world" leads you to websites for many countries, detailing sites, species, books, and other information on the birds in each region

http://www.fatbirder.com
Fat Birder is a superb portal to 15,000 birding website links and has a page for every country and all U.S., Canadian, and Australian states and provinces

http://www.surfbirds.com
A joint American-British website that includes breaking bird news items, articles of interest, rare bird reports, identification features, and more

Specific groups

http://www.neseabirds.com
Natural history of seabirds and where to find them; includes hints for novice birders

http://www.oceanwanderers.com
Devoted to seabirds, shorebirds, and gulls of the world, including excellent images, news, where to watch seabirds, and useful links to other sites

http://www.birdstrike.org
Bird Strike Committee USA. Information on understanding and reducing bird hazards to aircraft

http://www.geobop.com/Birds/Anseriformes
An online guide to all the ducks, geese, swans in the order Anseriformes

http://www.owls.org
Website of the World Owl Trust, whose primary aim is to ensure the survival of all species of the world's owls

http://www.peregrinefund.org
A site containing information on many birds of prey

http://www.pheasant.org.uk
The central site for the World Pheasant Association, dealing with many critically endangered species

http://www.western.edu/bio/young/gunnsg/gunnsg.htm
An excellent site about sage grouse, with useful links to other sites

http://sssp.fws.gov/index.cfm
The Shorebirds Sister Schools Program is a U.S. Fish and Wildlife Service site linking schools, biologists, and shorebird enthusiasts

http://shorebirdplan.fws.gov
The U.S. Shorebird Conservation Plan, with maps and contacts

http://www.portalproductions.com
A site devoted to all aspects of hummingbirds, with links to other sites of interest

http://www.uia.ac.be/u/matthys/nuttxt.html
An introduction to the nuthatches

http://www.geobop.com/Birds/Piciformes
A resource dedicated to woodpeckers and their allies

http://www.zeebyrd.com/corvi29
For the Love of Crows: a website about corvids

http://eebweb.arizona.edu/faculty/hopp/vireo.html
The Vireo Home Page, with information about the vireo family and links to other sites

http://www.birdsource.org/warblers/idguide.html
A website detailing American wood warblers

Index

Bold common names, e.g.
bittern, American,
indicate illustrated main
entry. Bold page numbers,
e.g. **70–71**, indicate the
location of an illustrated
main entry. Page numbers in
parenthesis, e.g. (23),
indicate at-a-glance boxes.
Page numbers in italics, e.g.
35, indicate illustrations of
animals or topics not the
subject of a main entry.

A
Accipiter
  gentilis **70–71**, 76
  nisus 70
  striatus 70, 243
Acridotheres 245
Acrocephalus palustris 245
Agelaius phoeniceus 263
Agriocharis ocellata 109
agrochemicals (23), 29, 59,
  77, 87, 91, (91), 188,
  223, 235
air-sac (60)
Aix sponsa **44–45**
alarm calls (130), (213)
Alauda arvensis 218–19
Alle alle **158–59**
allopreening 33
Amazilia cyanura 238
Anas
  americana **50–53**
  laysanensis 47
  melleri 47
  penelope 50
  platyrhynchos **46–49**
  rubripes 47
  sibilatrix 50
  superciliosa 49
  undulata 47
anhinga *35*
Anhinga anhinga 35
anisodactyl 204, *204*
Apteryx 66
Aquila chrysaetos **72–77**
Archilochus colubris
  192–95
Ardea herodias 264
Arenaria
  interpres **128–31**
  melanocephala 128
auk
  black guillemot **160–61**
  little *see* dovekie
avocet, pied 238
Aythya 56
  americana 50
  valisineria 50

B
baldpate *see* wigeon,
  American
bird strikes (42)
birds of prey 68–91,
  178–89
  eyesight (77)
  feet 204, *204*
  size (76)
bittern, American 30–31,
  88
blackbird *88*
  American 264, 265
  red-winged 263, 264
  yellow-headed 264
blackpoll 253

bluebird
  Eastern 236–39, 248
  fairy 238
  mountain 236
  western 236
bluetail, red flanked 238
bluethroat, Eurasian 238
bobwhite, northern
  92–93
bog bull *see* bittern,
  American
Bombycilla garrulus 270
Bonasa umbellus 100
bonxie *see* skua, great
booby, blue-footed 238
Botaurus lentiginosus
  30–31, *88*
Branta
  canadensis **40–43**
  canadensis leucopareia
    (43)
  canadensis maxima 40
  canadensis minima 40
breeding colonies 15, 17,
  26, 28, *29*, 32, 34, 69,
  149, *149*, 157, 159, 165
brood parasitism 45, 50,
  57, 112–13, 259
brood reduction 261
Bubo virginianus 82,
  178–79
bullfinch, Eurasian 272
burrowing species 164–65,
  198–99
Buteo
  jamaicensis 179, 213
  lineatus 213

C
cage-bird trade 244
camouflage (182)
Campephilus principalis 200
canvasback 50
Caprimulgus vociferus
  190–91
cardinal (red cardinal;
  northern cardinal)
  254–59
Cardinalis cardinalis **254–59**
Carduelis
  pinus 274
  tristis **274–75**
Catharacta skua 19,
  140–43
Cathartes aura 59, **64–67**
Centrocercus urophasianus
  100–103
Cepphus grylle **160–61**
chat 226
chemical defense 14
chickadee
  black-capped 224–29
  boreal 228
  Carolina 224, 228
  chestnut-backed 228
  mountain 228, 231
Childonias niger 154
Chrysolophus
  amherstiae 94
  pictus 94
Cinclus mexicanus **234–35**
Circus cyaneus 122
Clangula hyemalis **56–57**
Coccothraustes
  coccothraustes 272
Colinus virginianus **92–93**
Columba livia **168–71**, 265

condor
  Andean *58*
  California 58–63
  in prehistory (62)
cooperative breeding
  278–79, *278*
Coragyps atratus 64
cormorant, great 24–25,
  32
Corvus
  brachyrhynchos 214,
    243
  corax **214–17**
courtship feeding (226)
covey 92
cowbird 207, 253, 259
  brown-headed 263
crane
  sandhill 116
  whooping 114–17
  Wood Buffalo *117*
crop 193
crop milk *171*
crossbill, red 270
crow, American 52, 214,
  253
cuckoo 172, 204, 259
Cuculus canorus 259
Cyanocitta
  cristata **208–13**, 243,
    259
  stelleri (211), (212)
Cygnus
  atratus 36
  cygnus 36
  melanocorypha 36
  olor **36–39**, 265

D
Dendragapus
  canadensis 100
  obscurus 100
Dendroica 250
  castanea 253
  discolor 253
  magnolia 253
  petechia 253
  pinus 253
  striata 253
  tigrina 253
dipper, American 234–35
diving *21*, (26), 27
domestication (48), 168–69
dove
  mourning 166–67
  rock 168–71
  white 169
dovekie 158–59
dowitcher
  long-billed 132
  short-billed 132–35
dread *154*, 155
drinking (170)
drongo 226
Dryocopus pileatus
  200–205
duck 181
  American black 47
  American wigeon **50–53**
  eider **54–55**
  Laysan 47
  long-tailed 56–57
  mallard **46–49**
  Meller's 47
  Pacific black 49
  wood 44–45
  yellow-billed 47
dunnock 237

E
eagle
  bald 78–83, 91
  golden 72–77
  Steller's sea eagle 78
  white-tailed sea-eagle
    78
Ectopistes migratorius 123
egret 32
eider 56
  common 54, 55
  king 54–55
Eremophila alpestris
  218–19
Erithacus rubecula 236,
  240
eyesight (77), 156–57, 184,
  191, (198)
eyrie *75*

F
Falco
  araea 188
  peregrinus 76, **88–91**,
    165, 187
falcon, peregrine 76,
  88–91, 165, 187
feeding flocks 227, 263
feet 200–203, (204)
finch 265
  rosy 272
flinthead *see* stork, wood
food caches 179, *208*,
  211–12, 215, 226, *228*,
  (229)
Fratercula arctica **162–65**
Fregata magnificens 22
frigatebird 22, 52
fulmar 149
  northern 14–15
Fulmarus 149
  glacialis **14–15**

G
Gallinago gallinago 133,
  136–37
Gallinula
  chloropus **110–13**
  chloropus cachinmans
    110
  chloropus chloropus
    110
  chloropus guami 113
  chloropus sandvicensis
    113
  nesiotis (112)
  silvestris (112)
gannet, northern 26–29,
  142
gaping 266
Garrulus glandarius 211
Gavia immer **8–13**
Geococcyx californianus
  172–77
goldfinch, American
  274–75
goose 181, 265
  Aleutian Canada (43)
  cackling 40
  Canada 40–43
  giant Canada 40
goshawk, Northern
  70–71, 76
grackle
  bronzed 262
  common 262–65
  Florida 262
  purple 262

great northern diver *see*
  loon, common
grebe, great crested 111
grosbeak, pine 268–73
ground sallying 236
grouse
  blue 100
  ruffed 100
  sage 100–103
  sharp-tailed 100
  spruce 100
  willow 181
grunt-whistling 48
Grus
  americana **114–17**
  canadensis 116
guillemot, black 160–61
gull *21*, 52, 123, 125,
  131, 165, 265
  Armenian 144
  glaucous *158*
  great black-backed 141,
    165
  herring 144–45
  kittiwake **146–51**
  laughing 22
  lesser black-backed 144
  yellow-legged 144
Gymnogyps californianus
  58–63

H
hacking (83)
Haematopus
  bachmani **124–25**
  palliatus 124, 125
Haliaeetus
  albicilla 78
  leucocephalus **78–83**,
    91
  pelagicus 78
hallux 204
harrier, hen 122
hawfinch 272
hawk
  American sharp-shinned
    70
  red-shouldered 213
  red-tailed 179, 213
  sharp-shinned 243
hearing, sense of 184–85,
  184
heron 32, 34, 179, 265
  great blue 264
heterodactyl 204
Hirundo rustica **220–23**
hummingbird 174, 264
  blue-tailed 238
  ruby-throated 192–95
hybridization (49), 125
Hydrobatidae 66

I
ibis, glossy 32–33
Icterus
  abeillei 266
  bullockii 266
  galbula **266–67**
  gularis 266
introduced species 42, 97,
  (188), 239, 244, (248),
  (278)
Inuit bird names (120)
Irena
  cyanogaster 238
  puella 238
iridescence (264)
ironhead *see* stork, wood
irruptions 230, (270)

J

jaeger 140, 142, 154
jay
    blue 208–13, 243, 259
    Eurasian 211
    Steller's (211), (212)

K

kestrel 188
kingfisher, belted 196–99
kite, Everglade (snail)
    68–69
kittiwake (black-legged
    kittiwake) **146–51**
kiwi 66
kleptoparasitism *21*, 22,
    29, 50, (52), 110, *141*,
    (142)

L

Lagopus lagopus 181
lark
    horned (shore) **218–19**
    skylark 218–19
Larus
    argentatus **144–45**
    armenicus 144
    atricilla 22
    cachinnans 144
    fuscus 144
    marinus 141, 165
leks 102, *102*, (102)
Leucosticte tephrocotis 272
Limnodromus
    griseus **132–35**
    scolopaceus 132
loon, common 8–13
Loxia curvirostra 270
Luscinia
    megarhynchos 242
    svecica 238
lyrebird 245

M

mallard 46–49
matched countersinging
    (258)
Megaceryle alcyon **196–99**
Meleagris gallopavo 64,
    104–09
Menura novaehollandiae
    245
migration (81), (153), (194),
    (222)
mimicry (213), (245)
Mimus
    gilvus 242
    grundlachii 242
    polyglottos **242–45**
mire drum *see* bittern,
    American
Mniotilta varia 250
mobbing (187)
mockingbird
    Bahama 242
    northern 242–45
    tropical 242
Molothrus 207, 253, 259,
    263
moorhen
    Christobal (112)
    common 110–13
    Tristan (112)
Morus bassanus **26–29**,
    142
mousebird 170, 204
muttonbird *see* shearwater,
    sooty

Mycteria americana **34–35**
myna 245

N

navigation (169), 170–71
nestboxes and conservation
    (239)
nightingale, European 242
nightjar 190–91
Numenius phaeopus 123
nuthatch
    pygmy 231
    red-breasted 230–31
Nyctea scandiaca 55,
    180–83

O

Occeanodroma leucorhoa
    18–19
oriole
    Altamira 266
    Baltimore 266–67
    black-backed 266
    Bullock's 266
osprey 84–87, 91, 264,
    265
Otus asio 243
owl 248
    barn 184–89
    bay 184
    eagle 178
    great horned 82,
    178–79
    pellets (186), 186
    screech 243
    snowy 55, **180–83**
oystercatcher
    American 124, 125
    American black
    124–25

P

pamprodactyl 204
Pandion haliaetus **84–87**,
    91, 264
parakeet 265
parasites 22
parrot 204, 245, 265
Parula americana 253
Parus
    atricapillus **224–29**
    carolinensis 224, 228
    gambeli 229, 231
    hudsonicus 229
    montanus 226, 227
    palustris 227
    rufescens 229
Passer domesticus 239,
    276–79
passerines 204, *204*
Pelecanus
    occidentalis **20–23**
    thagus 20, 21
pelican
    brown 20–23
    Peruvian 20, 21
pests, birds regarded as
    (265)
Phalacrocorax carbo **24–25**
phalarope, red-necked
    138–39
Phalaropus lobatus **138–39**
Phasianus colchicus **94–97**
pheasant
    common 94–97
    golden 94
    Lady Amherst's 94
    Reeves' 94
Phodilus 184

Picoides villosus 231
pigeon 265
    fantail 169
    feral (town; rock)
    168–71, 265
    passenger 123, 167
    racing 169, (169),
    170–71
Pinicola enucleator **268–73**
piracy *see* kleptoparasitism
play (217)
Plectrophenax nivalis
    260–61
Plegadis falcinellus **32–33**
plover
    American golden
    118–23
    black-bellied 118
    Eurasian golden 118
    Pacific golden 118, 119
Pluvialis
    apricaria 118
    dominica **118–23**
    fulva 118, 119
    squatarola 118
Podiceps cristatus 111
pollution 13, 29, 55,
    59–61, 75, 199, 235
    see also agrochemicals
polyandry 112, 237, 278
polygamy 237, 278
Polysticta 56
prairie chicken 98–99,
    101
    Louisiana race 98
    Massachusetts race 98
    Texas race 98–99
preening *39*
Procellariidae 66
protective umbrella (123)
puffin 154
    Atlantic 162–65
Puffinus
    griseus **16–17**
    puffinus 164
Pyrrhula pyrrhula 272

Q

quali 92–93
Quiscalus quiscula **262–65**

R

raven 125
    common 214–17
Recurvirostra avosetta 238
redhead 50
redstart, American
    250–53
Rissa tridactyla **146–51**
roadrunner, greater
    172–77
robin
    American 240–41, 263
    European 236, 240
roller 204
roosting *24*, 241, 247–48
Rostrhamus sociabilis
    68–69
    plumbeus 68
Rynchops niger **156–57**

S

sapsucker, yellow-bellied
    193, 255
scaup 56
Setophaga ruticilla **250–53**
shearwater 66
    Manx 164
    sooty 16–17

Sialia
    currucoides 236
    mexicana 236
    sialis **236–39**, 248
siskin, Eurasian 274
Sitta
    canadensis **230–31**
    pygmaea 231
skimmer, black 156–57
skua, great 19, 123,
    140–43
skylark 218–19
smell, sense of (66), 169
snipe (common snipe) 133,
    136–37
snow bunting 260–61
Somateria 56
    mollissima 54, 55
    spectabilis **54–55**
sparrow, house 239,
    276–79
sparrowhawk, Eurasian 70
Sphyrapicus varius 193,
    255
spinning 138, *138*
starling 128, 264, 265
    European 239, 245,
    246–49, 263, 265
Sterna
    dougalli 145
    hirundo 155
    paradisaea **152–55**
stork, wood 34–35
storm-petrel 66
    Leach's 18–19
Sturnus vulgaris 239, 245,
    246–49, 263
Sula nebouxii 238
sunning (63), 173
superspecies 46, 50
swallow, barn 220–23
swan
    black 36
    black-necked 36
    mute 36–39, 265
    Polish (39)
    whooper 36
swan upping (38)
syndactyl 204
Syrmaticus reevesii 94

T

talons 204, *204*
Tarsiger cyanurus 238
tern 52, 131, 143
    Arctic 152–55
    black 154
    common 155
    roseate 145
territorial aggression (10),
    95, *110*, 113, 131, 142,
    (143), (151), 231, 245
thermal updrafts 58, *64*,
    (81)
thrush 236, 238, 265
thunder pumper *see*
    bittern, American
tit 226
    marsh 227
    willow 226, 227
touch, sense of 34, 124
Tringa melanoleuca **126–27**
Troglodytes
    aedon 253
    troglodytes **232–33**
Turdus
    migratorius **240–41**,
    263
    vulgaris 88

turkey
    common (wild) 64,
    104–09
    ocellated 109
turnstone
    black 128
    ruddy 128–31
Tympanuchus
    cupido **98–99**, 101
    phasianellus 100
Tyto alba **184–89**

V

Vermivora
    celata 253
    peregrina 253
vireo
    solitary 206
    yellow-throated
    206–07
Vireo
    flavifrons **206–07**
    solitarius 206
Vultur gryphus 58
vulture
    American black 64
    turkey 59, **64–67**

W

warbler 226, 250–53
    bay-breasted 253
    black-and-white 250
    Cape May 253
    hooded 250, 253
    magnolia 253
    marsh 245
    northern parula 253
    orange-crowned 253
    pine 253
    prairie 253
    Wilson's 250, 253
    yellow 253
waxbill 170
waxwing, Bohemian 270
weaver 265
webbed feet 23, 56, 204,
    204
whimbrel 123
whippoorwill 190–91
wigeon
    American 50–53
    Chiloe 50
    Eurasian 50
Wilsonia 250
    citrina 250, 253
    pusilla 250, 253
woodpecker 204
    hairy 231
    ivory-billed 200
    pileated 200–205
wren
    house 259
    winter (common;
    northern) **232–33**

X

Xanthocephalus
    xanthocephalus 264

Y

yellowlegs, greater
    126–27

Z

Zenaida macroura **166–67**
zygodactyl 204, *204*

Picture Credits